SHEFFIELD
CITY
BATTALION

The 12th (Service) Battalion York & Lancaster Regiment

A HISTORY OF THE BATTALION RAISED BY SHEFFIELD IN WORLD WAR ONE

SHEFFIELD CITY BATTALION

The 12th (Service) Battalion York & Lancaster Regiment

A HISTORY OF THE BATTALION RAISED BY SHEFFIELD IN WORLD WAR ONE

PAUL OLDFIELD
RALPH GIBSON

Pen & Sword
MILITARY

First published in Great Britain in 1994 by Leo Cooper
Reprinted in this format in 2006 by Leo Cooper
and in 2010 by Pen & Sword Military
An imprint of Pen & Sword Books, 47 Church Street, Barnsley S70 2AS

ISBN 978-184884-344-8

Typeset by Mac Style, Beverley, E. Yorkshire

Printed and bound in the UK by CPI

Pen & Sword Books Ltd incorporates the imprints of Pen & Sword Aviation, Pen & Sword Maritime,
Pen & Sword Military, Wharncliffe Local History, Pen and Sword Select, Pen and Sword
Military Classics and Leo Cooper.

For a complete list of Pen & Sword titles please contact
PEN & SWORD BOOKS LIMITED
47 Church Street, Barnsley, South Yorkshire, S70 2AS, England
E-mail: enquiries@pen-and-sword.co.uk
Website: www.pen-and-sword.co.uk

Contents

View from the approximate site of the German front line on 1st July 1916. The village of Serre is out of sight to the right. The British front line ran along the forward edge of the trees on the left. Three of the copses (Mark, Luke and John) that existed in 1916 have since been joined together to form this continuous wood line, with John Copse on the right. In the centre middle distance is the Cross of Sacrifice in Luke Copse Cemetery and in the right foreground is Queen's Cemetery; both contain the remains of many City Battalion men. On 2nd June 1928 Monsieur Maurice Cocquet, the land owner, gave 6½ acres to Sheffield on the understanding that £37/2/- was paid to the tenant farmer in compensation. The path in the foreground leads to the entrance to Sheffield Park and Railway Hollow Cemetery beyond it (signposts on the extreme left of picture). Here the Sheffield Memorial building was erected having been designed by Mr F Ratcliffe (formerly 12/486 Corporal in B Company). It was inaugurated on 25th May 1931, but the building fell into disrepair and the land became badly overgrown in the 1940s and 1950s (see picture opposite). Following discussions between the Commonwealth War Graves Commission and the Sheffield Council it was decided to replace the ruined building with a more durable structure on the same foundations. Five acres of the original were sold off to leave the more manageable plot that remains today. The work was carried out by the CWGC in 1957 at a cost of £6,000, which included a sum for future maintenance.

Introduction

10th September 1914 the City of Sheffield officially raised its own battalion to fight in the war against Germany. After a number of changes its title was settled as the 12th (Service) Battalion York and Lancaster Regiment (Sheffield City Battalion). Just three and a half years later, on 28th February 1918, the Battalion was disbanded, never to be reformed. In that short space of time over 3,000 men passed through the ranks of the City Battalion. Of these almost 700 were killed or died of their wounds, and over 500 men were commissioned. This was a considerable achievement for a Kitchener Battalion.

Despite its short existance the Battalion made a significant contribution to the war effort. It distinguished itself in the heat and dust of Egypt, and later in the mud and misery of the Western Front.

One particular day stands out in the Battalion's history, 1st July 1916. That day was the biggest military disaster in terms of casualties ever suffered by the British Army. Over 50,000 men were lost, of whom 20,000 were killed. The City Battalion lost 248 men killed and over 300 wounded. This battle marked the end of the original Battalion that had formed in the heady days of the autumn of 1914.

The Battalion was rebuilt with men from Lancashire, Norfolk and Staffordshire, as well as the remaining volunteers from the early days. It continued to serve in France throughout 1916 and 1917, but the Army reorganisation of early 1918 brought an end to its short life. This book is the story of the Battalion, from beginning to end, and the men that formed it.

It may be questioned, some 70 years after the war ended, why a book on the City Battalion is needed at all, especially when Richard Sparling, an ex-soldier in the Battalion, wrote a history in 1920. Apart

HIGH STREET, SHEFFIELD.

from the recent resurgence of interest in the First World War, there were a number of other reasons why we felt this book was required.

Firstly there is a general lack of knowledge within the City about its own Battalion. Secondly, we wanted to commemorate all the members of the Battalion by name, or at least as many as we could trace, to ensure that the war service of every man was properly recognised. At the end of the book is a list of the members of the Battalion, together with the biographical information we were able to discover. The list is not comprehensive and has been compiled from the Public Records Office, Medal Rolls, Commonwealth War Graves Commission and the York & Lancaster Regiment Museum. The main reason for not being able to complete the lists is that the Luftwaffe destroyed most of the Army's records in a raid in 1941. We cannot claim to have exhausted every avenue of enquiry. For this reason we would be delighted if survivors, relatives and other interested people who can add to the lists would contact us through the *Barnsley Chronicle*. A few months after publication an up to date list will be lodged with the York and Lancaster Regiment Museum in Rotherham. The third reason, was the need to update Sparling's earlier work.

We have constantly referred to it in our own research, but sadly the book is now very dated and contains some obvious errors. The readers in 1920 had just lived though the war, and many aspects which needed no explanation then, would be lost on many of today's readers. We have also paid more attention to the exploits of the Battalion after 1st July 1916. After all almost 80% of its time spent on active duty was after this date. For all the faults in Sparling's book, it made our task an easier one and we are indebted to him.

Readers may be interested to know a little about Dick Sparling. Richard Arthur Sparling was born in 1890 in Bolton, and was one of the many *Sheffield Daily Telegraph* employees who enlisted in the City Battalion in September 1914. Because of his background he was selected to work in the Battalion orderly room. He was later awarded the Meritorious Service Medal (MSM) for his outstanding efforts under very trying conditions. He returned to the Telegraph after the war, and eventually became the Sports Editor.

The final reason for writing this book was to complete the history of the 94th Infantry Brigade, which consisted of 12th, 13th and 14th York and Lancaster and 11th East Lancashire. The history of the two Barnsley Battalions (13th and 14th York & Lancs) was written by Jon Cooksey and published in 1986; while Bill Turner had his book on the Accrington Pals (11th East Lancs) published in 1987. With the completion of this volume the 94th Brigade must be one of the best documented formations of the entire war.

There are many abbreviations in the text. To avoid confusion the first time a term is used it will appear in full followed by the abbreviation in brackets. Thereafter only the abbreviation will be used. Those readers unfamiliar with military organisations are advised to look over the appendices before starting the book.

We hope you will enjoy reading this book as much as we have enjoyed researching it.

Preamble

Sheffield in 1914 was a very different place than it is today. Before starting on the history of the Sheffield City Battalion we felt that readers should know a little about the City and its part in the industrial war effort.

During the 19th century the City had undergone a major expansion due to the steel industry, and by 1914 its population stood at 454,632. The quality of Sheffield steel for heavy engineering was renowned throughout the world, and about 98% of all British cutlery was manufactured there.

The people were mainly working class and still largely adhered to Victorian values and lifestyle. In the main people lived in overcrowded housing and the overall state of health was very poor. In the early stages of the war it became clear from the Army's enlistment medical tests that malnutrition was rife. One reason for so many men volunteering for war service was the attraction of three meals a day and to reduce the burden on the family budget.

Life was anything but exciting, for long working hours dominated most people's lives, the basic working week being 53 hours. The glamour of an Army uniform and the excitement of going to war was very attractive to many men. Thousands enlisted just to relieve the monotony of day to day life.

New tramway routes had opened up outlying areas of the City, and many people moved out of the polluted industrial areas to live in the clean air of the suburbs. A building boom had slowed considerably by 1914, and on the outbreak of war there was actually a housing shortage. This caused major accommodation problems later when people flooded into the City to take advantage of the well paid munitions jobs that the war created.

Before the war the political scene was dominated by the two main parties; the Liberals and the Conservatives. To most working class people the Liberals were too moderate. In 1903 the Federated Trades Council and the Labour Representation Committee joined forces to form a Labour Party with the intention of getting a voice on the City Council.

Churches and chapels exerted a much greater influence on people's lives than they do today. Not only were they places of worship, but for many people their social life was also centred on the local church. Whitsuntide was a particularly important event. On Whit-Sunday everyone went for a walk in their Sunday best and ended up in the local parks where hymns were sung. On Whit-Monday there would

John Brown & Co. Ltd., Altas Works, Savile St. East, as it was in 1903.

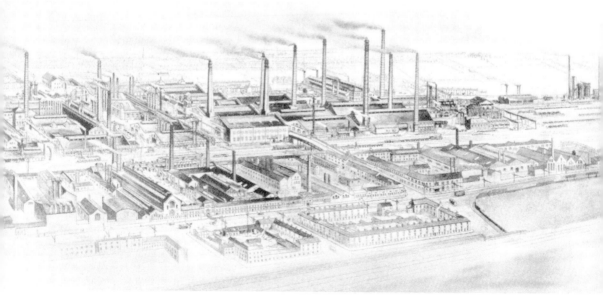

usually be a sports day followed by tea, often known as 'bun fights'. The Boy's Brigade was a church run organisation, designed to make better citizens out of its members. In 1914 it was very popular with young boys.

In the days before radio and television entertainment was limited to the theatre or music hall. The area around West Bar and Snig Hill was Sheffield's own Piccadilly. However, cinemas were already beginning to have a considerable effect on theatre takings, and by 1914 only five remained. At the junction of the Rivers Don and Sheaf in Blonk Street there was the Alexander Music Hall, with the largest stage in the City. In 1914 the Council purchased it and in 1915 it was demolished to make way for road improvements. The Hippodrome in Cambridge Street took over from the 'Old Alex' in putting on the large stage shows. Between the wars this theatre changed over to a cinema.

The Lyceum is the only one of the old theatres still in existence, and it stands close to the modern Crucible Theatre. The Lyceum was known as the 'High Brow' because it mainly put on ballet and opera productions. Nearby was the Theatre Royal, owned by the same company as the Lyceum. Sadly on 30th December 1935 it was burned down and never rebuilt. The site has been a car park ever since.

The Empire Theatre, known as the Palace of Varieties, stood at the junction of Charles Street and Union Street. It was damaged during the blitz in the Second World War, and later demolished.

On the left is the Lyceum Theatre and on the right the Theatre Royal.

While the theatres declined the number of cinemas was increasing. In Fitzalan Square was the Electra, and in Barkers Pool the Cinema. Prices were 1/– (5p), 6d (2¹/₂p) and 4d (1¹/₂p). Further out of town, however, prices were cheaper. At the Heeley Palace the balcony was 6d, the stalls 4d and the pit 2d. A private box for four cost 4/– (20p).

The war had a profound effect on Sheffield and its industrial output. In a booklet published by the City Council in 1918, Sheffield was described as the 'World's Arsenal', and the production figures lend some credence to this proud boast. Sheffield had been a world leader in heavy engineering and the production of armour and alloy steels. Yet in 1914 no one could have predicted the massive amounts of war material that would be required.

In 1914 there were six major armament factories in the private sector, and four of these (Firth's, Hadfield's, Cammell Laird and Vickers') were in Sheffield. In addition the government had three of its own factories. After the Boer War orders tailed off. Between 1900 and the outbreak of war in August 1914 less than 1,000 artillery pieces had been ordered, and most of them were in the period 1904–5. During the war Sheffield alone produced 16,500 complete guns, plus another 514,000 gun barrels, tubes and jackets.

Other types of military output were equally staggering. Sheffield produced 11 million shells. This may sound like a colossal amount, but it was only 6% of the 170 million shells expended by the British on the Western Front alone. Also produced were three million rifle barrels and seven million steel helmets.

Even to a City that made its living through steel the increased production caused many problems. One of the first to be encountered was a shortage of labour. Many farm workers came into the City to take on the higher paid factory jobs, but it was not enough. The French had begun to replace the men at the front with women at a very early stage in the war. When Lloyd George established the Ministry of

Cyclops steel and iron works, Charles Cammell Ltd. The photograph above is of the three storey building in the top right hand corner of the central Factory complex in the drawing below.

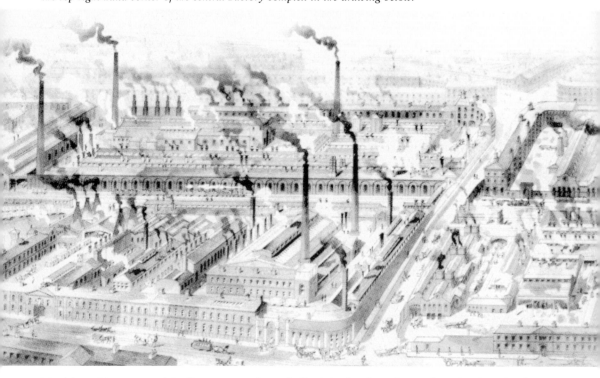

Munitions this was one of the first measures he took. Statistics for the ordnance factories show just how vital these extra workers were. In 1914 the work force had stood at 10,000 men. By 1918 it had grown to 100,000, and 27,000 of them were women. Without them the industry would have collapsed.

Producing shells in Sheffield at the end of the 19th century.

Test firing shells into armour plating in a Sheffield Steel works, 1891.

Bessemer furnace shop, Cyclops works, Sheffield.

Women began to replace men in some jobs as early as the beginning of 1915. Within a short time 124,000 had signed up for War Service. Girls as young as 14 were accepted for unskilled work, although they were not allowed to work on night shifts until they were 18. It was not just industrial jobs that women took over. When Pte Ernest Hough of the City Battalion got married in September 1915, his bride, Miss E. Beal, was described in the newspaper as a tram conductress. Such employment for a woman before the war would have been unthinkable.

Relying on volunteers alone was not good enough. It was soon found that the majority of skilled workers necessary to run the munitions industries, had enlisted in the army. During 1915 40,000 men were demobilised and sent back to their peacetime jobs because of this. But still this was not enough. The solution lay in the National Registration Act.

The Act required every person between the ages of 15 and 65 to register themselves, with details of their employment and age etc. False registration could incur a penalty of three months' hard labour plus a £20 fine, a lot of money when top wages for working men were about £4/6/6 (£4.32) a week.

From the register the authorities decided who was to be left to work in essential industrial jobs, and who was to be conscripted into the armed forces. This was the most efficient way of using the nation's manpower resources.

Tyler St.

Steel workers' accommodation, wooden huts erected at the beginning of the war, originally to house Belgian refugees.

Munitions St.

Because there was almost full employment during the war people had more money to spend. Unfortunately many chose to spend their earnings in the pubs. Lloyd George said that drinking during working hours was causing more damage to the war effort than all the U-Boats put together. In order to curb this habit he introduced the licensing laws, which with modifications remain in force to this day. Opening times were restricted to 12 o'clock to 12.30 and 6.30 to 9.30 p.m., whereas before they had been open virtually all day.

The influx of extra workers into the City caused a severe accommodation shortage. This was partly solved by converting huts, which had been erected for Belgian refugees at the beginning of the war, into family housing units. When internal partitions had been added they made adequate if somewhat spartan homes.

These huts were located just off Tyler Street and Petre Street, overlooking the main steel works. The first street of huts was aptly named Munitions Street, and it stood until the outbreak of the Second World War, when it was demolished as a fire hazard. Some of the huts found their way into Derbyshire, where they were erected as weekend homes. During the First World War the residents of the huts formed their own fire brigades, and even held competitions on a piece of flat ground behind Munitions Street.

The move towards full employment in the City was evident in the takings of the Tinsley route of the Sheffield Tramways Department. At the end of August 1914 takings were up by 25%, and by the end of 1916 had doubled, as more and more workers used the route to get to the factories.

It soon became evident that some form of local control was necessary to coordinate industrial efforts. It was inefficient just to let individual firms get on with their own production. The Sheffield Committee on Munitions of War was formed, with members from commerce, industry and the City Council. The Committee was responsible for organising sub-contractors, delivery dates and the supply of raw materials. It was also concerned with manpower problems and the release of essential workers from the forces.

It has already been mentioned that Sheffield produced seven million steel helmets. However, the story behind them is probably not that well known. Dr. C. W. Saleeby wrote to the Daily Chronicle in 1915 "After the ghastly failure of our 'victories' at Loos and Neuve Chapelle, many of us who count every soldier sacred urged that our men should be armoured. The French had profited by their helmet, and no other than armour to the machine gun was then or yet is in existence". He was joined in his campaign by Sir Arthur Conan Doyle, they pressed for the matter to be raised in Parliament. It was finally agreed by the Ministry of Munitions, that the development of a steel helmet was to be carried out. Lightness and strength were at the top of the requirements, also the material to be used should be capable of being pressed in one piece. This was decided after a study had been made on the French helmet, which was found to be constructed in three pieces, creating an in-built weakness, apart from the inferiority of the steel used allowing easy perforation by shrapnel bullets of low velocity. The only steel found to meet all of these requirements was discovered in 1882 by Sir Robert Hadfield of Sheffield after some ten years' research. It was called Manganese steel, an alloy which could be dropped stamped into the required shape. Dixons of Sheffield, the silver-smiths and cutlers, who are still in business today at the same location, were to be one of the biggest producers of the helmets.

By the end of December 1915 some 1,337 had been produced, but by the end of December 1916 the figure had reached 61,500 a week. Known as the "Soup Plate", the helmet became standard equipment in the British Army through to the end of the Second World War when the shape was changed. The soup plate name given to the helmet originated from Dixons' themselves. Whilst studying the

French steel helmet constructed in three pieces from inferior metal. Weight 23¹/₄ ozs. This helmet is easily performed by Shrapnel Bullets at as low a velocity as 350 feet per second.

Dixons of Sheffield producing the British steel helmet which was dropped stamped from a single sheet.

British helmet compared to the German version.

Weight 25½ ozs. This helmet keeps out Shrapnel Bullets up to a velocity of about 750 to 900 F.S. (feet per second).

Weight 37 ozs. This helmet, although 12 ozs heavier and 12 per cent thicker than the Manganese Steel Helmet, is perforated at lower velocities, it also cracks badly under impact.

No. 20—*1636*

This Certificate is granted to *Alfred Sanderson*
employed *on Gun Forgings* in the works of
Messrs. CAMMELL, LAIRD & Co., Ltd., SHEFFIELD,
in token that his services are urgently required in the manufacture of
Ordnance War Material for the defence of the Realm, in which service
he is required to exercise diligence and faithfulness.

Kitchener

(This Certificate is the property of H.M's. War Department.)   [OVER.

Document presented to men employed in munition production which excused them from military service.

required shape of the helmet it was found that a set of stamp tools which had previously been used in the manufacture of soup plates, with slight modification, could be adapted to make the first helmets. Later, of course, new tools were made.

We could go on about old Sheffield and its part in the war for much longer, but that is not the purpose of this book. If we have given the reader a taste of what life was like 70 or more years ago in the City then this short preamble will have served its purpose.

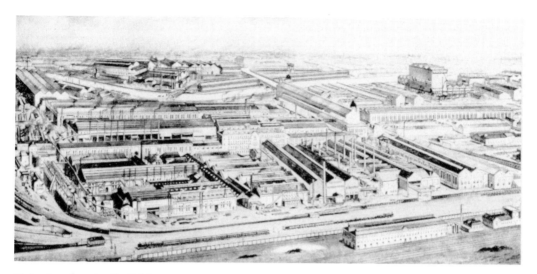

Vickers' steel works, Sheffield.

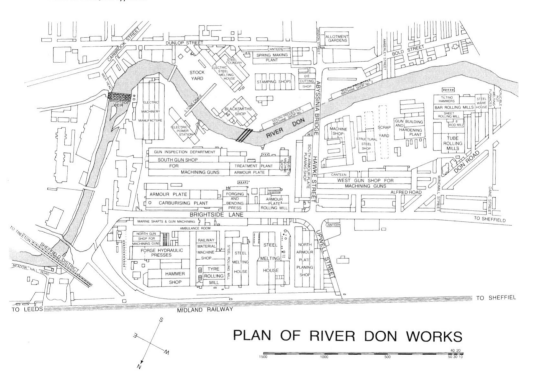

PLAN OF RIVER DON WORKS

Sheffield – the arsenal of Britain.

Producing 18 pounder shells.

Belgian refugees fleeing from the advancing German army.

Belgian infantry advancing to meet the invaders.

Chapter One

Raising the Battalion

On 4th August 1914 Great Britain's ultimatum to Germany ran out and war inevitably followed. It was to be the most bloody and savage conflict the country had ever fought. There had been hopes of staying out of what became known as the Great War, but sadly this was not to be.

A clash between the major powers in Europe had been threatening for some years. The inevitability of war lay in the growth of the German Empire after 1871, and its aspirations to dominate Europe and the world. Europe divided into two camps. Germany formed the Triple Alliance with Austria-Hungary and Italy; while France and Britain formed the Entente Cordiale in 1904 which was joined by Russia in 1907 to create the Triple Entente. The incident that finally sparked off the war was the assassination of Archduke Franz Ferdinand, heir to the throne of the Austro-Hungarian Empire, at Sarajevo on 28th June 1914. Austria-Hungary had become alarmed at the increase in territory won by Serbia as a result of the Balkan Wars of 1912–13 and the assassination gave Austria-Hungary the excuse to declare war on 28th July. Germany fully supported the Austrians, but Russia was not prepared to allow Austria-Hungary to extend its power in the Balkans, and mobilised her forces. Germany then declared war on Russia on 1st August, and France on 3rd August.

The alliance of France and Russia presented the Germans with the problem they most feared – a war on two fronts. They simply did not have the resources to strike against both countries simultaneously. The problem had exercised the minds of the German General staff for many years, and a solution was found, which was named after its author, von Schlieffen.

Von Schlieffen's plan was bold, but was also a considerable risk. Because the French were assessed as the greatest threat to Germany, he planned to deal with them first. The Russians were to be held with the minimum forces necessary to prevent them from breaking through the German defences. Meanwhile the bulk of the Army, working to a meticulously detailed mobilisation plan, was to concentrate in the west and settle with the French. The forces in the west would then be transferred to the eastern front to deal with the Russians.

Germans moving up to the border. Trains running to strict timetables were part of the war plan.

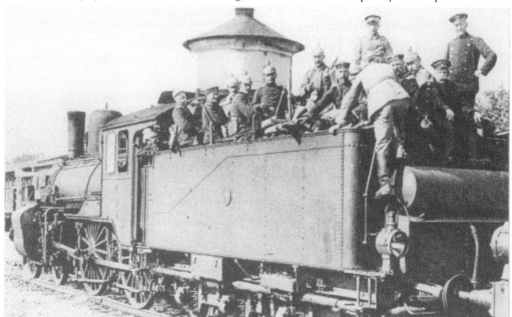

The Germans could not hope to achieve complete strategic surprise, since the mobilisation of such massive forces could not be hidden. But tactical surprise could be achieved if they attacked from an unexpected direction. France's defences were weakest along their border with Belgium. By ignoring the neutrality of the Belgians the Germans believed they would be able to outflank the French forces, envelop them, and end the war in a matter of weeks.

As the rest of Europe mobilised and marched off to war the British hesitated. Although morally obliged to help the French, the Liberal Government was not in favour of war. But the German invasion of Belgium, which commenced on 4th August, decided the matter. Britain had guaranteed the neutrality of Belgium in the treaty of 1839, and she had no option but to honour it. An ultimatum was sent to the German government, demanding the immediate withdrawal of their troops from Belgian territory. Unless a satisfactory answer was received by 11pm on the 4th then a state of war would exist between the two countries. The Germans made no reply; the Great War had begun.

There was a deep seated suspicion of the Germans in Britain at this time. The suspicion had been mainly caused by the expansion of the German Empire, which was seen as a threat to the security of our own Empire. At home propagandists stirred these fears up into a wave of anti-German feeling, and fuelled it with stories of German atrocities in Belgium. The atrocity stories have been written about often enough. Suffice to say that they were exaggerated out of all proportion, but they served the purposes of the propagandists well.

Patriotic fervour was already running at fever pitch and support for the war, when it came, was almost universal. The country had not seen the likes of it before. Even the jingoism of the South African War, at the turn of the century, paled into insignificance. The attitude of the majority of people was that the Germans had been asking to be taught a lesson for long enough. Now they were going to get it.

Few people stopped to wonder how we were to fight a major war with our tiny regular army. Indeed most believed that when the Germans saw our resolve they would back down anyway. Lord Kitchener, the newly appointed Secretary of State for War, did not share this unrealistic view. He knew that the Army was only strong enough to take part in a short campaign. He also rightly assessed that the war would be a long one.

Kitchener was already a national hero. In 1898 he had conquered the Sudan. During the South African War he was initially the Chief of Staff to Lord Roberts, and succeeded him as the Commander in Chief there, in 1900. He later became CinC in India, and in 1911 was appointed British representative in Egypt.

When war broke out Kitchener was on leave in England and was immediately appointed to his new position at the War Office. It was his vision which led to the formation of the New Armies. The Sheffield City Battalion was but a tiny part of this huge creation. Kitchener was not destined to see the results of his work. Before the New Armies fought their first big battle, in July 1916, he was drowned when his ship was mined on its way to Russia.

German infantry advance into Belgium.

German commander Von Arnim proclaimed: "German troops will pass through Brussels today and on the following days and are obliged by circumstances to demand from the city lodging, food and supplies. I expect the population to conform itself to these necessities of war." Here German troops are seen passing through Vise on their way to Brussels.

In the early years of the century the British and French Armies had made a joint plan, in case of both countries being at war with Germany. The plan, known simply as WF (With France), allowed for a small British Expeditionary Force (BEF) to cross the Channel to fight alongside the French on the continent.

The contingency plan was found to be very valuable when the time came to cross the Channel. When the operation to move the BEF began on 12th August it ran with a clockwork like precision. With a minimum of fuss and delay the force was quickly established on the continent, ready to counter the German invasion.

Although the BEF was quickly concentrated on the continent, it at first failed to impress the Germans. The Kaiser dismissed it as a 'contemptible little army', and on the face of it he was right. With a strength of only 125,000 men, in its six infantry divisions and one cavalry division, the BEF was tiny by continental army standards. In comparison the French Army had 1,071,000 men and the German Army had 1,485,000 men. Both these nations could also call on a vast pool of reserves, created by many years of peace-time conscription. Britain had always been against compulsory military service. She therefore did not have the luxury of a reserve of trained soldiers.

What the regular British Army lacked in size it made up for in its professionalism. The infantry were trained to fire 15 aimed shots a minute. Although they were often outnumbered by up to ten to one in the early days of the war, they inflicted a terrible slaughter on the massed ranks of the advancing Germans.

Belgian troops man a street barricade at Louvain in an attempt to block the German advance on their capital.

German Ambassador, Prince Lichnowsky and his wife seen here leaving London on August 6th, 1914.

Even so the Germans pushed the allies back almost to Paris itself. A desperate counter offensive helped to restore the situation somewhat in the allies' favour. The Germans realised they could not break through and so began the 'race to the sea', as both sides attempted to outflank each other to the north.

The fighting in the autumn and early winter of 1914, culminated in the indecisive First Battle of Ypres. Neither side could gain an overwhelming advantage, and there were no flanks left to turn. The troops on both sides dug themselves into the earth for the winter. The war of movement was over and would not recommence until 1918. For 470 miles the trenches ran from the Swiss border to the Channel coast. Barbed wire, machine guns and massed artillery would be the dominating factors from now on. Only when they could be overcome would the deadlock be broken.

While the BEF was desperately trying to stem the advancing Germans, Kitchener was devoting himself to the task of raising more men to continue the fight. The regular battalions in Britain were quickly formed into divisions and sent to France. Battalions on policing duties throughout the Empire were hastily recalled. As they arrived back in the country they too were formed into divisions and quickly dispatched to the front. Kitchener knew he would need many more men than this to see the war to a successful conclusion.

There was a large Territorial Force (TF), in Britain, but these 'weekend soldiers' were only embodied for home defence duties. Most of the first and second line TF units would eventually volunteer to serve abroad, but they were not immediately available. Kitchener knew that even with the TF the Army would still need more men.

On 7th August 1914 Kitchener launched his appeal for an initial 100,000 volunteers. The response was immediate and overwhelming. In a matter of days he had his men. But it did not

Lords Haldane and Kitchener arrive at the War Office. Lord Kitchener (on the right) was appointed Minister for War on the outbreak of war.

British troops arrived in northern France and were soon pitched into battle.

British regular troops trained to fire off 15 aimed shots per minute inflicted heavy casualties on the advancing Germans.

Belgian refugees took to the road before the advancing Germans.

end there. Within a month he had 500,000 volunteers, and by the spring of 1916, when conscription was finally introduced, 2,467,000 men had enlisted. They were to be a new type of soldier, previously unknown in Britain, who undertook to serve for the duration of the war only.

The volunteers were formed into what became known as the 'Pals Battalions'. They were very localised units and often the men came from the same social background, or even the same place of work.

The Army's regimental recruit training depots were unable to cope with the influx. But help was at hand; local councils and other influential bodies stepped in. They undertook the initial organisation and financing necessary to get training underway. For this reason the new battalions ended up with two titles. One was officially recognised, but the unofficial title was more popularly accepted, and better reflected the background of the members. The War Office allocated all the battalions to one of the established county regiments.

Barnsley recruited two battalions, known unofficially as the 1st and 2nd Barnsley Pals. They were absorbed by the local regiment, and became the 13th and 14th (Service) Battalions of the York and Lancaster Regiment, (13th & 14th York and Lancs). The Sheffield City Battalion became 12th York and Lancs. The title 'Service' indicated a unit raised purely for war service, and was not part of the regular army establishment. Over 550 Service battalions were raised during the war.

Sheffield was slower than many other cities in starting to raise a battalion. The local newspapers in August 1914 carried many letters advocating Sheffield's own contribution to Kitchener's New Armies. When the Battalion was eventually raised the critics then complained that the city could do more. It only managed to raise a single battalion, while a small town like Barnsley had raised two. However, it must be borne in mind that the City Battalion was very selective in its recruiting, and this made it difficult to find sufficient men for another battalion. An attempt was made but the lack of suitable volunteers never allowed it to be completed.

THE CONTINENT PLUNGED INTO WAR.

GERMANS INVADE FRANCE.

DECLARATION OF WAR UPON RUSSIA.

STARTLING RUMOUR.

"BRITISH CABINET DECIDES TO SUPPORT FRANCE."

VIOLATION OF LUXEMBURG NEUTRALITY.

REPORTED GERMAN DEFEAT.

BRITISH NAVAL RESERVE MOBILISED.

Headlines from Sheffield Telegraph.

It must also be remembered that the famous Territorial unit, the Hallamshires (1/4th York and Lancs), recruited exclusively from the Sheffield area. During the war the Hallamshires expanded and formed another two battalions, which became 2/4th and 3/4th York and Lancs. In addition many more men served in other units, and there was no question of Sheffield men shirking their duties.

TF battalions were distinguishable from the regular and service battalions by the prefix in their battalion numbers. The prefix indicates a first, second or third line unit. When there was only one battalion, as was the case pre-war with the Hallamshires, it would often be referred to simply as the 4th Battalion. To avoid confusion later in the war the prefixes were always used, and thus provide an easy identification for TF battalions.

The idea of forming the Sheffield City Battalion originated from two Sheffield University students. Their names are not known, but it is highly likely that they enlisted in the Battalion. They approached the University Vice-Chancellor, Mr H. A. L. Fisher, with the idea, and he readily supported it.

During August and September of 1914 Mr Fisher gave a series of very well received lectures on the war, at the Victoria Hall in Sheffield. As a result of the idea from the two students he took the matter up with the council and commenced talks with the War Office. He is credited as the moving force behind the formation of the Battalion.

A meeting at the War Office in late August 1914 was attended by the Duke of Norfolk, and Sir George Franklin, representing the University. Approval for the formation of the City Battalion was given, but on the understanding that Sheffield financed, fed, clothed and trained the Battalion until the War Office was able to formally take it over. No one could forecast then that the War Office would be unable to do this until the late summer of 1915.

Following the developments at the War Office, a meeting at Sheffield Town Hall was hurriedly arranged. This was attended by the Duke of Norfolk, Sir George Franklin, Sir William Clegg, Colonel H. Hughes and Mr H. A. L. Fisher. The Lord Mayor, Lt Col G. E. Branson JP, promised municipal recognition and assistance. Col Hughes offered to act as the Commandant of the Battalion, until a younger man

Colonel H. Hughes, C.B., C.M.G.

Colonel Herbert Hughes, the City Battalion's first Commanding Officer. He acted as Commandant until a younger man could be found. He had previously commanded the Hallamshires and was a member of the University Council. In 1905 he was Lord Mayor of the City.

H. A. L. Fisher, University Vice-Chancellor who supported the suggestion by two students to form a Pals' battalion in Sheffield and became the moving force behind the formation of the City Battalion. In 1918 he was the architect of the Education Act as President of the Board of Education in Lloyd George's government.

Pte Lewis Allen Hill, batman to Capt W. S. Clarke in A Company.

Sheffield University in 1914.

could be found to fill the position of Commanding Officer (CO). Col Hughes was a former CO of 1/4th York and Lancs, and a member of the University Council. He was therefore ideally suited to be the Battalion's caretaker.

At the same meeting the first title of the Battalion was settled upon as, 'The Sheffield University and City Special Battalion of the York and Lancaster Regiment'. It was soon changed to the better known version of 'The Sheffield City Battalion of the York and Lancaster Regiment'.

On 1st September 1914, at the end of one of his war lectures at the Victoria Hall, Mr Fisher made an announcement on behalf of the Lord Mayor. He told the audience that formal War Office approval for the formation of the City Battalion was expected to follow in a few days' time. In the meantime enrolment of volunteers would begin the following afternoon at the Town Hall. Volunteers were sought from the professional classes, and specifically from the University, ex-public school men, lawyers, clerks

Sheffield Town Hall. Note Queen Victoria's statue on the left.

Norfolk Barracks in 1987, little changed over the years. Headquarters of the City Battalion, September – December 1914.

and journalists. It was especially hoped that men who had tried to obtain commissions, and had so far failed to do so, would enrol.

The concept of men with similar social and professional backgrounds serving together was aimed at creating a happy and cooperative atmosphere. This in turn would lead to a more efficient unit. Most of the volunteers in the early days met the entry standards.

One of the exceptions was Lewis Allen Hill, who became 12/141 Pte L. A. Hill. When war broke out he was 21, and was employed as the second gardener at Whiteley Wood Hall, the residence of the Clarke family. One of the sons, William Spenceley Clarke decided to enlist, and took young Hill along with him. They both ended up in A Company, but shortly after enlisting Clarke was commissioned and went to B Company. Later, in 1915, he transferred back to A Company and Hill became his batman.

Postcard sent to all those who filled in the declaration forms at the Town Hall.

BRING THIS WITH YOU

University and City Special Battalion.

Town Hall,
Sheffield, 8th Sept., 1914.

You are requested to attend at the Corn Exchange, on Thursday, the 10th inst., between the hours of 2 p.m. and 8 p.m., for Medical Inspection and Attestation.

The pressure at Regimental Depots being very great, it is unlikely that the Battalion will leave Sheffield for some weeks. Training will begin in Sheffield, and meanwhile you will continue to live at your present residence.

By Order,

E. A. MARPLES,
Captn. and Acting Adjutant.

Letter to T. C. Hunter Pte 12/156, from his uncle. 6th September 1914.

Dear Tom,
I am writing to say how pleased we were to hear from your Father this morning that you had enlisted in the Sheffield Battalion and trust you will be given health and strength to do what ever falls your lot and to endure the change of life which you will experience to what you have been accustomed to. I am sure our Father and Mother, sisters and brothers will be (as we are) proud of you Tom and when the time comes for you to say goodbye it will be a great comfort to know we shall all have you in our thoughts from day to day and shall hope thr day will not be far distant when we shall have you back again amongst us all. It will be a thing you will never regret and when you march with your Battalion into Sheffield on your return, it will be the proudest day of your life to look back upon. If you are called upon to fight our enemies I hope you will not only think you represent Sheffield but will remember you also represent "The Houses of Hunter and Collinson" and if ever you should get near the German Emperor, don't come back without giving him what he is asking for. Well we wish you "Good Luck" Tom and speedy return. Of course I don't know what opportunity you will get for writing but do keep us well posted up, as we shall be so interested to know where you get to and what your duties are, and we will often write you if only we know where you are. It will be nice having so many friends with you. Far better than not knowing who you may have to be with. It would be nice to have a photo of you in your uniform before you go away, perhaps your Father has already arranged this. Auntie and Leslie go on Wednesday to Bridlington to join Grandpa and Grandma, and I go on Saturday and will return on the following Tuesday week. So our address will be the same as this is now. We are hoping when we return to have Grib (?) to come and stay with us for a time, we so much enjoy having any of you. Tell Willie we hope he will get on as well as you have done at Leicester. We know you will not be able to take many things with you, so please accept the enclosed so that you can get yourself anything you most need with our good wishes and love.
Give our love to your Father and Mother and congratulate them for having a son like you Tom, who has given up all his home comforts to go and defend his country and King.
Again wishing you Good Luck and a speedy return. I remain Your affectionate Uncle Ted.

Lewis Hill survived the war and shortly before his death wrote an account of his war service, which has been used in the research for this book. Clarke was not so fortunate. He was a Captain commanding A Company by November 1915. On the opening day of the Somme offensive, 1st July 1916, he was killed leading his Company over the top.

There were others like Lewis Hill, but by and large the men that were accepted came from the City's elite. Of the exceptions many came from Penistone, and included a number of railway men and miners. However, regardless of their backgrounds the men shared a common desire to serve their country and get to the front before the war was over.

Fifteen hundred forms declaring willingness to enlist were prepared, and a room in the Lord Mayor's Chambers was set aside for enrolment. On the afternoon of 2nd September a great crowd formed outside the Town Hall to watch the volunteers going inside to sign up. The Duke of Norfolk was in attendance throughout the afternoon's proceedings, and gave a word or two of encouragement to most as they enrolled.

The first man to complete the formalities was Vivian Sumner Simpson. A few months later, on 27th January 1915, he was commissioned, and remained with the Reserve Companies, at Redmires, when the Battalion departed in May 1915. In August 1916 he rejoined the Battalion in France, and won the Military Cross (MC), in 1917. He was killed in April 1918 serving with 13th York and Lancs.

The establishment of an infantry battalion in 1914 was just over 1000 men. By signing up 1,500 volunteers it was hoped to create the basis of a second battalion, if authority was later granted to form one. One of those who went to enrol was Reg Glenn:

> 'I worked for the Sheffield Education Department. My friend Ned Muxlow who worked in the same office as me came in and said. Shall we go and enlist in the City Battalion? I said alright we can go at dinner time, but he replied. No let's go now. So I got my cap and went and signed on. Instead of getting the King's shilling we received 1/6d. I don't know why and its worried me ever since. I still spent it though!' 12/928 L/Cpl J. R. Glenn

Reg Glenn became a signaller, and began his military career in D Company. Later he transferred to A Company to work in the Battalion Headquarters' signals section. All Battalion HQ elements were in A Company at this stage of the war. When the organisation changed in 1917, a separate HQ Company was formed. In 1917 he left the Battalion and was commissioned to the South Staffordshire Regiment (South Staffs). He has given many hours of his time to assist in the production of this book. Ned Muxlow became a Private in D Company, with Reg Glenn. On 1st July 1916 he went over the top with the rest of the Battalion, and was wounded and evacuated back to England.

Later in the afternoon of 2nd September a contingent of the University Officer Training Corps (OTC), marched into the Town Hall in column of fours and enrolled en masse. They then marched out and formally disbanded the contingent for the duration of the war, before going off to persuade friends and passers by to enroll.

A common joke at the time was about the drill sergeant who told three men to practice forming fours, while he went to find another man! Drill instructors were much maligned by the volunteers, but they did an excellent job of converting a rabble into a disciplined body of men.

On that first afternoon 250 men enrolled, and on the 3rd another 370 came forward. By the end of 4th September the total had risen to 790. A lot of excellent manhood was coming in, but there was precious little military experience. Capt E. A. Marples, the first Adjutant, made an appeal for retired regular and territorial soldiers to help out as drill instructors when the training began.

Enrolment slowed down after the initial rush, and measures were put in hand to keep momentum going. On 5th September another 187 joined, as recruiting was extended to areas outside the City itself. This did the trick. By the end of 7th September a total of 1,303 men had been enrolled at the Town Hall, well over the 1,000 required to form the first Battalion.

In an effort to encourage men to call in on their way to and from work, the opening times of the enrolment office were extended. It would be open from 8 o'clock in the morning to 8 o'clock at night whereas it had previously only opened from 10 until 5 o'clock. This measure apparently had little success since only 33 men were enrolled in the 12 hours that the office was open on the 8th.

Despite the slowing down in the number of men enrolling, there were enough names to proceed with. It was announced that proper enlistment would begin on 10th September. The enrolment lists however, were to be kept open, and any extra men would be used to fill in for those rejected on enlistment and also to create a reserve.

It is interesting that a Sheffield Daily Telegraph reader wrote to the paper at about this time, appealing to technical students to finish their studies before enlisting. The anonymous writer was proved to be more far sighted than most people. In 1915 there was a desperate shortage of technical experts to run the munitions industries. It was then that some City Battalion men were compulsorily removed from the Army and sent back to their old jobs.

The official formation date of the City Battalion was 10th September 1914, the day enlistment began. The Corn Exchange, on Sheaf Street, was chosen as the venue for the temporary recruiting office, because it was one of the largest buildings in the City. It will be well known to older Sheffielders. The huge building, erected by the Duke of Norfolk in 1881, stood on the site of the old Shrewsbury Hospital. It was gutted by fire in 1947 and demolished in 1964, to make way for road alterations at the bottom of Commercial Street.

SHEFFIELD UNIVERSITY
AND
CITY SPECIAL BATTALION

Col. Hughes, C.B., C.M.G., Acting Commandant.

Capt. E. A. Marples, Acting Adjutant.

For Professional Men,

For Business Men,

For Teachers,

For Clerks,

For Shop Assistants,

Etc., Etc.

Enrolment at the Town Hall

TO-DAY,

10 a.m. to 7 p.m.

ENROL NOW.

Badge of the Sheffield University Officer Training Corps.

Those men who had filled in the declaration forms at the Town Hall, received postcards which gave them reporting details. On arrival at the Corn Exchange they were greeted by a large sign inside which proclaimed, 'To Berlin via Corn Exchange'. In their naivity many of the men actually believed that they were going to push the Kaiser's Armies back to the German capital. The realities of the war would soon change their minds, but that was still some time in the future for them yet.

Forty-five doctors worked in shifts of eleven to undertake the medicals. They were organised by Doctors Scurfield and Forbes and controlled by Mr W. Swallow. It was easy to see who had passed by the smiles on their faces as they emerged from behind the screens.

There were forty volunteer clerks furiously filling in the masses of necessary paperwork. They had been organised by the Conservative and Liberal Parties and were under the control of Mr J. C. Skinner and Mr C. J. Preston; Col Hughes, Maj T. C. Clough and Capt Marples attested the volunteers as they completed the formalities and their medical examinations.

On completing the enlistment procedings each man was paid the King's Shilling by the acting Paymaster, Mr A. E. Jameson. He even paid his own son, Frank, who became a signaller and a Lance Corporal, firstly in C Company and then later in A Company. The Jameson family lived at 257 Glossop Road,

L/Cpl Frank Jameson.

where they ran an antiques business. The antique shop, still in the Jameson family until about 2000.

It was a long day for the staff of the recruiting centre. Enlistment commenced at 8 o'clock in the morning until 8 at night. By that time 600 men had been processed. The first man to complete enlistment was Eric S. Roberts. He was the son of the local MP, Mr Samuel Roberts, who took a great interest in the Battalion. Eric Roberts was commissioned into 2/4th York and Lancs in March 1915.

By the time the Corn Exchange closed on the 11th, 900 men had been accepted. Sadly some others had to be rejected, almost exclusively on medical grounds. The main reason was failure to come up to the minimum size for entry, which was 5'6" tall with a chest measurement of 35½". Another 74 volunteers were taken in on the 12th, and the same day it was announced that the first parade had been set for the following Monday.

The first parade took place at Norfolk Barracks, on Edmund Road, at 2.30 p.m. on 14th September. A few ex-regular soldiers and members of the OTC were the only ones in uniform, and they did their

Historic moments, first parade at Norfolk Barracks, 14th September 1914. The new recruits listen to the speeches from the gallery. A good looking crowd ... but at that stage just a crowd.

Colonel Hughes inspecting the new recruits on 14th September 1914 at Edmund Road. The man second right from Colonel Hughes is thought to be RSM J. S. Miller.

best to bring some order to the chaos. They organised the masses of men into groups, and after many lists had been compiled, provisional companies were formed and the men lined up. The process was complicated by friends insisting on staying together in the same company, the same platoon and sometimes even in the same section.

A Company was made up of many of the University men, some teachers, and a smattering of bankers. There were also some £500 a year business men. This was a lot of money in 1914, and they took an enormous decrease in salary to the Army's shilling a day (5p).

B Company had most of the men from districts outside the City, including a large contingent from Penistone and also some from Chesterfield. There were also a lot of bankers, a few teachers and students, some railwaymen, and an assortment of tradesmen associated with the mining and engineering industries.

The composition of C Company is not so clear cut as the other companies. There was a contingent of teachers, and some bankers and students. In addition there were some Town Hall clerks, accountants and at least one carpenter.

D Company was described by one of its members as the 'odds and sods'. Although there were only a few teachers in this Company there were still lots of bankers and students. D Company also had the large contingent of reporters from the Sheffield Daily Telegraph, which included Richard A. Sparling, who later wrote of the Battalion's exploits.

The formation of the provisional companies took over two hours to complete, and was made even more difficult by a constant stream of newly accepted recruits arriving from the Corn Exchange.

The Edmund Road Drill Hall, as Norfolk Barracks was popularly known, was on loan from the West Riding TF Association. It was the first 'home' of the City Battalion. In pre-war days it had been a popular venue for boxing matches, and was well known to the Sheffield men at least. The Barracks are still standing and are now used as a garage.

15th September 1914. Learning to form fours at Bramall Lane Football ground. The crowd begins to shape up. In the background is the recently demolished cricket pavilion. Third from right is 12/946 Sgt J. Hastings and 5th from right is Pte J. F. Wells.

When there was a semblance of order Col Hughes, and the Lord Mayor, inspected the men, watched by members of the organising committee. When the inspection was over speeches were made from the gallery overlooking the drill hall.

The Lord Mayor spoke first. He congratulated the men on their magnificent response to the call for recruits. He told them that they were of the very best material, and when trained the Battalion would be as good as any in the service of the King.

Mr Fisher spoke next. He quoted Kitchener's speech to his men at the end of the South African War, telling them they were about to 'taste the salt of life'. The war was the greatest the nation had ever been engaged in, he continued, and most momentous in its issues for the civilisation of the world. He concluded by saying, it was up to the Battalion to justify the hopes of their friends and to carve for themselves a niche in the temple of history. They would return to Sheffield having won honour for the City and their Country.

Col Hughes finished the speeches by offering the men three things. All ears were strained for the pearls of wisdom he was expected to deliver. Firstly he offered them work; secondly he offered them work; and finally he offered them work again. This brought a smile to many faces. He explained that because of their inexperience they would have to make up for it by working much harder than normal. He promised they would be spared nothing. The men he saw before him were a wonderfully good looking crowd, but that was all they were; just a crowd. He was going to make them into an equally good looking battalion of soldiers.

When the parade was over the men were dismissed. The barracks had been specifically built for the TF, and there was no accomodation for the Battalion. The men had to live at home for the time being, and continued to do so until moving into the camp at Redmires in December. Those from outside the City took lodgings, and many were put up by families in town. An allowance was paid for this, and also free passes were issued for public transport to get the men to and from the barracks. They were not slow to see the potential of this privilege and the passes were used extensively at other times too.

With the Battalion living all over the City it would have been very difficult to maintain contact with them without using the newspapers. Daily orders were printed in the press, and the first issue laid down the reporting times as 0850 and 1350. Work was scheduled to commence 10 minutes after these times, which allowed for a roll call to be taken.

Six hours drilling began to seriously damage the turf just prior to a new season. The Sheffield United directors soon regretted their initial generosity.

Training began in earnest at 9 o'clock on 15th September. The men were marched to Bramall Lane Football Ground where they were drilled by the few soldiers amongst them. The football ground itself was not big enough to take the whole Battalion, and so some waste land in Edmund Road and Queens Road was also put to use. For six hours that day, (9 until midday and from 2 in the afternoon until 5 o'clock), they pounded the turf under the hot autumn sun.

At first the performance of the recruits was a total shambles. But they were of a higher intellectual and physical quality than most Army entrants, and they quickly picked up the intricacies of this important introduction to army life. Drill was regarded as being fundamental in welding together a body of men into a team. It also taught them discipline, and to react without thinking to words of command. According to one man, 12/525 Sgt J. W. Streets, it was the 'foundation of the science of movement'.

Front row second from the left is 12/941 Pte Harry Harlow, and fifth from left is 12/883 Sgt Allan Buckley.

For most of the men drill proved to be a very tiring activity until they became fitter. Many complained of aching feet and backs at the end of the first day. It was still very hot and as photographs show much of the time they worked in their shirtsleeves. While the majority of the men sweated away, the last recruits arrived to bring the Battalion up to full strength. Recruiting still continued in the hope that a second Battalion might be formed.

The directors of Bramall Lane soon began to regret their generosity. Turf does not wear well when used as a parade ground, and with the new season approaching they had to reduce the area available for the Battalion's use. This did not unduly affect training since the men were now divided between various activities on a rotational basis. The area they now required for drill was therefore not so large as when the whole Battalion was involved.

There was no time to waste, and before long basic fieldcraft and tactical training were being carried out in Norfolk Park. The park keepers were not pleased by this, since the men practised rushing imaginary enemy positions with little regard to the park's flora, and even dug trenches in the beautifully kept gardens!

Col Hughes carried out the initial tests to select the first Non-Commissioned Officers (NCOs), in Norfolk Park. Candidates were usually assessed as they drilled their own squads. This was where the future sergeants and corporals earned their first stripe, and was also where some of the future officers were first identified.

The pace of progress was very rapid. An ex-Guardsman, who was an instructor in the Battalion, said that in three weeks they had achieved what normal recruits took three months over. This remark appeared in the local newspapers, and was misunderstood to mean that the Battalion would be putting in an early appearance at the front. But this was not to be the case. Most of the men were worried that the war would end before they got into it. With hindsight they need not have worried, the war would last long enough for them to be thoroughly sick of it by the end.

During the early days potential officers and warrant officers (WOs) were identified, and provisional lists were drawn up to be submitted to the organising committee for approval. Potential officers were usually chosen from those with previous experience in the Territorial Force or Officer Training Corps of Sheffield University. Some however, were selected after a simple oral examination. The future Capt Middleton for example was questioned, by the Regimental Sergeant Major (RSM), for an NCO's slot, or so he thought. But a few days later he was surprised to find his name on the list of officers.

WOs' posts were easier to fill. They invariably went to ex-regular NCOs. The success of the Battalion hinged very much on these posts, and it was important that suitably experienced men filled them. On 17th September three of the Company Sergeant Majors (CSMs), were appointed. They were C. Polden, J. W. Ellis and P. Doncaster.

Charles Polden had already served for 26 years in the York and Lancs as a regular soldier. He became the RSM in January 1915, and won the MC in March 1917.

"Company will advance, by the left! Quick march! Watch your dressing!"

Time out for a rest at the Shoreham St. end of Bramall Lane in September 1914. Lying in front is a member of the University OTC. Standing just right of centre with a bow tie is Arthur Clifford Baynes, the future radio comedian "Stainless Stephen". Behind him with hat on is 12/681 Sgt. H. N. Hobson.

Joe Ellis had also been a regular soldier, and had seen active service in the Matabele and South African Wars with 2nd York and Lancs. He had been attached to the Hallamshires for his final years of service, and he settled in Sheffield when he retired in 1911. It is thought he became the commissionaire at Walsh's store. Joe Ellis was a big man, as can be seen from photographs. He used to huff and puff on route marches, but was always in the lead. On winter marches a cloud of steam rose from his back, so the men always knew where he was.

CSM P. Doncaster was another ex-regular soldier, and had been a Gymnastics Instructor, (the equivalent of a Physical Training Instructor nowadays). He later became the Regimental Quartermaster Sergeant (RQMS). Before the war he had played for Sheffield United reserves.

The first list of officers, which is reproduced below, was published on the 22nd:

Commanding Officer – Col H. Hughes; Second-in-Command (2IC) – Maj T. C. Clough; Adjutant – Capt E. A. Marples; Captains – A. R. Hoette, A. Plackett, W. A. Colley, W. J. Armitage; Lieutenants – C. F. Ellwood, W. J. Jarrard, J. Kenner, A. N. Cousin, C. Elam, E. G. G. Woolhouse, J. L. Middleton; Second Lieutenants – N. L. Tunbridge, E. L. Moxey, R. E. J. Moore, G. J. H. Ingold, W. S. Clarke; Quartermaster (QM) – Honorary Lieutenant S. W. Maunder.

More officers would be appointed later. Before disbandment over 150 officers would serve with the Battalion. To finish off the initial appointments, J. S. Miller became the RSM on the 23rd. The same day Capt W. S. Kerr arrived from 1/4th York and Lancs, to take up the post of Medical Officer (MO).

RSM Miller was an ex-Coldstream Guardsman, and had only retired from the Regular Army in the June of 1914. He had served in the South African War, and was later seconded to the West African Regiment. In January 1915 he was commissioned to 20th Battalion Northumberland Fusiliers, in the Tyneside Scottish Brigade. Shortly afterwards he was appointed as the Adjutant, and later in the year was promoted to be the Officer Commanding (OC), the Brigade Machine Gun Company (MGC).

Having organised the men into companies and started on their training, the next priority was to clothe and equip them. For the first few months the men had to make do with their own clothing, but this was not very resilient to the hard wear of military life. They had to endure a lot of fun poking as they charged imaginary German trenches in Norfolk Park in their Sunday best suits.

The officers had to pay for their own uniforms and had them made by local tailors. The men were to be supplied with theirs, and measurements were taken on 6th October. They were all looking forward to getting into proper field service khaki, but they had a surprise coming to them. Issues of the first uniforms began on 16th November. The men were aghast! The uniforms were blue/grey and without

A few precious but obsolete rifles were used for drill purposes, but there were no belts to carry the bayonets yet.

pockets on the tunic. The hat was the same colour, cut in a glengarry pattern, with thin red piping around the edges.

Most thought they would be mistaken for postmen. However, there were those who thought much worse:

Bramall Lane, Shoreham Street end, showing the Kop under construction in 1914.

> *The Battalion was on a route march one day and was passing through the village of Bamford in Derbyshire. Two old ladies were standing at the side of the road watching us going by. One was overheard to say to the other, "Eee it must be a terrible war if they have to turn out convicts to fight in it!"* 12/664 Pte H. Hall

Fortunately the blue/grey uniforms were only a temporary measure until the textile industry could catch up with the sudden increased demand for khaki. Even so it would be mid-1915 before all the men were properly clothed. Ironically one of the reasons for the shortage was that in pre-war days the dye used in the manufacture of khaki cloth had been purchased from Germany!

Herbert Hall who described the delightful story above, was a bomber in C Company. On 1st July 1916 he went over the top carrying buckets of grenades, and described himself as a walking bomb. He

A novel way of providing back rests for these tired City Battalion members – professional men turned soldier.

survived the day and was later commissioned to the King's Own Yorkshire Light Infantry (KOYLI), and served in India.

During the course of October 600 obsolete Lee-Metford rifles were received. Until then all weapon training had been carried out with 23 rifles and a single machine gun, on loan from the Vickers company. It wasn't until June 1915 that every man had his own Lee-Metford. In the meantime rifles were passed from man to man to practise with. The first batch of modern Short Rifle Magazine Lee-Enfields (SMLE), did not arrive until 17th June 1915, when 80 were issued to NCOs for instructional purposes. But the rest of the Battalion did not receive theirs until November.

The SMLE was regarded as the best rifle of its time, although some people would argue in favour of the German Mauser. The version in use at the time was the Number 1 Mark III. The design was so advanced that the Lee bolt action was still used in the Army's sniper rifle until recently. The Lee action and the Enfield method of rifling the barrels formed the heart of the design. The rifle was 3' 8½" long and was supplied with a 14" bayonet for close hand to hand fighting. The magazine held 10 rounds of .303 ammunition, which could be loaded singly or by means of 5 round clips.

Before the war the British infantry had been trained to fire 15 aimed shots a minute with their SMLEs, and were also renowned for their accuracy. Such a combination of rapid fire and precision was devastating when used against troops advancing in mass. In the early days of the war the Germans were convinced the British had hundreds of machine guns, but in most cases it was actually rapid rifle fire that they encountered. The City Battalion, like most of the Kitchener units would be unable to reach as high a standard because of the shortage of training ammunition.

Reg Glenn with his fiancee Elsie. He is dressed in the temporary blue/grey uniform issued at first because of the scarcity of khaki. It was loathed by the men.

Personal equipment began to arrive in October, and by the end of February every man had his own set. Like most other items of military kit at this time, there was a shortage of the 1908 Pattern webbed equipment. To overcome this an interim version was made in leather by Hepburn, Cole and Ross of Bermondsey. It matched the webbing version in most respects and was named 1914 Pattern. This was to be the equipment that the Battalion was issued with. The major difference between 1908 and 1914 Pattern equipment was the size and quantity of the ammunition pouches. The 1908 Pattern had five small pouches, mounted two above three, on either side of a wide waist belt. Each pouch held three five round clips of ammunition, and thus 150 rounds were carried in easy reach of the rifleman.

In contrast the 1914 Pattern pouches were similar to those on the pre-Boer War Pattern equipment. There was only one either side of the waist belt, but it was much larger than the 1908 Pattern type. Each pouch held a 50 round bandolier, which contained 10 of the five round clips. The bandolier was folded so that all the clips were exposed when the flap was lifted. The main limitation was that only 100 rounds could be carried in easy access for the rifleman.

The Battalion was only a month old when the new CO arrived to replace Col Hughes. He was Lt Col C. V. Mainwaring, an ex-Indian Army officer, who had been commissioned to the Royal Inniskilling Fusiliers in 1883. He later joined the Indian Staff Corps and saw active service in Burma in 1887-8. Following tours of duty in Australia, and having gained further promotion, in 1910 he became the Aide de Camp (ADC) to the Governor of Singapore. In 1912-3, just before returning to Britain, he commanded the Mandalay Brigade. His wide experience of soldiering was put to good use in training the Battalion.

Lt Middleton's diary tells of the new CO arriving on 10th October. He concluded that Mainwaring, 'looks a terror', and a terror he turned out to be. The men worked harder than ever under Mainwaring's leadership, but they also had the greatest respect for him. The Battalion was deeply shocked when ill health prevented him from going abroad with them.

On the same day that Col Hughes handed over the Battalion to Lt Col Mainwaring, the Adjutant, Capt Marples, also departed. He went to 13th Northumberland Fusiliers, and was replaced by Lt E. G. G. Woolhouse.

Later in October Maj T. C. Clough arrived from 1/4th York and Lancs to assume his duties as the Battalion's Second in Command (2IC). He suffered from bad knees, and the ordeal of trench warfare rapidly worsened this complaint. He had to be sent home just before the opening of the battle of the Somme, in June 1916.

Another officer to leave the Battalion in October was Capt W. J. Armitage. He had been an officer in 1/4th York and Lancs, and later in the war became a Garrison Musketry Staff Officer, responsible for rifle training. He did not serve abroad, probably because he was too old.

The Battalion continued to make rapid progress, with fitness training forming a major part of the programme. Each day Swedish drill, better known as physical training, was undertaken, and on a rotational basis one of the companies would go out on a route march.

When the men had reached a basic level of fitness the whole Battalion went out together for route marches. The first of these Battalion marches took place on 15th October. The outward journey ended at Redmires,

Lt Colonel Charles Vaughan Mainwaring takes over command from Col Hughes in October 1914.

where the Battalion's future camp was already under construction. On arriving there the men were drilled in companies, on a flat piece of land which would later become their parade ground.

Lunch was served in the open and consisted of sandwiches and tea. It was a very wet, misty and miserable day. One of the wags in the ranks broke into song. Much to everyone's amusement he crooned, 'There's no place like home'.

By this stage training for the Battalion's specialists had begun. Reg Glenn became a signaller because of his experience of semaphore with the Boys Brigade. It was a common sight to see masses of waving flags in Norfolk Park. Later on, at Redmires, the signallers discovered how lucky they were, by avoiding some of the most gruelling work including many of the route marches.

The privileged position of the specialists annoyed some of the older soldiers, including the CSM of Reg Glenn's Company. One day he had had enough and shouted out in frustration: 'Those damned signallers and their blasted flag wagging. I can never get them for duties.' The signallers also liked to watch the rest of the Battalion marching about or practising bayonet fighting, while they settled down for a brew between training sessions. Not only was it an easier life than that of the average rifleman, but in France it often proved to be a safer one too.

'*On one Saturday morning the Battalion had a route march of about 15 miles over Bradfield way. We signallers acted as flank scouts on these marches. On passing by a farm house below Redmires, I was invited in for a drink of fresh milk and some biscuits. I watched the Battalion disappear into the distance and thought I'm not going chasing after them, so after a while I made my way back to the camp. I got myself washed and cleaned up ready to go out. About*

First Church Parade was held on 8th November. Here the Battalion march through the streets en route to attend morning service at St. Mary's.

an hour and a half later they came back and most of them were too tired to go out at all. On another occasion I was the signaller who marched behind the company commander. A car sped past us and the officer turned round on his horse and said, 'Signaller did you get the number of that car'. He was checking to see if I was alert or not. I had to admit that I hadn't seen it. Luckily there weren't many cars about in those days!' 12/928 LCpl J. R. Glenn

The first church parade was held on 8th November, when a contingent of 650 men marched from Edmund Road to attend morning service at St Mary's church. The Battalion did not yet have a band, and so the services of the Dannemora Steel Works Band were enlisted. After the service the Battalion,

St. Mary's Church at the bottom of Bramall Lane on St. Mary's Gate.

Church Parade of the Sheffield City Battalion,

Sunday, November 8th, 1914.

Hymn 1.

FIGHT the good fight with all thy might:
Christ is thy Strength, and Christ thy
    Right ;
Lay hold on life, and it shall be
Thy joy and crown eternally.

Run the straight race through God's
    good grace ;
Lift up thine eyes and seek His face ;
Life with its way before us lies,
Christ is the path. and Christ the prize.

Cast care aside, lean on Thy Guide ;
His boundless mercy will provide :
Lean, and thy trusting soul shall prove
Christ is its life, and Christ its love.

Faint not nor fear, His arms are near :
He changeth not, and thou art dear ;
Only believe, and thou shalt see
That Christ is all in all to Thee.

Hymn 2.

O THE bitter shame and sorrow,
    That a time could ever be
When I let the Saviour's pity
Plead in vain, and proudly answered,
    All of self, and none of Thee !

Yet He found me ; I beheld Him
    Bleeding on the accursed tree,
Heard Him pray, Forgive them, Father!
And my wistful heart said faintly,
    Some of self, and some of Thee !

Day by day His tender mercy,
    Healing, helping, full and free,
Sweet and strong, and, ah ! so patient,
Brought me lower, while I whispered,
    Less of self, and more of Thee !

Higher than the highest heavens,
    Deeper than the deepest sea,
Lord, Thy love at last hath conquered ;
Grant me now my spirit's longing,—
    None of self, and all of Thee !

Hymn 3.

JESU, Lover of my soul,
    Let me to Thy bosom fly,
While the nearer waters roll,
    While the tempest still be high :
Hide me, O my Saviour, hide.
    Till the storm of life is past !
Safe into the haven guide,
    O receive my soul at last !

Other refuge have I none,
    Hangs my helpless soul on Thee ;
Leave, ah ! leave me not alone,
    Still support and comfort me.
All my trust on Thee is stayed,
    All my help from Thee I bring ;
Cover my defenceless head
    With the shadow of Thy wing.

Thou, O Christ, art all I want,
    More than all in Thee I find !
Raise the fallen, cheer the faint,
    Heal the sick, and lead the blind :
Just and holy is Thy name,
    I am all unrighteousness ;
Vile and full of sin I am,
    Thou art full of truth and grace.

Plenteous grace with Thee is found,
    Grace to cover all my sin ;
Let the healing streams abound,
    Make and keep me pure within :
Thou of life the Fountain art,
    Freely let me take of Thee,
Spring Thou up within my heart,
    Rise to all eternity.

Hymn 4.

GOD save our gracious King ;
Long live our noble King ;
    God save the King !
Send Him victorious,
Happy and glorious,
Long to reign over us :
    God save the King.

O Lord our God. arise,
Scatter his enemies,
    And make them fall !
Confound their politics,
Frustrate their knavish tricks,
On Thee our hopes we fix.
    God save us all.

Thy choicest gifts in store
On him be pleased to pour ;
    Long may he reign ;
May he defend our laws,
And ever give us cause
To sing with heart and voice,
    God save the King !

under Maj Clough, marched back to Edmund Road. He took them on a deliberately circuitous route around the town to show the Battalion off, now that they could march properly. The route taken was along St Mary's Road, Hereford Street, the Moor, High Street and Commercial Street.

The band played a selection of popular military tunes, including 'Boys of the Old Brigade', 'British Grenadiers' and 'The Red, White and Blue'. On arriving back at the Drill Hall, Mr Samuel Roberts, the MP, presented a Union Flag to Maj Clough. The flag had been laid over the altar at St Mary's during the service. It was to be flown over Redmires Camp when the Battalion moved into it.

Lieut Gen Sir Herbert Plumer, General Officer Commanding, Northern Command in 1914.

Next day the Battalion was inspected by Gen H. Plumer, who was the General Officer Commanding (GOC), Northern Command. Born in 1857 Plumer had been commissioned to the old 65th Foot, which eventually became 1st York and Lancs. Later in the war he commanded Second Army and gained a remarkable success at the Battle of Messines on 7th June 1917. During his visit Plumer took a great interest in the Battalion and particularly remarked on the rapid progress being made.

Despite the very full programme of work the men still had time to enjoy themselves, and those that survived would look back on these days as some of the happiest of their lives. On 12th October Lt Middleton and the other subaltern went to the Grand Hotel to celebrate his 21st birthday. Afterwards they took a box at the Lyceum, where they saw the 'Pearl Girl'. D Company were particularly active socially, and they held a series of concerts at the King's Head Hotel, which proved to be very popular. All ranks in the Company, including the officers, produced turns. At the second concert, on 20th November, a Belgian soldier recovering from his wounds wandered in and spontaneously sang the Belgian anthem. He was rewarded with a standing ovation.

The formation period was now at an end, and the time to move into camp at Redmires was rapidly approaching.

Chapter Two

Redmires

There had been a military barracks in Sheffield since before the Napoleonic Wars. In 1854 the large barracks at Hillsborough were built, and it may appear logical to have lodged the City Battalion there. Before the outbreak of war a regular infantry battalion had been based at Hillsborough, but on mobilisation it had been sent abroad, thus leaving the barracks vacant.

The City Battalion, however, did not move in, and the reason is not known. It is possible that because the Battalion was not yet an official part of the Army, that the War Office would not allow it the use of normal military accomodation. On the other hand it may have been considered an unsuitable site for a unit under training, because it did not have easy access to open country.

Whatever the reason for not occupying Hillsborough Barracks, a new hutted camp was soon under construction at Redmires, on the site of an old racecourse. The Redmires area was not unaccustomed to military activity. In pre-war days this land had been used by the West Riding Division Artillery TF, at an annual rent of £100. In the 1880s the old Militia artillery used to fire their pieces, from Stannington, at targets in Wyming Brook, just below where the camp was built. This was in the days before Manchester Road ran along the intervening valley, and so there was no danger to the public. In 1914 one of the shells was found by two young boys, and some alarm was caused until it was discovered that it was a solid practice shot and did not contain explosives.

During the Second World War a Prisoner of War camp was established at Redmires. However it was not on the same site as the City Battalion camp, being further to the eastern end and therefore nearer to Lodge Moor. The remains of hut bases and crumbling masonry from this camp can still be seen amongst the trees of the plantation, which now stands on the site. The camp had a hard core of Nazi inmates who ran it internally with a brutal regime. On one occasion two prisoners were accused of informing the guards of a planned breakout. They were savagely beaten and one eventually died. After D-Day there were so many prisoners to house that tents had to be put up for extra accomodation.

Council contractors did the bulk of the construction work on the City Battalion camp, to War Office designs. They were assisted by the City Architect, Mr F. E. P. Edwards, and furniture plus other fittings were supplied by local dealers. All bills were initially paid for out of the fund set up to establish the Battalion. The City would be recompensed later by the War Office.

Hillsborough Infantry Barracks.

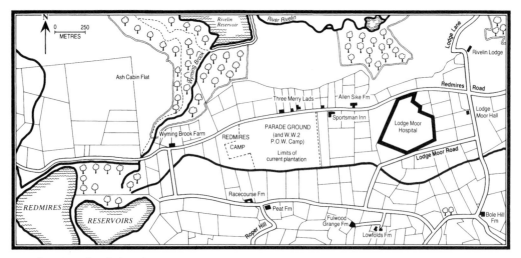

Exact location of Redmires Camp.

The carpenters who built similar camps on Cannock Chase were paid 10d (4p) an hour. The bricklayers received 9d (3½p), and the general labourers 6d (2½p). The builders of Redmires camp would have received roughly the same rates of pay. It is ironic that the men who were to live in the camp were only paid 1- (5p) for a whole day's labour!

The accomodation huts were of a standard design, known as Type No. 19. At Redmires they were constructed of wood, but in some other camps corrugated iron or asbestos sheeting was used instead. The huts were 60 feet long by 20 feet wide, with a single door at one end. There was a pot bellied coal-burning stove in the centre. The lighting was by gas, and the entire structure was raised off the ground on brickwork piles.

The huts were designated as being suitable for 34 men to live in, 17 along the length of each side. This would give each man just over 3 feet of wall space. It must have been very cramped if the hut was full. In practice there were normally fewer than 30 men allocated to each hut, but it would still have left little room for privacy.

Showers and ablution blocks were sited between the accommodation huts. There were also larger buildings such as the cookhouse and officers' and sergeants' messes. The only entertainment in the camp was a wet canteen, and soon after arrival a YMCA hut was opened.

However, when the men could get a pass they took advantage of being close to home and went into town frequently. There were also the two local pubs, the Three Merry Lads and the Sportsman, just a short walk down the road towards town. They proved to be very popular indeed!

Redmires Camp in the middle of 1915. The photo was taken from the bend in the road at Roper Hill looking to the North. The view is largely unchanged today save for the plantation.

The column climbs out of the City towards Redmires, though the driving rain. Some of the men are still in their civilian clothes.

On Saturday, 5th December, the Sheffield City Battalion marched out to Redmires in heavy rain and strong wind. At this point they are just about to turn into the camp. *(Inset below left) Major T. Carter Clough, the Battalion 2IC. (Inset below right) Honorary Lt S.W. Maunder the Quartermaster.*

The band pose for the camera near Dore and Totley Station. The drums were presented by local dignitaries.

Redmires camp was built at 1000 feet above sea level, and a bleaker and more godforsaken place would be difficult to find in winter. The weather was so bad in the early winter of 1914–15 that delays were caused in completing the camp. Towards the end of November, nightly work parties were sent up to Redmires to help finish the camp as quickly as possible. Appeals were made for blankets for the men and a number of articles in local newspapers said that life at Redmires would toughen the men up. This was true, but it turned out to be the death of a few of them.

For those who wish to visit the site of the camp it is easy to find at the western end of the plantation. It stood in the field to the south of the main road that leads to the reservoirs. Those with keen eyesight will notice the crop marks that denote where huts used to stand. A fairly good view can be had from Roper Hill to the south, and this is where the comparison photograph was taken from.

To mark the end of the time spent at Edmund Road, Mr Samuel Roberts MP, entertained the whole Battalion to supper at the Drill Hall, on the evening of 26th November. However the imminent move to Redmires was delayed yet again. The intended completion date of 30th November could not be met due to the atrocious weather. However, sufficient progress had been made by 3rd December for an advance party to move in. Lt R. D. Berry led the party of 50 ORs, who marched out to the camp to prepare for the arrival of the main party.

Lt R. D. Berry.

Lieutenant Reginald Douglas Berry was the OC of 12 Platoon. In October 1915 he became the ADC to the Commander of 94th Brigade. He missed the Somme battle due to sickness, but rejoined the Battalion later on. He was killed in action on 12th May 1917.

On arrival the advance party found the camp was far from complete, and they rushed about trying to make it barely habitable for the arrival of the main party. Even so there were still many essential improvements to be made in the early days of occupation.

At 1.30 p.m. on Saturday, 5th December, the main party marched out of Edmund Road with the newly equipped band at the head of the column, and the CO on horseback leading the way. They marched along Glossop Road to Broomhall and then up through Crosspool. As they climbed out of the City the heavy rain turned to sleet and then snow. After about an hour they swung into the new camp, soaked through and thoroughly miserable.

'Looking back across the years to our youth it makes you realise just how fit we were, when I remember the first night we arrived at Redmires

soaked to the skin, but not down hearted, in fact six of us decided to go into town, we had just been paid. There was no transport until we reached Nether Green where we then caught a tram to town. I don't remember which pubs we visited but we were merry when catching the last tram back. Needless to say we had to find a back way into camp, this being a hole in the wall which was used on numerous occasions, mainly when going to the Three Merry Lads after lights out.' 12/664 Pte H. Hall.

The first night was uncomfortable. The wind howled, and there was thunder and lightning all night. The stoves were of little use in these extreme conditions and they wrapped themselves in every available piece of clothing and blanket they could find. They were also not used to sleeping on straw palliasses, and since some huts had not yet had their windows fitted it is not surprising that they got little sleep. This was the first time most of them had been away from home, and they were very excited to be soldiering at last. The occupants of some huts chattered away until the early hours, or until a harsh rebuke by a prowling sergeant shut them up.

The winter of 1914–15 was very severe, and it was not uncommon to wake up in the morning to find the hut doors blocked by snow drifts.

'With the doors being outward opening, it meant we couldn't get out with all that snow. So, being the smallest man in the hut, it was decided that I should be pushed through the window to dig the snow away. I had my uses sometimes.' 12/928 L/Cpl J. R. Glenn.

The first priority was to make the camp habitable. The men were put to work quarrying stone to make proper roadways and paths. Until this was done there was mud everywhere, and CSM Polden took to wandering around the camp in Wellington boots. Most of the men were unused to hard manual labour, but it helped to strengthen and toughen them up.

'We had to make all the paths and roads in the camp from stone that we quarried nearby. I wasn't used to being a navvy, the work was really heavy and I was none too pleased with it. You groused at the time, not realising that all this hard labour was helping with your general fitness and hardening you for the rigours of soldiering.' 12/664 Pte H. Hall.

Another group of specialists now began to learn their trade, the cooks. Some of their early efforts were very good, but equally there were complete disasters. On one occasion a cook even tipped the ashes from the ovens into the stew!

'The food at first left a lot to be desired, after all the cooks were learning and it was 'Hobson's Choice' if it was edible or not. There was a chap in our hut at Redmires who seemed to be continuously hungry always asking if you had any spare food, he must have had hollow legs. Even when in the trenches he was a fearless scrounger, always on the look out for food. It could be said that food killed him. After the War when on holiday with his family he went for a swim in the sea after having had a big lunch, and drowned. I think his name was Meakin, he worked in the Town Hall Surveyor's Department.' 12/664 Pte H. Hall.

(Authors Note – 12/729 L/Cpl Francis Meakin was in C Company. He went over the top on 1st July 1916. He was discharged from the Army as being unfit for further service on 6th February, 1918.)

The morning after moving in reveille was at 6.30. After breakfast Maj Clough marched A and B Companies to church at Ranmoor, and the rest of the day was then free. As a rare

Winter snows drifted against the hut doors and prevented the men getting out in the mornings. The smallest man in each hut was pushed out of the window to clear the snow.

The cookhouse at Redmires. Standing sixth from left is 12/839 Sgt. R. Hutton.

privilege guests were allowed to visit the men in the camp. However on Monday morning work began in earnest, with road building, digging drainage ditches and clearing an area to the east of the camp for a parade ground.

With the Battalion living cheek by jowl the men got to know each other better, and a sense of belonging to the unit became more acute. Despite the poor conditions esprit de corps was fostered and

The camp gateway always attracted inquisitive crowds.

Opening ceremony of the YMCA. Lord Roberts Memorial Hut at Redmires on 30th December 1916. Sixth from the left is the Bishop of Sheffield, then the Mistress Cutler, the Lord Mayor, the Rev'd J. F. Colquhoun, Mr S. M. Johnson. Fourth from the right is Maj T. Carter Clough.

morale was very high. Friendships were forged at this time that would see them through the carnage, degradation and deprivations that were to come at the front.

Soon after arriving at Redmires the City Battalion, along with the 13th and 14th York and Lancaster Regiment, and 10th Lincolnshire Regiment, (10th Lincs), were formed into 115th Infantry Brigade, as part of 38th Division; (hereafter 'Infantry' will be omitted from brigade and divisional titles). The Brigade was commanded by Brigadier General H. Bowles CB. He set up his HQ at 7 Bank Street in Sheffield, and later moved it in February 1915 to 93 Brunswick Street. Back in October Army Order No. 388 had allocated the City Battalion to 21st Division, along with 14th Northumberland Fusiliers and 10th South Staffordshire Regiment. But Army Order No. 434 in November replaced the City Battalion with 13th King's Royal Rifle Corps.

A local dignitary, Mr S. M. Johnson, had the idea of opening a YMCA hut at Redmires, in memory of the late Field Marshal Lord Roberts. He organised the setting up of a fund for the purpose of providing recreational facilities for the City Battalion. Lord Roberts had been Commander in Chief in the South African War, before being succeeded by Kitchener. As a Lieutenant in the Indian Mutiny he had won the Victoria Cross. He died in France on 14th November whilst visiting troops at the front.

The bad weather caused a series of delays, but the YMCA hut was finally opened by Mr Johnson on 30th December. In attendance at the ceremony were the new Lord Mayor, Mr O. C. Wilson, the Bishop of Sheffield and the Mistress Cutler. The hut served many purposes apart from being a canteen. It doubled as a church and had quiet rooms where the men could write letters. There was also a Post Office.

The venture proved to be a tremendous success. From opening until the end of March 1915, 35 concerts were held in the YMCA hut. In the same period the Post Office dealt with 22,000 packages, and took in over £135 in savings. Although how the men managed to save anything out of 7/- a week is something of a mystery!

Over the Christmas period everyone was allowed home for a short leave. They were not all allowed to go at the same time, and the companies were staggered to retain some men at Redmires to carry on the routine duties. 12/1141 Cpl R. B. Henderson in D Company decorated his hut with the Battle Honours of the York and Lancaster Regiment, as well as the more usual seasonal decor. It is this hut that appears in the reproduced postcard photographs.

The Battalion Policemen with Sgt J. H. Kirk on the left.

Cpl Henderson was an old volunteer soldier from South Africa days. He was mortally wounded on the night of 26–27th June 1916, while rescuing a wounded comrade from No Man's Land. He died on 30th June, aged 39. He was one of the Battalion's characters and his loss was felt by everyone.

On Christmas day the men left at the camp were served their dinner by the officers, as is the tradition in the services. From photographs it appears they did not go short. New Year's Eve began as a quiet affair with lights out at 10.15 as normal. However, at midnight the men got up and gathered outside their huts to sing 'Auld Lang Syne', and they were joined by a number of the officers.

Cpl Henderson's hut decorated for Christmas. Above the centre window we can see one of the York & Lancs battle honours, Tel El Kebir.

For the Battalion New Year's Day 1915 began with a route march, but it had to be cut short. A violent storm blew up soon after leaving the camp, and they quickly returned rather than get wet unnecessarily. That evening Capt Hoette gave a lecture on his experiences in the South African war, using slide photographs he had taken there to illustrate his talk. This was very well received by the men who

Serving Christmas dinner at Redmires 1914, from left to right: Cpl R. B. Henderson, Capt J. L. Middleton, 2Lt R. E. J. Moore and C.S.M. Cavanagh. The officers are wearing double crossbelts on their Sam Brownes. This was introduced by Lt Col Mainwaring and was not usual in York & Lancs Battalions. After he left the Battalion the officers reverted to the normal single strap over the right shoulder.

attended.

Capt Albert R. Hoette was something of an adventurer. In his earlier life he had been a sailor, and later he had farmed in South Africa, Argentina and Australia. He was in command of D Company until being wounded on 1st July 1916. Sadly some years after the war he took his own life, probably as a result of his failing health.

January also saw the departure of RSM Miller. He was replaced by the legendary RSM C. Polden, who would remain as RSM until June 1917 when he became an Honorary Lieutenant and the Battalion's Quartermaster (QM).

There were a number of important visitors during the month. On the 13th Brigadier General Bowles called at Redmires and watched some of the men undertaking musketry training, while others took part in simulated attacks. He returned to Redmires on the 26th, this time escorting Gen R. B. Gainsford CB CMG, the Director of Infantry. They watched troops drilling on the parade ground and later saw others on physical training. They then left the camp and walked to Quarry Hill, beyond the 'Grouse and Trout Inn' which used to stand on the left hand side of the road from Redmires Camp. Here they saw two platoons of B Company digging trenches on land that had been loaned by Mr William Watson of Beauchief Hall and Mrs Wilson Mappin. The next day Col Josling arrived to conduct a

Digging trenches on the moors near Redmires.

Among the first men to die in the City Battalion was Pte Charles Haydn Hanforth. His funeral was recorded in 'The Sheffield Independent War Album'. The funeral took place February 12th, 1915. 1. Coffin entering the Cathedral. 2 and 3. The funeral procession passing through Nether Green. 4, At the Graveside. 5. Firing a volley in salute to their comrade.

routine inspection of the camp as the area medical supervisor. None of these visits found the Battalion lacking in any respect.

Although most men thrived on the arduous training, the atrocious weather conditions took their toll. Some contracted pneumonia, and at least one man died. He was 12/133 Pte C. H. Hanforth, who passed away in the 3rd Northern General Hospital in Collegiate Crescent on 8th February 1915.

Pte Hanforth's funeral was held at the Cathedral on 12th February. His father was the organist there. It was conducted with full military honours and A Company provided 100 men to line the route into the Cathedral. Following the service Pte Hanforth was buried at Fulwood Church. The Last Post was sounded and a party fired shots over the grave.

On 20th February another man died. He was 12/741 Pte J. C. Ortton. The cause of his death is not known, but it is likely to have been pneumonia. He was buried with full military honours, on 23rd February at City Road Cemetery.

There is some dispute as to who has the dubious honour of being the first man in the City Battalion to die in the service of the King. Before Ptes Hanforth and Ortton died the Commonwealth War Graves Commission (CWGC) record the death of 12/344 Pte E. Cuthbert, on

Capt H. W. Pearson.

12th October 1914. It is strange that there was no mention of this in the local press. It was an event unlikely to have been missed by the Sheffield area newspapers, despite Cuthbert being a Lincolnshire man. The City Battalion was big news at the time and a story such as this would undoubtedly have been published. Unfortunately it is a mystery that needs more research than we had time for.

The Battalion attracted many gifts from well meaning benefactors. Anyone who was anybody in the City wanted to be associated with it. These gifts varied from expensive items of military equipment to comforts for the men.

Samuel Roberts, the MP, had presented a Union Flag to Major Clough on 8th November, following the service at St Mary's church. When it was flown over Redmires camp it was rapidly reduced to rags by the vicious wind. So on 14th March 1915 Mr Roberts presented another one to the Battalion.

On 20th November, prior to the move to Redmires, on returning to Edmund Road from a route march the Battalion had been welcomed back by a corps of drums. These had been paid for by Colonel Hughes and Messrs A. J. Hobson, W. Hobson, A. Wightman and S. J. Robinson. They were decorated with the City crest.

Captain Colquhoun, the Padre, was invited to a meeting of the Sheffield Federation of the Church of England Men's Society, at Church House, on 11th February. At this meeting he was presented with a silver communion set for the use of the Battalion's chaplain. We wonder what became of the drums and the silver? They are not in the Regimental Museum.

The gifts did not stop arriving when the Battalion left Sheffield. In late May 1915, Mr Charles Crook of Gell Street, arranged for 1,500 packets of cigarettes to be delivered to the men; and as late as December 1915 there are articles in the Sheffield newspapers telling of further presentations.

One of the last gifts was photographed and appeared in the Sheffield Daily Telegraph on 18th December 1915. Three stretchers with a single centrally mounted wheel had been given to the Battalion by Sheffield notables. They were designed to ease the load on the shoulders of the stretcher bearers. The stretchers are not mentioned again, and it is assumed they were taken to Egypt, but were found to be useless in the confined space of the trenches in France.

Despite the war, and the lengthening casualty lists in the newspapers many of the men were married during the stay at Redmires. One of the first to take the plunge was 12/927 L/Cpl W. H. Giraud, some time in January 1915. His platoon bought him a set of cased pipes as a wedding present, and also presented his wife with a small iron cross, (not the German military decoration), in recognition of her courage. She would certainly need it, her husband would be killed at the front in May 1917.

The Battalion had a great reputation for its sporting prowess. Many famous local sportsmen were amongst its ranks, and some of them are shown below:

Redmires showing construction of roads.

Kit layout awaiting CO's inspection.

12/573 Pte G. G. Abraham – Noted Sheffield golfer

12/282 Pte J. H. Allan – Hallamshire Harrier and Yorkshire 440 yds champion

12/589 ACSM A. C. Baynes – Sheffield Road Club cyclist

Pte R. M. Davy – Noted Sheffield motor-cyclist

12/834 RQMS P. Doncaster – Sheffield United reserves

12/103 Pte F. Fowlstone – Otter's waterpolo goalkeeper

12/706 Pte W. H. Kettle – Secretary Sharrow Cricket Club

Capt H. W. Pearson – Noted Sheffield golfer and motorist

L/Cpl Gus Platts – Professional boxer

Capt V. S. Simpson – Sheffield Wednesday amateur

Pte F. Taylor – Sickleholme Golf Club pro

Cpl R. O. Wever – Northern England hockey team

Recreation time at Redmires.

The men took a great pride in their fitness, which stood them out from the rest of the Brigade. However, it is not surprising that they were so fit given the location of the camp. Marching over the moors, and up and down the steep local hillsides strengthened them very quickly indeed. It was not unknown to spend a morning in full battle order running up and down the track that follows Wyming Brook down into the valley below the camp. One veteran, 12/300 RQMS T. Bingham, even recalled running up and down Lodge Lane. Parts of this hill have to be negotiated in first gear in a car; in battle order it must

A route march near Stanedge Edge. The officer is thought to be Lt W. S. Clarke.

have been an exhausting ordeal. The harsh life they led at Redmires further enhanced their physical robustness.

The Battalion became well known for its sports teams. The soccer eleven was very strong. In a match, against 15th Battalion Nottinghamshire and Derbyshire Regiment, (15th Notts & Derby), on 22nd April, the Battalion won a resounding victory by six goals to nil. Despite the fact that the opposition was made up of bantams (undersized soldiers between 5ft and 5ft 5 ins) it was still a good result. The Notts and Derby Regiment was more commonly known as the Sherwood Foresters.

A rare chance for the men to show visitors around the camp.

Many other sports were played, but by far the biggest event was the Sports Day at Redmires, on 29th April 1915. As if arranged to order the weather on the day was glorious, and a large crowd, from the City, turned out to watch. The buses couldn't cope with the rush and many people had to walk all the way from town. An estimated 10,000 spectators attended. This was one of the few occasions when civilians were allowed into the camp, other than on business. Great interest was shown in the men's accommodation, and in their military equipment.

There were over 1,000 individual entrants, and the morning was spent in running heats to decide the finalists. Entrants were not restricted to the City Battalion and sizeable contingents turned up from both Barnsley Battalions and 15th Notts & Derby.

The five mile Steeplechase started and finished on the parade square after circumnavigating the Redmires reservoirs. This event, like most of the others, was won by a Battalion runner. A notable exception was in the 100 Yards, in which Pte Harrison of the Barnsleys was the winner in a time of 10.35 seconds.

The Victor Ludorum was Pte E. M. Carr of A Company. He won the High Jump and the 220 Yards, and was runner up to Pte Harrison in the 100 Yards. Eric Marcus Carr was a well known local schoolboy athlete from King Edward VII's School. He was commissioned on 27th June 1915, and commanded the rear details when the Battalion went to Egypt. He rejoined it in time for the opening of the Somme offensive, and was killed on 1st July 1916. He has no known grave.

A Company had a good day at the Sports. In addition to Pte Carr winning the Victor Ludorum, the Company also won the Tug-of-War and the football competition.

Probably the most gruelling event was the Inter-Platoon Mile. Each team was led by its platoon commander, and consisted of 16 other men in full fighting order with their rifles. They each carried about 50 pounds. The winning team was 16 Platoon, under Second Lieutenant A. J. Beal, in a time of seven minutes and 45 seconds. This was a truly remarkable demonstration of physical fitness.

RQMS Tom Bingham. Before and after the war he was a teacher.

Second Lieutenant Arnold James Beal had only been commissioned since 17th February, and had been the OC of the Machine Gun Section for a short time, before taking over 16 Platoon. He was killed on 1st July 1916 and is buried in Queens Military Cemetery at Serre.

The whole day was a tremendous success. At the end of the competitions Mrs Branson, wife of the Deputy Mayor, Col Branson, presented the prizes watched by the organising committee.

The Battalion's stay at Redmires had by this time almost run its course, and preparations were in hand to concentrate all of 94th Brigade into one camp. This would enable Brigade sized manoeuvres, which were the next stage of training, to take place. The selected concentration area was Cannock Chase near Stafford.

On 30th April the new General Officer Commanding of Northern Command, Major General H. Lawson CB, visited Redmires and was very complimentary about the state of training. He also remarked on how well the camp looked, which shows how hard the men must have worked to transform it from its original muddy state.

Training continued right up to the time of the move to Cannock. 12/525 Sgt J. W. Streets wrote of a particularly unpleasant night exercise on the nearby moors at the beginning of May. It was cold, wet and foggy. The scheme was one in which outposts were manned by piquets, while other troops were engaged

At the Battalion Sports Day, 29th April 1915. The RSM, Charles Polden holds the loudhailer. Capt Ellwood scrutinises the programme, Col Mainwaring is to his left. On the extreme right is CSM W. H. Marsden of Marion Road, Hillsborough.

A company on a route march into Derbyshire in early 1915. The officer on the right is Capt W. J. Jarrard, the Company Commander who later was to command the Reserve Companies of Redmires when the Battalion left for Cannock Chase. The other officer is thought to be 2Lt N. K. Peace.

Stacked rifles as the men brew up during field training.

in patrolling to try to penetrate the line of posts. Sgt Streets was luckier than some that night. At least he was in one of the heavily wooded plantations, and therefore not as exposed to the elements as the men out on the open moor.

The orders to move arrived on Sunday 9th May 1915. At the same time the Battalion learned that due to a reorganisation they were now part of 94th Brigade, under a renumbered 115th Brigade HQ. The Barnsley men in the 13th and 14th York & Lancs stayed with the City Battalion, but the 10th Lincs were replaced by 11th Battalion East Lancashire Regiment better known as the Accrington Pals.

The original Fourth New Army, (30th to 35th Divisions), was being broken up to provide reinforcements for the first three New Armies, (9th to 26th Divisions), which were already at the front or destined soon to be there. At the same time the locally raised battalions were included in the new Fourth New Army Divisions. These Divisions took over the old Divisional numbers, 30th to 35th. 94th Brigade was in 31st Division.

Until brigades were swapped around it was possible to work out which division a brigade belonged to. By dividing the brigade number by three, the nearest whole number gives the divisional number. In reverse the process works equally well. By multiplying the divisional number by three

Inside one of the shower blocks at Redmires.

A typical evening's entertainment at Redmires, in Cpl Henderson's Hut. Some faces have been identified: from the left - 3rd standing, 12/1133 Sgt F. G. M. Chambers, 4th standing, 12/1031 Pte F. C. Robinson, 7th standing, 12/877 Cpl O. Bradshaw, later a cartoonist with the Sheffield Daily Telegraph, 8th standing, Pte T. H. Moorwood, 12th standing 12/1058 Pte. R. A. Sparling, 13th standing is Cpl Henderson and 14th is thought to be 12/1110 Pte F. W. Wright. From the left sitting are 2nd, Pte Adam Kerr, 6th, 12/1043 Pte. W. R. Scott and 7th, 12/966 Cpl F. M. Hunt.

The inside of a Redmires' hut. During the day the beds are folded back to make space for the dining tables in the middle, which in this picture are set out ready for a meal.

Entertainment in the City Battalion was often of a higher quality than in the average infantry battalion! Little wonder the Barnsleys called them the 'Coffee and Bun Boys'. (Note the loaves of bread stacked on the shelf.)

Kit laid out for inspection.

you arrive at the middle brigade for that division. For example the 31st Division's brigades turn out to be the 92nd, 93rd and 94th. 115th Brigade was in the original 38th Division, which was now re-raised in the Fifth New Army.

Maj Clough went off to recce the new camp, which he found to be still under construction. On 11th May an advance party left Redmires under Capt Hoette, consisting of three officers and 100 Other Ranks (ORs). They marched down to Sheffield Midland Station where they joined forces with the

A relaxed route march from Redmires.

Top row, left to right :—Lieutenant WARD, Second Lieutenant W. D. BERRY, Lieutenants MIDDLETON, CLARK, MOXEY, COUSINS, ELAM, Second Lieutenants ATKINSON, T. G. BERRY, LUCAS, and TYZACK.

Middle row :—Second Lieutenants SIMPSON, WOODHOUSE, COOPER, Lieutenant INGOLD, Second Lieutenants EARL and BEAL. Captains KINNER, ALLAN, WOOLHOUSE, Second Lieutenants PEACE STORREY and PEARSON.

Bottom row :—Lieutenant MAUNDER (Quartermaster), Captains ELLWOOD, JARRARD, Major CLOUGH, Colonel MAINWARING, Majors PLACKETT and HOETHE, Lieutenant TUNBRIDGE, Captain BEELEY, Lieutenant MITCHELL (Medical Officer), Second Lieutenant PITT.

Insets :—Captain MOORE, Second Lieutenant GRANT, Lieutenant COLQUHOUN (Chaplain).

Top row, left to right :—Sergeants JONES, FAKER, BUCKLEY, UNWIN, FURZEY, REEVE, MADIN, BARDSLEY, TURNER, and R. G. ROBERTS.

Second row :—Sergeants ATKIN, FYFE, BINGHAM, WELLS, REGISTER, CROZIER, E. W. ROBERTS, WILKINSON, SIMPSON, and HORNCASTLE.

Third row :—Sergeants SLEIGH, PHILBEY, CHAPPELL, BEVINGTON, POWELL, HEPPINSTALL, KIRK, NUTT, BRIDGWATER, ATKINSON, CONNELL, and EVERITT.

Fourth row :—Company-Quartermaster-Sergeant BILBEY, Company-Sergeant-Majors MORLEY, CAVANAGH, and MARSDEN, Regimental-Quartermaster-Sergeant DONCASTER, Regimental-Sergeant-Major POLDEN, Company-Quartermaster-Sergeants CHARLESWORTH, BADGER, and SHEPHERDSON, Company-Sergeant-Major LOXLEY.

Insets :—Sergeant HUTTON (Regimental Cook), Company-Sergeant-Major ELLIS, Sergeant HENDERSON.

Group photographs of the Officers and Sergeants of the Battalion taken before leaving Redmires. Note that in the officers' photograph above a name is missing – Captain Colley sits between Captain Jarrard and Major Clough in the front row.

advance parties of the two Barnsley Battalions. The combined party was then seen off by Brigadier General Bowles, the Brigade Commander.

While packing up was in progress at Redmires on 12th May, farewell presents of cigarettes and chocolates were sent to the camp. They had been organised by the Matron and nurses of the nearby Lodge Moor Hospital. The imminent departure of the Battalion caused great excitement in the City. Arrangements were made to give the Battalion a good send off, but the day before departure the Midland Railway Company announced they were unable to lay on trains at the required times of 11.20 and 11.35. Instead the departure would take place earlier in the morning.

There was great disappointment in the City as a result of the change in plans, but even so many people turned out early to see the Battalion off. The soldiers were woken at 4.30 a.m. on 13th May. After breakfast they put on all their equipment and marched off at 6.15. On Manchester Road they were met by two bands, one from the Sheffield Engineers and the other provided by the Hallamshires. Together the two bands played them to the Town Hall.

As they swung along the streets discipline was relaxed and mothers, wives and sweethearts of some of the men joined them arm in arm. At 7.30 they turned into Surrey Street and were drawn up opposite the Town Hall entrance. A platform had been erected for the speakers, and a crowd of over 5,000 people crammed into the remaining space on the pavements to listen.

The Lord Mayor, Mr 0. C. Wilson, and his deputy, Colonel Branson, both wished the Battalion good luck in the trials that lay ahead. They also hoped that they would bring glory to the City. The Commanding Officer called for three cheers and then the Battalion was on the march again, along Fargate and High Street to the Midland Station. As they passed by, a regular soldier home on leave, said the bearing of the men was as good as the Guards. A fine compliment indeed.

At the Station the men's families crowded in to see them. There were many touching scenes of farewell amid the clamour and bustle. Most of the families thought that this was the last time they would see their menfolk before they went abroad. No one knew then that every man would get leave before embarkation, nor that going abroad was still some seven months away.

The officers and NCOs eventually sorted out the chaos, and the first train with A and B Companies aboard, plus Battalion HQ, left at 8.25 a.m. They were followed at 9.50 a.m. by C and D Companies. For miles along the track people turned out to wave to them.

In the middle of the afternoon the trains disgorged their loads of stiff soldiers at the small Staffordshire town of Rugeley. The Battalion then marched up the hill onto Cannock Chase to its new home, Penkridge Bank Camp. Lieutenant Middleton's reaction to the place was typical, he said the camp was, 'half finished and very cold'.

Regimental crest outside guardroom at Redmires.

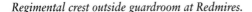

Awaiting the Battalion prior to seeing it off to Cannock. The Lord Mayor Mr O. C. Wilson and local dignitaries take their places on a specially constructed platform in front of the Surrey Street entrance to the Town Hall.

The Battalion is drawn up in Surrey Street to hear the farewell speeches.

After a resounding three cheers the Battalion marched off to the Midland Station for the journey to Cannock Chase.

Chapter Three

Advanced Training

After enduring the rigours of a Redmires winter the Battalion might have been expected to be pleased with the move, but at first they were not. Although they had been in the Army for eight months they had been close to their homes and friends and still saw them regularly. They also felt cheated; having worked hard in the harsh winter to make Redmires habitable, they expected to reap the rewards when the good weather came in the spring. But instead they had been uprooted into unfamiliar surroundings, and the new camp was a complete mess. To cap it all there was no handy 'Three Merry Lads'!

Penkridge Bank Camp was one of two huge military complexes to be built on Cannock Chase; the other one was called Brocton. When they were both completed there was space to accommodate two entire infantry divisions; about 35,000 men plus numerous transport animals. In May 1915 however, it was still under construction. 94th Brigade was the first formation to move into the Penkridge Bank complex.

Cannock Chase is an area of high ground standing between Stafford and Rugeley. In 1915 it was mainly scrub and moorland, and was full of wildlife including many deer. The soldiers were constantly startling them while out on training manoeuvres. Today the Chase is mainly covered by coniferous plantations.

The inhabitants of the nearby towns and villages were very apprehensive at the prospect of having tens of thousands of high spirited young men billeted in their midst. However, by the time 94th Brigade left they had nothing but praise for their temporary visitors. Rugeley Urban District Council even passed a resolution conveying their compliments to the troops for their good behaviour.

This reputation had not been easy to achieve and some drastic measures had been necessary. On one occasion cork matting and straw had been laid along a stretch of road, outside the house of a seriously sick person, to deaden the noise of troops marching past.

Cannock Chase: Looking along the road from Broadhurst Green towards the White House on the right of the road to Penkridge Bank Camp on the horizon. This whole area today is completely covered in trees.

Signallers take it easy training while behind them the riflemen do physical drills. On the left is Reg Glenn and on the right is Frank Jameson. The man in the centre is thought to be Pte F. H. Carpenter. They are using a type of Morse field telephone which employs an earth return circuit. A similar device was used by a staff officer on 1st July, 1916, to send the message which the Germans intercepted to discover that the British offensive was imminent.

Full Brigade exercises took place, especially in attacks and tactical movement. For the signallers there was also an increase in the amount of communications training. Night operations were particularly well covered, and they dug trenches all over the Chase. The tempo of fitness training was increased and route marches became more frequent and longer. The hard slogs around Redmires in the early days now paid off. On Brigade marches the Battalion was always outstanding.

> 'On one march we were passing a road sweeper, who must have been an old soldier. He looked up and did a marvellous present arms with his broom, and our officer returned the salute.' 12/928 L/Cpl J R Glenn.

By the end of the war Cannock Chase had a large complex of long and short rifle ranges, but they were still under construction at this time. There was an immediate need for a shorter range on which to zero rifles, and the Battalion was set the task of building a 100 yard range for this purpose.

Training on the SMLE. The men are in a mixture of blue and khaki at this stage.

The Battalion pauses during construction work on the Zeroing range on Cannock Chase.

Zeroing is a process which brings the rifle barrel and the sights into synchronisation. It is necessary because of minute variations in manufacture, and because every man has peculiarities in the point of aim he takes.

The method of zeroing has not changed since the First World War. It relies on the rifleman firing five carefully aimed shots at a target, using the same point of aim throughout. When the target is examined it is simply a case of adjusting the sights to bring the fall of shot onto the target centre. The sights would normally be adjusted by the armourer. Zeroing always took place at 100 yards, because at greater ranges errors could mean missing the target altogether, thus making adjustment very difficult.

Soon after arriving at Penkridge one man was given the job of constructing a large mosaic York and Lancs badge on the parade square. It would be exactly the same as the one that stood outside the guardroom at Redmires. The parade ground itself was covered by thousands of stones, which had to be laboriously picked up. There was however, a practical use for the stones; they went to make pathways between the huts.

More equipment arrived at Penkridge, in particular rifles and transport. Sixteen hundred Lee Metfords were supplied in total. Of these only 1,100 were found to be reasonably serviceable, even if in poor condition. The remainder were too dangerous to fire and had to be returned! The Battalion's transport was also made up to scale at this time. Draft horses and pack mules, wagons and carts came in little by little. Within a few months the full complement had been received.

The Transport Officer, Lt Middleton, was dogged by always moving into camps which were incomplete. Since the priority was always to house the men first, his animals came off second best every time.

At Penkridge the animal lines were not completed until a few weeks after the Battalion's arrival. The situation would be the same at the other camps the Battalion occupied before going abroad.

Zeroing new rifles.

The concentration of 94th Brigade at Penkridge Bank brought its units into close contact with each other for the first time. Because of the different backgrounds of the Battalions, relations between them, at soldier level, were not always harmonious. The City

The Machine Gun Section with the Vickers on loan to the Battalions. Before going abroad the Vickers were withdrawn to form Brigade Machine Gun Companies and Battalions, were issued with the lighter Lewis Guns instead.

The location of the camp on Cannock Chase.

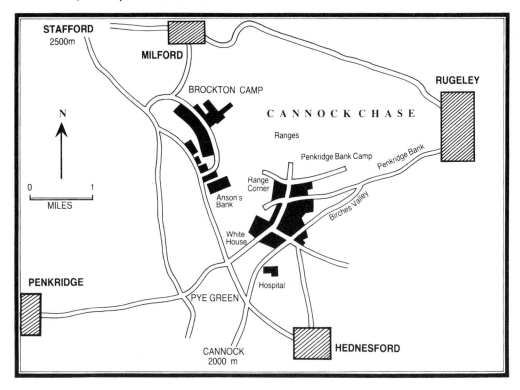

Battalion regarded the Barnsley men as a rough and ready lot. The Barnsley men were equally unimpressed by this white collar bunch from Sheffield, who they called the 'coffee and bun boys'. Slowly a mutual respect was built up, and the Brigade soon had the reputation as the best in the Division.

In addition to the heavy training programme, the men were often called upon to put out fires on the Chase. The hot summer frequently caused the outbreak of large conflagrations. Eventually a large fire piquet had to be provided by the Brigade. It was about 100 men strong, and was manned by Battalions in rotation.

Fire fighting on the Chase.

Although the men had to work very hard at their training, and other duties, there was the compensation of generous amounts of leave. Every weekend while at Penkridge, 15% of the Battalion were allowed to go home. And as a bonus, on 2nd – 4th June, the whole Battalion was stood down in recognition of the King's birthday.

Now that the men could no longer slip home as easily as at Redmires, the volume of mail that the Post NCO had to deal with increased enormously. Up to 1,100 letters per day were sent out, and incoming mail arrived by the sack load. Included were hundreds of parcels of food and other goodies, sent by doting mothers and wives to supplement the dreary Army fare.

Members of the Battalion continued to take the plunge into marriage. One of the officers who did so was 2Lt V. S. Simpson, who took Miss M. Belcher as his bride at St. Mark's Church, Sheffield on 19th June. The ORs were not to be left out either. Pte George Senior was even given special leave for his wedding on 2nd July.

Just under a year since its formation the Battalion was formally taken over by the War Office. On 13th July at a very long parade and inspection, all the men's personal equipment was carefully checked over. This was done to assess how much the Sheffield Corporation was to be reimbursed for the financial support they had given the Battalion during the preceding 11 months.

The organising committee had done a magnificent job. No one could have foreseen in September 1914 that they would have to look after the Battalion for so long. Despite this protracted caretaking period the committee continued to maintain a very high standard, and the War Office took over a well equipped and trained Battalion. The formal take over date was 15th August 1915.

Men of 11th East Lancs, at bayonet drill. The remnants of construction materials are evident around the hurriedly erected camps.

A long and dusty route march near Cannock Chase.

Wind of another move was soon going around, and at the end of July orders were received to move to Ripon. As its farewell to Cannock Chase the Battalion went on a 16 mile route march, in full kit, on 30th July. Part of the route went cross country, and it was a blazingly hot day. On previous marches the Battalion had never before lost more than four men. But on this day 80 fell out with heat exhaustion. It took six hours, including halts and the lunch break, to complete the course. At the end those who had made it all the way were just about verging on exhaustion. But there was no time to rest, they then had to prepare to leave Penkridge that same evening.

On their return to camp the men had two hours to clean up, pack up, have a meal and get ready to move out. They then had another march of four miles to Rugeley Station. At least it was a little cooler

Stafford. Greengate.

12TH (SERVICE) BATTALION, YORK & LANCASTER REGIMENT. (SHEFFIELD).

B A T T A L I O N   O R D E R S.   N O 231.

By

Lieut-Colonel J.A. Crosthwaite, Commanding.

Headquarters: Hurdcott Camp. Salisbury. Tuesday. September 28.1915.

PART I.

1. COMMAND.
(a).

In relinquishing the Command of the Battalion on account of having been found unfit for active service, due to nearly thirty years spent in the Tropics, Colonel C.V. Mainwaring desires to place on record his appreciation of the way all ranks have worked during his period of Command.

He thanks the Officers and N.C.O's for the assistance they have given him in instructing those below them in rank, and he thanks the rank and file for the keenness which they have shown to master all the details of their new profession.

It is a great grief to him to sever his active connection with the Battalion, but he can assure all ranks that he will take the very greatest interest in their future.

Wherever it goes, he feels sure that the Battalion will uphold the grand traditions of the British Army, and be a credit to Sheffield.

(b). In accordance with War Office letter No 100/Gen No/ Infantry 3388 (M S I) K, dated 25/9/15, Lieutenant Colonel J.A. Crosthwaite, late Durham Light Infantry, assumes command of the Battalion from September 28th, 1915, vice Colonel C.V. Mainwaring, retired.

2. DUTIES.   Orderly Officer for Wednesday: 2nd Lieut. J.C. Cowen.
             Next for Duty.   : 2nd Lieut. A.J. Beal.

3. PARADES: WEDNESDAY.

Company Commanders' Parades.

4. SICK LIST. The under-mentioned Officer is placed on the sick list September 28th. 1915:-
             2nd Lieut. C.H. Godwin.

5. PIONEERS.
(a) No 12/1323, Private W.R. Carter. "A" Coy, batman to Brigadier-General Bowles, returned to duty 24/9/15, and is placed on the Pioneer staff as saddler from 28/9/15.

(b) No 12/693, Private E. Jeffcock. "C" Coy, is added to the Pioneers from this date as Cold Shoer, vice No 12/310 Private G. Bramham. "B" Coy. (released for munition work).

(c) No 12/490, Private J. Richardson. "B" Coy, is removed from the list of Pioneers from this date, and returns to duty accordingly.

6. BRIGADE ORDERS. The following extract from Brigade Orders is re-published for information:-

No 1034. Bounds: Hurdcott Farm is out of bounds. Troops will on no account leave the gates of fields open, or damage hedges in the vicinity of this farm, or in any other locality.

Battalion orders with Lt Col Mainwaring's farewell message. Also notice in paragraph 5b Pte Bramham is released for munitions work.

While he was home on leave he received notification of his new appointment as CO of 12th York and Lancs.

Unlike the other regular soldiers in the Battalion, the new CO had actual combat experience in France. The others could draw on their experiences of previous conflicts, but much of what they had taught the men was only relevant to frontier wars and policing actions in the Empire. They knew almost nothing of the tactics and realities of a major continental war. This was not surprising, since the last time Britain had fought a war in Europe had been in 1815, at Waterloo! Many hours were spent out on Salisbury Plain on Brigade and Divisional exercises. The aim was to bring them up to a standard ready to go into the trenches in France. The intensity of the various schemes they undertook was always being increased. They never worked harder than at this time until actually at the front itself.

Leave was cut to the barest minimum, but some men managed to get some. The Sheffield Daily Telegraph of 11th October carried a photo of some City Battalion men snapped the previous day in the City.

Having just arrived in a new area the usual VIP visits began again. The most notable was by Gen Sir A. H. Paget, Commander of Salisbury Training Centre, in early November.

Lt Col J. A. Crosthwaite.

The Brigade and Divisional Commanders also called in on a fairly regular basis.

Towards the end of 1915 the Munitions Scandal began to have an effect on the Battalion. Since the outbreak of the war the artillery had been unable to properly support the infantry in France because of a shortage of high explosive shells. The crisis had come to a head at the Battle of Loos, when attacks by British infantry had failed with heavy losses because the artillery had no shells with which to support them. At home Col Repington, the Times Military Correspondent, wrote articles about this scandalous situation. But at first Kitchener refused to believe that a problem even existed, which shows how out of touch he had become.

Besides inefficiency on the part of the military procurement system, one of the major reasons behind the shell shortage was a lack of trained labour in the munitions industry. Many of the skilled workers required to run the factories had volunteered in 1914 and were now serving at the front in Kitchener's Armies.

A Ministry of Munitions was set up under Lloyd-George. One of the first actions it took was to claw back many of the skilled men into their old jobs. Representatives from the Ministry visited every unit and interviewed the men about their previous employment. If they considered that a man was essential to industry they arranged for him to be released from the Army.

The training of the City Battalion was so far advanced by this stage that to withdraw too many men would have seriously impaired its fighting capabilities. Specialists, whose training and experience could not easily be replaced, were jealously guarded and in the end only about 50 men were taken from the Battalion. But throughout the Army over 40,000 men were returned to their pre-war jobs.

Having been forcibly returned to work was not always the end of the story. One of those who was sent back was 12/743 Pte John William Parker, known as Willie. With his brother Reg, (12/744 Pte R. Parker), he had enlisted in the Battalion in September 1914. Some time later Willie was returned to Armstrong-Whitworths where he had been an engineer before the war. He steadfastly refused to believe that he was helping the war effort more in industry than he would have been as an infantryman in the City Battalion. He pestered the Army and his employers persistently, and even petitioned the Mayor, until his factory manager finally gave in and allowed him to go back. He rejoined the Battalion just in time for the opening of the Somme offensive in July 1916.

On 16th November the Battalion, along with the rest of 31st Division, made its way to Larkhill passing Stonehenge on the way. On arrival they took over No. 10 Lincs recently vacated by a Canadian

GD3101 10,000 11/16 HWV(P)

MINISTRY OF MUNITIONS OF WAR

In view of the immediate importance of the output of certain Munitions Works, the Army Council at the request of the Ministry of Munitions have given orders that the enlisting of workers in such works should be so arranged as to ensure a minimum of inconvenience. All workers in this establishment, whether they are or are not in possession of a War Service Badge Certificate, are therefore required to notify the Management immediately they receive a summons to the Colours.

M.M. 94a.

A relaxed hut group. Front row from the left, 12/976 Pte H. G. Kidney, unknown, 12/889 Pte C. F. Chamberlain, 2nd row sitting 2nd from left, 12/953 Pte H. Hickson. Standing extreme left, 12/965 Pte W. Hutton. Standing in centre of door with rolled sleeves and crossed arms, 12/1042 Pte N. Scaife. Standing in doorway on left, 12/847 Pte W. G. Alflat, centre 12/1040 Pte R. Sanderson. Standing to right of door 12/1022 Pte O. Price.

Battalion, which was on its way to France. Everyone in the Battalion was expecting to be there soon themselves.

The reason for moving to Larkhill was to fire Parts 3 and 4 of the Musketry course. In addition there were good facilities for the machine gun crews to practise their deadly trade on the Larkhill ranges.

At Larkhill the long awaited SMLE rifles were issued to the men. They could now get used to their own personal weapon, get the zero spot on and settle down to classify with it. The shooting tests in Parts 3 & 4 were of a more practical nature than their previous training, involving firing from trenches, as well as more traditional firing positions.

In 94th Brigade the City Battalion won four out of the five prizes for shooting. This further enhanced the Battalion's already high reputation within the Brigade and Division.

Signallers on Salisbury Plain. 2nd from left is Sgt. Gus Simons.

None of the camps that the City Battalion had occupied could be described as luxurious, but Larkhill proved to be the most primitive and uncomfortable of them all. In a letter Sgt Streets tells of the bitter cold, made worse by no coal being available for the stoves. He also mentions the practice trenches and the chalky mud that everyone was plastered in. Within a few months he would be familiar with other chalky and muddy trenches, but these would not be for practice.

12/525 Sgt John William Streets was a self educated man and a well known war poet. This is especially remarkable since he was a miner from Whitwell in Derbyshire. He passionately believed in the righteousness of the British cause in the war, and his ardent patriotism comes through clearly in his poetry. On 1st July 1916, he was killed while returning to NML to rescue a wounded comrade. He is believed to be buried in Euston Road Military Cemetery at Colincamps. An anthology of his poems was published in 1917.

While training continued at Larkhill orders began to come through for the whole Division to move to France. Lt Middleton first heard of it on 20th

November, although it is not known when the Battalion received its official notification. Capt A. N. Cousins was selected as the Battalion's representative on the Divisional advance party. He accompanied the Divisional Staff, the four Brigade Majors and the other unit representatives when they left England on 29th November.

Capt Arthur Norman Cousins originally enlisted as a soldier in the Battalion, but by 1st November 1914 he had been commissioned. His rise was rapid and on 1st October 1915 he was promoted to Captain. On the arrival of the Battalion in France he was seconded to HQ 94th Brigade as the Intelligence Officer, a post he held from 7th April to 20th August 1916. Soon after becoming the Adjutant, at the end of November 1917, he was killed and is buried in Roclincourt Military Cemetery.

The news of going to France caused great excitement in the ranks, mixed with not a little apprehension. On 30th November as the Battalion marched back to Hurdcott, the Musketry course completed, runners brought the news that the move to France had been cancelled, and the advance party was returning.

There is a discrepancy in dates here. The 94th Brigade War Diary (WD) records the cancellation order being issued on 2nd December, yet a number of diarists record being told of the change on 30th November. It is possible that the order mentioned in the WD was purely confirmatory to back up earlier verbal orders. Whatever the reason the Battalion was not slow to take advantage of the respite, and the men were sent on leave.

Half the Battalion went on leave on 2nd December, returning late the following evening. The rest went on the morning of 4th December and returned on the evening of the 5th. Each party therefore had less than 36 hours leave, which was precious little. But if they had been going to France there would have been no leave at all, so they were thankful for what little there was.

As the second half of the Battalion was making its way back to Hurdcott after its short break, Lt Middleton was being issued with a new sola topee, or sun helmet. The destination was to be Egypt. Lt Middleton was disappointed; he still wanted to go to France, but he would have his wish soon enough.

The Battalion was to leave England on 21st December, about halfway through the movement programme for the 31st Division. The first units began leaving Devonport on 7th December, and the last unit did not arrive in Egypt until 23rd January 1916.

Such was the level of activity in the Battalion that not one of our diarists recorded anything in their journals for the period 6th-16th December. We can only assume they were far too busy. By the 18th most of the preparations had been completed, and that afternoon many of the men were allowed out of the camp to go into Salisbury.

12/535 Pte Gilbert Unwin and his companions in C Company caught a bus into town. They went to the YMCA and 'The Haunch of Venison', where they ate a 'hearty tea'. Pte Unwin only kept his diary for a fortnight, ending on 30th December. It is thought that he obeyed the order banning the keeping of diaries on active service. Fortunately not everyone was so disciplined. He was killed on 4th May 1916 at the age of 25, and is buried in the Sucrerie Military Cemetery.

During the morning of Sunday the 19th the men packed their kit bags and loaded them onto the transport carts. Later a church service was held.

Salisbury High Street Gate. (Dodging the Redcaps). Jameson.

Movements of the City Battalion in England 1914–15.

After lunch they were again free to walk out until 6 p.m. Since the Battalion was due to leave in the early hours of the next morning, the canteen remained open all night.

On this final day before departure farewell messages were received, most notably from the King, and also from Mr Samuel Roberts MP. The telegram from Roberts read: 'My warmest good wishes to you all. May God's blessing and protection be with you.'

The Battalion replied: 'All ranks convey many thanks for your kind wishes and your past interest in the Battalion.'

Before and after. Scrubbing out a hut in the top photograph prior to an inspection by CSM Ellis at the bottom.

The King's message was much longer and was to compensate for the disappointment he felt at not being able to personally review the Division before it departed. He had been injured on a recent visit to France and was not able to travel. His message read:

> '*Officers, NCOs and men of the 31st Division, on the eve of your departure for active service I send you my heartfelt good wishes. It is a bitter disappointment to me that owing to an unfortunate accident I am unable to see the Division on parade before it leaves England, but I can assure you that my thoughts are with you all. Your period of training has been long and arduous but the time has now come for you to prove on the field of battle the results of your instruction. From the good accounts that I have received of the Division I am confident that the high tradition of the British Army is safe in your hands and that with your comrades now in the field you will maintain the unceasing efforts necessary to bring this war to a victorious ending. Goodbye and God Speed. George I?'.*

The port of embarkation for the Battalion was Devonport, and the journey from Hurdcott was made in three separate parties. On 20th December A and B Companies marched out of the camp to a rousing send off from the other 94th Brigade units. At Salisbury they collected their kitbags from the transport carts, and boarded the train which departed at 5 a.m. Just before 10 o'clock the train halted at Exeter, where the Mayor gave out cigars and cigarettes, and the Lady Mayoress served out sandwiches and tea. By midday the train had been shunted alongside the SS Nestor at Keyham Dockyard, Devonport and embarkation began.

The Nestor was a Blue Funnel ship out of Liverpool, weighing 15,500 tons. Prior to this voyage, her first as a troop ship, she had carried passengers and cargo on the Australia run. The cargo decks had been converted into a series of troop messes, each big enough for about 18 men. The officers and senior NCOs used the original passenger cabins.

C and D Companies left Hurdcott at 2.30 a.m. and the train departed Salisbury at 6.25. They also halted at Exeter to receive the Mayor's hospitality, and by 2 p.m. they too were boarding Nestor.

They stowed their kitbags and rifles, and drew hammocks and blankets, and were then free to wander the decks until 8 p.m. when they bedded down for the night.

The men went to sleep early that first night aboard, due to having been up all the previous night. The hammocks

The mule lines at Hurdcott.

Mobile field kitchen.

Section of City men kitted out for sunnier climes.

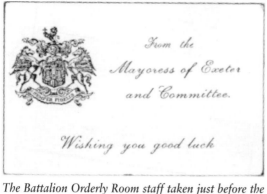

The Battalion Orderly Room staff taken just before the departure for Egypt in December, 1915. From left to right, standing, 12/1058 L/Cpl R. A. Sparling and 12/797 L/Cpl G. Teather, sitting, 12/1054 Sgt H. R. Sleigh, Capt N. L. Tunbridge, the adjutant and 12/806 Sgt H. H. Turner.

proved to be a problem for many of the men, and quite a few fell out during the night, with the ship still firmly tied up at the dockside! The third party, made up mainly of the Battalion's Transport, left Hurdcott at 5 p.m. and arrived at Devonport after midnight. The three officers (Capt Moore and Lts Middleton and Atkinson), and 43 ORs in this party together with the animals and carts were to travel in a different ship to the rest of the Battalion, the HMT *Malakoota*. The ship was shared with the Divisional artillery and their equipment.

John Learn Middleton was one of the Battalion's original officers. He wrote a very full diary of his war service, and extensive use of it has been made in the research for this book. He was originally OC

Lt T. L. Ward's Platoon show off their new headgear.

Final group photographs of the Sergeants and Officers at Hurdcott. Note the officers' Sam Brownes have reverted to normal with the arrival of Lt Col Crosthwaite.

14 Platoon in D Company, and became the Transport Officer on 4th January 1915 retaining this post until 15th January 1916. He then went to B Company to command 5 Platoon. On occasions he commanded B Company, but was left out of the attack on 1st July 1916 and employed as an observer instead. At the end of that day he was one of only five officers from the Battalion left on his feet. In 1917 he transferred to the RFC and was later awarded the DFC.

Capt Reginald E. J. Moore had been a trooper in the Royal Devonshire Yeomanry. At various times he served in B, C, and D Companies. He was severely wounded on 1st July 1916 and did not return to duty until May 1917. In September of that year his eyesight was found to be defective and he left the Battalion for less strenuous duties.

Lt S. J. Atkinson took over from Lt Middleton as the Transport Officer in January 1916. He remained in this post until taken seriously ill in October of the same year. There is no mention of him thereafter, and it is assumed he was either discharged on medical grounds, or transferred to another unit on recovering.

Battalion transport cart. The driver may be Sgt Atkins.

Life jacket drills on Nestor prior to sailing from Devonport.

The strength of the Battalion on embarkation was:

Officers	29 + 2 attached (the Padre and Medical Officer).
WOS	6
SNCOs	46 + 1 attached (the Armourer, Sgt Beckett).
JNCOs	125
Ptes	817 + 18 attached.
TOTALS	31 officers + 1,013 ORs (incl. 2+19 attached).

In addition there were 89 horses and mules, 23 carts and wagons and nine bicycles. The Battalion's WD was opened on 20th December, and from now onwards we are much more certain of the circumstances of various events.

On board Nestor the morning of 21st December was spent conducting life jacket drills, and all the men were vaccinated against cholera. At 11.45 a.m. the ship slipped its moorings and inched its way out of the harbour escorted by two destroyers.

Devonport turned out in force to give the troops a proper send off. In addition to the soldiers on Nestor's decks cheering for all they were worth, the harbour tugs blew their whistles, naval guns fired salutes, and the crews of the other ships and the naval barracks turned out to cheer as well. On Nestor the Battalion band tried to compete with the noise by playing the Regimental March, 'Keep the Home Fires Burning', 'Auld Lang Syne' and the National Anthem.

It was a very moving and emotional moment for the men as they headed out into the unknown. At the backs of their minds they all knew that some of them would not be coming back. There would be many dangers to face in the future, not least of which was the immediate problem of the menacing U-Boats.

Allied forces prepare to withdraw from Gallipoli.

Chapter Four

Egypt

Before continuing the story of the City Battalion it is necessary to pause and consider why the 31st Division was sent to Egypt. Most of the men believed that Egypt was merely a prelude to being sent to Gallipoli. The situation there had deteriorated throughout the summer of 1915. Rather than opening up the Dardanelles, as had been the purpose of the venture, the force which had landed on the Gallipoli peninsula was desperately clinging to its meagre gains.

The element of surprise and the initiative had been lost almost immediately the initial landings had taken place, and no further progress could be made.

By the end of 1915 the only option left was evacuation, and the acceptance that the whole campaign had been an expensive failure. A major implication of evacuation was that the large force of Turkish troops at Gallipoli would be freed to turn against Egypt through Sinai.

The British could not afford to let Suez fall so the Canal had to be better defended. It may be thought that the troops evacuated from Gallipoli would have been sent to thicken up the Canal defences. Indeed they eventually were, but immediately after being evacuated they would be in no fit state to defend anything. Some of the men had been in the thick of it at Gallipoli for almost eight months, and were utterly worn out. They needed time to rest; to bring their units back up to strength; and also to be re-equipped and retrained, before they could be usefully employed again.

Apart from the men to be evacuated from Gallipoli, there were another 100,000 British and Empire troops in Egypt. On paper this was a considerable force, and one which should have been able to make a great contribution to the defence of Egypt. However, in this total there were only 12 trained infantry battalions. Some of the Australian battalions which were completing their training in Egypt, didn't even have rifles. Clearly the forces in the Middle East would need reinforcement if they were to withstand a Turkish offensive over the Suez Canal.

A German postcard produced for her ally Turkey, depicting British troops being repelled from Gallipoli.

To fill the gap three infantry divisions were to be sent to Egypt; the 31st Division from England, and the 14th and 46th Divisions from France. To withdraw troops from France was indeed a desperate measure. Every man on the Western Front was considered to be vital, and the loss of two whole divisions from the order of battle would have been deeply felt. But within a short time it became obvious that the forces in Egypt would be able to cope after all, and the move of the two divisions in France was cancelled. The 31st Division began to arrive in Egypt on 22nd December.

During the night of 19th-20th December, while the City Battalion was dozing on the train heading for Devonport, the remaining troops at Anzac and Suvla on the Gallipoli peninsula were silently evacuated. The other beach-heads were not finally given up until the night of 8th–9th January 1916. The evacuations, unlike the rest of the operation, were a masterpiece of planning and ingenuity, and were a complete success.

'V' Beach was evacuated under fire. A Turkish shell is seen here to strike close to the transport ship River Clyde.

Even though sufficient forces had been found to reinforce Egypt, the Canal was still not safe. The defences were extremely weak consisting only of earthworks on the Canal banks, and it was wisely decided to construct a series of new defensive lines, on the eastern, i.e. Turkish, side. These new lines were to be 11,000 and 4,500 yards forward of the Canal, with a third line constructed only around the crossing points.

The aim of pushing the defences forward was to deny the Turks the opportunity to fire their artillery directly at shipping in the Canal. However, there was a major problem in that there were very few military engineers in Egypt, and no suitable labour force to undertake the enormous amount of construction work required. Apart from digging trenches and erecting barbed wire obstacles, there was

Abandoned stores ablaze at Suvla Bay, as viewed from HMS Cornwallis.

Turkish attempt to cross Suez Canal on February 3rd, 1915, was thwarted with some 400 killed. German made metal pontoons abandoned on the Canal side and Turkish casualties.

a need to build light railways, lay water pipelines, and construct ferries to connect the two banks of the Canal.

The problem of finding the engineers to plan and supervise the work, was solved by putting many of Egypt's Public Works Civil Servants into uniform. The labour shortage was solved by using infantry soldiers as organised work parties under their own officers and NCOs, but working to the direction of the engineers. Much will be heard later on about the back-breaking work undertaken by the Battalion as part of this work-force.

The threat of a Turkish attack was a very real one. On 3rd and 4th February 1915 they had made an attempt to cut the Canal, but had been pushed back quite easily. What was alarming was the way in which the Turks had got so close to the Canal before being detected. To gain advance warning of any future Turkish advance, mobile patrols mounted on camels were pushed forward up to 20 miles into the Sinai desert, and planes were used to search deeper into Turkish territory.

On its arrival in Egypt the 31st Division was put in XV Corps, commanded by Lt Gen H. S. Home. They were to serve side by side with the Gallipoli veterans of 11th and 13th Divisions. XV Corps was responsible for No. 3 Sector, the northernmost of the three defence zones, which stretched from Port Said on the Mediterranean coast, southwards along the Canal to El Ferdan.

The Division spent just over two months on the Canal, until it was relieved by reformed Gallipoli units. It was then transferred to France. We will now rejoin the Battalion as the SS *Nestor* nosed out of Devonport into the rough waters of the English Channel.

Once out of the shelter of Devonport the rough sea soon made itself felt. Many of the men suffered terribly from seasickness, and few of them could face that evening's meal. Those who were especially badly affected tried to sleep on deck during the day, where they could at least get some fresh air. But there was little else to alleviate their suffering. The decks were often washed with spray and it was very cold in the howling winds of the storm, but this was far preferable to the stuffy warmth below.

After dark all external lights were extinguished against the submarine threat, and at 10 p.m. the escorting destroyers turned for home. Nestor had the sea to herself, and as far as the men were concerned she was welcome to it! Next morning a hearty breakfast of porridge and herrings was served up. One man commented that it was the best food they had had since joining the Army. Ironically most of his friends were not in a position to take advantage of it. It would take a few days for them to find their sea legs, and in the meantime the storm continued to batter the ship unceasingly.

The first full day aboard was taken up with practice alarms, and in the evening there was a sing song on deck. At one point during the day it was so rough that the sea crashed in through the hatches down onto the mess decks below.

The weather on the morning of 23rd December was not as bad as on the previous two days. There were parades and physical drill on deck, and the armourer, 12/2008 Sgt W. Beckett, began rifle inspections. Sixty men at a time were detailed off for submarine guard, 15 to each corner of the ship, armed with their rifles and 50 rounds each. They would have been of limited use against a submarine unless it surfaced fairly close to the ship, and they could then have fired at its gun crew. The ship did have its own guns but these would have been of no use against a submerged attack. The best defence was bad weather, because it prevented the U-Boats from finding their targets in the first place. The ship's gunners took advantage of the good weather on the 23rd to have some target practice at rubbish thrown overboard.

Another storm blew up in the afternoon, but in the evening the weather turned out fine again. Most of the men were now getting over the initial bout of seasickness and began to show interest in the rations.

Breakfast on most days consisted of porridge, plus one of the following on each day; herrings, cheese, tripe, stewed meat, liver or bacon. Lunch was almost invariably a stew, followed by a pudding. In the evening tea would be a more haphazard affair of bread, jam, cheese and tinned fruit.

Christmas Day 1915 was the strangest that most of the men had ever experienced in their lives. A voluntary church service was held on the upper deck in the morning, with the Brigade Commander and the CO reading the lessons. Throughout the day Nestor steered a circular course to pass the time until darkness fell. The ship had to pass through the Straits of Gibraltar at night because the relatively narrow sea lane was a favourite hunting ground for U-Boats. It was too dangerous to attempt passing through in daylight hours.

By 7 p.m. the men on deck could see the Rock with its sweeping searchlights, and the flashing of lamps as signals passed between the naval signalling station and shipping in the strait. To the south was the North African coast, where a lighthouse and the lights of numerous little towns could be seen. Very soon though Gibraltar was behind them, and the ship was in the calmer waters of the Mediterranean. The troops were very relieved to be out of the Atlantic.

Nestor kept close to the coast of North Africa and a number of diarists commented on the spectacular sunrises over the mountains. Now that the weather had become kinder the men organised belated Christmas celebrations, and one event was a concert on deck.

A close watch was always maintained against the submarine threat.

Minesweeper accompanying SS Nestor.

Views from SS Nestor *as she arrives at Valetta Harbour, Malta, on 29th December, 1915.*

During the afternoon and evening of the 27th *Nestor* changed course and headed back towards Gibraltar. No explanation was given, but it was later learned that a ship called the Suffolk had been torpedoed and sunk nearby. Nestor's Captain was sensibly avoiding the area for the time being. At 9 p.m. he turned back onto the eastward course, but going at best speed to outrun any prowling submarines.

Nestor made good time and reached Valetta in Malta at lunch-time on 29th December. There was lots to see in the crowded harbour, and the troops crowded the decks. They bought chocolate and postcards from the vendors in the bum-boats, and enjoyed watching the cat and mouse game they played with the naval police, who regularly chased them off. They always came back and managed to do a roaring trade. They sold cigars at 1/- (5p) for 25, and 100 cigarettes for 9d (4p). There were a few English newspapers to be had as well.

Wounded soldiers who were convalescing on the island rowed small boats around the harbour, and exchanged news with the men on deck.

Young Maltese boys provided entertainment by diving for coins the troops threw overboard. Apart from the Captain, who went ashore to receive his orders, and a few of the Battalion's officers, no one else was allowed off the ship, and at 5 p.m. Nestor put out to sea again.

HMS Cornwallis *anchored in Malta after covering the British withdrawal from the Dardanelles.*

The next few days were spent playing sports on deck and in physical drill. It was now much hotter during the day, although they would have it hotter still in the coming weeks.

The submarine threat did not diminish, and on New Year's Eve the SS *Ionic*, with 11th East Lancs on board, was attacked by a U-Boat in broad daylight. Although they were in sight of the Ionic at the time the troops on Nestor were unaware of the immediate

danger. The submarine fired a torpedo from 500 feet of Ionic's port side, missing its stern by about 100 feet. Ionic then proceeded at full speed and outran the German boat.

1915 passed into 1916 and early on New Year's Day Nestor sailed into Alexandria harbour. It has always been a contentious point that members of the City Battalion are not entitled to the 1914/15 Star, since they didn't land in a war zone until 1st January 1916. They were in constant danger of being drowned, as a result of enemy submarine torpedo attacks, from 21st December 1915 onwards. This however, did not qualify them for the medal. Many of the men felt very bitter about this to the end of their lives.

Before continuing with the story, it will be recalled that a small party, mainly from the Battalion Transport, were travelling on the H M T Malakoota. We will now see how they fared on the journey to Egypt.

The Malakoota sailed the day after Nestor, on 22nd December. It was a much more uncomfortable ship, and space was very limited. The officers lived in wooden huts bolted to the deck. Down below the animal accommodation was so cramped that the poor creatures could not even lie down.

The storms, which Nestor passed through in the Bay of Biscay, also hit Malakoota. A lot of damage was caused and by 26th December there was only one lifeboat left. The rest had been torn from their mountings and washed away. A number of the animals died of pneumonia, including Capt Allen's charger, and they had to be thrown overboard.

Christmas Day arrived but it was impossible to hold any celebrations because of the atrocious weather. Instead, Christmas was observed on 27th December when conditions were calmer. That night Gibraltar was passed and once into the Mediterranean the journey became much easier. The officers passed the time with pistol practice, and on one occasion used a dead mule as a target, as it was towed behind the ship.

Malakoota arrived at Valetta at midday on New Year's Eve. Lt Middleton was one of the few who managed to get ashore to welcome in the New Year. The journey continued next day, and they arrived at Alexandria on the morning of 4th January, docking later in the afternoon.

Due to very high winds it was not possible to unload the animals, and so disembarkation was delayed until 7th January. It was still a risky business transferring the animals and carts onto shore, and one mule was lost when it fell into the sea. By the afternoon of the 8th Lt Middleton had supervised the unloading of his animals and equipment, moved to Port Said and settled into the transport lines. The Battalion was once again complete.

The main body of the Battalion had arrived at Alexandria on 1st January to a rapturous reception from the other ships in the harbour. During the afternoon, while they waited to disembark the men watched the arab street vendors on shore selling oranges and British newspapers. They were periodically

Arab vendors selling their wares to the Sheffielders.

Egyptian policeman sorts out an Egyptian trader.

moved on by native policemen, dressed in blue uniforms and red fez type hats. The police were very fond of dishing out liberal beatings with their long sticks to the layabouts on the dock side. However, they were not too proud to join in the scramble for coins which the troops threw overboard.

In the early evening the Battalion disembarked and boarded two trains bound for Port Said, leaving Alexandria at 7.30 p.m. and 9.30 p.m.

12/1299 Pte A. H. Hastings.

They did not arrive until 7.10 a.m. and 9.30 a.m. the next day. In his diary Pte T. C. Hunter, wrote that he was sad to leave Nestor, but it must be pointed out that he was one of the few not affected by seasickness. Although many of his companions later expressed an affection for the old ship most were very relieved to get back on dry land.

12/156 Pte Thomas Collinson Hunter served in 3 Platoon, A Company. He was wounded on 1st July 1916, and in November 1917 he was commissioned into 3rd West Yorks.

On arrival at Port Said the men were served tea by English ladies and then they were allocated tents. Thirteen men had to share each one and it was very cramped, but in the chilly Egyptian nights it helped them to keep warm.

That night some men were issued passes to go into town. It was a Sunday and they were very surprised to find all the cafes open, and their small orchestras playing the latest tunes from home. The diarists are unanimous in their criticism of the Arabs, who they regarded as filthy creatures. None of them, however, took the trouble to notice the hopeless poverty that they had to endure.

12/847 Pte W. G. Alflat.

The third day of January brought the men back to earth with a bang. There were rifle inspections, route marches and physical drill, and even lectures on their conduct while in Egypt. It was a harsh environment for the men, unused as they were to the climate.

The wind blasted their faces with sand during the day. At night the temperature plunged, often to below zero, and they huddled together in their tents for warmth.

There were no proper facilities for bathing, and the only way to get a good scrubbing down was to jump in the sea or the Canal. Much of their free time was spent swimming. On one of the frequent bathing parades, Pte A. H. Hastings provided a little light relief, by putting a crab in a friend's sock! 12/1299 Pte Alan Howard Hastings was a signaller in A Company. Before the war he had been employed in the family auctioneering business. On 1st July 1916 he was badly wounded by a shrapnel ball which went through his jaw. When he recovered he was transferred to the Labour Corps and served in Italy.

Local native traders arguing a point with City Battalion men.

There was no time for a lengthy acclimatization period, and almost immediately the Battalion began to play its small part in the defence of the Canal. On 5th January during a violent gale, D Company left Port Said in open railway trucks for outpost duty at Tineh. En route Lt Ingold's Platoon was dropped off at Ras El Esh, where it remained until relieved by a platoon from C Company two days later. It then rejoined the rest of the Company to bring it back to its full strength of 4 officers and 201 ORs.

Geoffrey J. H. Ingold was commissioned in the City Battalion because of his experience with the Sheffield University OTC. He was very seriously wounded on 1st July 1916, and never rejoined the Battalion.

The outpost duties at Tineh mainly involved picquets guarding the Canal, and patrolling along its banks. It was certainly not an easy assignment. 12/847 Pte W. G. Alflat was in D Company at this time, and his experience shows just how tiring the work was. A few months later he was very seriously shell shocked in France, and was granted a medical discharge almost immediately afterwards.

On the night of 5th-6th January Pte Alflat was on guard duty manning an observation tower on the Canal bank. The ships passing along the Canal were going by within feet of him, and he could see their searchlights lighting up the water for miles ahead.

Next morning he was allowed to sleep from 9.00 a.m. to 12 noon, and was then woken to help collect stores from the railhead with 50 other men. At 6 p.m. he went over the Canal on the chain ferry for another spell of piquet duty. At 4.30 a.m. on the 7th he 'stood to' and manned the local defences in case of a surprise dawn attack. For the rest of the morning he worked on the ferry.

In a defensive position every man is allotted a position to be held in case of an enemy attack. The order to man these positions was, 'Stand to your posts', and this was usually shortened to just 'Stand to'. The best times to launch an attack were at dawn and dusk, when the poor light made accurate shooting difficult for the defenders. Consequently everyone had to stand to at these times.

The Canal was crossed by a series of chain ferries. These were simple pontoons linked to both banks by chains. Propulsion was provided by a team of soldiers hauling on the chains. It was backbreaking work, and the soldiers spent many hours doing it since the ferries had to be manned 24 hours a day. The only available manpower were the infantrymen. It was a familiar situation that the men would become accustomed to in France. Any labouring tasks or dirty and heavy work always fell to the 'Poor Bloody Infantry' (PBI).

After his morning's work on the ferry, Pte Alflat was free for the afternoon, but by 5 p.m. he was back across the Canal again. This time he was on the worst duty of all in this area, No. 2 Canal Patrol. This involved a seven mile march through the shifting sands, to an advanced patrol base. From here the men were sent out on seven mile patrols into the desert. At 6.00 a.m. the following morning he marched the seven miles back to the ferry, having covered a total of 21 miles during the night.

The patrols were designed to cover all the possible approaches to the Canal, and consequently an enormous area had to be watched over. The only effective way to do this was to organise a series of numbered patrol areas, which overlapped on their flanks. It just turned out that No. 2 Canal Patrol was the most gruelling of them all.

After his 21 miles overnight march, Pte Alflat was given the day off until 1400, when his next task was to stand guard while some of the men relaxed on a bathing parade. The next evening he went back over the Canal for another night on No. 2 Patrol. On this occasion he was very unlucky, and instead of doing the usual one patrol he had to do two. There were never enough men to go around on these patrols and someone always drew the short straw. By the time he returned to the ferry, early on the morning of the 10th, he had marched 28 miles through the sandy desert and had probably only managed to snatch a few minutes' sleep here and there.

When he got back to the camp, Pte Alflat could still not relax. That same afternoon the whole Company had a drill parade in full kit. In the circumstances this seemed very harsh to young Alflat, and it put him and his comrades in a foul temper.

Life was not always so bad, and when it was possible, Sundays were left free for the men to rest. Most managed to get a few evenings out in Port Said in the early days in Egypt. In his diary Lt Middleton tells of the officers having dinner parties at the Eastern Exchange Hotel or at Maxim's. When not on duty they also went horse riding in the desert.

On 10th January it was the turn of A Company to go on detachment. Their destination was the Salt Island Redoubt, where they relieved a battalion of the East Yorkshire Regiment (East Yorks). The Company at this time had a strength of 5 officers and 208 men, and was under the command of Capt D. C. Allen. In addition it also had 12 men attached from C Company. It will be remembered that Capt Allen's horse died on the outward journey from England. A battery of the RFA, which travelled out to Egypt with the Battalion Transport on the Malakoota, very kindly replaced the horse from its stock of surplus mounts.

Douglas Charles Allen commanded A Company until the Battalion went to France. He then went to the 31st Division School as an instructor, where he remained until recalled to temporarily command the Battalion after the disaster on 1st July 1916. He then served as the Battalion 2IC.

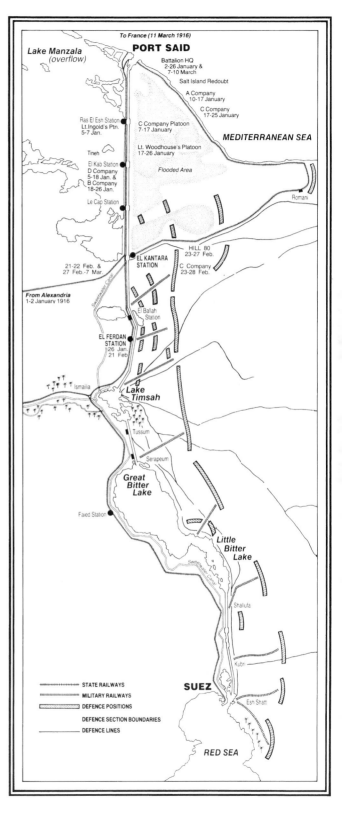

Port Said.

In January 1918 he transferred to the Tank Corps.

The Salt Works position also contained the premises of the Vacuum Oil Company and Shell Motor Spirit. The land surrounding the redoubt had been deliberately flooded. It stood on the old caravan route to Palestine, and the flooding prevented it being used by the Turks as a line of attack.

Soldiers the world over, from ancient times to the present day, have always complained about the food they received. The City Battalion men were no exception. On arrival in Egypt there had always been bacon at breakfast; at lunchtime there had been a filling and tasty stew; and for tea there had been jam and cheese.

But the standard of the rations went steadily downwards, while the amount of grumbling went steadily up. On 14th January, 12/1137 Pte J. Dixon in D Company wrote in his diary what the rations actually consisted of. There was always bully beef (corned beef) and Army biscuits for breakfast and lunch, and there was only jam and bread at tea time. The cheese ration had been stopped because, 'there was milk in the tea!' There is a perverse sort of Army logic behind this statement somewhere.

Pte Dixon's diary covers the period from December 1915 to April 1916. He was left out of the attack on 1st July 1916, and survived the rest of the war. When the Battalion disbanded in February 1918, he transferred to 13th York and Lancs.

The time soon came to relieve A and D Companies. On 17th January C Company under Capt Colley, took over from A Company at the Salt Works. On the return journey to Port Said, A Company detached Lt Woodhouse's Platoon at Ras El Esh.

Capt William Arthur Colley was an ex-TF officer in the Royal Engineers (RE). He was 47 in 1916, and really too old for the command of a company. Before the war he had been a leading businessman in Sheffield, and a member of the council. On 1st July 1916 he was killed outright by a shell just seconds

Method of crossing the Canal using floating pontoons pulled across by chains, hauled by soldiers.

No. 10 Platoon C Coy at Ras El Esh. Jan. 17th, 1916.

after leading his Company over the top. His body was never identified and he is commemorated on the Thiepval Memorial.

Lt, later Capt, Cecil Herbert Woodhouse has the dubious honour of being the first officer casualty in the Battalion. He received a minor wound on 9th April 1916, during the first tour of duty in the trenches in France. He was soon fit again and took part in the attack on 1st July, and was wounded again. This time it was more serious and he was evacuated to England. He recovered again and went back to the front for the third time. The odds were now very heavily loaded against him, and on 6th June 1918 he was killed in Belgium. It is thought he was serving with 1/4th York and Lancs at the time. He has no known grave and is commemorated on the Tyne Cot Memorial near Passchendaele.

B Company marched out of Port Said on the 17th, destined for Tineh to relieve D Company. They broke the march with an overnight stop at Ras El Esh. Having been relieved D Company did the same journey in reverse, also spending a night at Ras El Esh. They arrived back in Port Said at 11.00 a.m. on the 19th.

The previous day the GOC Canal Forces, Gen Sir Archibald Murray had inspected A Company and Battalion HQ. The same day there was great joy when the first mail since leaving England arrived. There

were many belated Christmas gifts, and lots of good things to eat and share around. Over the next few days the mail was got out to the detached Companies.

On 17th January Maj F. J. C. Hood, of 14th York and Lancs, presided at the Field General Court Martial of 12/80 Sgt Colin Crammond of the City Battalion. The WD does not record the crime or the verdict, although we do know from other sources that he was reduced to the rank of Pte. Maj Hood later became CO of the City Battalion.

One of the administrative duties which the officers now had to carry out, was to censor their soldiers' mail before it was sent home. Because of their other duties this proved to be a major problem, and a limit of three letters per man per week had to be imposed. This still meant the Platoon Commanders read an average of 20

Small gauge military railway.

A patrol prepares to set off into the desert. Notice the sandbags around the banks to form a hasty defence line in case of a surprise attack.

letters per day. They must have become tired of reading the same old tales time after time, and one wonders if after the first few the letters got more than a cursory glance.

From 20th January onwards all of the diarists make mention of the arrival of units withdrawn from Gallipoli. On the night of 23rd-24th January Pte Alflat was on Town Patrol, and helped to carry home many members of the 29th Division, who had been out celebrating with their back pay. They had lived through hell, and told many an horrific story to the eager City Battalion men. It must have made them very apprehensive as to their own future.

On 26th January the Battalion moved by train from Port Said to El Ferdan on the eastern bank of the Canal. C Company had been relieved at Salt Island the previous day, and as the train travelled south it picked up the detachments at Tineh and Ras El Esh. The Battalion was then complete for the first time in three weeks. Those who travelled all the way from Port Said had an early start at 4.30 a.m., but were compensated by having eggs for breakfast for the first time since landing in Egypt. By midnight the Battalion had crossed the Canal and settled into its new camp.

The Battalion now became part of the huge labouring force that was working on the Canal defences. Such was the intensity of the work that

The Signallers in Egypt, with severe haircuts. The caption on the original reads: "Corned in Egypt." From left to right; back row, Pte F. H. Carpenter, 12/513 Sgt C. G. B. Simons, 12/928 Pte J. W. Jago, 12/151 Pte A. E. Horrabin. 2nd row; thought to be Pte F. A. Ruddock, 12/961 Pte J. H. Holmes, 12/928 Pte J. R. Glenn holding a hard tack biscuit. 3rd row; 12/152 Pte L. A. Horrax, thought to be 12/499 L/Cpl G. Rose, 12/697 L/Cpl F. Jameson. Lying on the floor is 12/373 L/Cpl J. A. S. Froggatt.

Lt Middleton complained in his diary that they were handymen not infantrymen.

On the first day at El Ferdan 800 men were provided by the Battalion for Brigade and Divisional fatigues. Pte Dixon was among them, carrying rails for the construction of a light railway. The next day he was carrying supplies from the Army Service Corps (ASC) depot to the Battalion stores. Other men erected barbed wire entanglements, dug trenches or manned the chain ferry. Each night one of the companies was stood by on three minutes' notice to move, and had to sleep fully clothed. This company also manned the local defences at the dawn stand to.

Despite the grinding monotony and the sheer hard graft some things did improve. The mail seemed to get through on a more regular basis, and the quality of the rations improved considerably.

The daytime temperatures were now rising steadily, and at the beginning of February the men were allowed to cut their trousers down into improvised shorts. Despite the climate the men were still dressed in the khaki serge uniforms they had been wearing when they left England. They should have been issued with the more comfortable and cooler khaki drill uniforms, but these arrived too late to be issued before they moved to France. The only item of proper tropical uniform they had was the sola topee helmet, which had been issued at Hurdcott. Some of the officers had ordered tropical uniforms from the local tailors in Port Said as soon as they arrived in Egypt. Most had them delivered just in time to pack for France!

On the last day of January 2Lt T. E. A. Grant and a party of 125 men were detached from the Battalion to build a light railway. It was to run for a distance of five miles from the camp to the nearest

El Ferdan Station on the Suez Canal.

Queueing for the mid-day meal.

railhead. The track was of the two foot Decauville gauge, which was very versatile and many thousands of miles of it were laid in all theatres of the war. Next day the party left the Battalion's camp to live closer to their work. Not only did they lay the track, but the party also had to dig cuttings and construct embankments along the route. The line was completed on 14th February, and it was largely due to 2Lt Grant's efforts and organisation that it was finished so quickly.

2Lt, later Capt, T. E. A. Grant was the OC of 9 Platoon. In France he was the 94th Brigade Pioneer Officer from 20th May to 19th August 1916, and was Mentioned in Despatches (MID) for his work.

The chain ferry at El Ferdan was officially described as a medium ferry bridge. It was capable of transporting cavalry and medium artillery, as well as foot passengers and stores. Like the other chain ferries it was powered by teams of men hauling on the chains, which connected it to both banks. This particular ferry needed 13 men on each of its two chains. The job was arduous, and not without its dangers either. Between 11th and 17th February the ferry was rammed three times; twice by the same French ship on two separate occasions! Fortunately there were no casualties and the ferry was quickly repaired after each incident.

Squatting in the sand to eat the inevitable bully beef. One of the soldiers has "borrowed" the turban.

There was always something happening on the Canal, and it provided a source of entertainment for the men. There were even a few moments of light relief in the endless round of work and fatigue parties. Nestor passed along the Canal on 6th February, on her return journey from India. The Battalion band immediately turned out to play 'Auld Lang Syne' and 'Keep the Home Fires Burning'. The ship's bugler returned the compliment. The following Sunday, while the men were attending an open air service close to the Canal banks, a liner passed by with its decks crammed with young ladies. They had not seen any girls for weeks and discipline broke down as the men ran shouting and laughing to the Canal bank, to get a closer look. The Padre's reaction is not recorded!

Hyderabad Lancer. They were used for deep patrols into the desert.

The signallers, due to their other duties, managed to avoid some of the backbreaking toil. There were numerous telephone and signal stations to be manned, and occasionally they were asked to stand in for the Brigade HQ signallers, while the HQ was moved to a new location. A few signallers were even detached to the Mysore and Kashmir Lancers. These proud warriors were described by one man as, 'splendid tall fellows'. But they had a weakness since they '... would do almost anything for a cigarette!'

Of all the arduous jobs given to the Battalion, perhaps the worst one of all fell to D Company. On 14th February the engine on one of the light railways broke down. It could not be repaired immediately and there was no spare available, so D Company had to replace the engine. The men pushed heavy trucks laden with water pipes four miles out into the desert. The trucks often jumped off the rails and had to be manhandled back on again. This job lasted into the early hours of the next morning. Two days later Pte Alflat records doing the same job again. Obviously the fault on the engine proved difficult to rectify.

On 19th February units of the 11th Division began to arrive to relieve 31st Division. On the 20th the Battalion handed over the garrison duties to 14th York and Lancs, and moved camp onto the west bank of the Canal. Next morning they set off on a gruelling 18 mile march to Kantara under the blazing heat of the sun. On arriving there they crossed the Canal back onto the east bank.

The best part of 22nd January was given over to the soldiers to rest. But at 4 a.m. on the 23rd they once again shouldered their 60 pound loads, and this time marched out into the desert to a position known as Hill 80. Here they relieved 15th Battalion West Yorkshire Regiment (West Yorks).

Crossing ferry bridge over the Canal.

The seven mile march to Hill 80 took almost four hours to complete. The slow pace was due to the heat, their heavy loads and the fine sand they had to march through. Luckily they had started early and so avoided the worst heat of the day. Hill 80 was, and probably still is, a desolate pinpoint on the map surrounded by a sea of featureless desert. Each day parties of men would be marched a further two miles into the desert where they spent eight hours digging trenches and erecting barbed wire entanglements.

At first they were rationed to a single canteen of water each per day for drinking, washing, shaving and cooking. A canteen only held two pints, and a few days later the ration had to be increased to two canteens per day. Even so, in the heat it was precious little. However, the problems of transporting sufficient water for a thousand men were immense. Every drop of it had to be brought across the seven miles of desert from the Canal in tanks mounted on the backs of camels.

Lancers' camp.

During the evening of 26th February most of the men were asleep after a hard day working in the desert. But at 10 p.m. they were woken by their officers to carry out a kit inspection. This was somewhat perplexing for the men and caused a lot of consternation amongst them, but the reason was sound enough. The Division had just received orders to proceed to France, and any worn and deficient equipment had to be replaced quickly if the men were to be properly clothed for the colder and damper climate of the Western Front.

Next day the Battalion marched back to Kantara, leaving C Company behind at Hill 80 to be relieved on the 28th by units of 155th Brigade. Pte Alflat's diary for 27th February says that news of going to France caused a lot of excitement in the Battalion. He then went

A canal bathing party.

on to ponder about how many of them would be alive in six months time. How many indeed!

Life at Kantara was much easier than before. Each morning there were parades followed by some form of refresher training, such as bayonet fighting, physical drill and route marching. There was also some shooting practice in the desert with each soldier firing 30 rounds. It was so hot that some men actually blistered their hands on their rifles. Most afternoons were free or for sports, and a lot of swimming was done in the Canal. On 4th and 7th March water sports competitions were held against the Barnsley Battalions. The City Battalion upheld its high sporting standards and won almost every event on both days. In the evenings the band played while the men sat around camp fires listening to the music and singing, or chatting about old times and what the future might bring.

The move of the Division to France drew ever closer. On 28th February the advance party left Egypt, and gradually the ex-Gallipoli units began to take over. Medical inspections were conducted, including the hated 'short arm' inspection for signs of venereal disease.

The CO addressed the Battalion on 3rd March to thank the men for all the hard work they had done while being in Egypt. The officers entertained the men with a football match on 6th March, in which A and B Companies played against C and D Companies. The final score is not known but C and D Companies won.

Arab camel herders loading their beasts with supplies for the men in the desert outposts.

At 6.00 p.m. on 7th March the camp at Kantara was struck and the men slept on the ground until the early hours of the following morning, when they marched off to the railhead and entrained for Port Said. On arrival they were served tea and buns by the Mayor and English YMCA ladies, and from 9.00 a.m. were free to wander around the town. Some went shopping and bought local souvenirs, such as carpets, which were sent home by post. Some just relaxed and went for a swim. Pte Furniss, in a letter to the Sheffield Daily Telegraph, mentioned that he used the time to take his watch in to have the sand of the Sinai desert cleaned out of it. It has not proved possible to identify this soldier, since there were four soldiers called Furniss in the Battalion at this time.

Camp at El Ferdan railhead with the arid and featureless desert beyond.

Arab prisoners, woman with child with her hand out to the City Battalion men.

Signallers at the Battalion HQ dug in on Hill 80.

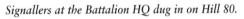

Cleaning equipment at a desert camp.

Kantara Station.

Heliograph Station at Hill 80.

All three methods of Battalion communications are shown here. Sgt Gus Simon sits behind the telescope used to read heliograph or lamp flashed messages. Behind him a signaller uses flags for semaphore, and on the left is a field telephone in its case.

Despite the many interesting sights to be seen most of the men were happy just to relax in the cafes, bars and restaurants. Having spent two months in almost unbroken toil, and with the prospect of many months to come in the trenches, they were determined to have a good time. Next day the sun helmets were handed in, and after a few other administrative tasks had been completed they went back into town once again. Pte Alflat confided to his diary that he was not looking forward to going to France. Despite the hard work he had enjoyed Egypt. He was not destined to have a happy time in France.

Embarkation on HMT Briton took place on the morning of 10th March. The ship was anchored in the harbour and the men were ferried out to it on lighters. As well as the City Battalion there were also two companies of 18th West Yorks and two companies of 14th York and Lancs on board.

The Briton was a Union Castle liner and had seen service as a troop ship during the Boer War. It was much more crowded than Nestor had been, but at least the journey was shorter.

At 5.00 p.m. the ship slipped out of the harbour amid the cheers from the men on board. That night and the next day were stormy, and most of them again suffered from the debilitating seasickness that had afflicted them on Nestor.

A work party pauses from digging trenches. Bottom left is Reg Glenn.

The 12th dawned bright and calm, and the men were much more cheerful as a result. That afternoon wreckage was sighted in the water and a corpse was seen floating amongst it. The guns were manned, but the ship did not stop in case a submarine was in the area. Nothing came of the incident and the next day Malta was reached. On this occasion the ship did not even go into the harbour, and very soon they were on their way again.

Arab lad in army cast offs tending supply camels.

Deck sports were held on the afternoon of the 14th, with 14th York and Lancs winning the Tug of War. As the ship passed Cape Bon it was learned that a French ship had been torpedoed and sunk there not eight hours previously. There was a lot of anxiety on board, but there was no sign of a U-Boat.

The men were in a cheerful mood as the Briton docked at Marseilles on the afternoon of 15th March. The band played the 'Marseillaise', and the men followed this by singing 'Keep the Home Fires Burning'. This song was very popular at the time, since it stirred memories of loved ones at home in England, and it became an inevitable part of any occasion such as this.

There was a pleasant surprise awaiting them on the dockside, an accumulation of three weeks' mail. This made up for being kept on the ship overnight. A French general came aboard to formally welcome the men to France, and they spent the evening on deck listening to the band and singing.

The Battalion disembarked at 7.30 a.m. on the morning of 16th March, with a strength of 30 officers and 986 ORs. Eight men had been left in Egypt because they were too ill to travel. They all eventually caught up with the Battalion when they recovered, except for 12/987 Pte Hugh Marshall. He remained in Egypt forever having died of appendicitis on 17th March. Pte Marshall was a Rotherham man but worked as a reporter on the Sheffield Daily Telegraph. He was 23 when he died, and is buried in Port Said Military Cemetery.

Later in the morning the Battalion marched through the docks to the railway sidings where a train was waiting to transport them northwards. On the way through the docks they saw some German prisoners working there; their first sight of the enemy. Some of them looked miserable, but others appeared to be happy to have escaped the nightmare of the Western Front. A few of them just gave the Battalion a knowing look as if they were watching more cannon fodder heading for the front. As it turned out of course that is exactly what they were looking at.

Sheffielders on their way to France passing a hospital ship in Valetta harbour.

Chapter Five

Early Days in France

The train awaiting the Battalion at Marseilles on the morning of 16th March, was made up of a collection of passenger coaches, cattle trucks and horse boxes. There was space for 2000 troops in all. The lucky ones, including the officers and senior NCOs, were squeezed eight into each coach with all their luggage. The majority of the men, however, had to travel in the horse boxes.

The horse boxes were labelled, 'Hommes 32/40. Chevaux (en long) 8'. There was thus room for 32-40 men or eight horses. The straw on the floor was invariably dirty from the previous occupants, who as often as not had been horses anyway. The straw was lousy as well as filthy, and it did not take long for the lice, or chats as they were known, to settle into their newly found homes. Before long everybody was itching and scratching for all they were worth.

Following a two hour delay the train departed to a great cheer from the men on board. There was a lot to see and they crowded around the open doors of the horse boxes. The land was green and beautiful after the drab and arid monotony of Egypt. The journey was to be typical of all rail journeys endured by soldiers during the war, it was slow and interspersed with frequent halts.

> 'We got used to all this stopping and starting, and it wasn't long before we discovered that if we were quick enough we could run down to the engine and get the driver to give us some boiling water from the engine to mash our tea. On reflection it makes you wonder how we survived, drinking that filthy water and the muck that we swallowed over the years.' 12/928 L/Cpl J. R. Glenn.

The route was one which tourists would have gladly paid to see. They travelled north-westwards at first to reach the Rhone valley, which was the route to the north. Arles was the first stopping place famous for its Roman remains, and it was here that they got their first glimpse of the great river.

In every village and town the train passed through they were enthusiastically greeted by the women and girls. There were very few men to be seen; they were all at the front. Much to the delight of the men on the train the women blew them kisses and waved to them. Only the odd soldier noticed an old woman crossing herself as they went by.

They passed through ancient Avignon with its famous bridge, and beyond the town there was more beautiful countryside to see. The Rhone valley was crowned with numerous castles, which were testament to troubles in more ancient times.

The next stop was at Orange, where they were met by pretty Red Cross nurses, who received more attention than did the tea they provided. The tea had been strongly laced with rum against the cold night to come. The nights were no colder than they had experienced in Egypt, but the atmosphere was damper. The men had to huddle together for warmth as the train slowly continued its way northwards.

The train went straight through the great industrial town of Lyons during the night, but it failed to raise any interest. At

German prisoners assisting with gangplank at Port of Marseille.

6 o'clock next morning they halted for one hour to have breakfast at Macon, but even so not everyone got the tea which was being served up by enthusiastic French soldiers.

Lt Middleton managed to find time to get a shave at Macon, but soon they were all back in the trucks again. Shortly before they stopped for lunch at Dijon, they had halted in a siding alongside a trainful of French wounded. They were a pitiful sight, and the men again began to brood about their own fate. A few who could speak a little of the language tried to converse with the Frenchmen. Not much could be gleaned from them except that they had been at Verdun, where a massive German offensive had been raging since 21st February.

Tea was taken at Les Laumes at 5p.m., where there was an hour long break to allow the men to stretch their legs. The tea had again been strongly spiked with rum. In his diary, Pte Alflat says it was a fearful mixture.

French cattle truck which would hold 32 to 40 men seen here beseiged by British soldiers – on this occasion it is carrying bread.

In one of the trucks 12/922 Pte R. E. Gapes poured his tea and rum mixture into his water bottle. Seeing this the other soldiers began to make fun of him. Before long he was thoroughly sick of this gibing and threw the contents of the water bottle over his companions. One of them, Bill Taylor, was all for punching him on the nose. But he was restrained by the rest of the men in the truck. This soldier could have been one of two Taylors in D Company. They were both killed on 1st July 1916. The long journey was obviously beginning to tell on the men, who were cold, tired and not a little apprehensive about their immediate future.

During the night they passed through Fontainebleau, the outskirts of Paris and Versailles, and breakfast was taken at Epluches. The train made a short stop in the large Cathedral city of Amiens, which was the main centre for the British Army behind the Somme front. It was packed with troops. Some of the men who had spare tins of bully beef threw them to the children in the streets.

Just before 3 p.m. the train journey came to an end at Pont Remy. It had taken 53 hours. The men disembarked stiff and tired only to be told they now had to march to their billets, seven to eight miles away in Huppy. Some got away quickly and began to arrive in the early evening, but the men detailed to unload the train did not arrive until after 10.00 p.m. But at least they could ride on the transport wagons.

12/922 Pte Rowland Ernest Gapes. Lived on Barnsley Road, Sheffield. He was killed on 1 July 1916 at Serre. His remains were recovered and buried in March 1917, but could not be found after the war.

When the billets were allocated some were lucky like Pte T. C. Hunter. He and his companions found themselves allocated to a house that still had a billiards table in it. Others were not so fortunate. Pte A. H. Hastings for example, was given space in a barn. So too was Pte Dixon, who wrote in his diary that at least it was dry.

British troops take advantage of a stop to get hot water from the French engine driver. The fur coats indicate this picture was taken in the first winter of the war.

Pont Remy Station in 1988.

The countryside was not unlike parts of England. The area around Huppy was unspoiled and looked as if time had stood still for centuries. The cottages were whitewashed and had thatched roofs. The larger houses had red tiled roofs, and long narrow windows. The well was covered by a log hood, green with age and algae. The picture of peace and serenity was completed by the women dressed in traditional black dresses with white bonnets.

The peaceful atmosphere was soon shattered by the arrival of a thousand soldiers, but relations with the villagers were very good in spite of the invasion of their privacy. The day after arriving the men had their kit bags returned to them and were left to rest and settle in.

Pte Dixon took the opportunity to have a flea hunt. He wasted his time, for within hours of finishing more eggs hatched out and he was no better off than before he started. Apart from a rifle inspection the rest of the day was free. Pte W. G. Alflat was billeted in a farm and although he and his mates were not sleeping in the farmhouse itself, the farmer allowed them to use his kitchen, where they spent the day drinking cider and singing for the farmer's family.

Monday 20th March was the day the men returned to reality. They had a 10 mile route march and later the order went out that all cameras were to be sent home. It was considered a grave risk to security if the enemy got hold of film taken behind our lines. Sadly everyone, as far as we know, obeyed this instruction, and there are few known photographs of the Battalion from now onwards.

After the route march morale was raised by an issue of mail.

Whilst on the route march the Battalion passed a contingent of Indian cavalry. They were used to seeing them in Egypt, where they patrolled the desert searching for the elusive Turks. In France however, the uses for cavalry were somewhat limited. In the early days of the war they had charged the enemy, but such death or glory tactics came to nought in the face of machine gun fire. Often they were used dismounted as infantry, as they had been in the desperate days of the German invasion in 1914. A charge did take place at High Wood later on in 1916, but this too was a failure. It would be well into 1918 before the cavalry could get mobile again. The advent of mechanised warfare would herald the end of mounted troops within the next two decades.

The next day there was physical drill in the morning, followed by bayonet fighting in the afternoon, and later they played their first football match in France. In reality it was little more than a kick about. The troops would play a lot of football in their spare time, there was precious little else to do.

The next few days were mainly spent on a temporary range at Poultieres, about a kilometre from Huppy. Most of the men fired 15 rounds to check their weapons were functioning properly. Sgt Beckett,

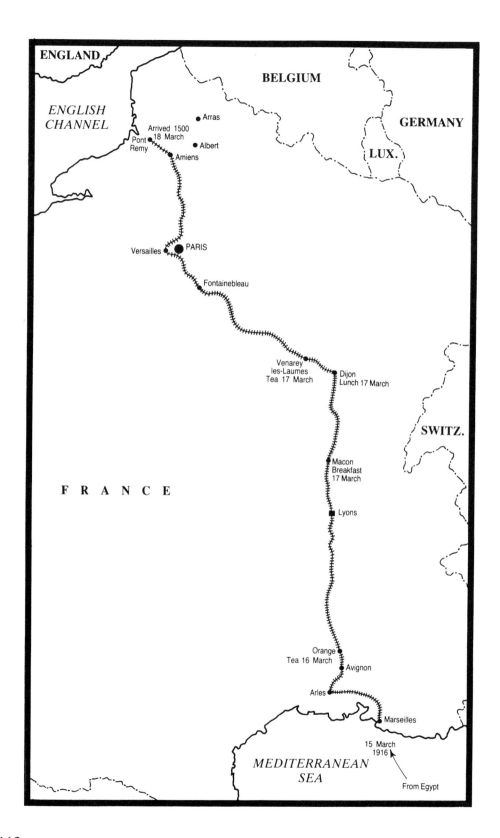

ENGLAND

ENGLISH
CHANNEL

BELGIUM

GERMANY

LUX.

● Arras

Arrived 1500
18 March

Pont
Remy ●

● Albert

● Amiens

Versailles ●   ● PARIS

● Fontainebleau

Venarey
les-Laumes
Tea 17 March

● Dijon
Lunch 17 March

SWITZ.

● Macon
Breakfast
17 March

■ Lyons

F R A N C E

Orange ●
Tea 16 March

● Avignon

Arles ●

● Marseilles

15 March
1916

MEDITERRANEAN
SEA

From Egypt

the armourer, stood by to rectify faults as they occurred. Some rifles were found to be defective and Pte Alflat did not get his back for two days.

Meanwhile training for gas warfare had begun. The Germans had been the first to use this very effective weapon in April 1915 at Ypres. At the time it had caused a complete panic in the ranks of the French Algerian troops against whom it had been released. The first protection against chlorine gas had been to soak handkerchiefs in urine and tie them around the nose and mouth. It was not very pleasant and neither was it all that effective.

By 1916 an effective gas helmet had been developed and this was the type issued to everyone in the Battalion between the 22nd and 24th March. Lectures on its use and drills to fit it were carried out over the next couple of days.

While all this had been happening some men had been granted leave. One of those who went home was Capt Colley. He had only a few more weeks to live and this would be the last time that his family saw him.

On the 24th a long route march took place. Accounts vary from 8 to 16 miles as to its exact length. The weather was atrocious, and most of the time they tramped through slush and snow. They then discovered that the heat and dryness of Egypt had ruined their boots; they all leaked like sieves.

Saturday 25th March saw an endless succession of inspections, as everything from

If der York & Lancs.
haf gone by, den I kan kom out.

Popular postcard sent home by Sheffielders (note the Regiment changed according to the affiliations of the sender).

their mess tins to their new gas helmets were checked. Many of the men were told to have an interview with the barber. Some old soldiers will remember a crusty Sergeant Major coming up behind them and saying, 'Am I hurting you soldier?'. 'No sir.' 'Well I blinking well should be I'm standing on your hair'! Also on this day a batch of parcels arrived, containing a selection of luxury goods, courtesy of the Sheffield Independent newspaper. The parcels were shared one between eight men. As an extra bonus the farmer's wife where Pte Alflat was staying, baked him and his companions an apple pie.

All the men agreed that Huppy had been a cushy billet, and only the weather had ruined it. They would look back to these few days with longing in the months to come. Orders were received to start to move up to the front, and the first stage was a four day march to Bertrancourt.

The first day of the march commenced with reveille at 5.00 a.m., and to make matters worse it was raining hard. They did not leave until 8.00 a.m. due to all the fatigues that had to be done. Those that had made friends with the people of Huppy marched off with their water bottles filled with cider, to cheer them up on the 13 mile march to Longpre close to the River Somme.

At Longpre they halted for the night and took full advantage of the cafes there. The next day two officers and 18 NCOs from each company, were due to go to the trenches for instruction under an experienced battalion.

Next morning the bulk of the Battalion continued the march. The next halt was at Vignacourt which was reached at 12.30 p.m. They had covered another 13 miles that morning. Pte Alflat's boots were still wet after the journey and he despaired of them ever drying.

Vignacourt proved to be good for one thing at least, there were eggs and real bread for dinner. That night Pte Alflat was shocked to wake up with 12/885 Pte C. W. Budds wrapping his arms around him.

Budds was apparently having a pleasant dream, thinking that Alflat was his girlfriend. Sadly Pte Budds was killed in September 1918 serving as an officer with 5th KOYLI.

Next morning Lt Middleton was the only officer left in B Company. Capt Woolhouse and 2Lt Cowen had gone up to the trenches, and 2Lt A. J. Beal was temporarily acting as the Adjutant. Like most of his men Lt Middleton had to spend the night in a barn, but some others were less fortunate and were allocated a railway goods house.

The party going to the trenches for instruction were looked after by 1/8th Battalion Worcestershire Regiment (1/8th Worcesters). The party was smaller than had been intended, consisting of 10 officers and 40 NCOs. In the original plan there were 72 NCOs. The party travelled the first part of the way up to the front by bus, via Flixecourt and Doullens. They were billeted at Courcelles au Bois overnight before going into the line. Just after midnight on the 28th, the trench party marched to Colincamps under the command of Maj A. R. Hoette. Here they were met by guides from the Worcesters who took them up to the front line. The aim was to become familiar with trench routine, and generally learn the ropes. For the officers this included learning the reams of written Trench Standing Orders.

The WD of 8th Worcesters says that they were suffering heavy casualties at this time, mainly caused by the infamous German mortar, the minenwerfer. It was not an easy introduction to trench warfare for the City Battalion men.

The minenwerfer fired large rounded projectiles, known to the British troops as 'flying pigs', or 'oil cans'. Like all mortars they were high trajectory and low velocity weapons. By day the shells could be seen quite plainly tumbling through the air, and at night the burning fuse could be seen instead. With practice the troops could judge approximately where the bombs would land, and then had a few seconds to take avoiding action. Of course they didn't get it right every time, and minenwerfers caused many casualties. There were seven different types of the weapon, varing in calibre from 7.6 cm to 24.5 cm.

For the rest of the Battalion on the morning of the 28th, it was back on the march again. There were 12 men who were not fit enough to walk any further and they rode in the transport wagons. The long march and heavy loads, plus their feet being constantly wet, caused great problems. Despite their feet being hardened many of the men still suffered badly with blisters.

The Battalion marched behind 14th York and Lancs to Beauquesne, 14 miles away. During the march distant gunfire was heard for the first time. Every day brought them nearer to the front, and with the background noise of gunfire they began to feel more like proper soldiers.

In war rumours are always spreading amongst soldiers. The rumour of the day on 28th March was that an entire platoon of an East Yorks battalion had been wiped out on the march by a single shell. Whether this was true or not it was soon forgotten as the first rum ration was issued since getting off the train. One thing they had to watch out for was that the person issuing the ration did not have his thumb in the measure, thus keeping more for himself at the end.

The rum issued at the front had the consistency of treacle, and was not for the faint of heart. It was often called "VC mixture" because some units issued it just before the men went over the top to steady their nerves. It came in large earthenware jars with the initials "SRD" stamped onto them, which stood for "Services Rum Diluted". The troops however, soon changed this to "Soon Runs Dry", or "Seldom Reaches Destination".

The final day's march to Bertrancourt was only nine miles long, much to the relief of everyone concerned. While on the march the troops halted for 10 minutes in every hour. The old sweats knew that the best thing to do at these halts was to lie back on their packs, and put their feet in the air to let the blood drain back. It also took the weight of the packs off their shoulders. It sounds stupid, but it does help to relieve tired leg muscles. Before long the whole Battalion was at it, and at a rest stop they looked like a host of dead insects.

Bertrancourt was to become familiar territory to the Battalion, but first impressions were not good. The village did at least have a YMCA hut, but the area was a little too hot for comfort. During the afternoon a German aeroplane flew low overhead and was fired on. That first night in Bertrancourt they drifted off into a fitful sleep to the sounds of gunfire, much closer to them than ever before. In places they could actually see the shelling going on, day and night.

More mundane matters than enemy planes or shelling occupied most of the men during the day. Getting dry straw to spread over the muddy barn floors was a high priority, or there would have been nowhere dry to sleep. Most of the men however, lived in wooden framed huts with stretched canvas walls which were situated just outside the village. Snow fell during the day but it soon melted, and added to the muddy mess that was already all around them. The hut dwellers were kept busy blocking holes in the thin canvas walls of their temporary abodes to keep the melting snow out.

The officers of A, B and C Companies dined together that evening in a barn. Lt Middleton went out to buy a chicken for the occasion. It is to be hoped that it was a big one, or it would not have gone far between all of them.

On the 30th news arrived from Egypt that one of the sick men left behind there, Pte H. Marshall, had died. Also that day, Pte Dixon was detailed off for a burial party for an East Yorks soldier. Otherwise it was a fairly routine day, and not at all like being at war. The men were paid later on, and one group of 10 men got a 100 Franc note between them. They had to take it to the nearest canteen to get it exchanged before they could divide it up between them.

There was a lot of aerial activity in this area, and a number of the diarists mention German planes being shelled at breakfast time. Fortunately they were more inconvenient than dangerous. The enemy artillery fire however, began to get nearer to them. On the 31st Pte T. C. Hunter watched a nearby village being shelled and burning, probably Colincamps.

Also on the 31st the trench instructional party returned. They were eagerly questioned by those left behind about conditions at the front. Sgt J. W. Streets told of standing for 24 hours up to his knees in water and going into NML on a wiring party at night. He said it was a trying but valuable lesson. The Worcesters had been good teachers, having had 12 months' experience at the front by then.

For the rest of the men there were lectures on gas from Maj Clough, followed by a gas mask check. There was only one way to be sure that a mask fitted properly and that was to subject it to a dose of gas; with the owner wearing it of course. This was done by filling a disused house with a non-lethal gas, (probably lachrymatory), and then the men went into it a couple at a time. There were some very tense faces, but it was better to get a whiff of gas where they could quickly get away from it, than to find the mask didn't work in the middle of a real attack.

Some leave was granted. Sheffield Midland Station 1916. First soldier on the right is 12/941 Pte Harry Harlow. Next to him is his brother (1/4th Y & L). Both are home for a funeral. Note the difference in Pte Harlow's appearance from the photograph on page 33. Next to him is his wife who was still living in Hillsborough in the late 1980s.

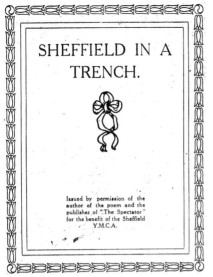

SHEFFIELD IN A TRENCH.

Issued by permission of the
author of the poem and the
publisher of "The Spectator"
for the benefit of the Sheffield
Y.M.C.A.

Another trench party was being organised to depart on 1st April, and Lt Middleton was detailed off for it. Capt Woolhouse was also going, as were Lts Ward and Storry and 50 NCOs. However, next day Middleton and Ward were sent on leave instead. No one else mentions going to the trenches and there is nothing at all about it in the WD. With the first trench tour for the whole Battalion only a few days away it was probably thought wiser to do without another instructional trip.

On the 1st the men did a little training, and later they watched Colincamps getting a good going over by the German artillery. This cannot have done morale too much good, since the Battalion was under orders to move there the next day. The Germans were trying to search out two 9.2″ guns, which they knew were hidden somewhere near the church. They failed to hit them, but did hit the church tower, a canteen run by the REs, and the Brigade grenade store, which by a miracle did not explode. A shell actually passed through the Brigade Commander's bedroom without going off.

April 2nd dawned and the men prepared to move up to the front. At 1.00 p.m. they moved off in open order, or artillery formation, and took about two hours to get to Colincamps. The village was only two miles from the front line and was a constant target for the German artillery. It was the usual location for the brigade reserve battalion in that sector.

There were no civilians left in Colincamps, save for a few roughly dressed peasant girls who made a living selling eggs to the troops. The rest had fled the incessant enemy artillery fire for safer areas. The village stands in the middle of a large common, which was called 'Colincamps Plain' by the British. In 1916 it bristled with every calibre and type of gun the Army possessed in preparation for the forthcoming Somme offensive.

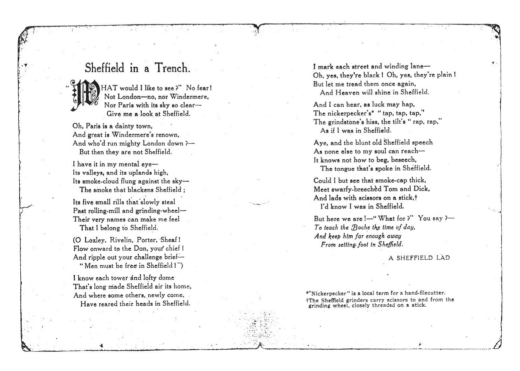

Sheffield in a Trench.

"WHAT would I like to see?" No fear!
Not London—no, nor Windermere,
Nor Paris with its sky so clear—
    Give me a look at Sheffield.

Oh, Paris is a dainty town,
And great is Windermere's renown,
And who'd run mighty London down ?—
    But then they are not Sheffield.

I have it in my mental eye—
Its valleys, and its uplands high,
Its smoke-cloud flung against the sky—
    The smoke that blackens Sheffield ;

Its five small rills that slowly steal
Past rolling-mill and grinding-wheel—
Their very names can make me feel
    That I belong to Sheffield.

(O Loxley, Rivelin, Porter, Sheaf !
Flow onward to the Don, your chief !
And ripple out your challenge brief—
    " Men must be free in Sheffield !")

I know each tower and lofty dome
That's long made Sheffield air its home,
And where some others, newly come,
    Have reared their heads in Sheffield.

I mark each street and winding lane—
Oh, yes, they're black ! Oh, yes, they're plain !
But let me tread them once again,
    And Heaven will shine in Sheffield.

And I can hear, as luck may hap,
The nickerpecker's* " tap, tap, tap,"
The grindstone's hiss, the tilt's " rap, rap,"
    As if I was in Sheffield.

Aye, and the blunt old Sheffield speech
As none else to my soul can reach—
It knows not how to beg, beseech,
    The tongue that's spoke in Sheffield.

Could I but see that smoke-cap thick,
Meet swarfy-breechèd Tom and Dick,
And lads with scissors on a stick,†
    I'd know I was in Sheffield.

But here we are !—" What for ?" You say ?—
*To teach the Boche the time of day,
And keep him far enough away
    From setting foot in Sheffield.*

A SHEFFIELD LAD

*"Nickerpecker" is a local term for a hand-filecutter.
†The Sheffield grinders carry scissors to and from the grinding wheel, closely threaded on a stick.

When the war ended in 1918, there was not one stone standing on another in Colincamps. But when the Battalion arrived there were still some undamaged buildings, one of which was the school in which Battalion HQ was set up. Overall the village was fairly typical of French farming communities, being rather gloomy, poor and cheerless.

While most of the men were trying to get to sleep in Colincamps, amid the noise of snipers, trench mortars and artillery, Lt Middleton and the leave party were making their way home. They took the mess cart as far as Acheux where they boarded the train for Le Havre. On arriving there at 5.30 a.m. on 2nd April, they were greeted with the news that there was no leave boat that day. They managed to scrounge accommodation in a hospital that night, but did not get on a boat until the early hours of the 5th. In the meantime they entertained themselves at the Folies Bergeres. Lt Middleton said the show was incomprehensible, but he judged by the applause that it had been very naughty.

By 11.00 a.m. on the 5th Lt Middleton was in London. He spent the afternoon in the Hippodrome, and arrived home in Sheffield at 10.45 p.m. Because he was not expected he had to wake everyone up to get in. As he drifted off to sleep that night the Battalion was beginning its third day in the trenches.

The Battalion went into the trenches on the evening of the 3rd. During the day they went for baths by companies in Courcelles. Every man stripped off and handed over his uniform for cleaning. He then had 10 minutes in a large vat with eight other men. On getting out he was given clean underwear and his uniform, which by then had been fumigated. By the time they had marched back to Colincamps they were as lousy and dirty as before they started off.

Later in the day rubber gas capes and steel helmets were issued. At that time there were not sufficient steel helmets for every man to have his own. On coming out of the line units handed them on to the next battalion going in.

The final hours were spent writing letters home, or in the YMCA. They handed in their kit bags, packed with spare clothing and equipment that was not required in the line, and at 6.00 p.m. formed up to march off. It was a pitch black night and progress was slow. At the entrance to the trench system they were met by guides, but it still took an hour from there to get to the front line. It was very tiring forcing a way along the narrow trenches in full kit; stumbling against the man in front, and all the time trying to stop oneself from panicking at the unusual noises and smells.

The heavily laden men were further hampered by the trenches being in a poor state of repair, as a result of repeated attention from the enemy artillery and the weather. The journey up to the front line knocked the edge off the men's excitement and apprehension, as it became nothing more than a physical battle against the mud. It built up on their boots, and became so thick that they actually stood a few inches taller than normal. Once the thick glutinous stuff was stuck on it was a devil to try and kick off. The memory of the first trip up to the front line tended to remain with all soldiers.

> '*I remember my first visit to the trenches. It was on a carrying party, trench mortar bombs were the load. We were all a bit jumpy to say the least. In fact every time a shell exploded we would duck down. They could have been exploding in Abbeville for all we knew, but we still ducked. Another thing was that when we entered the communication trenches there hadn't to be any smoking. But when we had dropped off our loads we left a trail of smoke behind us on our way back we moved that fast!*'
> 12/928 L/Cpl J. R. Glenn.

German troops dig in on the Somme front.

The Battalion took over part of the front previously occupied by elements of 18th DLI and 1/8th Worcesters. In the front line D Company was on the right, and C Company on the left. In support at the rear A Company was on the right and B Company on the left. To the right of the City Battalion was a battalion of the King's Own Scottish Borderers (KOSB), and to the left 14th York and Lancs. The Battalion's frontage was 1300 yards long and it had taken over the right hand portion of the Colincamps sector. It was some 1,400 yards west of the German held village of Serre. The Germans had taken full advantage of what had until that stage been a comparatively quiet sector to dig themselves in firmly. When the time came it would be a very difficult task to dislodge them.

Serre lay on the opposite side of a low valley to Colincamps, and had been in German hands since 1914. The French tried to retake the village in 1915 and the Germans had given a little ground. This was because they wanted to improve their positions and not due to any success on the part of the French. The trenches which the Battalion had taken over were in fact part of the old German defences. They had very strongly built dugouts, but were completely dominated by the new German lines around Serre which looked down on them.

The Germans were not complacent about their situation. They constantly worked to improve the already fine position they occupied, and proceeded to turn Serre into a seemingly impregnable fortress. It was one of a number of village strongpoints that the British infantry would have to take when the expected offensive got under way in the summer.

Serre's importance lay in the all round observation it afforded. To the south it overlooked the Redan and Hawthorne ridges, and even beyond to the fortress at Thiepval. To the west it overlooked the British trench lines and the approaches to them. To the north everything as far as Gommecourt was open to view. To the east the land was also wide open, but this was behind the German lines.

Elaborate construction in the German trenches on the Somme.

However, if the British ever took the village they would then be in a position to overlook the Germans. Because of this they were determined to hold onto Serre at almost any cost.

The tactical importance of Serre had little relevance to the soldiers at this stage. They were quickly detailed off to their posts where they were briefed on the layout of the local area by the outgoing troops. As soon as the briefing was over they left, often with a cheery word of encouragement, but often as not they just hurried away, glad to have survived another tour of the trenches. Very soon the Battalion was left on its own.

After 18 months in the Army the men had at last arrived at the war. The first thing they learned was that trench warfare meant lots of work and comparatively little actual fighting. Sentries were posted, always in pairs at night, and then the work parties began. There were always hundreds of jobs to be done in the line, and because of the danger of attracting enemy fire by day, work parties invariably did not start until after dark. The trenches had also been neglected for some time, so the men were immediately set to work repairing them.

The trenches needed deepening to provide better cover, and the sides strengthening to prevent artillery fire from collapsing them. Isolated posts needed proper communications trenches digging to connect them to the main trench system. The front line was not even continuous at this point and this too had to be rectified. In addition more dugouts were constructed and disused trenches opened up again.

Maj Clough, in the absence of the CO who was on leave, set up Battalion HQ in a trench called Bow Street off Cheerio Avenue. All trenches, including those occupied by the Germans, were named for ease of identification and for giving directions. It was unusual for a battalion on its first tour of active duty in the line, to have its CO absent. It is known that Lt Col Crosthwaite was not a well man and it may be that he was on sick leave.

We will now leave the Battalion on its first night in the trenches, to explain some of the terminology

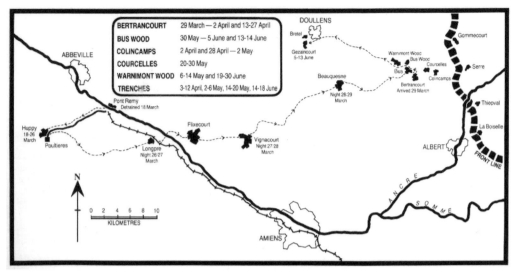

BERTRANCOURT	29 March — 2 April and 13-27 April
BUS WOOD	30 May — 5 June and 13-14 June
COLINCAMPS	2 April and 28 April — 2 May
COURCELLES	20-30 May
WARNIMONT WOOD	6-14 May and 19-30 June
TRENCHES	3-12 April, 2-6 May, 14-20 May, 14-18 June

City Battalion's route towards the Front.

of trench warfare. The jargon at first sight appears to have more in common with the days of Vauban and the massive forts of the 17th and 18th centuries, and indeed there are parallels.

There were two types of trenches. The first type was properly prepared for defence and was called a fire trench. The second type was basically a sheltered walk way known as a communications trench. Generally the fire trenches ran parallel with the front, while communication trenches ran from front to rear.

Fire trenches were ideally at least eight feet deep and about six feet wide at the top, tapering down to about four feet wide at the bottom. To prevent the walls from collapsing they were revetted with any suitable materials that were available. Such things as sandbags, corrugated iron, wickerwork fascines and timber were used. The subsoil in the Somme area was chalk and the trench walls were therefore already quite strong and required the minimum of revetting. In other areas the soldiers had a constant battle to prevent the trench walls from collapsing, due either to the weather or enemy shellfire.

The spoil created when digging the trenches was thrown out to the front and rear. The heap at the front was shaped to allow clear fields of fire, and was called the parapet. The rear heap was called the parados, and was deliberately made higher than the parapet for two reasons. Firstly to give protection against shells which burst behind the trench; and secondly to create a background behind anyone peering over the parapet so they would not show up against the skyline.

Fire trenches were not constructed in straight lines, because a single shell landing in a trench would have wiped out a long stretch of it. Similarly if the enemy got into a trench they could enfilade fire right along it. Instead they were built in a series of zigzag steps, which when viewed from the air looked like the crenellations on top of a castle wall. The bays thus formed were called fire bays if they were on the enemy side of the trench, and traverses if they were on the friendly side. Each traverse would be no more than 10 yards long, and the double corner between each greatly lessened the effects of blast.

White chalky soil thrown up on the parados, typical of soil in the Somme region.

At the bottom of the enemy side of the fire trench was a step, which allowed the sentry to see over the parapet. Known as the fire step, it was manned by every man during an attack and at dawn and dusk stand to. Also on the enemy side of the trench were shelters, called dugouts. Some of these were elaborate affairs and proof against all but the highest calibre shells. In the main, however, they were little more than splinter proof sleeping holes. The Germans were much better than the British at shelter construction, often digging down 40 feet below the surface, and even installed bunk beds and electric lighting.

Because the British lines opposite Serre had been originally dug by the Germans, many of the dugouts were set in the rear wall of the trenches. This had disastrous results later when by a thousand to one chance artillery shells went straight through the entrances of two dugouts.

Running out from the front line were short lengths of trench called saps, which led to isolated posts in NML. In these posts were listening patrols to give advanced warning of the enemy approaching the main position. If an attack developed the posts were not normally defended, although they could be used to fire into the flank of an enemy advance. They were always exposed and dangerous places to be in.

As a general principle fire trenches were constructed in three lines; from front to rear these were the front line, the support line and the reserve line. Each line was sited so that the men in it could fire on the line in front and thus support it in the event of an enemy attack. In some places there were many more than just three lines of trenches. On the Somme in early 1916, the Germans were constructing four separate trench systems, one behind the other. To break through to open country the British would therefore have had to overcome at least 12 trenches.

Communication trenches were not normally prepared for defence, but could not be constructed in straight lines for the same reason as the fire trenches. Instead of the crenellations, which were laborious and difficult to dig, they had a simple zigzag pattern.

To control the flow of men and materials into the forward trenches it was often necessary to designate up and down routes, similar to modern one way streets. This was usually done during an offensive, when reinforcements and ammunition were going forward, and casualties were being taken to the rear. To have everyone pushing against each other in the narrow confines of a trench, while being fully laden would have caused serious delays. In some places a traffic trench was dug just to the rear and parallel with the front line. The aim was to keep lateral movement along the front line to a minimum, to avoid attracting attention from the enemy, and to leave the garrison undisturbed to fulfil its duties.

Life in the trenches could be tolerable, but it very much depended on how 'cooperative' the enemy were and the weather. In some areas there was a mutual understanding that for an hour or two after the dawn stand to neither side would make any aggressive actions. This allowed everyone to have breakfast and a wash and shave in peace. The French were particularly prone to this attitude, but it was discouraged by the offensively minded British senior officers.

> 'I liked to have a shave every morning, even when we were fighting. If I was going to be killed I wanted to be clean. I had to save some tea if we didn't have any water. I even had a shave on 1st July 1916, with a cut throat razor of course. Every time a shell went over my hand shook and I got nicked. Later on a Sheffield razor manufacturer sent us all a safety razor, but we had to keep the cut throats for kit inspections.' 12/928 L/Cpl J. R. Glenn.

During the day a watch was constantly kept over NML, usually through a periscope. It was also the time to get some sleep or prepare for the night's activities. An hour or so before dawn, and until the enemy parapet could be clearly seen, all the men stood to their positions on the fire step ready to repulse an attack. At dusk they did the same, manning the fire step until the enemy parapet could no longer be discerned. But it was not until darkness fell that the real work of the day took place. Wiring parties went out into NML to construct or repair the protective entanglements. Carrying parties came up from the rear with rations, ammunition and water etc. There would always be a work party of some description, digging, building or draining, in an attempt to improve the trenches. Often there were more warlike activities, such as patrols in NML or raids against the enemy positions.

One of the unsavoury aspects of life in the trenches was having to cope with the rats and the flies. There was so much waste lying around that it presented a major health hazard. The rotting corpses from previous battles, the contents of the trench latrines, and waste food, were all breeding grounds for flies.

The rubbish also provided a plentiful source of food for the rats. Consequently they bred rapidly and grew to enormous sizes. They were not shy of men, often rifling a man's pack while he slept next to it, and if challenged they would fight back ferociously. A source of amusement in the front line was rat hunting. During the first tour in the trenches 12/144 Pte T. W. Holmes in A Company shot a rat when his rifle went off accidentally, or so he claimed!

During its first night in the trenches the Battalion, literally working in the dark, had made a good start on the programme of work set for them. At dawn this was evident by the amount of white chalky mud stuck to the soldiers' clothing. They soon got used to this, and to stop their greatcoats getting too thickly coated in the mud they cut them down to thigh length.

Everything was very strange and danger was ever present. Snipers fired at known gaps in the line and periodically machine guns would sweep along the parapet trying to seek out a dozy sentry. Flares shot into the night sky illuminating NML, and any man out there had to freeze if he was to escape detection. Some of the sentries on the first night made a common error for inexperienced troops, by staring into the darkness. If they stared long enough in one direction they would see static objects apparently moving and this caused many false alarms. Shells had passed overhead all night, sounding like express trains, and some had landed close by. They soon got to know the difference in sound between one of ours going out, and more importantly one of the Germans' coming in.

Pte A. McKenzie's grave in the Sucrerie Military Cemetery near Serre.

Despite their inexperience and the frightening happenings of the night they were glad to be there. The Battalion was in excellent spirits and quickly began to gain in confidence.

The Germans welcomed them after breakfast on the first morning with a 'hate session' of rifle grenades and canister bombs. The firing increased in tempo during the course of the day and the German snipers joined in as well. At one stage a man ran along the trench passing Pte Alflat, shouting that the Germans were about to blow up a mine beneath them. Nothing happened, and Pte Alflat did not see the man again.

Because it was a chalk area the Somme was very suitable for mining operations. Around Serre both sides were actively involved in tunnelling, but the British were especially busy at this time making preparations for the forthcoming offensive. At that stage of the war the Germans were far better at this strange form of warfare than the British. In the critical seconds following a mine explosion the Germans almost always got to the crater first and by occupying the high lips gained the upper hand. They even managed to do this when the British had the advantage of knowing the time the mine was to be blown.

British tunnellers were however, very technically proficient. Some men from the Barnsley Battalions had been transferred to RE Tunnelling Companies earlier in the war. Their labours and sacrifices, along with those of the other tunnellers came to fruition in 1917 at the Battle for Messines Ridge. At zero hour the top of the ridge was blown off by the simultaneous firing of 20 very large mines. The infantry attack which followed quickly took control of the ridge with very light casualties.

During the first morning the Battalion suffered its first fatal casualty. A rifle grenade landed in a trench and the explosion killed 12/991 Pte A. McKenzie. That evening he was carried out of the line by three of his comrades. Ironically two of them were themselves killed before the war was over. As the burial party made its way out of the trenches Pte Alflat saw them pass by, and observed the Germans firing at them.

The burial party were met at the Sucrerie Cemetery by the Padre who conducted a simple service. A wooden cross was put over the grave with the words, 'Gloriously Killed' roughly written on it. That night Maj Hoette wrote to Pte McKenzie's parents telling them of his death and the inscription on the cross. Attitudes were different then, but it is difficult to believe that they would have agreed with the wording. Later on death would become commonplace, but the loss of the first man in action deeply shocked the whole Battalion.

The morning of 5th April was similar to the 4th. After breakfast the Germans again fired a hate session, but it did not last as long as on the previous day. Pte Alflat wrote in his diary that the enemy had obviously given them their welcome and were now settling down to normal routine again. The rest of the day was relatively quiet, but on the 6th all hell broke loose.

The morning bombardment was so heavy that an attack was feared, and troops were rushed forward from the reserve trenches. In the afternoon snipers engaged each other in a duel, but by and large it was quieter than the morning. Sparling described the evening of 6th April as the Battalion's baptism of fire. At 8.00 p.m. the German artillery began shelling the trenches to the south, and slowly moved the barrage northwards. By 8.58 p.m. shells were landing in the Battalion's area, mainly on the support line. The Germans were firing everything from their heavy artillery down to rifle grenades and machine guns. Hundreds of flares were sent up which lit up the area almost as brightly as if it were day.

Gas helmet 1915-16 pattern.

The British artillery retaliated by firing onto the enemy's front and support lines. The duel went on for almost three hours, but by 10.45 p.m. work parties were able to start repairing the damage to the trenches. Incredibly no one in the Battalion was killed, and only one man was wounded. The Battalion acquitted itself very well under fire that night, and was very steady despite the torrent of shells falling around it. The Corps Commander himself, Lt Gen Sir Aylmer Hunter-Weston KCB DSO, sent his congratulations.

During the bombardment 12/1388 Sgt H. C. Clay of A Company thought he could smell gas and putting on his gas helmet ran along the front line shouting a warning to everyone else. What he didn't realise was that one of the eye-pieces had fallen out rendering the helmet completely useless.

As it turned out there was no gas, but he must have had his leg pulled about the incident by the rest of the Sergeants' Mess. Sgt Clay was a Sheffield policeman, who had previous military experience in South Africa as a regular soldier. He was killed on 17th June by a shell fragment, and is buried in Bertrancourt Military Cemetery.

Although gas is not mentioned in the WD, Ptes Dixon and Hastings both make mention of it being used against them in their diary entries for 6th April. Pte Hastings even specified it as being tear gas. It is however, strange that there is no official mention of the incident.

On Friday 7th April the companies rotated their positions. Those in the front line went back into the support line, and vice versa. Nothing much happened during the day, but in the evening a canister bomb fell straight into the front line trench injuring two men. A shell had landed at exactly the same spot during the previous evening's bombardment. The Germans obviously had the range of that portion of trench down to the metre. It was only a matter of time before serious casualties would be caused. The next evening at 8.30 p.m., another minenwerfer bomb dropped into the trench killing two men and wounding another seven. All the casualties were in B Company.

One of those suffering from shell shock was 12/425 Pte C. F. Kerr. Immediately after the incident he was told to get a grip on himself and stick it out. But he was unable to settle down and the next day was sent out of the line, to recuperate with the cooks, in the rear areas. The psychological effects of shellfire, known as shell shock, were not properly understood at that stage of the war. However, they could be every bit as debilitating as a physical wound, and often their effects lasted much longer. Pte Kerr was returned to full duties on 19th April, but he was still complaining of headaches. On 3rd October he was

Dubbed a 'sniperscope' this contraption enabled the operator to get off a shot without showing his head.

sent back to England for rest and returned to France on 27th November. He was still having the headaches even then, over seven months after the shell had exploded.

There is an amusing twist to this story, which Pte Kerr tells in his diary. Although he was not physically wounded on 8th April the left heel of his boot had been hit by a shrapnel ball. Pte Kerr was a tall man, over 6'2" and his comrades, surprised to learn that he had been hit so low down, started the rumour that he had been standing on his head at the time.

The two men that died in this incident were 12/358 Pte W. A. Emmerson and 12/388 Pte H. Handbury. They were both buried in the Sucrerie Military Cemetery. This burial ground was just to the rear of the trenches, near a sugar refinery and hence its name. After the war the men buried there were undisturbed and the cemetery was taken over by the CWGC.

After this tragic incident it was sensibly decided to hold that section of trench with only small groups of men at either end of it, thus avoiding further unnecessary casualties.

A number of other significant events occurred on 8th April. The Battalion detached 2Lt F. A. Beal and 120 ORs to the newly formed 94/1 Light Trench Mortar Battery, (94/1 LTMB). All the Brigades in the BEF were adding a LTMB to their order of battle at the same time, but the manpower had to come from the battalions in each brigade. 2Lt F. A. Beal was the brother of 2Lt A. J. Beal, who has already been mentioned. He did not join the Battalion until September 1915, having previously served in the Manchester Regiment (Manchesters).

Also on the 8th the first batch of telescopic sights arrived. The Battalion snipers were then able to take on the troublesome German marksmen on equal terms. Very soon it was noticed that the enemy's fire slackened, as they realised that their own fire was now being returned accurately.

In trench warfare sniping became a very carefully developed art, and special sniping schools were set up. The snipers themselves were chosen as much for their initiative and intelligence, as for their shooting skill. The work was dangerous often involving staying out all day in NML, but it was attractive to some men because once out of the trenches they had complete freedom of action. Snipers were a continual nuisance to both sides, and sometimes artillery barrages were laid down to flush out the most troublesome ones.

There is a superstition of never accepting the third light for a cigarette, which stems from the First World War. The theory was that at night a sniper would see the glow of a match being struck, and by the time the third man was lighting his fag the sniper would have him in his sights.

The weather, during the first few days in the line had been quite kind to the men, but it now turned much colder and the dreaded rain began to fall heavily. Pte Alflat was in the support line, which was little more than a series of linked shell holes. As the rain fell the holes slowly filled up with water. There was nowhere to go to escape the rain. Pte T. C. Hunter was in the front line, and on Sunday 9th April celebrated his 20th birthday soaked to the skin. Everyone was soon thoroughly wet through and fed up.

As soon as the weather turned bad any form of work became harder, and much of the men's time was directed towards stopping the trenches from collapsing. As if to counter the morale sapping effects of the rain, a batch of mail arrived on the 9th and was distributed in the trenches. The Battalion also suffered its first casualty amongst the officers, when Lt C. H. Woolhouse was slightly wounded, but he was soon returned to duty.

The rest of the tour of duty in the trenches was characterised by the wet and mud. The Germans were much quieter, perhaps because they were being relieved, or maybe because the weather caused them as many problems as it did our own troops. The shell hole which had become home to Pte Alflat steadily filled with water, and to get away from it he volunteered for any duty that kept him moving. One afternoon he was detailed for a ration carrying fatigue and after stand to he volunteered to stay on the same detail. He was up all night and did not return until dawn, but at least he avoided having to spend a night in the flooded shell hole. Sadly Pte Alflat's diary got wet soon afterwards and the last readable entry was on 11th April.

Relief came on the 12th. At 1.30 p.m. 13th East Yorks began to take over the line, and by 10.30 p.m. that night the hand over was completed. There were no casualties. The Battalion had achieved a lot in its first nine days in the trenches, (a long tour by later standards), and learned much of value for later trench tours. They marched off to Bertrancourt singing as they went, such was their relief to be out of the line. They arrived at Bertrancourt tired and wet through. As soon as they were dismissed they collapsed into their huts and slept properly for the first time in over a week.

The rest was short lived, and the next day training began at once. The subjects covered included erection of barbed wire obstacles, bombing and patrolling. Work parties were tasked to dig new trenches, mainly in the Colincamps area, and this task went on until 27th April.

Lt Middleton returned from leave the same evening the Battalion came out of the line. He heard on arrival that all leave had been cancelled, because someone had failed to salute the Brigadier. Even on active service the hierarchy were determined to maintain proper military decorum. Lt Middleton was lucky, having had his leave, but the rest had to wait until the Brigadier rescinded his ban.

On the 18th parties of soldiers went to Bus to see a practical demonstration of the German flamethrower and tear gas shells. On returning to Bertrancourt Lt Middleton found out that one of the other officers, Capt W. S. Clarke, had contracted measles. Lt Middleton and seven other officers who had been in close contact with Capt Clarke were isolated from the rest. This was necessary in the circumstances to prevent an epidemic in the Battalion. Throughout the war sickness and disease accounted for more casualties than did enemy action.

They were all lodged in one room which was sprayed the next day. They were allowed out for exercise, and took long walks in the rain and even went riding to the nearby villages of Sailly au Bois or Courcelles. Isolation was not as bad as they had feared it might have been.

When the men were not working they entertained themselves as best they could. One evening at an impromptu concert in the church hut, L/Cpl F. Jameson told some old jokes. He explained afterwards that he had to tell old ones because the men were too tired to work out any new ones!

Most of their time however, was spent either working or snatching a few hours sleep. Sgt J. W. Streets wrote a detailed account of one particular day. It was raining as usual, as it had been for a week. His party had a march of eight miles through the mud to where they were to dig trenches. It was so muddy that at one point it took him 15 minutes to move along 50 yards of trench. He also said it was rumoured that the navy was about to take over the line! Despite the atrocious conditions he could still see the humorous side of things, although there was precious little to laugh about.

The 'rest period' was soon over and arrangements were made to go back into the line. Rest is a deceptive word when used in this context. Being out of the line did not mean they could rest in the normal sense of the word. The troops actually in the trenches needed a vast administrative back-up to support them. Each division had a thirteenth battalion assigned to it, the Pioneers, to do the general dogsbody work of lifting, carrying and digging. But they could not cope on their own, and therefore battalions out of the line were co-opted to work as well.

B Company were the first to go back into the line on the morning of 28th April. They were sent to support 11th East Lancs because a company from that Battalion had been detached on other duties by the Corps HQ. B Company occupied the same stretch of the line as in the previous trench tour. The remaining three companies marched to Colincamps. On arrival there two and a half platoons of D Company were sent to occupy reserve posts at Fort Hoystead, Ellis Square and Hittite Trench.

The Battalion was in Brigade Reserve, but the work parties continued. One man was later wounded by machine gun fire while clearing out a new communications trench. Late on the evening of the 29th the men were ordered into their billets. The whole of the Division's artillery were to shell the enemy front for an hour commencing at 11.30 p.m. The purpose of this is not known, but it was probably a routine 'brassing up' of the enemy. The men were confined to their billets to avoid casualties in the forward areas if the Germans retaliated with a heavy bombardment of their own.

The weather improved considerably and the days were as hot as Egypt, according to Lt Middleton. But it would take a long time for the ground to dry out. In the trenches Pte Hunter was still up to his knees in mud.

There were lots of tasks in the forward areas to be done, even though the Battalion was in reserve. Pte Hunter went on a patrol led by 12/1123 Sgt R. Gallimore on the night of 29th-30th April. The next night six men went out on a wiring detail, again led by Sgt Gallimore. The wiring parties went on for another two nights. All of the parties in NML were harassed by Maxim machine gun fire and rifle grenades.

The work parties in and behind our own lines also had a rough time. Lts Ingold and Storry took a large work party to Ellis Square on 1st May. They were heavily shelled and one man was killed. He was 12/1216 Pte Frank Haywood senior, a Sheffield University student who was born in Neepsend. He is buried in the Sucrerie Military Cemetry like so many other City Battalion men.

Trench map of the Serre area. British trenches were rarely shown as accurately as the German lines in case maps were captured. The shaded circles round Serre were planned British strongpoints after the attack on 1st July 1916.

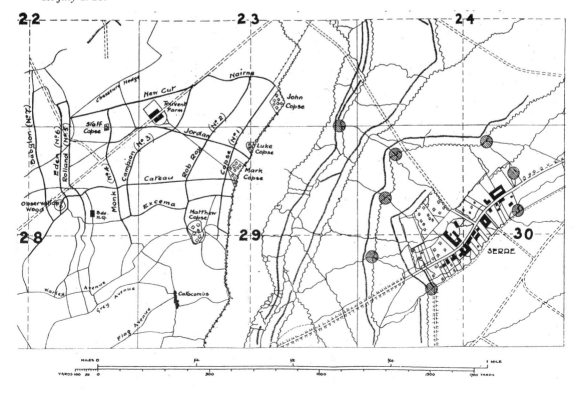

The Battalion relieved 14th York and Lancs on 2nd May. One company of the outgoing Battalion was retained, to replace D Company which had been sent off as a work party for 223rd Field Company RE until 16th May. On the left of the Battalion was a company of 11th East Lancs and on the right 6th Battalion Gloucestershire Regiment (Gloucesters).

The area the Battalion took over was where they would attack Serre from on 1st July. The front line ran along the forward edges of a series of small woods. These had been named Matthew, Mark, Luke and John Copses by the troops. From the British front line the ground rose gently towards the German lines. Behind the front line the slope continued downwards, into what later became known as Railway Hollow, then rose again towards Colincamps and the British rear areas. It was a far from ideal position, since the Germans overlooked the whole British forward trench system. Nothing could move in daylight without the Germans immediately seeing it. At this time the copses were battered, but still recognisable as small woods. Over the next few months they would be almost erased by artillery fire.

The routine of trench life, learned in the first tour, was quickly resumed. Work began immediately, and went on unceasingly, to repair and improve the defences. Assembly trenches were also dug in preparation for the forthcoming offensive, and masses of stores were brought into the line to be stockpiled ready for the big day.

The men especially hated carrying poison gas cylinders up to the front line. They were very heavy and difficult to manoeuvre in the narrow confines of the communications trenches. They were also very dangerous since shell splinters could easily pierce them and gas anyone nearby.

The officers who had been quarantined with suspected measles were cleared by the MO on the 3rd. They packed their kit and made their way into the line to rejoin the Battalion. Lt Middleton had been on leave during the previous trench tour, and this was to be his first visit to the trenches. His initial reaction was that the trenches were 'very ordinary', but at that stage he had not heard of the disaster that had just befallen C Company. When he was told about it he soon came back to earth and quickly appreciated that even in ordinary looking trenches danger lurked everywhere.

Earlier in the day three men in C Company had been wounded by a minenwerfer and were being tended in the Company telephone dugout in John Copse. While their wounds were being dressed another minenwerfer shell landed amongst them. The dugout had been constructed by the Germans, and although it was a sturdy structure the entrance faced towards the enemy. By sheer bad luck the shell went straight through the dugout entranceway.

Six men were killed instantly and a seventh died soon afterwards. The only other occupant of the dugout was badly wounded. Amongst the dead was 12/560 CSM J. W. Ellis, one of the old sweats who had trained the Battalion from the very beginning. The RSM saw a stretcher with a covered body being carried to the rear and he asked who it was. On hearing that it was CSM Ellis, he simply said, 'Poor old Joe', and walked away. Although it must have been a shock to the RSM, for the sake of discipline and morale he could not afford to let his feelings show.

The other men killed were: 12/1238 Pte A. D. Frost from Dore, aged 21; 12/668 L/Cpl S. Hardwick of Maltravers Road, Sheffield; 12/757 Pte P. C. Richards, a signaller, aged 23 from Grafton Street, Sheffield, previously a Town Hall employee; 12/767 Pte E. G. Rodgers aged 20; and 12/807 Pte G. Unwin aged 25, of Oxford Street, Sheffield, who had kept a detailed diary of the journey to Egypt.

Another man died of his wounds while being rushed to the dressing station. He was 12/802 Pte H. Todd. He had been hit in the leg in the earlier minenwerfer attack and was being attended to when he was wounded again. Before the war he had been a bank employee with the forerunner of the Midland Bank. He was 25.

All the dead were buried in the Sucrerie Military Cemetery. The CWGC give the date of death as the 4th. It is likely that the incident was not written up until the following day, and the casualty return would therefore have the wrong date.

CSM J. W. Ellis killed when a minenwerfer shell landed in a dugout. He was born in 1872. Following his previous military service as a Regular and TF soldier he became Commissionaire at Walsh's Store in 1911.

Throughout the next day both sides were very active. In the morning the rear areas around Le Cateau Trench and Touvent Farm were hit by German artillery. Later on German trench mortars fired into Matthew Copse and Blencarn Avenue. The British artillery registered targets on the enemy lines in the afternoon and in the late evening the Germans fired showers of rifle grenades into the right flank of the Battalion's front. The grenades were fired from NML, just outside the German wire, but the British artillery soon silenced the enemy grenadiers. There was another fatality during the day when 12/110 L/Cpl F. Gee of A Company, was killed by a sniper.

When the initial impression of calm had passed, Lt Middleton admitted in his diary that the shelling 'put the wind up him'. A heavy shell had landed close to him during the day and this would be sufficient to put the wind up anyone. During the day he was warned that a raiding party from 14th York and Lancs was to be sent out through B Company's lines that evening. The indications were that the Germans were making preparations to counter the raid and at 5.00 p.m. it was cancelled, much to Lt Middleton's relief. Raids invariably attracted heavy retaliatory artillery fire onto the trenches opposite the raided sector. Having had his first experience of what it was like to be on the receiving end of heavy artillery that day, he was quite naturally in no hurry for a repeat performance the same evening.

The cancellation of the raid brought no respite from the shelling which continued throughout the 5th. John and Mark Copses received a lot of attention on this occasion. No. 4 Post was blown in for the third day running, but there were no casualties. The night however, was quiet. Next morning the troops had a boost for their morale when low flying British planes machine gunned the German trenches.

Nowhere in the trenches could be regarded as being safe. Battalion HQ was situated in a dugout called the Monastery in Monk Trench. Despite being a long way behind the front line it was constantly being showered with bullets from long range machine gun fire. They landed in the trench at that point due to the curvature of the ground, and made a loud thwack against the trench walls. The Adjutant offhandedly called them 'blood spuds'. A few weeks later the Battalion HQ dugout was destroyed by shellfire.

Relief by 12th East Yorks came on the 6th and was completed by 7.30 p.m. The Battalion marched to a camp at Warnimont Wood, which was in surprisingly good condition at that time, and an idyllic setting when compared with the trenches. The Battalion WD says it was a new camp, one of many erected to cater for the thousands of extra troops who were beginning to arrive for the offensive.

Although it was only five miles from the front Warnimont Wood could have been in a different world. The birds sang and the grass was green, as yet untouched by the ravages of concentrated shellfire. The fields were full of crops and the local population had not left the area. After a tour in the trenches it was just what the men needed.

Training recommenced the next morning after the usual inspection. A draft of 20 new recruits arrived and they were immediately put into quarantine, although the reason for this is not known. Later in the day there was a church service.

At noon on 10th May the Commander of the BEF, Gen Haig, called to see the Battalion while it was training. He did not inspect the whole unit but walked around informally and took an interest in the various activities. He spoke to a number of officers and men, and expressed his pleasure at the way the Battalion had acquitted itself during its recent baptism of fire.

When the Battalion had come out of the trenches, D Company had been left behind to work for the REs. The Company was accommodated in Colincamps and marched to where it was to work as and when required. On the 11th a man was injured by shell fire in Rob Roy Trench, but otherwise the Company came off quite well.

Lt Ingold, who commanded 14 Platoon in D Company, was sent on leave on the 12th and his place was taken by Lt Middleton. The next day Lt Middleton took the Platoon digging in Rob Roy Trench in the pouring rain. The Germans shelled the area but there were no casualties. The weather was so bad that the digging party for that night had to be cancelled. Lt Middleton was relieved to hear this, since he had been due to accompany it. The following day he went with 2Lt E. M. Carr, to visit the graves of the men who had been killed over the past few weeks. He does not specify where he went, but it was almost certainly to the Sucrerie.

Orders to return to the trenches and relieve 16th West Yorks were issued. The relief was completed by 7.30 p.m. on 14th May. Two platoons of D Company remained with 223 Field Company RE at Colincamps. The other two platoons had been relieved by the East Lancs.

During the first night in the trenches the Battalion was subjected to one of the most devastating bombardments it was ever to endure. At 12.20 a.m. without warning the Germans suddenly commenced a heavy bombardment on the front line trenches, from Mark Copse to John Copse and the area to the north of it. Everything from the lightest trench mortars up to the heavy 15 cm guns were used.

At 12.50 a.m. a red flare shot into the air from a point in NML close to John Copse, and this appears to have been the signal to intensify the fire on the support lines. Immediately heavy fire was opened on Observation Wood, Le Cateau, Excema and Nairne Trenches, and on the communications trenches. The front line continued to be hit and the din and confusion was increased when the British artillery fired back in retaliation. The soldiers in the front trenches manned the parapet and fired a hail of bullets towards the German lines in case an attack was developing.

For an unknown reason many of the Battalion's senior and experienced officers were not in the trenches. The two front line companies (B and C), were commanded by Lt Middleton and 2Lt T. E. A. Grant respectively, and the support company behind them was commanded by Lt F. C. Earl. Despite their inexperience they performed very well and the men remained steady.

Although unknown at the time they were being subjected to a box barrage, as the Germans launched a raid on the trenches to the north occupied by 4th Battalion Royal Berkshire Regiment (4th Royal Berks). A box barrage was designed to seal off the area to be raided, so that reinforcements could not reach the defenders quickly.

> 'We were in the Rob Roy support trench. The Germans were shelling the supports to stop us getting to the front line. It was quite hot. I said to this chap at my side let's get in this dugout for shelter. It was an ammunition store stacked with boxes. We had only just got in when a shell landed in the trench blocking the dugout entrance and burying us. It took an hour to dig our way out with our bare hands.' 12/70 Cpl D. E. Cattell.

Aerial photo of the sector raided by the Germans on the night of 15/16 May 1916.

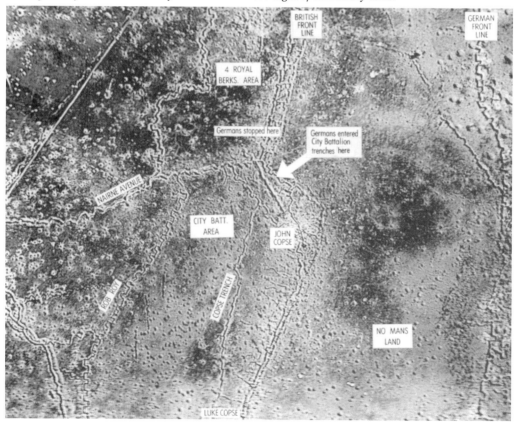

The events of the next few hours were very confusing, and some of the accounts of the raid are conflicting. The account that follows is a compilation from many sources. The raid itself seems to have started at about 1 a.m., when the bombardment slackened slightly and a party of Germans were seen entering the northern end of the Battalion's trenches, at John Copse. They had gained entry to the front line from the rear, due to the right angle bend at that point in the line. These Germans were at the southern end of the raid, the majority being directed towards the trenches of 4th Royal Berks. A bombing party from C Company cleared the Germans out after a fight lasting 15 minutes. The Germans left several casualties behind.

Sparling mentions Germans being seen wearing British uniforms with white arm bands. The same story has been heard from other sources, although it is not known if they were merely repeating what appeared in Sparling's book. The WDs of the City Battalion and 4th Royal Berks say nothing about this. Had there been clear evidence it would have appeared in the after action reports of both Battalions. There is never smoke without fire, but the truth of this incident will probably never be known.

The raid had some success in the 4th Royal Berks area. They suffered the brunt of the bombardment and the weight of the German attack. When the red flare went up the fire on the Royal Berks trenches slackened. Visibility was by then down to about 15 yards, due to the smoke and dust of the bombardment. The front line troops offered little resistance because they had virtually ceased to exist, and the Germans soon overcame one post which had survived. The Germans then divided their force into two; one party went along Jones Trench and the other followed the parados side of the front line.

The party moving along the front line was halted by some riflemen under the command of a Royal Berks Lance Corporal. The other party headed towards Nairne Avenue, and disposed of five front line posts in the process. They were prevented from taking the post closest to the junction with the City Battalion by the efforts of the Sergeant in charge. The collapse of the Royal Berks front line caused urgent appeals for reinforcements, and officers' servants and runners from the City Battalion were rushed up to prevent the enemy breaking through the trench lines and threatening Colincamps. There was actually no danger of this happening; the German raiders were too weak for such an ambitious project, but this was not known at the time.

Meanwhile the City Battalion was recovering from the initial shock. The greatest danger was still to C Company on the left, nearest to the centre of the raid. Its temporary commander however, was not unduly worried:

> 'I was not disturbed by the Royal Berks retiring. I felt confident the Boche could not get into my line. I went along my line and found everything in order to ward off an attack. I stopped for a while at No. 12 Post and observed the fire. A continual rain of High Explosive (HE) and shrapnel was falling in No. 11 Post, and the line of the barrage was at the time from No. 11, behind No. 12 to Rob Roy Trench, where it joined Nairne Trench, and then to our left. I asked for a couple of volunteers from each of Posts 14, 13 and 12, to help dig out the dead in No. 11 Post. After I left a number of Sappers in the mine gave efficient help. I went back along the line and along Nairne to Rob Roy to find out the extent of the damage. The men stood to until dawn when we removed the casualties. Rations were buried but we salvaged them all. The men behaved splendidly and showed fine spirit.' 2Lt T. E. A. Grant.

The mine mentioned by 2Lt Grant was being constructed by the REs from John Copse underneath NML in preparation for the forthcoming offensive. He was right about the behaviour of the troops. Apart from the baptism of fire earlier in the month this was their first battle of any consequence, since it was the first occasion when they had actually come face to face with the enemy. No one could doubt their spirit or their courage.

According to the WD a Lance Corporal was killed attacking a German officer with his fists. The CWGC record only one Lance Corporal dying on 16th May, and we know from another source that he was killed by a sniper later in the day, while passing a gap in the parapet. As to who the heroic NCO was remains a mystery. It might be expected that such a display of gallantry was rewarded with a posthumous bravery award, but this was not to be.

Seven MMs were later awarded as a result of this action. The full details are in the appendix at the end of the book. The recipients were: 12/742 Pte R. T. Owen, 12/825 Pte R. Wilson, 12/822 Pte B. C.

Wilkinson, 12/785 Pte E. Spencer, 12/1358 Pte G. Hanson, 12/392 Cpl M. C. P. Headeach, 12/548 L/Cpl F. E. Watkins.

At 2.10 a.m. the intense artillery fire began to abate and by 2.20 a.m. the front had returned to normal. By this time the German raiding party had withdrawn. In the wake of the attack was a scene of utter devastation. Many trenches had been levelled, in particular Excema close to Observation Wood, Le Cateau, Rob Roy, Nairne and the front line itself. There was much to be done to restore the trenches to normal, but the first priority was to evacuate the wounded and dig out the dead.

Even while the bombardment had been going on some men had risked their lives to begin rescuing those who had been trapped in dugouts or buried by collapsing trenches. Later men from 14th York and Lancs and the REs would assist, but in the first place it was up to the few men who had survived the direct hits, to dig out their comrades. They were themselves shaky from the effects of the bombardment and still under fire. With their bare hands they desperately tore at the mud and timbers to get at the trapped men before they suffocated.

One of those who had been buried was 12/1434 Pte L. McIvor. He related his story in a letter to the parents of the man who tried to rescue him. His would be rescuer was 12/568 Re R. H. B. Matthews, and an extract from the letter is printed below:

'It was my First time in the trenches, and Matthews took me in hand and gave me cheery advice, promising to keep an eye on me and answer any questions. Later when the bombardment commenced, he got me at his side. The parapet was blown in and buried me completely, but I found that I was getting air through a small hole, and so called for help. Matthews was surprised to find I was alive I think, and set about to try and extricate me. He found the weight too great, so discovered my air hole and scraped at it for some time. This gave me more scope for breathing. To this act I think I owe my life. The hole supplied me with air for about an hour and a half, when a working party found me on hearing my call. While your son was clearing out the hole his hand found mine, and with a strong grip on it, he assured me that he would get me out somehow. At this moment I heard a loud bang, and the hand went limp in mine. I cannot express how sorry I am at being the cause of this sad accident, but believe me I shall always think with gratitude of my one time comrade and his noble sacrifice on my behalf.'

Pte McIvor was himself killed on 1st July 1916. He was 24 years old and had lived at 133 Channing Street, Sheffield. His body was never identified and his name is commemorated on the Thiepval Memorial.

The rescue work went on as quickly as possible. Lt Middleton tells of one man being recovered as late as 8.00 a.m. He was 12/1397 Pte F. Earnshaw. Sadly the efforts to get him out were to no avail; he died of his wounds on 20th May, and was buried in the Military Cemetery at Etaples.

A number of men were particularly noted for the gallant way in which they helped to dig out their comrades without regard to their own safety. They were: 12/851 Pte F. 0. Appleby, 12/755 Sgt B. J. Register, 12/608 Pte S. Brown, 12/758 Pte F. 0. Rideout, 12/615 Pte N. W. G. Chandler, 12/774 Pte J. 0. Schofield, 12/628 Sgt H. C. Crozier, 2Lt J. Thompson, 12/180 Cpl J. H. Marsden, 12/1069 Sgt W. Thompson, 12/747 Pte F. J. Pennington. None of them were decorated for their bravery, and Sgt Register was also killed. Of the other 10, four were killed on 1st July 1916, and another died later in the war.

The Battalion lost a total of 15 men killed and 45 wounded, during the two hour long raid. All those killed were buried in the Sucrerie Military Cemetery. They were: 12/25 Pte A. E. Arrowsmith, 12/755 Sgt B. J. Register, 12/291 Pte W. Barlow, 12/516 Pte A. Slack, 12/1267 Pte P. Burch, 12/1057 L/Cpl R. E. Smith, 12/1469 Pte G. G. Cook, 12/1480 Pte J. Strickland, 12/638 Pte H. B. Dowty, 12/1145 Pte T. W. Stubley, 12/651 Pte E. Furniss, 12/805 Pte W. H. C. Tucker, 12/700 Pte C. Johnson, 12/1268 Pte R. H. Walker, 12/568 Pte R. H. B. Matthews.

The battalion at the centre of the raid, 4th Royal Berks, also suffered many casualties. There were 18 killed, 51 wounded and 29 missing. Most of the missing were later found to have been killed.

As it got light the true scale of the devastation became apparent. Trenches were blown in, and in many places had been completely levelled. Dugouts had collapsed. The wire in NML had been brushed away in places by the power of the bombardment. The signallers had to begin the unenviable task of going out to trace breaks in the telephone cables. This was a nerve-racking job that had to be done in the open and often in full view of the enemy. Pte Hastings wrote in his diary that he had 'a rotten job repairing them'.

> *'You got quite expert at tracing the faults at night. Also you learned your way around, often moving about out of the trenches. In fact I knew the ground like the back of my hand.'* 12/928 L/Cpl J. R. Glenn

Very little work could be done in daylight without drawing fire from the Germans. The wounded were extracted and taken to the rear, and preparations were begun for the repair work to be completed that night.

It was a very trying night's work indeed, and the men had little respite during the 17th, with the artillery on both sides active throughout the day. Carrying parties were again organised to remove the dead, and replenish supplies of food and ammunition. It was while on one of the parties removing the dead that 12/1585 Pte H. Johnson was killed by a sniper. This was a particularly sad loss since he was one of the last draft to arrive in the Battalion, and should not have been in the trenches at all.

That night work continued. Lt Middleton spent most of his time in NML supervising the repair of the wire. Capt Moore had by that time returned to resume command of the Company. The work done to restore the trenches did not go unnoticed by the Divisional Commander. On a tour of the trenches he complimented Pte Hunter and his companions on their splendid efforts.

The Battalion snipers took revenge for the raid. On the 18th they hit two Germans in their trench, in front of John Copse. The next evening, at 9.30 p.m., Lt Middleton took out a patrol to try to locate the body of a German who had been shot by 12/491 L/Cpl 0. G. Richardson during the day. The patrol found no trace of the German, despite having L/Cpl Richardson along with them for directions. They did however, hear the Germans at work on their wire obstacles. L/Cpl Richardson was a little hard of hearing and while the rest of the patrol were acutely aware of the proximity of the enemy he seems not to have heard them. Probably a combination of his deafness and the excitement of being in NML caused him to raise his voice. Whatever the reason he insisted on shouting to the other members of the patrol when a very quiet whisper would have been more appropriate. Lt Middleton was very pleased to get back to the trenches safely.

Lt Middleton spent a lot of time in NML during this trench tour. At 3.30 a.m. that same day, under the cover of a thick fog, he had explored the area between the front line and the wire. He and Lt Cowen had found an unexploded 'oil can' bomb, which Cowen blew open with a Mills grenade. They then scooped out the explosive from it. The purpose of this dangerous exercise is not known.

The trench tour came to a thankful end when 11th East Lancs began to take over the line in the early hours of the 20th. By 7.15 p.m. that evening the Battalion was clear of the trenches and marched to Courcelles. As usual the rest turned out to be more work than pleasure.

For the next nine days the Battalion provided daily and nightly work parties to the front line trenches. The work was concerned with the forthcoming offensive, and consisted mainly of digging assembly trenches and improving the existing system.

Lt Middleton was sent on an artillery observers' course run by 165 Brigade RFA. The aim of the instruction was to teach him how to direct the fire of the gun batteries behind the trenches, from an Observation Post (OP) close to the front line. For the next couple of days he practised on Serre from the OP in Monk Trench.

A number of men were wounded on the work parties and on 27th May 12/1084 L/Cpl Frederick Walker was killed by machine gun fire. Before the war he had been a fish and poultry dealer in Sheffield.

On 30th May the Battalion marched to a rest camp at Bus Wood, and on arrival were rejoined by the D Company work party, which had been in Colincamps with the Sappers. The Battalion was once again complete. Lt Middleton says he arrived at the rest camp at 1100 and complained in his diary that the place was not clean. Later in the day he spent some time taking a German rifle grenade to pieces. He must have been bored!

The men did not yet know it but there was only a month left before the great offensive, the Big Push as they called it, commenced. 94th Brigade was out of the line to train, and to carry out full scale rehearsals for its part in the assault on the fortress village of Serre.

Germans move up men and supplies for the coming British offensive on the Somme.

Chapter Six

Preparation for the Somme Offensive

The First Day on the Somme, 1st July 1916, was the blackest day ever for the British Army. No single day, either before or since, has resulted in so many killed and maimed. Over 57,000 men were casualties, and of these over 19,000 were killed or died of wounds. The spirit of Kitchener's Armies also died on the battlefields of the Somme.

No other battle has aroused so much emotion, or left such a lasting effect on the British people, as the First Day on the Somme. Whole communities at home were devastated by the casualties.

To put the British losses into perspective, they equate to three infantry divisions, or the fighting element of 70 infantry battalions. As Martin Middlebrook points out in his book, 'First Day on the Somme'; the British Army suffered more casualties on 1st July 1916 than in the whole of the Crimean, Boer and Korean Wars combined.

The Battalion's part in the battle will be related in the next chapter. This chapter is devoted to the Allied plans for 1916 and the preparations for the battle itself. To do this we must firstly turn the clock back to December 1915.

On 19th December 1915, Gen Sir Douglas Haig was appointed Commander of the BEF. He replaced Gen Sir John French who had been in command since August 1914. Haig was ultimately responsible for the British part in the Somme offensive, and because of this he deserves some attention.

Haig was a cavalry officer, and had served in the 7th Hussars and 17th Lancers. He failed the Staff College entrance examination in June 1893. However, he was selected to attend the College by

(Left) British Front Line prior to the 'Big Push' on 1st July, 1916. (Right) Somme section of the Front, showing first day objectives.

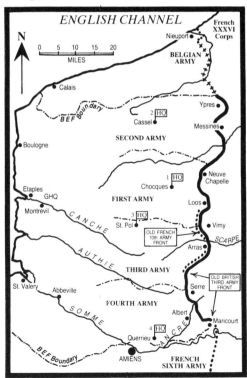

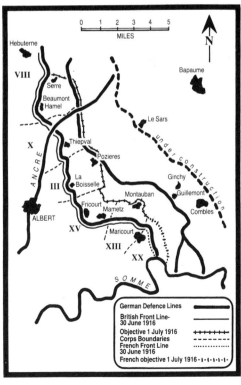

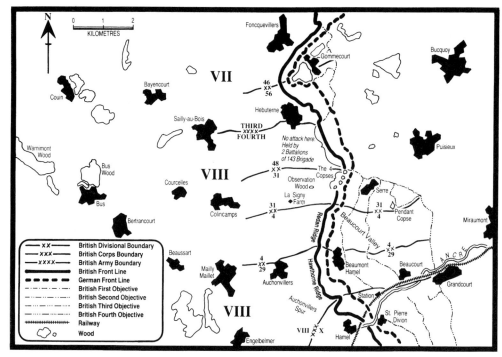

VIII Corps front showing 31st Division area on the extreme left flank of the whole British attack.

nomination in February 1896, because of the excellent reports he had written on the French and German Armies. It has been suggested that he used his friends in high places to get into the Staff College, although nominated places were perfectly normal at the time and a couple of officers each year gained entry by this means. Despite this setback he managed to make his way up the promotion ladder. Some would say

Gen Sir John French, BEF Commander August 1914-December 1915.

Gen Sir Douglas Haig who took over command of the BEF in December 1915.

he achieved this by devious means, but despite the criticism levelled at him, he proved to be a very competent Corps Commander in the First Battle of Ypres in 1914.

Haig has been accused of engineering the recall of French in order to gain command of the BEF for himself. There is no doubt that French had to go. It is also clear that Haig's criticism of French's handling of the war was a contributory factor in his recall. However, whether Haig's criticism was a means of securing command of the BEF for himself, or because he genuinely believed that French had to be replaced, is a matter for debate. This book is not however, the place for such a discussion.

The conduct of the war on the Western Front under Haig's command has attracted much criticism. His protagonists say he fought a war of attrition with no thought of the casualties involved. His supporters on the other hand, maintain that there was no alterative. Until technological solutions were found to overcome the stalemate, caused by barbed wire and machine guns, there was no other way to defeat the Germans other than to bleed them white.

Whatever opinions readers may have of this cold and somewhat aloof Scot, some facts are indisputable. Under Haig's command BEF casualties were higher than ever before in the war, and often they could have been avoided. But it must be remembered that Haig was successful in bringing the war to a victorious end, albeit under the auspices of a French Supreme Commander. In the latter stages of the war the Army had the technological and tactical means to break the trench deadlock, and under Haig's generalship overcame the enemy and sent him running for home. That is enough of Haig. We will now look at the planning for the Somme offensive.

Apart from their offensive at Ypres early in 1915, the Germans spent the rest of the year on the defensive. They had failed to crush the French in 1914, but had occupied almost the whole of Belgium and a sizeable portion of north-eastern France. The Germans were content to sit out 1915 in the knowledge that the onus was on the Allies to regain their lost territory. The Germans dug in and prepared for the French and British to waste themselves against their strong and in-depth defensive positions.

The Western Allies duly obliged the Germans by launching a series of offensives. Nothing was achieved, except for lengthening the casualty lists. By the end of 1915 the French had suffered almost 2,000,000 casualties and the British 500,000. Neither country had anything to show for their losses.

A meeting of the Inter-Allied Military Conference took place at Chantilly on 6th December 1915. At the conference the French put pressure on Britain to make a bigger contribution to the war on the Western Front. It was agreed that as British New Army divisions completed their training they would be sent to France. The British were gradually to take over longer stretches of the front to relieve the pressure on the French.

At the same meeting it was agreed that the Allies would launch simultaneous offensives in 1916. They reasoned that if the Central Powers were attacked on the Western, Italian and Russian fronts at the same time, they would crack and sue for peace. A target date for the opening of the offensives was set for as soon as possible after the end of March.

Haig was in full agreement with this policy. He was a 'Westerner', a supporter of the view that the war could only be won by defeating the German Army on the Western Front. He regarded all other fronts, such as the abortive Gallipoli campaign, as mere side shows which diverted men and supplies from the crucial theatre of operations in France and Belgium.

The great expectations the Allies had of their combined offensives were not to come to fruition. The Central Powers were well aware that a simultaneous attack on all three fronts would leave them in a very grave position. The French had suffered badly in 1915, but still posed a greater threat to the Germans than did the Russians, whose forces were disorganised and poorly equipped at the best of times. The Germans therefore decided on a pre-emptive strike and attacked the French at Verdun on 21st February 1916.

The offensive went on unceasingly throughout the spring of 1916, and more and more French troops had to be sent to hold the Germans at bay. As the attacks went on the French ability to launch a separate offensive in concert with the British became less and less. By May Haig was warning the government in London that the offensive could not be expected to achieve great results.

By that stage of the war the British Cabinet had accepted the principle that the Allies must attack in order to win. There was therefore no question of the British part of the offensive being cancelled, despite the greatly reduced French contribution. There could be no victory for Britain until the Germans had been thrown out of their conquered territories.

The Austro-Hungarian forces also pre-empted the Allies by attacking in the Trentino in mid-May. The Allied plan began to falter badly, before it had even been put into action. Both France and Italy appealed for help. The Italians begged the Russians to attack to prevent the Austrians withdrawing troops from the Eastern Front to use against them in the Tyrol. The French turned to the British, urgently requesting an offensive to take the pressure off Verdun.

We will now focus attention on the British sector of the Western front to set the scene for the battle. By the end of 1915 the British Third Army had taken over the area north of the Somme from the French. The Army front stretched from the River Somme in the south, northwards to a point about 10 miles south of Arras. This area, with minor boundary changes, would later become the territory of the Fourth Army, which was destined to launch the offensive in July 1916.

Between the Third Army area on the Somme and the rest of the BEF in Flanders was the French Tenth Army. Because of the Verdun offensive the planned British takeover of this area was

Gen Sir Henry Rawlinson, commander of the British Fourth Army.

brought forward and completed by the middle of March. The British line then extended continuously from Ypres in Belgium southwards to the River Somme. As the bullet flies the distance is about 60 miles, but there were actually 90 miles of front to be held.

At the beginning of March the Fourth Army was formed, under the command of Gen Sir Henry Rawlinson. He set up his HQ in the château at Querrieu, five miles east of Amiens on the Albert road. The Fourth Army took over the right of the Third Army front, from the River Somme northwards to Fonquevillers. The name of this village was impossible for most British soldiers to pronounce, and some readers may have sympathy with them! It was quickly renamed Funky Villers. The length of the Fourth Army front was 20 miles. Third Army shifted northwards and took over most of the old French Tenth Army area. On taking over Rawlinson was immediately made responsible for the planning of the offensive.

The opening date for the offensive was repeatedly changed in the early months of 1916, but by the end of May it had been settled as 1st July. At that stage the level of French participation was unknown and depended on the future actions of the Germans at Verdun.

However, it was clear that their involvement would be far short of what had originally been planned.

The situation at Verdun took a decided turn for the worse at the beginning of June, and the French

Heavy fighting at Verdun. French troops about to go "over the top".

urgently requested Haig to bring forward the opening of his attack to 25th June. Haig agreed to try. But soon afterwards the situation at Verdun improved and Joffre, the French CinC, asked for the date to be put back to 1st July again. Haig refused since his preparations were well advanced by then, and he did not intend to have any further changes. Eventually he settled on the 29th and not a day later. However, it was to be the weather, not Haig or the French, that dictated the actual date of the attack.

The Somme was chosen for the offensive because it was where the French and British forces met, and the combined attack would present the Germans with a longer frontage to deal with. The British attack was to be north of the River Somme. The countryside undulates gently and is very similar in appearance to the countryside around Salisbury Plain. The sub-soil is chalk and ideal for digging deep defences because it drains so well. The land is interspersed with large, dense woods and small villages. The town of Albert was about 2 miles behind the British lines and Bapaume, an important centre of communications, stood about 10 miles behind the German forward positions.

The Germans occupied the tops of spurs and the high ground, and had also made full use of the villages, converting those in their defence lines into strong fortresses. The Germans had also constructed a second position 2,000 to 5,000 yards behind the front line. Although in range of artillery the second

Strongly revetted German trenches like these would have to be overcome in the July offensive.

position could not be seen from the British lines. It was therefore impossible to bombard it accurately. Behind the second line a third was under construction. Each defence line consisted of at least three mutually supporting lines of trenches with thick barbed wire defences in front of each one.

Unlike British divisions, which tended to move periodically from area to area, the German divisions on the Somme had been there since the end of 1914. They had not wasted their time. Their trenches were deep and strongly revetted against shellfire. Deep dugouts had been constructed which could withstand all but a direct hit from the heaviest calibre shells. Within these dugouts the German infantrymen could shelter with impunity while a storm of steel flew about above them. Even if an entranceway was

destroyed there was always another for emergencies. Some of the shelters, usually officers' quarters, were fitted out with all sorts of creature comforts such as beds, electric lights, easy chairs, dining tables, wooden wall panelling and gramophones. Despite the protection the shelters afforded, the German soldiers suffered terribly during the bombardment preceding the offensive.

The Germans built deep shelters to protect themselves from artillery.

The first plan to emerge after Rawlinson took over was to rush the first German defence line after a 72 hour bombardment. Haig was not impressed, and said it lacked imagination. He told Fourth Army to consider advancing to the second position on the first day, but did not allocate more troops for this extra task.

Haig also instructed Third Army to plan an attack against Gommecourt, to divert attention from Fourth Army's open northern flank. Haig favoured a short, intense barrage just prior to the attack, but this approach left unresolved the problem of how to cut the thick belts of barbed wire in front of the German lines. Wire was usually cut by artillery fire prior to an offensive, but the absence of a preliminary bombardment would obviously leave it intact.

German soldiers constructing deep wire defences.

There was a possible alternative. Lt Eberle, an engineer officer in 48th Division, had developed the Bangalore Torpedo. Originally it was little more than a plank of wood with explosives fastened onto it which was pushed into the wire entanglements. When detonated it cleared a path for the infantry to pass through. Later developments resulted in steel tubes filled with ammonal. The first operational use of this type was in March 1916, when a 12 feet wide gap was successfully cleared through barbed wire for a trench raid. The Bangalore Torpedo proved to be very successful for small scale attacks and raids, but for a large offensive was impractical given the number of gaps required for the attacking troops to pass through.

There was a fundamental difference in philosophy between Haig and Rawlinson. Haig saw the objective of the first day's attack as being the occupation of the first German line along a 25,000 yards front. Subsequent operations would then be launched to capture the important Bazentin to Ginchy ridge, before the Army drove eastwards and a breakthrough was achieved. Rawlinson did not envisage a breakthrough, he only foresaw a limited offensive. His plan was to bombard 2,000 yards wide strips of the front which would then be occupied by the infantry. When the artillery had been moved up, another strip would be pounded and then occupied. This would go on until the Germans either broke or the British attacks ground to a halt.

Haig wanted to gain as much territory as possible while the Germans were still reeling before the initial blow. He wanted to capture the German heavy artillery, but this was sited behind the German

A typical shelter arrangement in the German forward trenches. Even in the heaviest bombardments a sentry was left at the entranceway to warn of an attack.

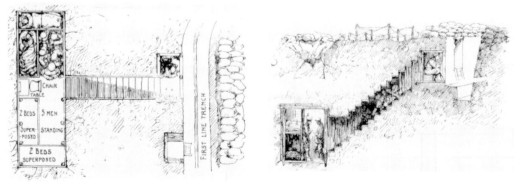

second line which was not visible to the artillery observers. The wire defending the second line therefore could not be cut until after the first line had been taken.

After much discussion it was decided to include the second position in the first day's objectives. The preliminary bombardment was to be as long and intensive as possible, but this was entirely dependent on the amount of ammunition available. It was calculated that there were sufficient shells for a five day bombardment. If a breakthrough was achieved then Gen Gough, commanding the Reserve Army, was to take over the right flank and drive it forward as hard as possible.

Preparations for an offensive on this scale could not hope to be concealed from the Germans. The start date however, could have been kept secret had it not been for a diabolical lack of security.

Soldiers at home on leave were constantly pestered by people asking when the 'Big Push' would begin. On 2nd June a speech by a British minister was reported in the newspapers. In it he said, 'I am asked why the Whitsuntide holidays are to be postponed until the end of July. How inquisitive we all are! It should suffice that we ask for a postponement of the holidays until the end of July. This fact should speak volumes'. British newspapers were freely available to the Germans through neutral countries, and to them the speech did speak volumes. The munitions industry was to be kept at full production in readiness for an offensive around the beginning of July.

Wire cutting by the artillery would pinpoint the limits of the attack since there was not enough artillery ammunition for diversionary cutting bombardments elsewhere. Even if there had been sufficient shells the Germans would not have been fooled. Other preparations stood out so clearly a blind man could have predicted exactly where the attack would occur.

> 'A few days before the attack I pointed out to Gen Hunter-Weston that the assembly trenches stopped dead on the left of the 94th Brigade, and that not a spade had been put in the ground between me and the subsidiary attack at Gommecourt.
>
> Worse still no effort at wire cutting had been made on that stretch either. A child could see where the flank of our attack lay, to within 10 yards.' Brig Gen H. C. Rees DSO.

Stockpiling trench mortar bombs (toffee apples) for the offensive.

A British 8" howitzer is moved up to the front by tractor.

The Germans had also been given many other clues. However, the German Supreme Command was not convinced that the Somme was the venue for the offensive. To von Falkenhayn it seemed that the preparations were too obvious. He believed the attack would fall in the Alsace-Lorraine region to relieve pressure on Verdun, or further north near Arras.

The local German commanders on the Somme could see clearly where the blow would fall, and wasted no time in making preparations to receive the attack. A British prisoner captured at Gommecourt told them that the artillery bombardment would go on for five days before the infantry attacked. On 26th June the Military Attaché in Madrid reported that the offensive would start on 1st July. On the 27th the Germans counted 14 observation balloons tethered in the area between the River Somme and Gommecourt. There was one balloon for each of the 14 assault divisions.

All the Germans were missing was the exact time of the assault, and even this was given to them. A British staff officer failed to observe elementary security precautions, and against all the regulations sent Rawlinson's eve of battle message over a field telephone. These instruments used an earth return circuit, and could be easily intercepted. A listening station codenamed 'Moritz' in the village of La Boisselle, on the Albert to Bapaume road, picked up the gist of the message at 2.45 a.m. on 1st July. The Germans had no doubts that the British would attack later that morning and the news was rapidly disseminated to all units.

Having looked at the overall British plan and its fatal flaws, we will now look at the detailed plans made by Fourth Army. On 17th May Rawlinson issued the general outline of his plan to the five attacking Corps. They were to assault simultaneously on the first day of the offensive to capture the line Montauban – Pozières – Serre.

Having achieved this the three Corps on the left British 8" howitzer were to secure a strong flank while the two other Corps were to push on eastwards to capture the high ground Guillemont – Ginchy – Combles.

The Corps commanders were left to get on with their detailed planning and rehearsals.

If there was no breakthrough Haig warned Rawlinson that he was considering opening another attack in the Messines area, where plans for an offensive were well advanced. Ironically when the Messines plan was put into action in June 1917 it was a resounding success.

Behind Fourth Army Gen Gough assembled his two cavalry divisions. In addition Haig had another cavalry and two infantry divisions in GHQ reserve, seven to ten miles behind the front. If Fourth Army succeeded in taking Bapaume then these divisions would be pushed into the battle to keep a hold on this important communications centre.

At the final Fourth Army conference before the attack, Gen Rawlinson emphasised the lack of experience, traditions and discipline of the New Army Divisions. He maintained that the only way to succeed was to rapidly reorganise on objectives immediately they fell and consolidate the gain. If this was not done then the more experienced German troops would counter-attack and push our troops back. There was a lot of truth in Rawlinson's assumptions.

The New Army Divisions had less than two years' experience, and many of the men still regarded the war as an adventurous crusade against the wicked Hun. They had yet to be exposed to the shock of a full scale offensive. The German troops opposing Fourth Army were mainly pre-war regulars or reservists, and had been in the Somme area since late 1914. They were very well trained and had a wealth of experience to fall back on in a tight situation.

The Fourth Army battle plan therefore developed from the premise that the infantry's role must be as simple and uncomplicated as possible. The theory of the assault was laid down in 'Fourth Army Tactical Notes', and was the basis for all tactical planning for the attack. In essence the artillery was to do the work by systematically destroying the German defences. All the infantry had to do was to move forward when the artillery fire lifted and occupy the remnants of the German positions. While the infantry mopped up isolated pockets of resistance the artillery would adjust their fire onto the second line of trenches. When this had been pulverised then the infantry would move forward again. This would go on until the Germans ran out of defence lines and the infantry broke out into open country.

Little initiative was left to individual commanders. However, a notable exception was that each Corps commander was to decide if advanced trenches were to be dug in NML to reduce the amount of open ground to be crossed. If they were dug the Germans would be warned that an attack was imminent. With hindsight it is easy to criticise the VIII Corps decision not to dig advanced trenches. The Germans knew the attack was coming so it would have been better to have dug them.

The infantry attack was to be made in waves, with each wave leaving their trenches at set times. The advance was to be made at marching pace, with a gap of two to three yards between each man. In some places NML was so wide that it meant several waves would be advancing simultaneously, normally with a 100 yard gap between them. This was a deviation from the old method of skirmishing forward in small groups covered by the fire of other infantrymen. Because of the lack of faith in the capabilities of the New Army Divisions it was decided not to risk losing control by allowing the men to charge the German trenches. They would obey the instructions to walk to the letter, but thousands were to die as a result.

The timing of the attack also caused a major controversy. The British wanted to attack at dawn or soon after, when the light would be poor for the Germans' aim. The French however, wanted to make full use of their heavy artillery and needed daylight for their observers. A compromise was reached with

Guns of all calibres were massed for the bombardment. Here is a 6" howitzer with its limber.

Heavy shells being prepared. One reason for the failure of the attack was a lack of heavy artillery to destroy the German shelters.

Zero hour at 7.30 a.m. The troops would be attacking into the full glare of the morning sun, with the Germans having the advantage of the light to their rear.

In the actual attack the artillery, in which so much faith was placed, was to work to a set timetable. These were the days before battlefield radios, and there was no easy or quick method to redirect artillery fire in the case of a hold up. Even so the guns amassed for the attack made an impressive list. Across the whole attack front there were 1,010 field guns (one for every 21 yards of front), and 467 heavy guns (one for every 57 yards of front). On the VIII Corps front the concentration was even greater with a field gun every 20 yards and a heavy gun every 44 yards. Impressive as this sounds there were not enough heavy guns. The German dugouts were invulnerable to field artillery. Only a direct hit from a heavy shell stood any chance of penetrating them.

Over 4,500,000 shells were allocated for the offensive. Of this staggering total 1,732,873 were expended in the preliminary bombardment alone. This figure was exceeded the next year in the successful storming of Messines Ridge, in which the opening barrage expended over 3,200,000 shells. However, prior to the Battle of the Somme the British had never before attempted a bombardment on this scale. Behind the lines the troops marvelled at the build up of artillery as new batteries arrived, and the stockpiles of shells grew daily.

The preliminary bombardment was planned to begin on 24th June, and last for five days. A whole series of tasks had been allocated to the artillery. The German wire had to be cut along the 25,000 yard frontage of the attack. Enemy batteries had to be sought out and destroyed so that they could not interfere with the attack. Trenches had to be collapsed, machine gun posts put out of action and supply dumps destroyed. At night German supply routes were to be hit to prevent reinforcements being brought up to the line. The gunners fed shells into their guns almost continuously during the bombardment. Many were deaf for days afterwards, while others had blood running out of their ears from the continual concussion.

One particular aspect of the bombardment needs to be highlighted. Every day at 6.25 a.m. all the guns were to intensify their fire into a stupefying barrage lasting for 80 minutes. The idea was to get the Germans used to a set pattern every morning. On the day of the attack the bombardment would be 15 minutes shorter, in the hope of catching any surviving enemy in their dugouts. As will be seen the message intercepted by 'Moritz' negated this ruse.

VIII Corps was the most northerly of the five assaulting Corps, and was to form a defensive flank for the rest of Fourth Army. Three of the Corps' divisions were to attack in line. The fourth division, the 48th, was in reserve apart from two battalions which held the two miles of front from 31st Division's left boundary to the junction with Third Army in the north. No attack was to take place in this sector. From south to north the assaulting divisions were; the 29th, of Gallipoli fame; the 4th, made up of regular troops; and the 31st. The 29th and 4th Divisions were given three and a half hours to reach the German second position, about 4,000 yards away. At the same time 31st Division was to pivot on its left flank at John Copse, swing left and establish a defensive flank to the north of the village of Serre. For the troops on the right of 31st Division this entailed an advance of about 3,000 yards, and for those on the left about 2,000 yards. Troops were to leave their trenches at the discretion of divisional commanders, but were to reach a point 100 yards from the German front line by zero hour.

In the VIII Corps area the Germans occupied almost perfect positions overlooking the whole of the British lines. The front line ran along the eastern slopes of the Auchonvillers Spur, across Hawthorne Ridge, over the Beaumont Hamel valley, then up and along Redan Ridge, crossing the head of Beaucourt valley and over the forward edge of the knoll on which Serre stands. Behind the German lines the reserves were accommodated in dugouts in the reverse slopes of hills making it almost impossible to shell them.

VIII Corps' supporting artillery was scheduled to step back in six lifts, with the heavy guns lifting five minutes before the lighter field artillery. The field guns were to step back 100 yards at each lift then continue to move back at a rate of 50 yards and three rounds per gun every minute. This was almost a creeping barrage, the techniques of which were perfected later in the war.

The task of knocking out machine gun posts was allocated to the 4.5″ howitzers. It was later found that the shell fired by these guns was not heavy enough for the job and many of the posts were scarcely damaged at all.

Apart from the diversionary attack at Gommecourt, two miles to the north, 31st Division were at the extreme northern end of the offensive. Two brigades were to attack with the third brigade, the 92nd, in reserve. 94th Brigade was to assault on the left and 93rd Brigade on the right. The commander of 93rd Brigade chose to attack with a one battalion frontage, whereas 94th Brigade went for the more usual option of two battalions leading with two in reserve behind them.

To fully understand the Battalion's part in the offensive it is necessary to examine the 94th Brigade plan in some detail. The final operation order was issued to battalions by Brigade HQ on 20th June. The City Battalion's own operation order was signed by the Adjutant, Capt Tunbridge, at 10.30 p.m. on 26th June. Apart from a number of minor changes the orders laid down in these two documents form the basis of the description of the 94th Brigade plan which follows.

The Brigade frontage stretched from the northern tip of John Copse, where it joined 48th Division, southwards to the southern tip of Matthew Copse, where it joined 93rd Brigade. The two assault

German rear areas on the Somme. Note equipment hanging from the roof of the nearest hut.

Gunners manhandling a Mark 7 naval gun into position. The carriage was adapted to allow the gun to be used outside its normal environment.

battalions were 12th York & Lancs on the left and 11th East Lancs on the right. In reserve on the left was 14th York & Lancs, and on the right 13th York & Lancs. The assault battalions were to attack in four waves, with a 100 yard gap between the 1st and 2nd waves. The 3rd wave was to advance when the 2nd wave reached the German front line, and the 4th wave was to follow 100 yards behind.

Three separate bounds were stipulated. In the first bound the assault battalions were to advance to and consolidate the German fourth line with their two leading waves. In the second bound the 3rd and 4th waves were to leapfrog forwards onto the second objective, which in the case of the City Battalion was the line of a German communications trench facing northwards. The third bound was for 11th East Lancs to advance to the orchard north east of Serre village. The troops were forbidden to enter trenches until they reached their allotted objectives.

The time the attack was to be launched was designated Zero Hour, and in the orders all times were referred to as being plus and minus of it. The exact time of Zero was not to be notified to the troops until the last possible moment.

Ten minutes before Zero the first wave of four platoons, (two each from A and C Companies), a platoon from A Company 14th York & Lancs and two gun crews from the LTMB were to leave the trenches and lie down in NML. They were to get as close to the German wire as the bombardment would allow them. At the same time the rest of the trench mortars would commence firing the final part of the barrage, at the rate of 10 rounds per gun per minute.

A few minutes later at Zero -5 the 2nd wave, consisting of the remaining four platoons of A and C Companies and another platoon of A Company 14th York & Lancs, were also to advance into NML and lie down 50 yards behind the 1st wave. A minute before Zero the 3rd and 4th waves were to leave Campion and Monk Trenches respectively and advance towards the front line.

At Zero the artillery was to lift and the first two waves were to launch their attack. On reaching the objective they were to consolidate it and send bombing parties forwards 80-100 yards along all communications trenches to block them. The 3rd and 4th waves were to wait at the German third trench. A platoon of A Company 14th York & Lancs was to advance in file at the rear of the left flank of each of the City Battalion waves. They were to occupy the German communications trench that would become part of the new front line.

Before Zero these troops were to shelter in Nairne and a short section of the front line traffic trench. Two platoons of B Company 14th York & Lancs were to advance from Copse Trench to clear the German trenches as the City Battalion passed over them.

The two other platoons from B Company 14th York & Lancs were to follow A Company out of Nairne and occupy the Russian Sap in NML. C and D Companies were to advance in waves over the open and take up positions in the British front line.

At Zero +20 the artillery was to lift onto the western edge of Serre and the second bound was to begin with D Company on the left and B Company on the right passing through the first two waves and swinging left onto the Battalion's final objective. At the same time A Company was to establish a defensive flank facing south east towards Serre village, by occupying the trench running around the perimeter of the village and an orchard. A platoon of 12th KOYLI were attached to A Company. As soon as the fighting allowed this platoon was to commence building a new trench to link the orchard with the rest of the village perimeter trench system. The 3rd and 4th waves were instructed to keep as close to the barrage as possible as it lifted at Zero +40, until they reached their objective at the planned time of Zero +80.

While the City Battalion was securing its final objective 11th East Lancs would swing left to clear the village of Serre from the south west along the line of the main street. As they advanced behind the artillery barrage at a rate of 100 yards every four minutes, they were to secure the trench running along the south east edge of the village. Behind them two companies of 13th York & Lancs were to cross NML and establish themselves in the third German trench. The remaining two companies were to occupy the British front line.

The third and final bound was to begin at Z+100, and only involved 11th East Lancs. They were to occupy the orchard to the north east of the village, supported by a platoon of B Company and some bombing teams from the City Battalion. By the end of the third bound all the battalions would be in their final positions. The new front line was to run from John Copse along the line of the Russian Sap to the German front line, then along a German communications trench around the north of Serre to the Puisieux road. From John Copse to the fourth German line would be held by 14th York & Lancs. Then the City Battalion was to hold up to the extreme northerly tip of Serre, from where the final stretch was to be held by 11th East Lancs. 13th York & Lancs was to be in reserve throughout the operation.

It was stressed that consolidation was to commence immediately. B and D Companies each had a party to construct and man a strong point on the new front line. The strong points were designated 'C' for D Company and 'H' for B Company. Each party consisted of an NCO and 12 men, plus five pioneers from 12th KOYLI and a machine gun detachment of one NCO and six men from the Brigade Machine Gun Company. In addition Strong Point 'C' had an officer from the Machine Gun Company to command it.

Originally the assault battalions were instructed to go into action with a minimum bayonet strength of 600, including the Lewis gunners and bombers, but excluding signallers and runners. Brigade HQ later realised that this was impossible to achieve and so battalions were ordered to go into action with the maximum possible strength. However, some men were purposely to be left out. Past experience had shown the need for keeping a small nucleus out of action in case of a disaster, with which to form the

German map showing the position of 169 Regiment at Serre.

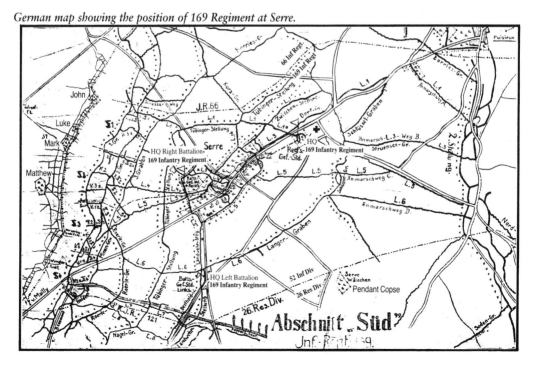

basis of a new battalion. To this end each battalion left 16 NCOs and 84 men with the Transport, and they became known as the first reinforcements.

Other men were detailed for tasks other than the assault. For example 15 men were detailed off to act as carriers for the LTMB. An NCO and 10 men were allocated to the Brigade Bombing Officer in Dunmow Trench to move forward supplies of bombs as required. The RSM also had a party of 2 NCOs and 20 men at the Battalion dump at the junction of Jordan and Jones Trenches. This dump held 75,000 rounds of small arms' ammunition, 1,625 man-day rations, 104 water cans each containing four gallons, 5,000 grenades, 2,000 rifle grenades and 100 trench mortar bombs.

The Regimental Police were given two main tasks. An NCO and two men were to establish a Police Post at the junction of Sackville Street and Jordan Trench. Other battalions were given the task of establishing other Posts at trench junctions along Sackville Street, thus forming an effecting control system for movement into and out of the trenches. In addition the Police Sergeant and six other men were to patrol the trenches within the Battalion's area to stop stragglers, direct the wounded and ensure that the one way system was adhered to. To avoid congestion and chaos communications trenches were designated as outward or homeward routes. Forward of Sackville Street the outward trenches were Nairne and Excema, and the homeward were Jordan and Le Cateau.

A considerable amount of preparation was required to cater for the extra men that the trenches were going to hold prior to Zero hour. Assembly trenches had to be dug deeper and revetted, and in addition many bombardment slits were dug off the main trenches.

Leading out from the front line into NML were three saps and a tunnel known as a Russian Sap.

The saps, known as C, D and E, were the basis of new communications trenches for when the enemy trenches had been consolidated. In side branches off these saps were sited the trench mortars which were to fire the final bombardment 10 minutes before Zero, together with 3,000 bombs.

The Russian Sap left the British lines at John Copse. It was a shallow tunnel and the idea was that once the forward German trenches had fallen the thin earth cover would be removed to create a new fire trench. This would become part of the new front line facing north. All of the saps were constructed by 13th York & Lancs with engineer advice and assistance.

Plan of attack showing objectives of 94 Brigade and the positions of its four battalions: 11th East Lancs (Accrington Pals), 12th York & Lancs (City Battalion), 13 & 14th York & Lancs (Barnsley Pals).

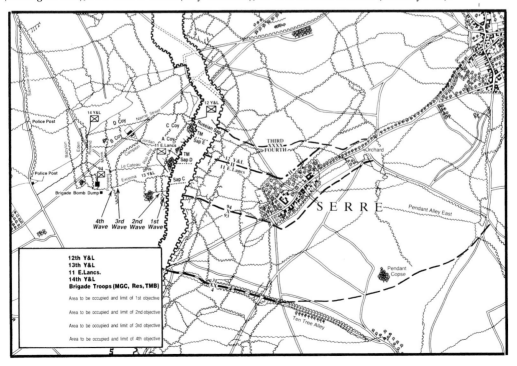

The wire in front of Serre was thickly constructed and the Germans had at least six machine guns covering it on the 94th Brigade frontage. Each line of trenches had its own wire defences in front of it and the artillery planned to blow seven lanes through each belt for the infantry.

Elaborate preparations were made for communicating with the assaulting troops. There were five methods of passing messages at Battalion level: telephone cable, visual means, runners, pigeons and an emergency procedure using flares etc.

From Divisional HQ in Courcelles a telephone cable ran forwards via Red Cottage and Le Cateau to Brigade HQ in Dunmow Trench. From there it went on to Mark Copse where a Signal Office was set up. Wires then branched off to the battalion HQs of 12th York & Lancs and 11th East Lancs. Four cables were to be laid by the assaulting companies as they advanced, with the 2nd and 4th waves of each battalion laying one cable each. The City Battalion was to lay its two cables from Mark Copse and the junction of Copse and Jordan Trenches.

Each battalion was to set up a visual signalling station with the facilities to use flags, lamps or a system using discs. The station was to be sited so that it could be seen from the area of Brigade HQ where observers would continuously look out for messages. On the left the German positions were given code letters, for example the four trench lines were coded W to Z from back to front. On reaching each line the signallers were to repeat this letter for three minutes to ensure Brigade had seen it.

Runners were allocated to companies and battalions. They were trained specifically for this dangerous task and wore much lighter equipment than other troops to preserve their mobility. A relatively high proportion of these men were decorated for their courage.

Almost as a last resort each battalion HQ had four pigeons. The loft for these birds was at Bus, so the passage of information by this means would be slow at the best of times.

An emergency procedure was devised to communicate with isolated bodies of troops cut off from the main force. Rifle grenades without warheads were prepared in two modes. The first was designed to throw a telephone cable up to 100 yards, and the second type was used as a message container, and could be fired up to 200 yards. These grenades were painted blue and white to distinguish them from the normal explosive types. Battalion HQs carried eight and each company another two. In addition every NCO and officer carried four emergency flares.

At Bus on 31st May the Battalion began training for its part in the forthcoming offensive. Next day the GOC inspected the men and congratulated them on their fine performance on the night of 15-16th May.

Bringing up supplies on the Somme front.

Rehearsals for communicating with aeroplanes were held on 3rd June. It had been realised that it would be difficult to make contact between air and ground forces in the thick of battle. To avoid the aviators directing artillery fire onto our own forces a system for communicating between aircraft and troops on the ground was devised. The aeroplanes swooped low over the battlefield and sounded a klaxon horn. On hearing this signal the troops would display a pre-arranged sign, such as coloured streamers, to identify their positions.

On 5th June the Battalion marched to Gezaincourt near Doullens, where full scale Brigade rehearsals were to be carried out on ground resembling the area around Serre. For the first time since arriving at the front they were out of earshot of gunfire. D Company was billetted in the village of Bretel, a little way out of town, because of lack of space in Gezaincourt. For the next week the men worked very hard during the day, but were allowed into town in the evenings. Even the weather was kind to them. For the survivors of the attack this period would bring back many happy memories.

According to the WD the Battalion practised moving into assembly trenches, shaking out into assault formation and attacking an imaginary objective on six occasions in four days. For some reason all the exercises were held in daylight, whereas the actual move into the trenches would be at night. In reality it turned out to be a much longer process than the rehearsals suggested it would be.

Rehearsals took place on ground similar to that around Serre. Trench lines were depicted on the ground by white tapes, and the Sappers went to a lot of trouble to ensure that all the points they would expect to see on the day were depicted on the ground. The artillery barrage was represented by men advancing with flags at the same rate as the lifts planned for the attack. Each wave advanced at a brisk walking pace, with rifles at the high port held across the chest with the long bayonets uppermost. In 94th Brigade the two leading waves were separated by only 30 yards, with successive waves following in section columns until they arrived at the front line. Within the waves each man was two to three yards from his neighbour. If the artillery failed to destroy the German defences then their machine gunners would be presented with an almost perfect target. It must be remembered that the attack philosophy had been designed to cope with inexperienced troops, and this was the simplest solution to the problem, as unrealistic as it might sound today.

At first the men did not take the rehearsals seriously. This was understandable given the good weather, the lack of danger and for once having no heavy fatigues to perform. However, it was not good enough for the staff officers observing the rehearsals. They rushed about shouting at the men and cajoling them to get it right. There was after all a lot at stake. The commanders publicly said the attack was going to be a push over, but privately they had grave reservations. The 94th Brigade's role was especially important since failure would leave the left flank of the whole offensive wide open to German counter attacks.

On 7th June the news came through that Lord Kitchener had been drowned. He had been on his way to Russia on the cruiser HMS Hampshire when it struck a mine in heavy seas off the Orkneys. His death came as a terrific blow to the men of the New Army battalions, who regarded Kitchener as their founding father. It was a bad omen for the coming offensive.

While the reheasals were in progress reinforcements arrived from the base to make up for the casualties the Battalion had already suffered. Amongst them were two officers, Lt H. Oxley and 2Lt C. H. Wardill. Also to arrive at this time was 12/743 Pte Willie Parker, who had been forcibly returned to his engineering job with Armstrong-Whitworth in 1915. He had eventually bullied the authorities into releasing him and was now as pleased as punch to have made it back to the Battalion in time for the 'big show'. His brother Reg was in C Company, detached to the Battalion Transport.

The brief respite at Gezaincourt came to an end on 13th June when the Battalion marched back to Bus. Billets for the men were split almost equally between huts in the wood and the village itself. Next morning the advance party left for the trenches and began the task of taking over from 10th East Yorks.

The sector the Battalion moved into was the same one they would attack from two weeks later. While the advance party waited for the men to arrive the Battalion HQ dugout, the Monastery in Monk Trench, was destroyed by a shell, as was a section of Rob Roy Trench. One of the main tasks of this trench tour was to strengthen, repair and deepen the trenches themselves. The Germans appeared to be nervous, firing frequent and seemingly pointless bombardments. This was another sign that they expected the offensive to begin at any time.

By 6.10 p.m. the Battalion had taken over and the East Yorks began to thin out. Later that night a ration party was hit by a shell in Excema Trench, killing 12/1354 Pte F. Gleave and wounding three others. A fourth man was badly shell shocked.

Despite periodical nuisance shelling over the next few days it was quiet enough for the men to get on with repairing the trenches. The weather remained fine and the worst of the wet areas dried out. Lt Middleton was not particularly busy, and spent some time amusing himself by shooting the detonators off a couple of German rifle grenades with his revolver. How this officer escaped serious injury is something of a miracle, given his liking for dangerous pursuits.

The quiet period did not last long. On the evening of the 16th Le Cateau Trench was blown in, and on the 17th the Germans shelled the front line with heavy guns all day. Although the fire was at a slow rate it was accurate and caused several casualties.

One of the shells scored a direct hit on the dugout at Post 35. 12/2 CSM W. H. Marsden was sleeping in the dugout at the time and the shell blocked the entrance. Before anyone could react three more shells hit the same spot utterly destroying the dugout. Frantically a rescue attempt was made but to no avail. The would-be rescuers had to expose themselves to get at the remains of the dugout and this attracted a shower of 77 mm shells and rifle grenades. Another attempt was made in darkness, but the men failed to get through the twisted and shattered remains of the dugout. A major work programme was required that night involving one of the reserve companies being brought forward. The front line and traffic trench behind it both needed considerable effort to repair them.

During the day 12/1388 Sgt H.C. Clay and 12/249 Pte E. C. Thomas of A Company were also killed, and were later buried in Bertrancourt Military Cemetery.

In the afternoon a battle developed in the air over the trench lines and at one stage a Fokker flew low over the British trenches.

It is interesting to note the German attitude to their airmen.

> '*You have to stay in your hole all day, and must not stand up in the trench, because there is always a crowd of English over us. Always hiding from aircraft, always with about eight or ten English machines overhead. But no one sees any of ours. Our airmen are a rotten lot.*' Extract from captured German report.

In the early hours of the next morning the Germans succeeded in blowing in one of the galleries of the Russian Sap being dug from John Copse towards the German front line. The Sappers were involved in this project but much of the work was undertaken by miners from the Barnsley Battalions. Three men were killed by the blast. It was intended to form a fire trench by opening up the tunnel after the assault on 1st July had cleared Serre. The idea was that troops would be inserted into the tunnel, then they would cut away the surface layers to form a ready made trench. The potential of using these tunnels to get closer to the German lines seems not to have been considered. The GOC realised that the John Copse Sap could not be completed on time since its position had been compromised. Next day he ordered the end of the Sap to be converted into a sap head and sentries posted there.

The Germans were by this stage wise to what was going on. They had seen the massive troop movements and observed the stockpiling of ammunition and other stores. The discovery of tunnels under NML only served to confirm their suspicions that an offensive was imminent.

There was digging going on all over the trench system. Masses of stores had to be pre-dumped in the trenches prior to the attack, and dumps constructed to accommodate them. The dumps contained rations, water and ammunition. Extra assembly trenches had to be dug for the assault troops to shelter in during the last few hours before the attack was launched. Running out from the front line were a variety of tunnels. Some of these were to become fire trenches, like the one from John Copse, while others were to be communications trenches. In addition underground emplacements were dug for the trench mortars forward of the front line.

Throughout Sunday 18th June work went on to recover CSM Marsden's body. The attempt was called off in failure at 11.00 a.m. The

12/2 CSM Marsden, who lived at 13 Marion Road, Hillsborough.

following day the Brigade Chaplain attempted to get into the lines to read a burial service over the dugout, but was prevented from doing so by the heavy shelling. CSM Marsden's body was never recovered and he is commemorated on the Thiepval Memorial. His remains are probably still lying in the little group of copses which mark the British front line in front of Serre.

The fact that the Chaplain failed to reach the forward trenches is not surprising. The War Diary states that 160 15 cm shells, (equivalent to 6") landed in the area of the front line during a six hour period that day. These heavy shells caused considerable damage. Retaliatory fire by the British artillery quietened things down by 3.00 p.m. when relief by 11th East Lancs began. Mist allowed part of the Battalion to withdraw in daylight, and by 7.00 p.m. the relief was complete. Just after midnight the whole Battalion was in billets in the hutted camp at Warnimont Wood. The trench tour cost the Battalion four killed, nine wounded (including 2Lt Lumb), and 12 shell shocked.

By this time Lt Middleton knew that he was out of the attack, and had been assigned to Divisional HQ as an artillery observer. A few weeks prior to this he had been suspected of having measles. Thus when it came to deciding which officers were to go and which to remain he was a clear candidate to leave out. This little coincidence probably saved his life.

From 23rd June onwards the Divisional OP was manned by two officers continuously on 12 hour

The Golden Virgin of Albert. The leaning statue could be seen from the British trenches in the Albert area. It fell in the fighting of 1918 and in accordance with the legend the war ended soon afterwards.

shifts. They were to keep a close watch on the movement of German troops and in particular on where the German batteries were registering targets.

The pace now began to gather as the opening of the offensive due on the 29th drew closer. From the Divisional OP in Wagram Trench Lt Middleton watched the gunners registering targets in preparation for the preliminary bombardment, which was due to commence on Saturday 24th June. The Battalion was being worked harder than normal to make the final preparations. They were in the trenches every night carrying ammunition or gas cylinders forward and there was always a digging task to be performed. There was also the march to and from the trenches every day, about 10 miles in total. It is little wonder the men were always dog tired. One soldier, 12/416 Pte C. G. Ibbotson of B Company, was killed on one of these fatigue parties. Lt Middleton knew him very well and his death upset him very much.

> 'It's little wonder why they called us the 'Poor Bloody Infantry', with spells in the line, providing carrying parties, general labouring, in between training and practice for the Big Push, that was common knowledge would be in the near future.
>
> The higher ups seemed to take delight in keeping us busy and on the go all the time.' 12/664 Pte H. Hall.

Some soldiers were not as badly off as others. Given the opportunity and a little initiative some of them managed to get some free time.

> 'It was some time in June that I received a letter from my sister informing me that her boyfriend was in France with 8th KOYLI in 8th Division. Being in the signal section we were responsible

for telephone communications and being connected to Brigade it was surprising what you got to know. When things were slack you could pass the time talking to the chap on the switch-board. I asked if he knew if 8th KOYLI were in our area.

It wasn't long before he came back on and told me they were in Albert. The next day I borrowed a bike, put on my blue signals armband denoting I was on duty, and to make it look more official I stuck a brown envelope in my belt, and off I went to Albert.

'We were camped in Warnimont Wood at the time some miles from Albert. The countryside was swarming with troops and transport, all part of the build up for the forthcoming battle.

Nobody bothered about me and my bike, but once or twice I had to get out of the way of lorries and gun teams. On approaching Albert on the Doullens road I saw the results of the German shelling and the damage it had caused to the Basilique, a huge church on top of which was a golden statue of the Virgin holding at arms length the baby Jesus. The statue had been knocked over and was leaning parallel with the ground. The engineers had lashed it to stop it falling. It was said that when the statue fell the war would end. It didn't fall quick enough for us! The 8th KOYLI HQ was in a street at the back of the Basilique. It didn't take me long to find my sister's boyfriend and we had the rest of the afternoon together. Poor lad he was killed on 1st July when the Battle of the Somme opened.' 12/928 L/Cpl J. R. Glenn.

Much of the hard work was undone on 23rd June when the weather broke and a violent storm flooded the trenches. Tethered observation balloons near Serre were wrenched free of their moorings and were not brought under control until they got to Sailly au Bois.

At 5.00 a.m. on Saturday 24th June the preliminary bombardment commenced. It was known as 'U' Day. On the first day of the bombardment only the field guns were involved. The 18 pounders were given the task of cutting the German wire, and in the City Battalion area seven lanes were planned for the troops to pass through.

The task was almost impossible except for the most skilled of artillery observers. The shells were fitted with a mechanical time fuse, and contained 375 half inch wide lead shrapnel balls set in a resin matrix. At the time set on the fuse a pusher charge blew the balls out of the nose of the shell in a cone shaped pattern. A small error in setting the time fuse would result in the shell plunging harmlessly into the ground before exploding, or alternatively it went off too high and the concentration of balls was ineffective against the thin wire.

The standard of manufacture of British ordnance at this time left a lot to be desired. Many soldiers later commented ruefully that the German wire was littered with dud shells. If you wander the battlefields today after ploughing you will still see evidence of this, piles of unexploded shells at the roadside waiting to be collected by the Army for destruction.

Sadly the British had insufficient artillery for all the tasks required of them, and for this reason the 18 pounders had been given the wire cutting mission. During the day the Germans reacted by trying to knock out the British guns with their own 15 cm artillery. Lt Middleton watched this tense cat and mouse game from the Divisional OP with Lt Foers from 13th York & Lancs.

Each day prior to the opening of the offensive was given a code letter: Saturday 24th June-U Day, Sunday 25th June-V Day, Monday 26th June-W Day, Tuesday 27th June-X Day, Wednesday 28th June-Y Day and Thursday 29th June-Z Day – the day of the assault.

On V Day the heavy artillery joined in. Their job was to destroy the elaborate German defences and communications. They were also tasked to destroy German gun batteries so they would be unable to interfere with the attack. The troops in and behind the lines were to be treated to a fireworks display of gigantic proportions over the next few days, as over 1,700,000 shells were fired into the German positions. Surely nothing could live through such a pounding? The sound of this concentrated fire could even be heard on the south coast of England 100 miles away.

'A tremendous cacophony which shook the ground and at times you could not hear your own voice, almost deafening.' 12/928 L/Cpl J. R. Glenn.

While the bombardment was in progress the German observation balloons were systematically destroyed by the RFC, to deny the enemy observation, and the ability to direct accurate retaliatory fire. This does not seem to have been particularly effective. Lt Middleton saw Colincamps being badly hit during the day.

On the last Sunday before the offensive the Battalion held church services in the YMCA hut and Warnimont Wood. Although it was clear that some of them would not survive the battle the mood was generally optimistic. They believed nothing could withstand such overwhelming strength. The troops had seen the massive build up and were eager to take part in this battle which was to end the war. However, some soldiers were also feeling very mortal by this stage:

12/70 Cpl D. E. Cattell.

'I had always been a church goer. In fact I sang in the Sheffield Cathedral choir, boy and man, so I thought I would go for communion before the battle. Up to that point the forthcoming event hadn't bothered me, but at that church service held in the wood, seeing as we could the build up of marching men, guns and horses moving towards the front, then I had this feeling of awe. It must have been the effects of the service and seeing all this movement that you got this feeling, just as if something was coming at you.' 12/70 Cpl D. E. Cattell.

That night Lt Middleton was awakened in the Divisional OP because of a gas attack. He wrote in his diary that it was a false alarm. Most probably it was because gas was being released from cylinders brought up by City Battalion fatigue parties the previous Thursday evening. Periodic gas attacks were part of the overall plan to wear down the Germans, as were releases of smoke. In 31st Division's area smoke was released on five occasions in the period 26th-28th June. The aim was to unsettle the Germans and cause them more casualties as they left cover to man their trenches.

During Monday the Battalion did some extra training for the attack and went through the motions of the assault on Serre once again. At 5.15 p.m. the GOC, Maj Gen R. Wanless O'Gowan, came to speak to the men taking part in the attack. He told them the Germans had brought up their reserves because of the barrage and they had fallen foul of a gas attack, probably referring to the same release that disturbed Lt Middleton's slumber. Never before, continued Wanless O'Gowan, had the British had such a preponderance of arms and superiority in numbers. Serre would be taken he promised.

Even within the Battalion it was evident by this time that all was not well. That night at 11.55 p.m. two patrols, under the command of Lt F. W. S. Storry and 12/352 Sgt F. Donoghue, went into NML to check the state of the German wire. Their reports in the War Diary are contradictory in that they say the wire was badly damaged, but go on to report only two gaps on the right and damage on the left only where the wire was thin. The patrols went out with Bangalore torpedoes but were unable to fire them because the men trained in their use were seriously wounded. The wounded men were 12/1141 Sgt R. B. Henderson, 12/375 Pte H. Story and 12/1378 Pte T. E. Gambles. At 1.10 a.m. the patrols returned to the British lines having recovered their wounded. It is worth noting that the War Diary of 169 Brigade RFA records the episode as a raid and not just a patrol. All three of the wounded died of their wounds within a few days. Sgt Henderson was hit by the nose cap of a shell and his leg was amputated. Before he died on 30th June he sent back a last message to his platoon, 'Tell the boys not to mind, but to buck up and give the Boches hell'. The date of this fatal patrol is recorded in the War Diary as the night of 26-27th June. Sparling and other sources record it as being on 27-28th June. We have taken the War Diary to be definitive. The other members of the patrols were 12/970 L/Cpl G. W. Jones, 12/493 L/Cpl A. Rixham, 12/1026 Pte A. K. Rigg, 12/542 Pte G. F. Wagstaffe, 12/1064 Pte J. S. Swift and 12/1481 Pte J. H. Kelk. Of these men only Pte Wagstaffe survived the war.

On X Day the bombardment was intensified. At 2.45 p.m. the shelling was supplemented by another release of gas from the front line. The Germans retaliated with heavy artillery, but they did little damage, and many of the shells that fell on Bus were duds. It wasn't only the British who had the problem of defective ammunition. The WD of 169th Brigade RFA records that the German wire was still uncut and that the Trench Mortars assisting with the task were a total failure.

Y Day dawned wet and miserable, and heavy rain flooded the trenches. Rob Roy, one of the assembly trenches for the attack was so badly damaged by the water that it had to be abandoned. The troops that were to have started the attack from this trench had to be diverted to another one further back, thus increasing the time they would be exposed to German fire.

The rain had saturated the ground so badly that the decision was taken to delay the start of the attack for 48 hours to allow it time to dry out. The extra two days were called Yl and Y2 Days. The offensive would therefore begin on 1st July as originally planned.

Later in the day the temporary Brigade Commander, Brig Gen H. C. Rees, (15th June to 2nd July), sent out his Special Order of the Day:

'You are about to attack the enemy with far greater numbers than he can oppose to you, supported by a huge number of guns.

Englishmen have always proved better than the Germans when the odds were heavy against them. It is now our opportunity. You are about to fight in one of the greatest battles in the world and the most just cause. Remember that the British Empire will anxiously watch your every move and that the honour of the North country rests in your hands. Keep your heads, do your duty and you will utterly defeat the enemy.'

Despite the optimistic note of the eve of battle messages the bad news continued to come in. That night a raid by 12th East Yorks failed to get into the enemy lines, and the following evening another raid failed. In spite of the bombardment the Germans were still in their trenches, they were alert and prepared to resist any attempt to break into their lines. It was not looking good for a daylight attack.

The senior commanders were by this stage in the hands of their soldiers. They could do little except wait for events to unfold. Many of them left diaries revealing what they really thought at this time, or their beliefs were recorded by others.

Brig Gen H. C. Rees, Commander 94th Brigade for the Somme offensive.

'The Corps Commander (Hunter-Weston), was extremely optimistic, telling everyone that the wire had been blown away, although we could see it standing strong and well, that there would be no German trenches and all we had to do was walk into Serre.' Unknown Brigade Major in 31st Division

'The weather report is favourable for tomorrow. With God's help I feel hopeful. The men are in splendid spirits. Several have said that they have never been so instructed and informed of the nature of the operations before them. The wire has never been so well cut, nor the artillery

The bombardment goes on for 7 days. At the end of it many of the gunners are deaf.

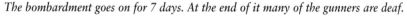

12th(S) BATTALION, YORK & LANCASTER REGIMENT.
(PRELIMINARY) OPERATION ORDER. NO 14.

Reference HEBUTERNE Trench Map.   26.6.16.
   1/10,000.

1.   GENERAL .

1. Outline.   The troops of the 4th Army are about to attack the
         German first line system.

         The duty of the 31st Division will be to form a
         defensive flank for the remainder of the Army.

         In order to be in a position to form this flank, they
         must first capture the village of SERRE. The taking of
         the village is essential to the success of the general
         operations.

         It will be the duty of the 94th Infantry Brigade to
         carry this operation to a successful conclusion.

2. DISTRIBUTION   The attack of the 94th Infantry Brigade will be
   of Troops.   carried out by two Battalions. 11th EAST LANCS.
                      REGT., on the right and the 12th YORK & LANCS.
         REGT.,on the left. The 13th YORK & LANCS.REGT., will be
         in reserve on the right,14th YORK & LANCS REGT., on the
         left.

3. Division of   The dividing line between the 11th East Lancs.Regt.,
   Line.   and the 12th York & Lancs.Regt., will be as follows:

         For purposes of Attack:The line North corner of MARK COPSE
         at Point K 29 a 98 65,Point K 30 a 21 20,Point K 30 c 66 91.
         North-Western boundary SERRE,to Point K 30 b 50 68.Point
         (68) as shown on sketch map already issued to Companies.

4. Conduct of   THE ATTACK WILL BE MADE ACROSS THE OPEN .
   Attack.
                      TROOPS WILL NOT ENTER TRENCHES UNTIL THEY HAVE
         REACHED THEIR OBJECTIVE.

                      ALL MOVEMENTS OF TROOPS IN REAR OF THE TWO LEADING
         WAVES WILL BE IN LINES OF SECTION COLUMNS.

                      The attack will be carried out in three "bounds",
         11th East Lancs.Regt.,completing its task in three and the.
         12th York & Lancs.Regt., in two.

                      As soon as troops have reached the objective of any
         "bound",immediate steps will be taken to consolidate prior
         to further advance. Special parties have been detailed for
         the construction and garrison of 9 Strong Points,positions
         of which have been indicated on map previously issued.

12th S. Battalion YORK & LANCASTER Regiment.
OPERATION ORDER. No. 15.

June 27/1916.

REf. Map. FRANCE.
57 D.N.E. 1/20,000,
& Special Trench Map
of COLINCAMPS Sector,
1/10,000.

1.   The Battalion will march to its area of assembly tomorrow
          June 28th as under:-

UNIT.	STARTING POINT.	TIME OF LEAVING.	DESTINATION.	ROUTE.
"A" Co.)				(
"H" Strong)	Cross	'7-20 pm '	Front Line	(
Pt party.)	Roads	'	COPSE.	(Through BUS Wood to road
	'J 20 '			(junction J 20 d 52 - cross
"C" Coy.	'C.22.	'7.25 pm.'	Do.	(roads-J 26 b 90 - track
	'			(junction J 27 b 61 - follow
"B" Coy.)			ROB ROY, JONES	(track to J 28 a 76 - across
3 Platoon)	"	'7.30 pm.'	&	(Country to track at J 28
12 KOYLI.)			CAMPION.	(b 81 - cross roads J 29 b
				(28 - road junction J 29 b
"D" Coy.)			JONES.	(65 - across country to MILL
"C" Strong)	"	'7.35 pm.'	&	(at J 30 b 76.
Pt Party.)			CAMPION.	(

(a)   All ranks will start with full water bottles; no water will be
          drunk until after the assault, and then only on orders from
          Company Commanders.

2.   (a)   Captain W.S.Clark and one subaltern from "C" Coy and six other
               ranks from both "A" and "C" Coys, will be at the junction, in
               front line, of Battn areas,(N.edge of MARK COPSE), at 11 pm.
               on June 28 (Tomorrow).

      (b)   At this hour parties from 92nd Brigade commence cutting our
               own wire. The 10th East Yorks will cut wire in front of our
               Battalion front and the Officer i/c of the 10th East Yorks
               wire-cutting party will report completion of the work on our
               front to Captain W.S.Clark, who will satisfy himself that the
               wire is properly cut, and will request the Officer i/c of the
               10th East Yorks. party to withdraw his party on completion.

      (c)   Party detailed in para., 2a. will then place a tape, or line
               of pickets, in "No man's Land", parallel to the enemy
               trenches, and distant about 100 yards from our own fire
               trench. This line will enable attacking troops to adjust their
               alignment before finally advancing.

      (d)   On completion of the task, a report will be sent to Brigade
               Hdqrs in DUNMOW and the party will rejoin their respective
               Coys.
                    The Assault will take place at <u>Zero</u> hour June 29.

141

DISTRIBUTION.	A	B	C	D	TOTALS.
Available for Assault.	115	127	116	125	483
Coy. Signallers and Coy. Runners	9	9	9	9	36
Headquarters Details, Runners 12, Bombers 9, Signallers 9, Observers 10, Stretcher Bearers 21.	24	14	12	11	61
Carriers. (Battalion)	5	6	6	6	23
-do- (Brigade)	11	11	11	11	44
26 Signallers.	6	6	6	7	
16 Machine Gunners.	4	4	4	4	
16 N.C.O.s.	4	2	4	3	
1st Reinforcement. 16 Bombers.	4	4	4	4	126
4 Runners.	1	1	1	1	
22 O.R. (Detail other side)	6	8	6	6	
26 Draft.	15	1	10	–	
Brigade and Divisional Employ.	22	12	13	8	
Command.	1	5	3	2	
Schools of Instruction.	–	–	–	2	
Trench Mortar.	5	7	6	7	93
Police.	1	5	2	3	11
Salvage.	3	3	3	2	11
1st Line Transport and Grooms.	5	18	9	9	41.
Sanitary Corporal.	–	–	–	1	
C.Q.M.S.	1	1	1	1	
H.Q. Servants.	2	2	–	1	
Water Men.	2	–	1	1	
Pioneers.	9	–	–	1	
Battalion Base Details. R.Q.M. Sgt.	–	–	–	1	33
Armourer. Sgt.	–	–	–	1	
Shoemaker Sgt.	1	–	–	–	
Cook Sgt.	–	–	–	1	
Band Sgt.	–	–	–	–	
Medical Orderly.	1	–	–	–	
Orderly Room Clerk.	–	–	–	1	
L.Cpl. Stoppani G.	–	–	–	1	
Post Corporal	1	–	–	–	
Hospital. Sick and Dentist, and too young.	6	–	7	5	18
TOTAL STRENGTH.	264	247	234	235	980

1st June 29th 1916.

preparations so thorough. I have seen personally all the Corps Commanders and one and all are full of confidence. The only doubt I have is regarding VIII Corps which has had no experience of fighting in France and has not carried out one successful raid.' Gen Sir D. Haig's diary, 30th June 1916.

'The artillery work during the bombardment and wire cutting has been done well except in the VIII Corps area, which is somewhat behindhand.' Gen Sir H. Rawlinson's diary, 30th June 1916.

Chapter Seven

1st July 1916

'No braver or more determined men ever faced an enemy than those sons of the British Empire who went over the top on 1st July 1916. Never before had the ranks of a British Army on the field of battle contained the finest of all classes of the nation in physique, brains and education. And they were volunteers not conscripts. If ever a decisive victory was to be won it was to be expected now.' Official History of the Great War 1916 Volume 1.

This chapter is devoted to the Battalion's part in the Battle of the Somme, from 29th June until being relieved on 3rd July. We have drawn the information from a variety of sources including personal interviews, diaries and official accounts from British and German sources. We believe we have ended up with a balanced and objective account of the sometimes confusing events of those momentous few days.

The last 48 hours before the attack were spent in issuing orders, collecting stores and drawing up the final list of who was to go and who would stay behind in reserve. On the 29th the assault state was typed by the clerks and the men knew their fates soon afterwards. Dick Sparling kept a copy of the assault state which is reproduced in the book. Of the total strength of 980 men, not including the officers, only 483 are shown as being available for the assault. This is deceiving because many other soldiers were in the trenches, and in some cases went over the top. They included the company signallers and runners, HQ details, stores carriers and trench mortarmen; a grand total of 697. The remaining 283 were in reserve, on base details or employed outside the Battalion.

'At first I was detailed to stay back at camp with those who were not going into the attack. More or less at the last minute orders were changed and I was told that I would be going with the HQ party. I didn't know if I was pleased or not. Most of the men accepted what they were told. You didn't bother with the whys and wherefores, you just got on with it.' 12/928 L/Cpl J. R. Glenn.

On the eve of the battle the CO, Lt Col Crosthwaite, succumbed to the immense pressure he had been under. He had been badly wounded earlier in the war at Ypres, and was too worn out to go on. At 10.00 a.m. on 30th June he was evacuated to hospital and Maj Plackett was recalled to take command. At this crucial moment the Battalion was robbed of its only professional officer when he was most needed.

Maj Plackett was the commandant of the 31st Division School where specialist techniques were taught to unit instructors. He arrived at Warnimont Wood just in time to parade the Battalion for the visit of the Corps Commander, Lt Gen Hunter-Weston, at 11.00 a.m. After the parade the General drew the Battalion around him in an informal circle and spoke to the men about the battle, and the difficult task ahead of them. He also spoke of the good chances of success and their superiority of numbers in men, guns and equipment.

Lt Gen Hunter-Weston, Commander of VIII Corps. Known widely as Hunter Bunter.

'But your lot is a very heavy one and a huge responsibility is shared by every individual. No individual soldier may say he has no responsibility. The 29th Division performed glorious feats of arms in Gallipoli, the 4th Division on your right did wonders in the great retreat from Mons. The feats of these divisions will never be forgotten as long as the world endures. You are Englishmen, even as they, and now you have your opportunity to shine. You will have to stick it. You must stick it. I salute every officer, NCO and man.' Extract of speech by Lt Gen Sir A. G. Hunter-Weston, 30th June 1916.

The General's talk had profoundly different effects on the men. Perhaps the passage of time and the events which followed changed some men's memories. Afterwards 12/1299 Pte A. H. Hastings wrote in his diary that he felt optimistic and superior. But others have different recollections.

'I remember some big wig came and spoke to us, all decked out in medals. He gave us some sort of pep talk and that we were for it.

After it was over the band played 'When You Come to the End of a Perfect Day'. What a bloody tune to play.' 12/1298 Pte D. C. Cameron.

12/1298 Pte D. C. Cameron of A Company.

The weather on this final day was dry but overcast. However, the ground was still very wet and in places the trenches were flooded. There was mud everywhere.

At 3.00 p.m. a message arrived from Brigade HQ confirming that Z Day was Saturday 1st July and Zero Hour was set for 7.30 a.m. At that stage only the company commanders knew the time of the attack. The rest would not be told until they were in the trenches.

The men did their last minute preparations and packed the final few items into their field kits. They went into action in Field Service Order, less their large packs. The small pack or haversack was worn on the back instead of being slung around the shoulder. Inside the haversack were mess tins, a complete day's rations, a haversack ration and iron rations only for use in emergency. They also carried a spare pair of socks, a cardigan and a 'housewife', the Army's name for a sewing kit. Fastened on the back of the haversack was a tin triangle cut from biscuit boxes. Every rifleman carried 150 rounds of ammunition in his pouches and an extra bandolier of 50 rounds in his pack.

They all carried four empty sandbags and two grenades. The latter were not to be thrown, but given to trained bombers when they had exhausted their own supplies. Two gas helmets were also taken, and the groundsheet was rolled up and fastened to the rear of the waist belt.

By the time they went into the line every man was carrying at least 60 pounds, and some were detailed off to carry extra items such as cable drums or ammunition, making their load considerably heavier. It has been calculated tha some men carried 90 pounds. Even if they had been ordered to attack at the charge they would have been physically unable to do so.

Popular picture of soldiers on the Somme front. Seated figure in foreground has been identified as 12/289 Pte Joseph Bailey by his daughter. If this is correct, then this is a picture of "B" Coy City Battalion ration party. The photographer claims it was taken on the morning of 1st July, 1916. If this is Joe Bailey then the picture could not have been taken on 1st July 1916. He was killed in the attack that morning and therefore could not have been in the ration party as well. Other sources state that the photo is of an Irish Battalion.

'I was detailed as a bomb carrier. The bombs as we called them were Mills hand grenades, a fragmentation type. RSM Polden was in charge of the bomb carrying party of four NCOs and 40 men. The idea was that we would carry the bombs forward to support the attack and supply the bombers, not use them ourselves. When the Battalion arrived at its assembly area near Euston Road the night before the attack, the bomb carriers left their respective companies and moved to the dump with the RSM. The dump was in front of the gun lines which were banging away all the time, as they had been for the past six days. We were issued with two white canvas buckets with bombs in each one. With these and our equipment, along with rifle and extra ammunition I don't know about being pack donkeys, we were more like walking bombs. All it needed was one piece of shrapnel in those buckets and up we would have gone.' 12/664 Pte H. Hall.

Digging tools were essential to the success of any operation in the First World War. Every soldier went into action carrying either a pick or shovel in the proportion of two shovels to each pick. The digging tools were fastened across the men's backs, and prevented them from bending easily. Every platoon took two mauls or mallets for hammering in pickets. Wire cutters were another essential item, and these were attached to the men carrying them by a lanyard. In case they became casualties the carriers wore distinctive yellow bands on their right arms, so other men could go and retrieve them.

Stretcher bearers and runners were exempt some of the heavy equipment, but more than made up for this with their hazardous jobs. Stretcher bearers carried no arms nor ammunition. Runners only carried a rifle, a bandolier of ammunition, haversack and water bottle.

The supply of bombs has already been touched upon. There were literally thousands of these devices in the Battalion, and they were essential for the close quarter fighting encountered in trench warfare. 466 riflemen carried two bombs each, and each platoon had a bombing party carrying 100 Mills bombs plus 25 rifle grenades. The bombing parties carried their bombs in canvas buckets and kept two empty ones in which to collect spare grenades from the riflemen. If there was a shortage Battalion and Brigade dumps had already been established in the forward British trenches, and as Pte Hall has related the RSM had a party of carriers, some of whom were dedicated to the supply of bombs. Disregarding the dumped bombs the Battalion went into action with about 3,000 assorted grenades.

In order that the observers could keep track on progress, each unit wore distinctive signs. Within the City Battalion the men wore 18" by 3" coloured ribbons denoting the furthest bound they were to advance to. The ribbons were fastened to the right shoulder strap. Capt Clarke wrote in his briefing notes that A Company wore red ribbons. We do not know the colours for the second bound troops in B and D Companies. Other units wore sacking over their steel helmets or badges on their backs.

The two leading assault companies, A and C, each carried a Bangalore Torpedo, and the two companies following in reserve carried two. It may seem strange that the reserve companies carried more of these assault weapons than the leading companies. It was probably done this way because the wire in front of the German front line was expected to be well cut, whereas further back it was expected to be in better condition. As things turned out all the men trained in using the torpedoes were wounded or killed. When the torpedoes were needed no-one knew how to use them.

At last everything was ready and at 7.20 p.m. the first company marched out of Warnimont Wood, watched by the men staying behind. Those who had been apprehensive about the future soon cheered up again, glad to be doing something at last rather than sitting around brooding on what might be in store for them. As part of the overall security plan the march was to be conducted in silence with no smoking and no lights were to be shown.

The companies left at five minute intervals and joined the Brigade column.

Bangalore torpedo in position across barbed wire.

The route they took is shown on the map. At the crossroads north-west of Courcelles the whole Brigade halted and hot tea laced with rum was served from field cookers. Here the men ate one half of a day's ration. This would be their last food and drink until after the attack.

Each company detailed one NCO to keep a sharp lookout for aeroplanes, and everyone was briefed to get under cover if one was spotted. No aeroplanes were seen, but just as the men sat down to drink their tea at the roadside, two German observation balloons were seen flying high in the sky watching the British troop movements. They could not fail to notice the roads thronged with men heading for the front, nor could they fail to conclude that the expected offensive was imminent. Despite the efforts of the RFC over the previous weeks the Germans had managed to fly these two balloons at the moment when it mattered most.

German observation balloon over the town of Bapaume prior to Somme battle.

At 9.40 p.m. the march resumed after watches had been synchronised. The battalions then began to peel off the Brigade route for the final approach to the trenches. The last two miles to the front line were in the trenches themselves.

A small group from the Battalion commanded by Capt W. S. Clarke and consisting of another officer and six ORs from A and C Companies, moved into the trenches before the rest of the Battalion. At 11.00 p.m. where the northern edge of Mark Copse joins the front line, they met up with a party from 10th East Yorks who were tasked to cut lanes through the British wire. Next morning the Battalion was to use these lanes to reach NML. Once Capt Clarke had satisfied himself that the lanes had been properly cut he detailed his small party to go into NML to lay out white tapes parallel with the front line and about 100 yards from it.

The first wave was to lie down on the tapes prior to Zero Hour in order to align themselves for the advance towards the German lines. By 12.30 a.m. the tapes had been laid and the party made its way through the trenches to join up with their companies.

> 'Our little party were in the front line about 11 o'clock at night. My platoon officer told me to go out and lay this white tape about 100 yards in NML across the Battalion's front. We were supposed to join up with other people on our right and left, but we didn't see a soul. It was quiet, not much shelling apart from star shells lighting things up as we crawled amongst the rubbish and shell holes. I was in the first wave in the morning but I never saw that tape again. The Germans must have been out later and took it in. They had it all worked out, they were waiting for us.' 12/70 Cpl D.E. Cattell.

Cpl Cattell was not the only man in the Battalion who feared the worst for the morrow. As he hurried back from his 12 hour stint in the Divisional OP, Lt Middleton ran into Lt Elam waiting to check off A Company as it entered the trenches. They had a short chat before Lt Middleton continued on his way. Later that night he filled in his diary.

> '...On the way back met Elam seeing A Company in. Didn't see any of A Company. Wonder what they are in for? Ran through a bombardment in Colincamps, the Germans know we are coming.' Lt Middleton's diary 30th June 1916.

The Battalion entered the trenches at Northern Avenue and made its way forward via Pylon and Nairne. Because of the wet weather the trenches were waterlogged in places. The pace was much slower than expected and most of the men were two to three hours late reaching their positions.

> 'It was still daylight when we set off, round about 7.30 p.m., all loaded up like pack mules with all the extra equipment that we had to carry. By the time we reached the communications trenches it was quite dark, apart from the gun flashes lighting up the sky. It was a struggle moving down the trenches loaded up like we were. We signallers knew this section of trenches like the backs of

our hands, as one of our jobs was to find broken telephone lines at night and repair them. We couldn't climb out of the trenches with all that weight of equipment, so we had to sweat and toil at the mud and water that was knee deep in places. The going was difficult and it took us much longer to get into position than planned. We got there just before first light.' 12/928 L/Cpl J. R. Glenn.

By the time the men got into the assembly trenches they were exhausted. The eastern end of Nairne, the front line and the traffic trench behind it, and Copse Trench were all smashed up by artillery fire. Monk and Campion were found to be in a very poor state due to the weather.

At 3.45 a.m. Lt Elam reported to Battalion HQ in the tunnel at John Copse that the Battalion was in position. Twenty minutes later, at first light, the German artillery opened fire on the front line and John Copse. When the British barrage began on the previous Saturday the Germans had initially retaliated, but soon realised that it heralded the opening of the offensive. Thereafter some German batteries had been silent and remained undiscovered in readiness for this moment, despite the close attention of the RFC.

It was no coincidence that the Germans should choose first light to fire this bombardment. They had been given enough clues about the forthcoming attack, and probably surmised that the British would attack at dawn. Daylight also revealed the lanes cut in the British wire, thus confirming their fears that the attack was to take place that morning.

The soldiers cowered in their assembly trenches to wait out the remaining three and a half hours before Zero. The first wave of A and C Companies was in the front line, with the second wave sheltering in bombardment slits between the front line traffic trench and Copse Trench. The third wave of B and D Companies was in Campion and the fourth wave in Monk.

'Battalion HQ was in John Copse, in a big dugout. You can imagine how hectic it was with all the tooing and froing, people making last minute arrangements, little nervous reactions wanting to get everything right. Our barrage was still banging away but in the light of morning the Germans started shelling our trenches. Funny thing about being in a barrage was being frightened and trying not to show it to your mates while trying to get used to it. The least amount of cover gave you a sense of security, even a sheet of brown paper over your head would have been sufficient!' 12/928 L/Cpl J. R. Glenn.

The German artillery fire had by this time destroyed the telephone lines to Brigade HQ in Dunmow Trench. All day the Battalion had to rely on runners. One of the first messages sent to Brigade, at 6.00 a.m., reported that the front line in C Company's area was being shelled by the British artillery, and casualties were being caused. By 6.30 a.m. C Company had eight men killed and another six wounded.

It was not only the British troops that were cowering in their trenches. The Germans had been shelled and gassed for a week, and despite being worn out they were eager to give the Tommies back as good as they gave when the opportunity came. The following extract comes from the WD of a German company about one mile to the south of the City Battalion.

'If the English thought they could wear us out by the unprecedented fire of the past few days they had badly miscalculated. Never was the enthusiasm for battle or cameraderie

Waiting in support trenches for the word to move forward for the attack. Photograph taken soon after dawn on 1st July 1916, a few miles from Serre.

greater than in these days of terror and privation. The most ardent wish that we all cherished was that they would finally come....Now everyone knows that the hour of retaliation will soon come. Ammunition and hand grenade reserves are made ready; everything is ready.....'
War Diary 7th Company 169th Infantry Regiment 1st July 1916.

Whenever possible the Germans went out into NML to repair the wire, and spent a lot of time and effort on strengthening damaged trenches and keeping them open for use. In the sector opposite 94th Brigade a whole engineer company was sent in to assist with the work. But despite these efforts the destruction went on. Many trenches and dugouts were flattened, but the deep shelters were largely unaffected. The 169th Regiment's WD is justifiably proud of the fact that not one British raid penetrated its lines during the lead up to the attack.

The news the Germans had been waiting for arrived at the HQ of 169th Regiment at 3.30 a.m., (Authors note – all times have been changed to British time to avoid confusion). The message was from the HQ of 52nd Division and contained the information gleaned by the 'Moritz' listening post at La Boisselle. It also stated that the attack would begin at 4.30 a.m. Although the time was wrong it was close enough. The information was reinforced minutes later when the 1st Battalion of the 169th Regiment (1/169), opposite the City Battalion reported that patrols during the night had noticed a lot of activity in the British trenches. It was not mentioned, but it was probably one of these patrols that removed Cpl Cattell's tape.

At 6.30 a.m. the British artillery began firing the final heavy bombardment. To the men in the assembly trenches the effect was almost stupefying. There were no separate explosions, just a solid wall of sound. Speech was virtually impossible. Looking over the parapet all they could see were the flashes of exploding shells and a growing cloud of smoke and dust that gradually obscured the German trenches.

Ten minutes before Zero three events occurred concurrently; the first wave left the front line trenches; the trench mortars opened up a hurricane bombardment; and a huge mine was exploded to the south.

The men in the first wave were ordered to leave the trenches at this time to take advantage of the barrage. While the Germans still had their heads down it was thought to be an ideal opportunity to narrow the distance between themselves and the German trenches. They struggled up ladders and stakes driven into the trench wall. Behind them other men pushed them out while those already in the open helped to pull up their companions. It was a strange feeling to be standing upright in NML in daylight, something no-one in this sector had done for almost two years. They made their way through the gaps in the wire and lay down in extended line in the middle of NML to await the end of the bombardment. The platoon of A Company 14th York & Lancs in Nairne advanced just behind the left end of C Company and lay down in single file. Almost immediately the Germans opened fire with rifles and machine guns from their front line.

While the men were struggling under their heavy burdens to get out into NML, the LTMB opened up a hurricane bombardment to cover the final few minutes. The previous afternoon three sections had been brought into the line. Two sections were set up with guns in the front line and in Saps C, D and E. The third section was held in reserve in Eden Trench. In the ten minutes before Zero the two forward sections fired an incredible 1,150 rounds at the enemy

A German artillery Brigade headquarters on the Somme. The Germans had hidden their guns awaiting the moment when the attack was launched.

trenches.

The fire from the trench mortars was impressive, but the explosion of the mine under Hawthorne Ridge surpassed anything the men had yet seen. The mine had been dug under an important German position commanding the approaches to the village of Beaumont Hamel, and packed with 40,000 pounds of ammonal. Not even the roar of the barrage could shut out this earth shattering explosion. Those soldiers who were looking to the south at this time witnessed a column of smoke and earth rising hundreds of feet into the air.

The timing of the explosion was a major contributory factor in the failure of the attack in this area. The Corps Commander had wanted to fire it much earlier as part of a preliminary operation to secure the crater before the main attack went in. There were another six large mines in the Fourth Army attack area, but the commanders responsible for firing them decided to set them off at 7.28 a.m. They knew that all the debris would land within a minute of the explosion and so the troops could safely advance at Zero, giving the Germans only two minutes to react.

After much discussion it was decided to fire the Hawthorne Ridge mine at 7.20 a.m., and at the same time the heavy artillery in the immediate area was to lift back onto the second German line. For an inexplicable reason the whole of the Corps heavy artillery lifted at 7.20 a.m. leaving only a thin shrapnel barrage on the enemy front line. This gave the German infantrymen 10 minutes of relative safety to get out of their shelters and set up their weapons ready to repel the attack. The early firing of the mine was also the final confirmation that the attack was about to be launched.

All of this was of little relevance to the men lying out in NML waiting for the whistles to sound. At 7.25 a.m. the second wave also left the front line trench and advanced into NML. They too lay down in extended line about 30 to 50 yards behind the first wave. At this time the German front line was seen to be manned by a soldier every five yards. They emerged from their shelters when the sentries warned them the Tommies were coming, and opened a furious fire on the men in NML and threw showers of grenades at them. Casualties were caused immediately and soon began to mount up. One of the first to be hit was 12/1299 Pte A. H. Hastings in A Company. He was wounded by a trench mortar splinter in his cheek, and managed to make his way to the medical post in John Copse. He was lucky. Some of the men wounded at this time would not be able to get back until after dark, and had to endure untold misery lying under the hot sun without any form of shade.

At 7.29 a.m. the third and fourth waves began to move forwards from their assembly trenches, in section columns instead of extended order. The German artillery observers were spoiled for choice at this stage, with targets in NML, the British trenches and in the open behind them. They began by

Bringing up German reinforcements as the offensive got under way.

bombarding Monk Trench then brought the barrage back until it settled on the front line and a strip of ground 50 yards either side of it.

Zero arrived and the artillery lifted off the German front line. There was a momentary silence remembered by many of the men present. Then the artillery reopened fire on the German second line. When the whistles blew the first two waves leapt to their feet, looked left and right to check their dressing and set off at marching pace towards the German lines. Immediately they were met by a hail of rifle and machine gun bullets. The German artillery adjusted their fire onto the advancing lines and cut great swathes in the ranks with a mixture of high explosive and shrapnel shells.

'On 1st July at 7.30 a.m., after one and a half hours of very heavy 'Trommelfeuer' (literally drum fire), there is a pause in the firing on the foremost trenches. Now the English must come. We scramble out of the dugout which has survived the battering.....the whole front is covered in a continuous cloud of smoke, our barrage has begun.....in closed ranks come the attacking English, slowly, almost leisurely they trot along....

Extracted from Daring Heroic Deeds of the 5th Company, 2/169th Infantry Regiment.

'Zero hour was at 7.30 a.m. Just before it the first two waves got out of the trench and lay down in NML. There seemed to be an uncanny silence, you could even hear the skylarks singing. It was a beautiful morning, then the whistles blew. They all stood up and started to move forward in a straight line. They hadn't gone but a few steps when they went down again. I thought they had been tripped by a wire across NML, but it soon became obvious why, we heard the machine guns chattering away and all hell broke loose. At this time I ducked back down in the trench and moved back to Battalion HQ to await instructions. Things got a little chaotic with the rest of the Battalion trying to get forward with the attack and keep up with the timetable. The wounded struggled to get back and John Copse soon became full of dead and wounded.' 12/928 L/Cpl J. R. Glenn.

'....As our infantry advanced down came a perfect wall of explosives along the front trenches of my brigade and the 93rd. It was the most frightful artillery display that I had seen up to that time and in some ways I think it was the heaviest barrage I have seen put down by the defence on any occasion.' Brig Gen H. C. Rees.

'When the English started advancing we were very worried; they looked as though they must overrun our trenches. We were very surprised to see them walking, we had never seen that before. I could see them everywhere; there were hundreds.....When we started firing, we just had to load and reload. They went down in their hundreds. You didn't have to aim, we just fired into them. If only they had run, they would have overwhelmed us.' Musketeer K. Blenk 169th Infantry Regiment from 'First Day on the Somme' by M. Middlebrook.

At Zero the British artillery had lifted onto the second German trench leaving the German infantry in the front line with complete freedom of action. Some rushed forwards with machine guns to find better firing positions amongst the shell holes in NML. Others were clearly seen standing up to get a better aim

Posed shot from the film "Battle of the Somme". It purports to show British troops advancing to attack on 1st July 1916. However, they are carrying virtually no equipment. In the film the man falling to his knees lies down, crosses his legs and then turns to smile at the camera. It is an obvious fake.

at the advancing British, completely ignoring the dangers around them. Within the first 100 yards the attackers had all but melted away. The British counter battery artillery fire made no impression on the German artillery, since the positions of the concealed batteries were not known. At the crucial moment of the battle the assault troops had no supporting fire available to them.

> '*We had been told that the 31st Division were a young division who had never seen any real active service, and we were amazed and frightened when we saw this young Division attack in correct lines as if on parade. We could not understand why your artillery barrage had moved forward at zero hour on to our second line, which gave us time to come out of our front line dugouts and mass to receive you, but perhaps you had not realised that the concentrated fire of your trench mortars had little effect because our artillery had long before registered on their battle positions and reduced any barrage by them on our front line to very small proportions, but your men were so wonderful we feared it was a trap, and that you must have had divisions in reserve ready to attack later, and probably at night on our right wing.*' Ex-German Staff Officer to Lt Col Gurney in Spain after the war.

The Germans had six machine guns facing 94th Brigade, which were referred to by the name of their team leaders. They were Adelbrecht, Wilhelm, Kaiser, Schloss, Kolle and Ruck. The concentrated fire from these guns forced the British to veer slightly to the right where the fire was slackest. The few men that eventually got into the German trenches and returned, reported the machine guns were cunningly set into deltas at the junction of the communications and fire trenches.

They were also placed so they could not be fired on from the front, but covered arcs of fire across the front of the trenches thus enfilading the attackers in a deadly crossfire.

There was no wavering in the Battalion's ranks and no thought of retreat. But the waves were rapidly thinned down until only a handful were left. Those remaining plodded steadily onwards towards the German trenches and just as steadily lost more men with every step they took.

At last they arrived at the enemy wire expecting to be able to cross the last few yards and get into the German front line. Here they would have been on equal terms with the Germans. But the wire was still there! There were gaps, mainly on the right, but the Germans made a point of covering these where possible with their machine guns. Anyone who tried to rush through a gap met with almost certain death. The Official History says that the wire was 'effectively cut and blown into thick heaps'. This may have been true on other sectors of the VIII Corps front but was certainly not the case west of Serre.

Casualties were heaviest on the left due to a combination of circumstances, including the uncut wire, and the failure of a smoke screen released to the north to effectively mask the attack. The Germans north of Serre quickly realised they were not going to be attacked. They turned their full attention to firing

A German Maxim Machine Gun team set up in the open.

Capt W. A. Colley.

into the left flank of the City Battalion and A and B Companies of 14th York & Lancs advancing out of Nairne.

C Company on the left almost ceased to exist. Its commander, Capt W. A. Colley, had a premonition of his death just before going over the top.

Despite this he was undeterred and was first out of the trench, but soon after he was hit by a shell and killed. His remains were never identified. This gallant gentleman should not really have been at the front, and certainly should not have been leading a company into action at the age of 47.

A Company suffered the same fate as C Company, but on the right arrived at the German wire with fewer casualties. The trouble really began at this point. There were few ways through the wire and the men ran up and down it looking for gaps. While they were so exposed the Germans had a turkey shoot. One of those looking for a gap was the Company commander, Capt W. S. Clarke. He was killed by machine gun fire and left hanging in the wire. Another officer in A Company noted for his pluck and determination was Lt P. K. Perkin, who had only been with the Battalion since the end of April. He was twice wounded by grenade fragments but refused to give up until he was cut down by a burst from a machine gun. Another A Company man killed early on was Pte Willie Parker, who had moved heaven and earth to get back to the Battalion from his protected employment. Cpl Cattell was in the first wave of A Company.

'I was never afraid, I never saw a German and I never fired at one. Yet all this firing was coming at us. They must have been firing through loopholes or something from their front line trench.

It was a surprise really because we were told that we would walk straight over. They must have seen us get up judging by the amount of fire that hit us. The ground was pitted all over with shell holes. After about 30 yards I had lost all my platoon, I was on my own. Keeping going I couldn't see anybody either side of me, they were all on the floor. Managing to reach the German wire I was unable to get any further because it wasn't cut. The only thing I could do was to lay down. What else could I do? I was on my own so close to the wire I could touch it.' 12/70 Cpl D. E. Cattell.

CHALLENGE
by 12/525 Sgt John William Streets

Go tell you shadow stalking 'neath the trees
With silent-footed terror, go tell Death
He cannot with life's vast uncertainties
Affright the heart of Youth. For Youth cometh
With flush of impulse, passion to defeat,
Undaunted purpose, vision clear descried,
To counteract, lay at Death's unseen feet
The gauntlet of defiance. Far and wide,
Beyond the fear of that unknown exile,
That brim of time, that web of darkness drawn
Across Life's orient sky, there breaks a smile
Of light that swells into the hope of dawn,
A dream within the dark, like evening cool,
Like sunset mirror'd in yon darken'd pool.

The survivors went to ground and tried to root out the machine guns with grenades. However, the Germans had deliberately constructed the wire entanglements so that their trenches were out of hand thrown grenade range to anyone outside of it.

Some of the men were not intimidated by their predicament and quickly rallied. One of them was 12/226 Pte R. W. D. Seymour of A Company who found himself unable to get through the wire. He calmly knelt down as if on the ranges and opened rapid fire, until seriously wounded by a bullet through the jaw. Close to Pte Seymour was 12/1123 Sgt R. Gallimore, who had led many night patrols into NML the previous month. He stood up in full view of the Germans and fired like a man possessed. He eventually took cover in a shell hole and gathered a number of survivors together. Whenever the Germans showed themselves they fired back. At nightfall they were able to get back to the British lines. 12/1376 Pte R. Gorrill in the first wave found the wire very thick and undamaged. Taking cover in a shell hole he and five others were subjected to accurate bombing. Timing his moment perfectly Pte Gorrill jumped up and shot the German just as he was about to throw another grenade. The aggressive action displayed by the survivors had some effect on the defending Germans as this extract shows.

The deadly Maxim machine gun that caused so many casualties on 1st July 1916.

'As Unteroffiziers Reiner and Adelbrecht saw the enemy they opened fire immediately with the machine gun (MG), on the English who were advancing in groups of five to ten or more. Further waves followed. The MG fired with great success at the approaching enemy who pulled over to the left to escape the fire. Then the MG jammed.

As Unteroffizier Adelbrecht tried to clear it he was shot through the head and died instantly. Other members of the crew were also hit; Rifleman Pfahler was apparently killed by his own grenade (Author's note -possibly as a result of Pte Gorrill's quick shooting?), and Riflemen Walter, Stein, Gerbel and Buck were wounded.....The Company commander Oberleutnant Faller, ordered MG Wilhelm in the second trench forwards. This was done with great bravery. The MG was firing effectively when the team leader, Unteroffizier Wilhelm, fell with a head wound. Despite this the platoon leader Unteroffizier Reiner kept cool and allowed the MG to continue firing. In spite of this some of the English came close and threw hand grenades with great skill, however they did not silence the MG. The wounded who were lying in front of the trench were picked off separately by the infantry.' Battle Report, 1st Machine Gun Company 169th Infantry Regiment.

Once the immediate threat from the first two waves had been repulsed the Germans redirected their efforts onto the third and fourth waves. Because Rob Roy had been destroyed these two waves had begun their advance much further back than had been originally planned. The fourth wave had 500 yards to go even before it crossed the British front line, and it was in view almost the whole way. It may be asked why they didn't move up to the front line in the comparative safety of the communications trenches. The plan called for a rapid build up to secure the enemy trenches. To have moved through the communications trenches would have taken too long, giving the Germans time to regroup. With hindsight it is easy to criticise this decision, but if the artillery had destroyed the German defences the plan would have worked and no-one would have questioned it.

By the time the third and fourth waves of B and D Companies had reached the British front line they had already suffered 50% casualties. None took cover, indeed orders had expressly forbidden anyone to enter a trench until he reached his objective.

'We were to follow the fourth wave of B and D Companies. As we waited to go over the top standing in the bottom of the trench, the attackers stood by the ladders waiting for the whistles to sound.

Everyone was tensed up waiting for the off when the German barrage fell on our trench, which was called Monk. It seemed to move further forward thank the Lord. Anyway it was now time for D Company to advance. We had to wait a few minutes for them to clear the trench and get going. By the time we got out of the trench all hell had been let loose. Shells were falling all over the place and between the crash of the shells you could hear the chattering of machine guns. There didn't seem to be many people moving about, there were plenty on the ground, dead and wounded. But orders said you didn't stop to assist the wounded just keep going. By the time I reached what was supposed to be our front line it was obvious that it was useless going on, the Battalion had been wiped out.' 12/664 Pte H. Hall.

In D Company was the poet Sgt Streets. He was wounded in NML and was making his way back to the aid station when he heard that a soldier from his platoon had also been injured and was unable to move by himself. Without hesitating he turned about and went back into NML to find his comrade. He was never seen again, although his remains are thought to be buried in Euston Road Military Cemetery. In a letter written just before the offensive he wrote about his poetry and his thoughts on his possible death.

A posed photograph of British troops "winkling out" a German dugout.

"They were inspired while I was in the trenches, where I have been so busy that I have had little time to polish them. I have tried to picture some thoughts that pass through a man's brain when he dies. I may see the end of the poems, but hope to live to do so.

We soldiers have our views of life to express, though the boom of death is in our ears. We try to convey something of what we feel in this great conflict to those who think of us, and sometimes, alas, mourn our loss. We desire to let them know that in the midst of our keenest sadness for the joy of life we leave behind, we go to meet death grim lipped, clear eyed and resolute hearted.' 12/525 Sgt J. W. Streets.

Despite the horrific casualties and the carnage some men got into the German trenches and fought a savage hand to hand battle. The account of this fighting is confused and largely incomplete because very few of the men who got into the German trenches left alive. One who did was 12/371 Pte A. Fretwell, in a party of 12 men from B Company. After a few minutes savage fighting they were forced to withdraw. Only three got away. Pte Fretwell was hit in the face with a grenade, but fortunately the pin was still in it.

Sgt J. W. Streets. Despite his wounds he went back into NML to assist his comrade. His devotion to duty cost him his life.

A bomber who made it to the German front line and got back was 12/551 Pte A. Wenman of B Company. He bombed a dugout containing eight Germans and brought back valuable information about the construction of these shelters.

Many accounts contradict each other thus further confusing the story. We have attempted to relate the events of the rest of the day and to point out the established facts from the educated guesswork.

The British artillery brigades supporting 94th Brigade are unanimous in reporting the early success of the attack. At 7.39 a.m. 165th Brigade RFA (165 RFA) noted the first waves entering the enemy front line, although it was also stated that smoke made observation difficult. Three minutes later 170 RFA reported the infantry in the enemy front line.

A little later, at 7.50 a.m., 165 RFA reported the infantry in the second line, and this is backed up 10 minutes later by a similar report from the 94th Brigade observers. The advance continued well according to the artillery, and at 8.05 a.m. elements of 94th Brigade were seen in Serre by 170 RFA, while 165 RFA reported them in the 4th line two minutes later. This last report concerned the left side of the attack where the City Battalion had experienced

The objective – the fortified village of Serre – taken on the morning of the battle.

the heaviest and most deadly fire. Ten minutes later the same observer saw the infantry moving through Serre.

It was not until 8.41 a.m. that the artillery reports began to doubt the success of the operation. At that time it was noted that the third line was still held by the enemy.

Why is it that the artillery observers should report success when it was obvious to other observers that the infantry were being massacred? This is difficult to answer. The artillery observers had the best viewpoints, and knew the ground well. It is difficult to understand how they made such an error, if indeed they made an error at all. A fleeting glimpse through the smoke of a handful of men advancing into the village may have given the impression of being a larger body of troops.

By 7.50 a.m. all four waves of 11th East Lancs had gone forward and had entered the enemy front line on the right and left. At 8.20 a.m. they were reinforced by a company of 13th York and Lancs which in its advance over NML had suffered heavy casualties from enemy shell fire. It is unlikely that the East Lancs and 13th York & Lancs held out in the front line for long, and this was later confirmed. At 9.00 a.m. a wounded Cpl from the first 11th East Lancs wave got back to his own lines to report only seven men in his platoon had got to the enemy front line. After 20 minutes they had been bombed out and forced back into NML.

L/Cpl A. Outram.

The Germans were certainly worried by these moves. The first indication that the British had broken into the trenches was reported to the HQ of 169th Regiment at 8.00 a.m. Four minutes later the 12th Company was ordered to fall back into Serre, probably to form a strong fallback position in case of a breakthrough. This move was seen from the British trenches and is recorded in the City Battalion WD. At the same time the 2nd Company was ordered to counter attack against 11th East Lancs and the 1st Company was sent to restore the situation where the City Battalion had broken into the front line. While this was happening the 10th Company occupied the fourth line and also supported the 2nd Company. The experienced German troops were quickly able to assess the situation and launch effective and immediate counter attacks at the important points.

Pte Archie Brammer.

According to the German WD at 8.30 a.m. the front line across the whole front of the City Battalion and 11th East Lancs was back in their hands. However, at 8.35 a.m. 94th Brigade observed the Germans firing shrapnel shells into their own front line. Perhaps it was a little later by the time the front line was completely back in German hands.

The crisis for 169th Regiment was not yet over, because British troops were holding out between the front line and Serre. Maj Berthold the CO of 1/169, advanced to clear the forward trenches, and by 9.00 a.m. they were once again secured. A little later the Germans were confident enough to send their reserve battalion (3/169), to support 2/169 on the left. They could not have done this if they were still facing a major threat on their right.

But what of 14th York & Lancs on the left, how had they fared since the initial attack had broken down? By 7.58 a.m. both A and B Companies had left Nairne to occupy the Russian Sap and the German communications trench that were to form the new northerly facing front line. The Battalion WD estimated that only 20% of the two Companies got to the German front line. However, at 9.05 a.m. 94th Brigade WD records that six platoons of 14th York & Lancs were making good progress with the new trench. But at 9.30 a.m. the officer commanding the Russian Sap party returned to Battalion HQ wounded. His story was not so optimistic and he asked for two platoons as reinforcements. The CO ordered two platoons from the reserve companies forward, but they were unable to find the Sap. The CO then went to investigate for himself, and could not find the Sap either. At this he countermanded the order and the two platoons were put back into reserve. The devastating effect of concentrated artillery fire cannot be better illustrated than this. A whole trench had completely disappeared and its location could not be traced despite its position being accurately known.

It would appear that men from 14th York & Lancs got as far as the second line, but after that they were too weak to go on. Elements of the Battalion should have reached the fourth line, which was to have been the junction point with 12th York & Lancs.

By 8.35 a.m. the remnants of the City Battalion were taking cover in NML and the Russian Sap with survivors of 14th York & Lancs. But some men from the Battalion had penetrated the German trenches and a few actually got into Serre. In November 1916 their bodies were seen in the north west corner of the village.

One man that survived the battle as a POW was 12/469 L/Cpl A. Outram, from Eyam in Derbyshire. He said that the last two men left standing were himself and another signaller, 12/879 Pte A. Brammer.

The lucky wounded were quickly recovered in the trenches and were soon on their way to the Dressing Stations and Field Hospitals.

They signalled to each other and then L/Cpl Outram turned his head for a moment. When he looked back Pte Brammer had disappeared. This incident took place just in front of Serre, but not actually in the village itself. Perhaps the Sergeant Major of D Company at Redmires would have been proud to learn that the last two men left at Serre were, 'flag wagging signallers', both from his Company! Pte Brammer is buried in Railway Hollow Military Cemetery.

For those stuck in NML it was a very long and hot day. The wounded suffered terribly and many died before the stretcher bearers could reach them. Anyone that moved immediately attracted sniper fire, and it was usually deadly accurate. Cpl Cattell was under cover but his pack stuck up and could be seen by the Germans.

> 'My thoughts were of home and of the loss of all my friends. Later in the day our guns shelled the German front line and I didn't know what it was all about, except I was covered in yellow smoke. They had been using me as target practice, but they only shot my pack away. I could manage to turn my head so that I could see behind me, thus seeing all my friends lying dead and wounded. One chap I remember very well was in a shell hole. He had a big nose and I saw him lift his head up. A sniper shot his nose off. All day I stayed out there unable to move. It was after 10 o'clock at night when I got back into our lines. There wasn't a soul about, the Germans could have walked straight through. Anyway I found a dugout and went to sleep for about 18 hours.' 12/70 Cpl D. E. Cattell.

Other men in NML were slightly better off and found they could move about a little with care. One of them was 12/1521 Pte A. Greenaway, a man from Bermondsey in Surrey. He was seen moving wounded men into shell holes where they would be protected from the snipers, and giving them first aid. Sadly he was later killed and his body was never identified. No medal was ever awarded for Pte Greenaway's selfless bravery, probably because no-one in authority who saw him survived the battle.

Some of the men sustained injuries that were so severe it is a miracle that they survived. One man with multiple wounds was 12/1189 Pte C. F. Cavill. He was hit early on in the attack, but discarded his pack and went on only to be wounded twice more. He was hit in the chest about an inch from his heart, his left elbow was shattered and he was also hit in the fleshy part of the upper right inside leg.

He was found by stretcher bearers during the day but they had no stretcher to carry him on. They returned, as they promised they would, at night and collected him. The lorry he was taken away on was so crowded that despite the seriousness of his wounds he had to stand on the running board. On arrival at the hospital he was stripped and iodine poured into the wounds. He eventually spent two years in hospital. At one stage a doctor wanted to amputate his left arm, but other doctors and a nurse intervened. After 10 operations his arm was saved, although it was an inch shorter than the other. Pte Cavill eventually married the nurse that had helped to save his arm. Despite his injuries he lived until 1986.

Perhaps the most incredible survival story concerns a soldier in B Company. He wrote this article for the hospital magazine in the Huddersfield War Hospital at Royds Hall in September 1916.

> '.....I hadn't gone far before I was hit, being shot in the chest. I immediately rolled into a shell hole for better protection and imagine I lost consciousness for some considerable time. When I came to, I heard a voice and discovered that there was another fellow in a shell hole about 15 yards away, so I decided to join him. It was while crawling across that I got shot through the arm by a sniper. How long we were in that shell hole I don't know, for it must have been several days – we were parched with thirst and welcomed the heavy rain which came, and which we collected in our steel helmets..... All at once the other fellow decided to crawl in and off he went. That was the last I saw or heard of him. I decided then that it was impossible to stay out day after day and started to crawl in myself. I found it an agonising and exhausting job, and have no idea how long it took me. Eventually I got into an old disused trench. Here I discovered a dugout and turned in. All I wanted was rest and oblivion, and I slept..... In the dugout I found some bits of Army biscuits, and these soaked in rain water were the only food I had. I was absolutely too weak to do anything but lie and sleep, and did not move except when I crawled to get water. To sum matters up I was hit on 1st July and was discovered on the 15th..... for 15 days I was without food (practically) and with my wounds undressed.' 12/1475 Pte A. C. Stagg.

The ground in front of the village in March 1917.

Another man stuck in NML was 12/338 Pte B. Corthorn. He was the No. 2 of a six man Lewis gun team in B Company. Within 50 yards three of the team had been hit, and after 15 minutes Pte Corthorn was the only one able to carry on. He got to within 20 yards of the German front line but could get no further.

Taking cover in a shell hole Pte Corthorn began firing back with his Lewis gun until it was hit by a rifle bullet and knocked out. He then found a rifle and fired that until the barrel was glowing red. At about 8.50 a.m. he crawled into another shell hole and found a badly wounded companion from his gun team, 12/1125 Pte R. F. Brookes. He made Pte Brookes as comfortable as possible and risked his life looking for water and clothing in which to wrap him. He refused to leave his charge even when darkness fell. Pte Corthorn was himself wounded by shrapnel in his leg, and although it was not serious he was unable to carry Pte Brookes. He therefore hoped that the stretcher bearers would find them in the night. They didn't, and late the next day Pte Brookes died. Once it was dark Pte Corthorn made his way back to the British lines with the Lewis gun. He was evacuated to the base hospital at Rouen and later to Newport in Wales.

12/427 Pte W. Kirkham.

In the early part of the battle Capt R. E. J. Moore had tried to join up with Pte Corthorn. However, he was weak from loss of blood and could not make it. He saw how Pte Corthorn had behaved under fire, and as he was being taken away on a stretcher later on he mentioned what he had seen to Maj Plackett, the acting CO.

As a result of Capt Moore's observations Pte Corthorn received one of the three Distinguished Conduct Medals (DCM) awarded to members of the City Battalion for actions on 1st July. For ORs the DCM is the next medal down in merit from the Victoria Cross.

Apart from Pte Brookes, whose body was never found, two other members of Pte Corthorn's Lewis gun team died. 12/284 Pte S. E. Aspland was buried in Queen's Cemetery at Serre, and 12/427 Pte W. Kirkham died of wounds on 3rd July and was buried in Bertrancourt Military Cemetery.

Three members of another Lewis gun team were also decorated. They were 12/24 Pte H. C. Arridge, 12/923 Pte C. S. Garbett and 12/1164 L/Cpl M. B. Burnby. They had advanced with the first wave of A Company, and been forced to take cover in a shell hole. Throughout the day they fired back at a German machine gun post and also threw grenades into the German lines. After dark they crawled back with the gun intact. They were later awarded the MM.

The scene in John Copse by this stage was utterly chaotic. Earlier in the day a small first aid station had been set up there. As the morning progressed more and more wounded made their way to it and soon it was overwhelmed. One of the first to get there was Pte A. H. Hastings, who had been wounded at 7.20 a.m. A little later his cousin 12/946 Pte J. Hastings was brought in with a head wound. It was not until 2.00 p.m. that they were allowed to walk back to the CCS at Bus. In the meantime the little copse had been shelled to a pulp and no trees were left standing.

Maj Hoette, the Battalion 2IC, left the shelter of the Battalion HQ tunnel in John Copse to try to find out what had happened to the assault companies. At about 10.30 a.m. he was wounded, and a message was sent to Brigade HQ to the effect that the Battalion didn't know what was happening. The conditions became unbearable to work in and the Battalion HQ moved to a dugout in Mark Copse at noon. At some time in the morning L/Cpl Glenn was sent to the rear with a message.

'Some time during the morning Capt Moore told me to take a message back to the Transport lines at Colincamps, to tell them to stop the rations. (Author's note - it was most likely the Adjutant, Capt Tunbridge that sent him. Capt Moore was wounded, and as a company officer had no authority to give such an order). Colin Evans (12/9 Pte C. C. Evans) went with me; usually two men carried a message in case one got knocked out. When we approached Colincamps we saw the barbed wire cages which had been constructed to hold the prisoners we were supposed to capture. They were guarded by Military Police who asked us where we were going, but ignored what we said. They told us to get in the cage. They did the same with all stragglers they saw. It was said they were expecting a counter-attack and orders were that anyone moving back was to be held in case they were needed. Anyway we managed to sneak off when they weren't looking and delivered the message.....When we arrived back at HQ in the late afternoon it was apparent that the Battalion had been badly hit. There seemed to be more wounded and dead than there were living.....' 12/928 L/Cpl J. R. Glenn.

Three of the Battalion's runners were decorated for their actions during the battle. 12/275 Pte G. C. Wright was awarded the DCM, and 12/4 Pte R. Marsden and 12/354 Pte A. Downing were awarded MMs.

Pte Wright was given a message to take to Brigade HQ from the Battalion HQ, a distance of about half a mile. On the way he was three times blown up by shells and very badly concussed. No sooner had he delivered the message than he collapsed. Pte Marsden was actually buried by the debris from an exploding shell. He dug himself out and got his message through. Pte Downing seems to have had a charmed life. He braved the heavy German fire to deliver two messages to Brigade HQ, and escaped injury on both occasions.

As the morning wore on any realistic hope of success dwindled. At 9.00 a.m. it looked as if the Germans were massing for a major counter-attack into the British trenches. It is now known that this was not the case but the seriousness of the situation caused the Commander of 93rd Brigade, Brig Gen Ingles to bring the artillery fire of 170 RFA back to deal with them. There were so few men left in the British trenches that the Germans could have gone straight through them. There are several reports around this time of the Germans shelling Serre and their trenches. It is possible that this was the fire of 170 RFA. However, as late as 10.11 a.m. German bombing parties were seen at work in the communications trenches, and at 10.21 a.m. there was another report of the Germans shelling Serre.

Confusion reigned at Divisional and Corps HQs. The lack of solid information plagued decision making throughout the day, and the breakdown of telephone communications introduced such long delays that messages were usually hopelessly out of date by the time they were delivered. If this was not enough the fact that many reports contradicted each other further added to the confusion. For example at 11.30 a.m. 170 RFA reported that troops on either side of 93rd Brigade had met up behind Serre thus encircling the village. Just 20 minutes later 11th East Lancs were scrambling to put their front line into a state of defence in case of a German counter attack. The two reports sound as if they come from different battles, and illustrate the problems facing the staff at the higher HQs throughout the day. However, from the Divisional OP it was clear that the battle had not gone well.

> 'On the way up I passed hundreds coming back and learned things had gone badly. From the OP I could see NML covered in corpses, which was a terrible sight. I also saw some Germans in their trenches which were mostly destroyed.' Lt Middleton's Diary 1st July 1916.

What Lt Middleton could see was a patch of ground about 700 yards wide and 200 yards deep. Within this space were the dead, wounded and survivors of 94th Brigade. Approximately 2,000 soldiers had gone forward from the infantry battalions, the pioneers and the machine gunners, and over 1,700 had become casualties.

NML by this time was quiet. British machine gunners in the front line did their best to discourage the Germans from sniping at the wounded.

There were occasional flurries of artillery and trench mortar fire as each side nervously suspected renewed attacks by the other. But at 1 p.m. the Germans could only see stretcher bearers in NML, and were content to allow them to get on with their missions of mercy as long as there was no aggressive action from the British. This unofficial truce went on until about 4 o'clock when the British artillery opened fire again. After that the Germans were reluctant to let anyone wander freely in NML. It was not until 10.30 p.m. and the coming of night that the task of recovering the wounded once again got underway.

Just after midday 31st Division ordered 94th Brigade to send forward any reserves it had to join up with the troops that were thought to have taken Serre and Pendant Copse beyond it. Brig Gen Rees wisely declined the offer until he had more information to work on. He was not going to send more men to certain death unless there was a chance of success.

Reports from aeroplane patrols indicated that there were still British troops holding out between the German front line and Serre, although by this time it had been accepted that our troops no longer held the village or even parts of it. Maj Gen O'Gowan wanted to launch another attack to link up with these suspected pockets of resistance. He conferred with the commanders of 93rd and 94th Brigades and came to the conclusion that another daylight attack was doomed to failure. Later in the evening he passed on his thoughts to the Corps Commander who agreed with him and ordered the Division to clear up its trenches and reorganise. He also ordered two battalions of 92nd Brigade forward in preparation for a night attack at 2.00 a.m. the following morning. However, because of the state of the trenches these battalions could not get to the front lines and the attack was cancelled at 9.50 p.m.

After dark the trenches and NML once again sprang to life. The two assault battalions were relieved by 13 and 14th York & Lancs. The remains of the City Battalion moved back to Rolland Trench, and by 2.20 a.m. Battalion HQ had been established in a deep sap. The strength of the Battalion at this time was about ten men unwounded, mainly signallers and runners.

As soon as darkness fell search parties of stretcher bearers and men from all of the battalions went out into NML to collect the wounded. Others were detailed off to begin the enormous task of repairing the trenches, which in some places had been completely levelled.

Those who had been stuck in NML and could move by themselves began to make their way back in. Pte Gorrill who had shown such courage earlier in the day urged those in his shell hole who were not wounded to try to make it back to the lines, saying he would follow soon afterwards.

However, he considered it more important to stay with the wounded, and this he did for the next three days before going for help. He was also slightly wounded himself.

A group of four stretcher bearers had not managed to get into NML during the day. Just after Zero their trench was hit by a heavy shell which knocked it in. Having recovered from the blast they discovered one of their number dead and six other men killed around them. The three remaining stretcher bearers then began collecting the survivors into a sap where they would be better protected from the German shells. As the day wore on two of the medics were also wounded, leaving 12/727 Pte S. Matthews of C Company to care for 50 seriously wounded men in the sap.

For the next three days he attended to the wounded without any rest at all. One of his charges was an officer from 12th KOYLI, who despite his wounds insisted on going out to look for his men. Pte

Matthews dressed this officer's wounds four times before persuading him to go to the rear. Fortunately there was not a shortage of bandages and many walking wounded were quickly patched up, and sent back under their own steam.

During the night of 1st-2nd July the sap became busier as more men crawled in from NML. Pte Matthews was joined by a stretcher bearer from one of the Barnsley battalions, who also did very good work. Eventually the Battalion MO, Capt E. C. Cunnington RAMC, found them and thereafter made periodic visits to the sap. He could not devote more time to Pte Matthew's party since there were similar groups of wounded all over the trench system. The MO tried to keep alive as many men as possible until they could be carried back to the dressing stations and then to the field hospitals.

After 70 hours of continuous work with the wounded Pte Matthews was relieved and marched out with the rest of the Battalion. For his courage and devotion to duty he was awarded the DCM. With typical modesty he could not understand why he had been awarded the medal, since other men had done as much if not more.

The men who were left standing had no time for rest. They had to get on with rescuing their comrades and clearing up the appalling mess in the trenches. There were wounded men and corpses everywhere and the trenches were full of all sorts of rubbish.

> 'What a job of work clearing up the trenches was! A ghastly task having to clear the dead, poor blokes. It took days to carry them back up to Red Cottage which was an aid station. Close by mass graves had been dug prior to the battle. There wasn't enough space for the amount of dead which had to be buried, so we had to use some old trenches.' 12/1298 Pte D. C. Cameron.

> 'I was working with the clearing up parties, you know we had a lot to do. First priority were the wounded who had to be carried up to the aid station at Red Cottage. I came across ACSM Atkinson who had been wounded in the chest. He was still breathing so I stripped his equipment from him, put him over my shoulder and carried him to the aid station. After much huffing and puffing I finally made it. The doctor took one look at my charge and said, 'Put him over there with the others, you've wasted your time lad, he's had it'. The sequel to this story is that some years later I became a member of Abbeydale Golf Club and in conversation with the club professional I mentioned that I had served with the City Battalion. He said his brother had also served in it and told me his name, it was CSM Atkinson. I then told him I had left him for dead at the aid station. Apparently his brother had been brought back to York where he lived until 9th July.' 12/664 Pte H. Hall.

During the night 94th Brigade informed the Battalion they had information that about 150 men were still holding out in the German front line opposite Mark Copse. At 1.30 a.m. on the morning of the 2nd two patrols from 14th York & Lancs, led by City Battalion officers, went out to investigate. They found

A casualty is rushed to the rear. Despite all the efforts made this man died minutes after the photograph was taken.

no signs of British troops in the German lines. Wounded men they encountered informed the officers that the trenches were firmly in German hands. As if to reinforce this the German machine guns continuously swept NML and many Very lights were sent up. On the return journey the patrols picked up a number of wounded, and one of the patrol leaders, Lt Oxley, was slightly wounded.

During the night a number of men were accounted for. Just after midnight the Battalion reported that 21 men had been collected and another 5 had made their own way back. Many more were found before dawn.

The work of recovering the wounded and dead was monumental. Every body, whether dead or alive, had to be carried back through the shattered trenches to the area of Red Cottage, about 1,300 yards behind the front line. At least at night the men could work above ground and avoid the rubbish and carnage in the trenches. VIII Corps did not declare NML clear until 4th July, and this was not totally accurate since survivors continued to be found for some time afterwards.

After dark the leaders began to try to find out what had gone wrong. Some were sympathetic towards their men, but others were not so kind.

The magnificent gallantry, discipline and determination displayed by all ranks of this North Country Division were to no avail against the concentrated fire-effect of the enemy's unshaken infantry and artillery, whose barrage has been described as so consistent and severe that the cones of the explosions gave the impression of a thick belt of poplar trees.' Official History of the Great War 1916 Volume.

'I have never seen a finer display of individual and collective bravery than the advance of that Brigade. I never saw a man waver from the exact line prescribed for him. Each line disappeared into the thick cloud of dust and smoke which rapidly blotted out the whole area. I can safely pay a tribute also to the bravery of the enemy, whom I saw standing up in their trenches to fire their rifles in a storm of fire..... I saw a few groups of men through gaps in the smoke cloud, but I knew that no troops could hope to get through such fire. My two staff officers, Piggott and Stirling, were considerably surprised when I stopped the advance of the rest of the machine gun company and certain other small bodies now passing my HQ. It was their first experience of a great battle and all that morning they found it impossible to believe that the whole Brigade had been destroyed as a fighting unit.' Brig Gen H. C. Rees.

'North of the River Ancre, the VIII Corps (Hunter-Weston), said they had begun well..... I am inclined to believe from further reports that few of the VIII Corps left their trenches.' Gen Sir D. Haig.

This last quote from the diary of the BEF Commander has angered many soldiers since it was written. On 1st July 1916 VIII Corps had over 14,000 casualties. They could not have suffered so grievously by cowering in their trenches. This terse comment was never rescinded.

Early in the morning of 2nd July, 80 reinforcements for the Battalion arrived, under the command of Capt E. G. G. Woolhouse and 2Lt W. H. Rowlands.

They were quickly put to work with the survivors. Later in the day Lt Middleton went to the trenches to visit the men, who he could see were all exhausted. He stopped to speak to Lt F. A. Beal and was asked the awkward question of what he thought had become of his brother, 2Lt A. J. Beal. We do not know his reply. Frank Beal was evacuated to England on the 10th with a bad case of shell shock. His brother Arnold had been killed, but at that time was listed as missing with hundreds of others.

The strain of the battle and then clearing up the mess gradually began to take its toll. One soldier remembers seeing the CSM of his company standing at the rear of the trenches in a state of shock weeping. A stretcher bearer, 12/239 Pte J. W. Stevenson, and his mate were taking a short break after three days of continuously moving wounded out of the trenches. They were utterly exhausted, but the MO saw them and ordered them to get back to work immediately. Pte Stevenson's mate lost his temper and threatened to shoot the MO. At this Capt Cunnington who was under a great deal of strain lost his self control and threatened to shoot the soldier too. Pte Stevenson managed to part the two of them and they went back to work.

The Battalion remained in the trenches until the evening of the 3rd. Conditions gradually improved as bodies and rubbish were removed, but improvements were negated when the weather turned and flooded the trenches once again. On the 3rd the first reinforcements of 56 Derby men arrived at Warnimont Wood from the Base to commence the rebuilding of the Battalion.

At 8.00 p.m. on the evening of the 3rd the Battalion was relieved by 1/4th Oxfordshire and Buckinghamshire Light Infantry (1/4th Ox & Bucks LI), in 48th Division. They marched wearily back to Louvencourt to rejoin the rear details. The Battalion strength was 202 men, including the reinforcements who had gone into the line on the night of 1st-2nd July.

Only four of the 22 officers that went into the trenches marched out with it. They were Capts Tunbridge and Cunnington, Lt Moxey and 2Lt Cloud.

HQ 94th Brigade sent two reports to HQ 31st Division on what had been learned by bitter experience from the battle. Most of the points have been mentioned in this chapter already, however, it is worth spelling out the criticisms levelled at the original plan.

1. The wait in the assembly trenches was too long.
2. The first waves should not have sheltered in the front line since the trench mortars were also there and became an immediate target for enemy retaliatory fire.
3. More bombardment slits were required. There were fewer casualties amongst men in the bombardments slits than there were in the assembly trenches.
4. More men needed training in the use of Bangalore Torpedoes. By the time they were needed all the trained men were casualties.
5. Smoke bombs would have covered attempts to cut the German wire.
6. The assault should have been at dawn. The enemy had over four hours from first light to prepare, having seen the gaps in our wire and the tapes in NML.
7. The attack should have been in double time with the waves much closer together. As it was the enemy could concentrate all their efforts against each wave in turn.
8. Officers, NCOs and machine gunners were marked men.
9. The men that returned from the German trenches reported the following:
   a. The front line was 12 feet deep and was strongly revetted with basket work. There was no fire step or parapet, all the earth was thrown up into a very high parados, often up to 3-4 feet tall.
   b. The Germans had ingeniously concealed their machine gun positions in the parados where they were very well protected.
   c. It was suspected that there were tunnels running up to the front line. (Authors note – this was not actually the case, the defenders that surprised the City Battalion men had in fact emerged from the deep dugouts.)
   d. A couple of dugouts were seen. None had been destroyed by shell fire. One of them had 18 steps leading down to it and space for eight men to shelter.

Chapter Eight

Aftermath of the Battle

The men that came out of the line on 4th July were a sorry looking bunch. They had seen their comrades die in their hundreds, and had endured days of shelling while attempting to clear up the mess caused by the failure of the attack. Many had been back into NML at night on numerous trips to search for survivors. Sometimes they had been lucky, but most of the bodies they came across were dead.

There had been little chance for rest since going into the line and many were at the end of their tethers. All they wanted to do was sleep, but the stress and shock of the previous week would take time to wear off. Until it did they would be unable to rest properly. The Army did not allow them time in which to brood on what they had been through. In the circumstances this was probably a good thing.

Lt Middleton arrived at Louvencourt at 1.00 p.m. on 4th July, having been released from his observation duties. The Battalion had also just arrived and were still standing in the road. There were 202 ORs there, of which 80 were reinforcements. It was a tense time as those who had been through the horrors of the battle linked up again with the base details and those purposely left out of the attack. Lt Middleton went to find out what had become of his platoon; only six men had returned uninjured.

At 5.00 p.m. that night the Commander of VIII Corps came to speak to the survivors of 94th Brigade. Although he was very laudatory of their efforts nothing could disguise the scale of the disaster to the men.

The next day they had another shock. Those who expected to stay at Louvencourt to rest were sadly mistaken. At 10.00 a.m. they were fallen in for a 20 mile march to Longuevillette, south west of Gezaincourt. There were many halts on the way, not for their benefit, but to allow troops heading to the front to pass by. Lt Middleton did not know how the heavily laden men managed it at all, tired as they were and in the heat of the day. He was now a Company commander and therefore entitled to a horse, so he avoided the worst rigours of the journey. However, in the afternoon he let his batman, 12/505 Pte E. Scholey, ride because he was completely done in.

At Longuevillette they were to rest and reorganise themselves. The village was undamaged and no other troops were in the area. Lt Middleton says it was a very pretty little place. Capt Allen, in temporary command, ordered that a daily arms' inspection was to be the only parade held. One unpleasant task still had to be undertaken, the calling of the roll and accounting for the missing.

The men were paraded at 10.00 a.m. on 7th July and the roll call began. When names went unanswered enquiries were made amongst the survivors to find out what had happened to them. This was very important since inaccurate information could lead to unnecessary heartache at home when the news came through. It was also pointless to list a man as missing if he had definitely been seen lying dead on the battlefield. This would only needlessly raise the hopes of relatives.

Almost half the names were unanswered. Of the 36 officers and 980 ORs in the Battalion on 30th June only 18 officers and 485 ORs were accounted for at the roll call. 18 officers and 495 ORs had become casualties during the past week, not including 75 more slightly wounded but who remained at duty. Just over half of the entire Battalion had been seriously injured or killed. The situation was actually worse than this since only 747 ORs had gone into the line on 30th June. So the actual casualty rate was 66%; two out of every three men committed.

The breakdown of officer casualties is shown below, unless otherwise stated all occurred on 1st July:

Killed	Wounded
2Lt A. J. Beal	Lt F. A. Beal
2Lt E. M. Carr	Capt J. C. Cowen – 28th June
Capt W. S. Clarke	Lt F. C. Earl
Capt W. A. Colley	Maj A. R. Hoette
2Lt F. Dinsdale	Lt G. J. H. Ingold

Lt C. Elam   Capt R. E. J. Moore
2Lt P. K. Perkin   Lt H. Oxley – 2nd July
2Lt C. H. Wardill   Capt H. W. Pearson
                              Maj A. Plackett
                              Lt F. W. S. Storry
                              Capt C. H. Woodhouse

Six of these officers receive little or no mention elsewhere in the book, and warrant attention here. Three of them had only joined the Battalion in June, and they were Lt H. Oxley and 2Lts F. Dinsdale and C. H. Wardill. Lt Oxley took over as the Signals Officer from Lt Bardsley, and in October 1917 transferred to the Army Signal Service. We know little of 2Lt Dinsdale except that he was 23 years old when he died. 2Lt Wardill, of 18 Violet Bank Road, Sheffield, was 39 and one of six brothers in the Army. One of the other brothers, 12/816 Pte S. G. Wardill was also killed with the City Battalion on 1st July 1916. 2Lt P. K. Perkin had been in the Battalion since 23rd April. He originated from Tiverton, but lived in Sheffield where he worked for W. Hutton & Sons on West Street.

Capt H. W. Pearson was a noted Sheffield golfer and motorist pre-war. He was seriously injured in the face and back, and evacuated to hospital in Bristol. Lt F. C. Earl recovered to become the Adjutant of the Local Defence Battalion in Sheffield for the rest of the war. He was the stepson of the Reverend C. Ellis and lived at Wales Vicarage.

The breakdown of OR casualties resulting from the roll call was as shown in the chart below. Over the following months it changed continuously as missing men were accounted for, but the total number of casualties remained the same. Of the 201 men shown as missing all but 18 of them were actually dead. The final reckoning was to be 8 officers and 240 men killed in action (kia) or died of wounds (dow) on 1st July. Others died later, but it is more difficult to separate them from men who became casualties in later actions.

	A Coy	B Coy	C Coy	D Coy	Totals
Kia	6	15	8	16	45
Dow	1	2	2	7	12
Wounded	76	62	43	56	237
Missing	44	44	71	42	201
Totals	127	123	124	121	495

It is interesting to note that the companies suffered almost equal numbers of casualties.

Included amongst the killed were two pairs of brothers. Ptes A. and R. H. Verner, of Spring House, Calow, Chesterfield, are both commemorated on the Thiepval Memorial. L/Cpl F. R. and Pte W. W. Gunstone, of 11 Ashland Road, Netheredge, are both buried in Luke Copse Military Cemetery.

The other assault battalion, 11th East Lancs, had suffered even worse, with 21 officers and 564 ORs becoming casualties. The two Barnsley Battalions had not been so badly hit, but still had a considerable number of killed and wounded. Total casualties were 12 officers and 274 ORs for 13th York & Lancs, and 10 officers and 265 ORs for 14th York & Lancs. The Brigade lost 1,747 men altogether, including the casualties from the LTMB and the Machine Gun Company.

By way of comparison it is interesting to study the casualties sustained by the Germans. 169th Regiment had faced the whole of the 31st Division and some elements of 4th Division as well. During the period of the preliminary bombardment the Regiment had lost two officers and 224 ORs, and on 1st July 12 officers and 353 ORs. It can be seen how ineffective the bombardment had been when considered against the effort put into it.

The bodies in NML would lie there until the spring when the Germans withdrew to the Hindenburg Line. It was too risky to try to recover them. So they lay there rotting away in the summer heat.

The stench on the battlefields was unbearable, and everything became impregnated with it including the men's clothing. When they came out of the line they carried it with them. Of the 248 officers and men of the Sheffield City Battalion killed on 1st July 1916, 165 were never identified. They are still on the battlefield or buried in one of the graves marked simply, 'A Soldier of the Great War - Known unto

God'. Their names are commemorated on the Thiepval Memorial along with 73,412 others, who perished in the Somme battles of 1916 and who have no known grave.

At home it was the families of the missing that suffered the most. For the relatives of a man that had died there was a finality to the bad news. For those with a son or husband listed as missing, however, there would be a year of hoping and praying before the listing was altered to 'missing presumed killed'. After a few weeks many accepted the inevitable. But there were others who could not come to terms with their loss, and tried any means to find out what had become of their loved one. Soldiers home on leave were constantly pestered for information, one of them was Douglas Cattell.

'It was a harrowing time for me with the mothers of my friends asking for information about their sons. When I told them that they had been killed or were missing they wouldn't believe me. In fact in some cases it cost friendships.' 12/70 Cpl D. E. Cattell.

The newspapers in Sheffield printed photographs of the missing and appealed for information as to their whereabouts. It was hoped that wounded men evacuated to England would read the article and get in touch with the family. Some did but the news was rarely good. One who responded was 12/200 Pte J. W. Norton, of Fulwood Park, Sheffield. He was evacuated to Bristol, and in hospital he wrote to the Sheffield Daily Telegraph telling of the death of his friend 12/196 Pte F. Nichols, a machine gun team leader listed as missing. After the war his body was not identified and he is commemorated on the Thiepval Memorial. Before the war he lived at 23 Tom Lane and was employed by Hadfield's.

The Lord Mayor wrote to the War Office about the missing from the City Battalion, and a reply was received in early August. The War Office had been inundated with enquiries, and a list of the missing had been sent to Germany via the Red Cross, for circulation around hospitals and camps. In the Sheffield Daily Telegraph of 3rd August the Lord Mayor undertook to collate all the details from relatives of the missing through his own office, and to act as the link between the War Office and the families.

For most families confirmation of their loved one's death would be received in March or April 1917. The Germans retired their line early in the year to better positions on the Hindenburg Line, and the battlefields of 1916 were left exposed. At Serre the skeletons still lay in NML and many were identified from their ID discs or letters etc. Where possible the remains were buried, but many of the corpses could not be identified.

One body that was identified was that of 12/922 Pte R. E. Gapes. In March 1917 his remains were buried in a cemetery in front of John Copse, and the Padre wrote to his relatives telling them about the burial. Sadly when the war ended the grave could not be found and he is commemorated on the Thiepval

Burial of two British soldiers on the Somme front, 1916.

Memorial. There is still a cemetery in front of Luke Copse and it is more than likely that Pte Gapes lies in one of the 'Unknown' graves within it.

After a year of being listed as missing the War Office presumed a man was dead. It was only at this stage that many relatives finally accepted their loss. Some though could never accept it. 12/961 Pte E. Hough was the youngest of four sons. His mother lost the will to live soon after the news of his death came through, and died soon afterwards.

Even after the war there were those who still could not come to terms with their loss. The father of 12/851 Pte F. 0. Appleby searched the Serre battlefield in the forlorn hope of finding a trace of his son. He was not successful. Known as F 0, Pte Appleby before the war had worked for the Sheffield Savings Bank, and lived at 163 Ellesmere Road. On the night of 15th-16th May under heavy fire he had helped to rescue the men trapped in collapsed dugouts.

Some remains were found years after the war. Indeed an average of 10 men are recovered from the battlefields of France and Belgium each yea to this day. The most notable example in the City Battalion was 12/1831 Pte A. E. Bull. Hi remains were found on the site of the old Britisi front line at Serre on 13th April 1928, and were buried in Serre Road No. 2 Military Cemetery. A concrete cross was erected on the spot where his body was found and can still be seen just inside the Sheffield Memorial Park in Mark Copse.

The rebuilding of the Battalion began immediately. The same day as the roll call was held a draft of 56 men arrived. At about the same time a batch of parcels arrived, and many of them were for those missing or killed. Orders were issued to open the lot. Nothing was to be returned in order to spare the feelings of the people at home. At least the survivors had a decent feed of the contents of the parcels, which otherwise would only have been wasted.

> 'It was a sad day, many pals had gone and we had to start clearing up the effects of those who would not return. This task was mainly done by the officers. It was a mistake to form the Battalion from such a small area, as there was a greater feeling of loss all round.' 12/928 L/Cpl J. R. Glenn.

Having rested for only a day the Battali⸱ moved again on the afternoon of 8th July. (this occasion the march was of 15 miles Prevent via Doullens, arriving at 9.30 p.⸱ Here they boarded a waiting train. Most we so tired that they immediately fell asleep. T train pulled into Steenbecque station at 2.⸱ a.m. the next morning, and a cup of Bovril w served to the men before they resumed t march. They reached Merville at 2.00 p.⸱ The Division had by then passed to t command of XI Corps in his Army.

The Battalion was to spend the next fi days in Merville, but the men were not awa of this when they arrived there on 10th July. message was received that day from t Chancellor of Sheffield Universi⸱ congratulating the Battalion on its supe courage, while deeply deploring the seve losses. Although news of the disaster w

The dreaded notification forms sent out to next of kin. The form sent to relatives of the dead was very similar. Cpl Machen was also wounded on 1st July, 1916.

No._____
(If replying, please quote above No.)

Army Form B. 104

_____ *Infantry* Record Office,

_____ *York* _____ Station.

_____ 28-8- ____, 1916.

Sir,

I regret to have to inform you that a report has this day been received from the War Office to the effect that (No.) 12/1280

(Rank) *Corpl* (Name) *E. Machen*

(Regiment) 12/ YORK & LANCASTER REGIMENT was {*dangerously* *severely* *slightly*} wounded in action at *Ysenbte g General Hospital, Rouen* France on the 20th day of *August* 1916.

I am at the same time to express the sympathy and regret of the Army Council. *Contused Left Foot.*

Any further information received in this office as to his condition will be at once notified to you.

I am,

Sir,

Your obedient Servant,

_____

CAPTAIN,
I/c. No. 4 SECTION
FOR COL. I/c. _____
Officer in charge of Records.

(4 27 1) W 13081—273 400,000 3/15 H W V(P) Form/B. 104—S0/2

beginning to get through to Sheffield the Chancellor could not at that stage have really appreciated the true extent of the losses.

During the day at Merville the men undertook refresher training. All their equipment was carefully inspected and indents were prepared for replacement items. In the evenings they were allowed to go into the town, and visits to the Divisional baths were organised to remove the grime of the battlefield. Lt Middleton marched B and C Companies down to the baths on 12th July, and took the opportunity to have a bath himself.

That evening all the officers went to Callons-sur-Lys, where they were spoken to by the Commander of XI Corps. He was sympathetic towards them and promised to keep the Battalion out of the line for as long as possible. For all his good intentions this was only a few days away.

Meanwhile the training went on. Lts Middleton and Cowen went on a one day map reading course, which they claim taught them nothing new. There is a widely

Cross on the spot where Pte A. E. Bulls' remains were discovered in 1928. The ditch behind it is the remains of the old British front line.

held belief in the British Army that there is nothing more dangerous than a subaltern with a map! Probably for this reason the Army chose to brush up the skill at every available opportunity.

On 14th July the order came through to be at 30 minutes notice to move. Apart from this the men had another restful day. Lt Middleton was billeted with a French family and had become very friendly with the daughter. When she found out the Battalion was to move on she was very upset and cried. Before he left she gave him a gold locket which he hung on his ID-disc string.

Colincamps Sector 1.7.16

7/30 am

Barrage lifted from the German front line and first and second waves moved forward to the assault. They were immediately met with very heavy machine gun and rifle and fire and artillery barrage. The left half of "C" Coy was wiped out before getting near the German wire, and on the right the few men who reached the wire were unable to get through. As soon as our barrage lifted from their front line, the Germans, who had been sheltering in Dug-outs immediately came out and opened rapid fire with their machine guns. Some were seen to return to the second and third lines. The enemy fought very well throwing Hand grenades into his own wire.

NOTES: A great many casualties were caused by the enemy's machine guns; infact the third and fourth waves suffered so heavily that by the time they had reached No Man's Land they had lost at least half their strength. Whole sections were wiped out.

The German front line wire was found to be almost intact, particularly on the left.

A few men of both "A" and "C" Coys managed to enter the German trenches on the right of the attack, but in all other parts of the line men were held up, being shot down by the Germans in front of them. The few survivors took shelter in shell holes in front of the German wire and remained there until they could get back under cover of darkness.

The failure of the attack was undoubtedly due to the wire not being sufficiently cut. Had this been out the enemy's machine guns could have been dealt with by the men who managed to reach the front line. As it was, they could not be reached and there was no means of stopping their fire. Bombers attempted to silence them with grenades but could not reach them -consequent succeeding waves were wiped out and did not arrive at the German wire in any strength.

Summary of the actions of 94th Brigade on 1st July, 1916, from the after action report.

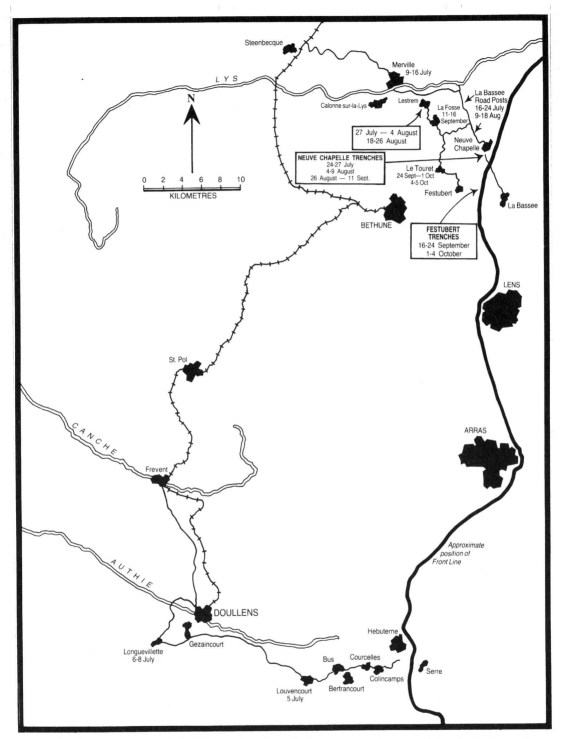

Map showing the movement of the City Battalion from the Somme to another part of the Line in the north.

Chapter Nine

Neuve Chapelle

3 1st Division was ordered to take over part of the front line held by 61st Division in the Neuve Chapelle area. 61st Division and the Australian and New Zealand Army Corps (ANZAC), were to attack Fromelles, and 31st Division was to hold the line while the preparations were made. Haig had ordered 1st and 2nd Armies to make small attacks such as this one in their areas. The intention was to wear down the enemy in readiness to break through when the offensive on the Somme eventually cracked the enemy front wide open. The plan was perfectly sound if the Germans were in danger of breaking. Sadly at this stage there was little real hope of such an event occurring.

Orders were received in the early hours of 15th July for the Battalion to take over a number of posts in the rear of the Neuve Chapelle area, astride the La Bassee road, 2,000–3,000 yards behind the front line. 2Lt W. H. Rowlands was selected as the officer in charge of the party. He had joined the Battalion in June, but had been left out of the attack on 1st July. At 7.00 a.m. he departed for the posts with 68 men of A Company and 28 men of D Company under his command.

The rest of the Battalion left Merville at noon the next day, and marched to Croix Barbee where they billeted awaiting further orders. Croix Barbee was one of the posts occupied by 2Lt Rowland's party. It was far enough behind the lines to allow the band to play for the men that evening, perched on top of a manure heap! The band was being given a good airing at this time. It played again on the evening of 17th July. On that occasion the venue was an orchard, somewhat more convivial than a dung heap!

The newly promoted Capt. Middleton toured the posts and noted in his diary that there was some shelling going on, but apart from that it was all quiet. The men were allocated buildings as billets, except for those manning outposts and the whole of B Company managed to cram themselves into one barn.

Advantage was taken of this comparatively quiet period to catch up on some essential training. This was important in order to assimilate the new draftees. Bombing was concentrated on, and 94th Brigade opened a Bombing School on 19th July. Courses of four days' duration were run under the instruction of 2Lt J. C. Cowen of the City Battalion.

German aircraft were particularly active in this area and several bombs were dropped on the Transport lines. No casualties were recorded. On the 19th a congratulatory message arrived from Lt Gen

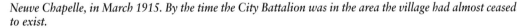

Neuve Chapelle, in March 1915. By the time the City Battalion was in the area the village had almost ceased to exist.

Another view of Neuve Chapelle in early 1915.

Hunter-Weston, the commander of VIII Corps. He had addressed the survivors of the attack on 5th July at Louvencourt and it is not known what purpose this written message served. In it he praised the heroism and discipline of the troops in their first big battle. He went on to say that they had proved themselves worthy to serve alongside the regular divisions. In Hunter-Weston's eyes there was no higher accolade than that.

The attack by the ANZACs and 61st Division went in on 20th July. The troops were ill-prepared for it and consequently the attack failed. 31st Division was not involved and spent the day confined to its billets, to avoid casualties from stray shot and shell. The following day a couple of posts were handed over, to 10th East Yorks, and on the 22nd the Battalion rotated the men in the remaining posts. Those coming out of the posts were sent to the rear for three days' rest.

Because the Battalion was still very weak 140 men from A, B and C Companies were formed into a composite Company under the command of Capt E. G. G. Woolhouse. They came under command of 14th York and Lancs and went into the front line trenches on the evening of 24th July. The area allocated to the City Battalion was between Church Road in the south and Oxford Street in the north, at a point not far from the famous Pope's Nose bulge in the line. In the meantime D Company moved into posts behind the front.

The front in this area was very active, and the Battalion was subjected to almost constant shellfire by artillery and trench mortars. During these bombardments a new type of trench mortar round was identified which proved to be far worse than the 'oil cans' they were accustomed to.

Wednesday 26th July brought the first batch of casualties since the attack on Serre. In the middle of the day the Composite Company reported that the Germans were registering targets behind the front line, just to the south of Neuve Chapelle. The targets were collections of buildings, and these were bombarded in the afternoon by the German heavy artillery. Many of the shells were duds, so although the shelling was troublesome it was of no particular danger.

Commencing at 5.15 p.m. German trench mortars began to fire on the front line and traversed along it from north to south. The fire was divided into three separate periods; 5.15–6.00 p.m., 6.30–7.00 p.m. and 7.45–8.15 p.m. When the firing was over the trenches had been blown in at many points and a lot of other damage had been caused. The WD reports three men killed and 18 wounded. Of the wounded two died over the next few days.

Next morning relief arrived and the men began to move to L'Epinette and Lestrem. The front line was taken over by A Company of 18th DLI, while D Company handed over its posts to elements of 15th and

16th West Yorks. By the evening of 27th July the men were settled into their new billets. The Battalion would lie out of the line for a week.

The weekend was spent resting, and on the Sunday a church parade was held in the grounds of a château. The GOC attended and the service was conducted by the Battalion's old Padre, Capt Colquhoun, who was by then the Divisional Chaplain.

Work began again in earnest on Monday 31st July. At 11.30 a.m. that morning Maj C. H. Gurney assumed command of the Battalion. He had previously served with 13th York and Lancs and was destined to command 11th East Yorks in 1918. The Brigade began running Field Work courses on the same day, assisted by 223rd Field Company RE. A six day programme was arranged to include wiring, sandbagging, revetting and demolitions. Capt Middleton and 2Lts F. H. Westby and W. H. Rowlands were sent on the course. On the first day they failed to find the place where it was being held. This tends to reinforce the theory about officers and maps not mixing well!

The rest of the Field Work course seems to have proceeded smoothly. The next day the men were shown models of the German trenches and later in the week erected barbed wire entanglements before going back into the line. Gen Sir Charles Munro, Commander of 1st Army, inspected the Battalion on 1st August, and watched the men being trained by the Sappers.

The rest was soon over and it was back to the trenches once again. This time the remnants of the City Battalion formed a composite Battalion with 11th East Lancs. The portion of line to be held was from Oxford Street northwards to Vine Street. It was just to the north of where they had been on the last trench tour.

The relief was completed by 5.30 p.m. on 4th August. The trenches in this area were found to be well constructed. Perhaps for this reason one of the newly joined officers, 2Lt Pirkis, confided to Capt Middleton his Company commander, that he enjoyed being in the line. Pirkis's experiences in the coming months would soon change his outlook on life in the trenches.

It was quickly realised that the length of line to be held was too long for the manpower available. B Company was therefore left isolated with both of its flanks open. Capt Middleton felt somewhat cut off because of this situation. His morale was not improved by a worsening medical complaint. For some time he had complained of sores all over his body. The complaint also affected his eyes and on the evening of 6th August the MO ordered him to rest. He was evacuated to the 2nd London Casualty Clearing Station (CCS) at Merville next morning, and 2Lt C. C. Cloud took over command of the Company.

Lt Col H. B. Fisher. CO of the City Battalion 18th August–3rd October, 1916.

While his kit was being sorted out at the hospital a medical orderly discovered two German rifle grenades and a Mills Bomb in his pack. The poor orderly almost had a seizure at the sight of these lethal pieces of ordnance in the peace and calm of a hospital. This demonstrates the gulf between the fighting soldiers and those who supported them. Capt Middleton had by then lived in danger for some months and had obviously grown accustomed to such items. Indeed many soldiers kept a frightening array of weaponry about their persons 'just in case' they ever came in useful!

Capt Middleton did not return to the Battalion, but recovered and went on to serve in the RFC in the Middle East and France, following a period with 1st York and Lancs in Salonica. With his disappearance from the scene we lose the last of our diarists, until the men wounded in July began to return to the Battalion in January 1917. For the next few months we are almost totally reliant on the WD for information.

In the trenches at Neuve-Chapelle the Battalion were subjected to frequent trench mortar 'stunts', but there are no reports of casualties until 9th August when one man was killed. The same day they were relieved by 13th York and Lancs and moved back to occupy the posts behind the front line trenches.

The next five days were spent in interminable fatigues and work parties. While some men manned the posts others humped loads of ammunition and rations to them to bring them up to their proper fighting scales. For at least one day B and D Companies did fatigues for the REs.

Relief by 2/8th Worcesters and 2/4 Gloucesters, of 188th Brigade, took place on 18th August and the Battalion marched to Lestrem. On the same day Maj H. B. Fisher arrived, to take over as CO. He had previously been the Brigade Major of 92nd Brigade. On 22nd August he was promoted to Lt Col. Maj Gurney became the Battalion 2IC.

Nothing of note took place in this period and on 26th August the Battalion was back in the front line, taking over from 2/4 Gloucesters. The position consisted of 700 yards of front line trench south of Church Road, and included Pioneer Trench and the Pope's Nose.

This trench tour was one of the longest the Battalion ever undertook. They manned the front line in this very active area for the next 16 days. In this time there were precious few quiet periods, and the tour of duty ended with a trench raid.

There was a constant bombardment of the Battalion's trenches which provoked counter bombardments of the German lines. This went on incessantly day and night. Often trench mortars thickened up the artillery fire, and at night machine guns played up and down the parapets in the hope of catching a careless sentry.

The WD does not record daily casualties at this time. There was a change of Adjutant on 16th August and this may account for the change in procedures concerning the entries in the WD. The Adjutant invariably made up the WD at the end of each day. Capt Tunbridge, who had held the position since the end of March 1915, had gone to 11th East Lancs as the temporary 2IC. He was replaced by Lt T. L. Ward, who later became a Staff Officer in the HQ of 94th Brigade in March 1917.

The CWGC record four men dying in the period up to 9th September. However, it is not clear if some of them died of wounds received in previous trench tours. The casualties were remarkably light in view of the heavy bombardments which were going on.

It was not always the Germans who started the artillery duels. Sometimes our own artillery began the tit for tat fire fights. Occasionally the routine was varied when the artillery lifted off the trenches and fired at the opposing side's gun positions. This counter battery fire was often reserved for just before an attack, in order to reduce the effectiveness of the enemy's artillery on the assaulting troops.

A raiding party of the York & Lancs enjoy a joke before the serious work begins. Notice the trench mortar bomb sticking up in front of the 4th man from the left. The 6th man from the left is holding a Mills hand grenade in his right hand. Most of the men are wearing single-piece suits to cut down on noise in NML.

The Battalion was ordered to mount a raid on the night of 9-10th September. During the previous day the medium trench mortars were kept busy cutting gaps in the enemy wire at the points where the raid was to enter the German trenches. This activity did not go unnoticed by the Germans and they took sensible precautions against an attack.

Just before midnight two raiding parties moved out into NML, commanded by 2Lt V. S. Simpson on the right and 2Lt J. Thompson on the left. In overall command of the raid was Capt T. E. A. Grant who remained in the front line trench to retain control. At 1.30 a.m. both parties launched their attacks.

Almost immediately the raid began to go wrong. A man in 2Lt Thompson's party started to choke in NML. Not unnaturally the men around him thought the Germans had released gas and about 20 of them withdrew. It proved to be a false alarm, but it caused considerable confusion. When 2Lt Thompson got to the wire he found it was damaged but not breached. From a shell hole he and 12/1412 Pte H. A. Wilson threw bombs into the German trenches a few yards in front of them. The Germans fired back and Pte Wilson was killed instantly by a shot through the head. His body was never recovered and he is commemorated on the Loos Memorial.

The other party had better luck and within a minute of Zero Hour 2Lt Simpson's men were in the enemy front line. They quickly discovered that the crafty Germans had evacuated their front line trench and blocked the communications trenches leading to the rear. 2Lt Simpson noticed that the trench was very strongly revetted, and the British artillery had made little impression on it.

The Germans held the trench 15 yards to the rear of their front line in considerable strength. A bombing battle took place, but despite the trenches being crowded neither side was particularly successful. About 15 of 2Lt Thompson's men also managed to get into the trench. Both parties spent about 15 minutes examining the trench and its dugouts for information. Once they had expended their bombs in the general direction of the flashes from the Germans' rifles and machine guns, they withdrew.

Occasionally the troops had the luxury of moving by bus.

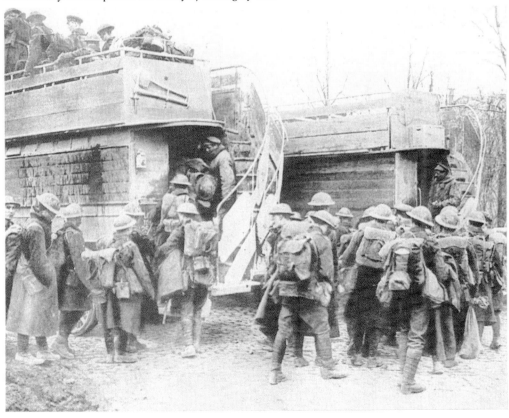

A German machine gun on the La Bassee road was most effective and caused a number of casualties in the withdrawal.

By 2.10 a.m. the parties had returned to their own lines and a check was quickly made to find who was missing. Stretcher parties were organised and went out into NML to search for the wounded.

Fortunately the supporting artillery was effective and for some unknown reason the Germans failed to properly utilise theirs. It was all quiet again by 2.30 a.m.

The Battalion lost four men killed, 20 wounded and four missing. One of the wounded later died. The four missing had in fact been taken prisoner, but this was not known for some time afterwards. It was estimated that the Germans had about 30 men killed and an unknown number wounded. However, not one prisoner was taken, which must have been disappointing after such an effort. Despite this a lot of valuable information was gained and the Army Commander sent his personal congratulations on a fine night's work.

During the early evening of the 10th patrols went out into NML, possibly to search for the missing from the raid. Just after 9 p.m. they spotted a German work party and dispersed it with machine gun fire. In the ensuing engagement a City Battalion soldier was killed.

While the patrols were in NML a curious discovery was made. A bundle of letters had been placed in NML in such a position that a British patrol was very likely to find them. A note attached to the bundle read, 'Letters of dead English soldiers'. They turned out to belong to men of the Royal Sussex Regiment, who had been in the area in June. It was assumed that the Germans had examined them and then put them back in NML so they would be returned to the soldiers' relatives. It was a kindly act which proved that there was some humanity even in the midst of the war's brutality.

The Battalion was relieved on 11th September by 18th DLI, and moved into billets at La Fosse. The next three days were spent in work parties for the forward trenches. Then totally unexpectedly they were warned to move to Festubert, four miles south west of Neuve Chapelle. During 16th September the Battalion moved by lorries and buses to relieve 18th Manchesters in the sector between Lothian Trench and Quinque Rue. One man was killed during the relief, which was a clear warning for the men to keep their heads down in this sniper infested area. The dead man was 12/105 Pte A. H. Foxon, a pre-war student at Sheffield University who lived at Sheldon Road, Netheredge. He was buried nearby in Le Touret Military Cemetery.

While the rest of the Battalion was moving to Festubert the men who won medals on 1st July went to have them presented. At a ceremony at Merville the Commander of XI Corps awarded MMs to six soldiers. They were: 12/1164 L/Cpl M. B. Burnby, 12/923 Pte C. S. Garbett, 12/24 Pte H. C. Arridge, 12/354 Pte A. Downing, 12/443 Pte R. Marsden and 12/1118 Pte S. Vickers. Details of their actions are in the Appendix Decorations 1916-18, at the end of the book.

Festubert in 1915.

On a sadder note 7595 Pte J. A. Haddock was executed by firing squad at 6.14a.m. on the same day for desertion and was buried in Vielle Chapelle Military Cemetery at La Courte. He may have been a former regular soldier and certainly served with 4th York & Lancs, the Sheffield Territorial Battalion (Hallamshires), for a time. He was recalled when war broke out and served at the front with 2nd York & Lancs from early in 1915. On 9th July 1916 he was transferred to 10th KOYLI and 11 days later was admitted to 99th Field Ambulance with shell shock.

Haddock was transferred to the City Battalion on 9th August in a draft of 28 soldiers. On arrival he was allocated to B Company by 12/481 RSM C Polden and this party was guided into the trenches by 12/275 Pte G. C. Wright (awarded the DCM for 1st July 1916). By the time the party arrived at B Company Haddock had disappeared. Five days later he was discovered seven miles from the Battalion's trenches by the Military Police.

Haddock's defence was that his feet were playing up and a medical officer had told him he needed rest. He lost his way trying to find the Transport and when apprehended he was looking for the Police to ask for directions. His evidence lacks any credibility. His orders were quite clear; to follow Wright into the

12/105 Pte A. H. Foxon.

trenches. Claiming he was looking for the Military Police for directions five days after disappearing and seven miles from his unit, while hiding in a civilian wagon having abandoned his equipment and rifle wasn't going to convince anyone.

Despite the damning case against him Haddock may have escaped with his life had it not been for a string of previous cases. He had absented himself seven times since August 1914 and had also been punished for being drunk on active service and refusing to obey an order. However, of greater consequence, on 3rd April 1916, he was found guilty by a Field General Court Martial (FGCM) of desertion and sentenced to 20 years penal servitude. The GOC of Second Army had reduced the sentence to five years suspended and he was to soldier on.

This time Haddock had gone too far. He was tried by FGCM on 24th August and the sentence was inevitable given his past record – death by firing squad. However, the court, which had no discretion on sentence given the circumstances, recommended mercy. The chain of command did not agree and the sentence was endorsed at entry level for the Brigade Commander all the way up to General Haig himself, who confirmed it on 12th September 1916.

Haddock was one of 300 soldiers executed on the Western Front during the war. It is easy to be critical when judged against today's liberal values. However, attitudes were different then and the judgement against Haddock needs to be considered with that in mind. In mitigation Haddock had been at the front for 16 months, may have been wounded (not proven), suffered shell shock and had recently lost his wife at home. But thousands of other men endured the same and came

Pte Haddock's gravestone in Vieille-Chapelle Military Cemetery.

through it. Understanding of combat stress was in its infancy in 1916, so rather than criticise the execution we should consider it against the circumstances of the time. In addition it must be borne in mind that he had been dealt with leniently on numerous previous occasions, contrary to the general impression most people have gained about the capital courts martial in WW1.

There is no mention in the Battalion WD of Haddock going missing, his discovery, the trial or execution. His name appears in the CWGC register but not in 'Soldiers Died in the Great War'. Most of the information about this case comes from the court maritla records held in the National Archive at Kew. An unconfirmed source says that Haddock's son was later adopted by a CSM from the Battalion. The family is said to have lived in the Lincoln area, but the CWGC register gives his father's address as Ranskill Road, Tinsley Park, Sheffield.

Apart from the snipers, who were a continous nuisance, and the occasional artillery exchange, the Festubert area was reasonably quiet. After a short tour the Battalion handed over to 14th York and Lancs on 24th September, and moved back to the defended village of Le Touret. Since losing Pte Foxon there had been no further casualties until the time came to move out. During the relief 12/2047 Pte J. S. Fairclough was killed and Capt T. E. A. Grant was wounded in the forearm.

Although they were officially out of the line, the Battalion sent 200-man work parties to the front line for the next three nights. On 29th September all the available officers and 100 ORs were sent to Pacaut to see a demonstration of the German flamethrower. It is always well to know the capabilities of your enemy's weapons, but the flamethrower had a terrible effect and the men probably left in a sober mood after seeing it in action.

On the morning of Sunday 1st October the Battalion went back into the trenches at Festubert to relieve 14th York and Lancs. The whole Division was by now under orders to move again, and the tour was to be a short one, but it ended in tragedy.

The CO, Lt Col Fisher, had been away at a conference at 1st Army School and got back to the Battalion on the afternoon of 2nd October. In the small hours of the 3rd he was touring the Battalion's position to get to know the layout and visit the men.

The defences in this area consisted of a series of disconnected breastwork posts. The ground was too wet to dig deep trenches so the only alternative was to build artificial ones above ground level. As Col Fisher was moving from one of these posts to the next a lucky shot from a rifle set up on fixed lines, hit him in the head and killed him instantly. He was buried that afternoon in Le Touret Military Cemetery. The service was attended by Brigade and Divisional representatives.

Next day the Battalion, commanded once again by Maj C. H. Gurney, was relieved by 1st Battalion Royal West Kent Regiment. The men returned to their billets in Le Touret. On 5th October they began the move back to the Somme area.

Chapter Ten

Return to the Somme

The Battalion was out of the line until the end of October, but it still suffered a number of casualties on work parties. Commencing on 5th October they started a slow move southwards, which ended in familiar surroundings at Warnimont Wood.

The journey was not difficult, and on the first day they only marched for three hours before billeting at Vendin les Bethune. Next day found them only six miles further on at Robecq. It was here that they heard a rumour that the Kaiser had hung himself. Although the men were pleased to hear this there was no truth in the story.

After a training day the journey resumed on 8th October, with a six mile march to Berguette. Here the Battalion entrained for Doullens, and on arrival they marched to Marieux and billeted there.

The journey south was broken at Marieux for eight days, during which time the Battalion rehearsed its part in an attack. On 11th October they practised communicating with aircraft from 5 Squadron RFC. Later on they took part in an exercise as the centre battalion in a brigade attack. Each battalion was formed into four waves with 100 yard gaps between waves, and battalions separated by 200 yards. The supporting barrage was represented by men with flags who advanced to simulate the various lifts the men could expect.

It is not known if this exercise was to rehearse a specific operation or for general refresher training. Certainly the City Battalion did not take part in an attack for some time after this. It is likely that they were practising for a particular operation which was later cancelled.

A number of changes took place whilst at Marieux. On 12th October Maj C. H. Gurney, who had been acting as CO since the death of Lt Col Fisher, departed for England. He attended the Senior Officers' School at Aldershot in preparation for taking over his own battalion.

Before he left a fête was arranged in his honour, but it was not without its complications. The Drill Manual laid down the correct method of executing every movement of arms drill, and the penalty for an officer who messed up an order was invariably a round of drinks for the Sergeants' Mess. Maj Gurney ordered the Battalion to fix bayonets while their rifles were at the slope, an impossible movement to carry out.

Maj Gurney's expensive mistake captured by 12/332 Pte George Leslie Tirebuck. His artistic talents were later put to good use when he joined the 94th Brigade Concert Party, "The Nissan Nuts", as a scenery painter.

> 'I had been told that day there was an important person of the French General Staff who would probably pass our way, and might visit and want to inspect us. It spoilt my morning, with a perfectly new Battalion of reinforcements, and to my horror I saw afar a most elegant French Officer on a lovely horse with red and gold trappings galloping our way. I gave a perfectly unusual order, as this caricature shows, and when the danger was over, I leaned over to my Sergeant Major and said, 'I fear this means free beer to the Sergeants' Mess tonight', and he replied most discreetly, but with a twinkle, 'I fear it does, Sir'. Maj C. H. Gurney DSO.

Maj Gurney was replaced by Maj C. P. B. Riall who had been 2IC of 13th York and Lancs. He was a regular officer with 18 years' service, including the South African war. He wasted no time on arrival. The next afternoon, following a morning of physical drill, weapon training and tactical manoeuvres, he took the whole Battalion on a route march. He followed this on 14 October by an inspection of the entire unit, including the Transport lines

Meanwhile other events had been taking place. Some of the officers and NCOs had made a familiarisation tour of the trenches in the Divisional area. There was a lecture to all available men on the latest weapon of war, the tank, at Sarton on the 14th. Throughout the period further drafts of reinforcements were coming through. Late on 15th October 93 men arrived. They had been intended for 1/6th North Staffordshires, and originated from the Burton on Trent area. On 17th October another 48 draftees joined the Battalion. This batch came from South Lancashire. The very regional background of the origina Battalion was gradually broken down.

These new men were never fully accepted by the old hands, even when they became the predominant part of the Battalion. After the war they were debarred from membership of the 12th Club unless directly elected, whereas the original members of the Battalion were automatically life members.

Lt Col C. P. B. Riall, CO of the City Battalion 12th October 1916–15th May 1917.

No sooner had the last draft arrived than the Battalion was moving again. In two days they marched to the camp at Warnimont Wood, with an overnight stop at Famechon. On arrival they had a difficult job carrying all the stores up the hill on which the Wood was situated. This had to be done by the light of hurricane lamps and took four hours to achieve.

The Battalion was split up for a few weeks. On 21st October C and D Companies were sent under the command of the acting 2IC, Capt D. C. Allen, as a work party for 93rd Brigade, which was going into the line. They were billeted at Courcelles in old trench shelters and canvas bivouacs. The area was very muddy and unpleasant.

At Warnimont Wood A and B Companies settled down to more training, which was frequently interrupted with more work parties.

On some occasions both Companies were sent in their entirety, but on other occasions only 50 men were required.

One aspect of training that was brushed up on was bayonet fighting. To ensure that the correct techniques were taught 94th Brigade had an expert attached to it. He was CSM F. W. Freestone of the Army Gymnastic Staff, the predecessors of the Army Training Corps.

At about this time the effects of winter began to be felt. Even though they were out of the line their living conditions were still poor, and some of the men began to go down with winter ailments. In the month of October 48 men had to be evacuated. This rose to almost 300 men per month in January and February 1917. From October to April a total of 887 men were sent to hospital, and it was a far more serious problem than battle casualties, which were negligible by comparison.

Many of the sick were quickly treated and returned to the Battalion, but equally many others were never to return to active duty. New drafts just about kept up with the incessant drain on the unit's manpower. They should have been restoring the Battalion to its full establishment, but due to the high sickness rate the City Battalion never regained its pre-July 1916 strength.

On 27th October C and D Companies returned to Warnimont Wood, and A and B Companies went to the mud and filth of Courcelles. The work they did was mainly to assist the Sappers.

Some of the new draftees learned about the bitter realities of war the next day. While working in the streets of Hebuterne a shell landed amongst a party of soldiers. One man was killed and seven others wounded, all of them were new arrivals. The man who died was 31342 Pte R. H. Yelf who was one of the draftees intended for the Northants Regiment. He was buried in Hebuterne Military Cemetery.

On the evening of the following day another party was hit by shellfire at the crossroads in Hebuterne. Another one of the new men died, and five more were injured. A further two soldiers were evacuated with severe shell shock. On this occasion it was one of the Lancashire men who was killed, 38042 Pte J. Pownall. He had originally enlisted in the Lancashire Fusiliers and was 28 years old. His final resting place is in Couin Military Cemetery.

Hebuterne village church.

At 1.00 a.m. on 31st October orders were received to take over the left of the Hebuterne sector from 18th DLI. The companies at Warnimont Wood went cross country, and those at Courcelles met up with their guides at Sailly-au-Bois. The weather was atrocious with very heavy rain, and there was thick mud everywhere. Even the roads were covered in it. Some of the trenches were two feet deep in mud and the front line itself was knee deep in water.

A and B Companies went into the front line and the other two companies occupied the support trenches. The Hebuterne sector was particularly nasty. The artillery on both sides were always busy, and the Germans were very fond of gas shells. Despite the dangers the relief itself was accomplished without casualties.

Two days later, on 2nd November, a chance shell hit the Battalion HQ mess kitchen at Kensington House in Hebuterne. 12/559 LSgt T. H. Wood and 12/889 Pte C. F. Chamberlain were killed, as well as the Orderly Room Corporal of 1/5th York and Lancs who was there on a visit. It is strange that the two City Battalion men were buried in different places. Wood is interred in Sailly-au-Bois Military Cemetery, and Chamberlain in Hebuterne Military Cemetery. It is possible that Wood was being evacuated to a CCS when he died, and this would explain why he is buried so far from the place where he was struck down.

On the 3rd the Battalion was relieved by 14th York and Lancs and went into Brigade reserve at Sailly-au-Bois. Four days later they went out of the line for a rest at Thievres. For a change they had the luxury of moving by bus instead of the usual route march.

The rest period was uneventful and by the 12th the Battalion was billeted in huts at Warnimont Wood. The next day saw the opening of the Battle of the Ancre. The Battalion was held in reserve and took no part in the battle. However, two battalions of 92nd Brigade, 12 and 13th East Yorks, were included in the attack on the left flank of 3rd Division.

The circumstances of this attack had a number of similarities with that of 1st July. 92nd Brigade attacked from John Copse on a frontage of 500 yards northwards, to protect the flank of the main assault. Covered by the neutralising fire of 36 machine guns positioned to the south of Hebuterne, the two battalions initially did well. Unfortunately the main assault on Serre failed, and the Germans were soon able to give them their full attention.

They fought a desperate fight but were gradually bombed out of their limited gains and forced to withdraw. 92nd Brigade ended the day having suffered 800 casualties. One of them was a former City Battalion soldier, 12/647 ACSM F. L. Faker, who was killed. He had taken over as the CSM of C

Company when CSM Ellis had been killed in May 1916. Shortly before this attack he had been commissioned to 12th East Yorks. Another man in the same Battalion, Pte J. Cunningham, won the Victoria Cross for his actions on this day by repelling two German counter attacks single handed.

The day after the ill fated attack on Serre the Battalion went back into the line. They relieved 18th West Yorks in the same trenches they vacated 11 days previously. In the next two days five men were killed but the WD does not record the circumstances.

Very late on the evening of 16th November a patrol in NML, commanded by 12/304 Sgt W. H. Boot, ran into an enemy patrol just in front of the British trenches. Sgt Boot's men exchanged fire and grenades with the Germans, but were outnumbered and had to beat a hasty retreat, with one man killed. Later a strong fighting patrol left the cover of a sunken road to the north of the contact position, to sweep NML clear. It found no trace of the Germans nor of the body of the dead man. The CWGC record one man killed the following day with no known grave. Because of the late hour of the action on 16th November it is likely that the missing man from the patrol was listed as dying the next day. If this is so he was 38036 Pte J. Mylchreest, a 24 year old Manchester man, whose name is commemorated on the Thiepval Memorial.

Having been relieved by 14th York and Lancs, on 18th November, the Battalion took over the dug-outs and temporary huts in Sailly Dell. The Dell was about half a mile west of the village, and became a familiar rest area to the men over the coming months.

An uneventful rest period was soon over and on 22nd November the Battalion was back in the same trenches again. There was great excitement on the 27th when the first prisoner taken by the Battalion was brought in. A soldier of the 8th Bavarian Infantry Regiment was seen outside our wire and gave himself up.

14th York and Lancs relieved the Battalion in daylight on the 29th. This was unusual and was only made possible by a thick fog. Normally all approaches to the Hebuterne front were in full view of the German lines, and reliefs after dark were the norm. While the relief was in progress the fog momentarily lifted, and a party of A Company men were caught in the open by a German machine gun. Luckily the gunner judged his aim poorly and only one man was killed. He was 31291 Pte R. J. Heading, a St Albans' man who had originally enlisted in the Northamptonshire Regiment. His body was carried back by the men coming out of the line, and buried in Sailly-au-Bois Military Cemetery.

The period of rest at Sailly Dell was uneventful, however a number of changes among the officers occurred around this time. Maj Allen was evacuated to hospital on 1st December, and the CO went on a long leave commencing on 3rd December. His position was filled by Maj F. J. C. Hood from the 14th Battalion.

It will be recalled that Maj Hood had presided at the Court Martial of Sgt Crammond in Egypt. He had served in the South Africa War, in Paget's Horse and the Imperial Yeomanry, resigning his commission at the end of the conflict. On the outbreak of war in 1914 he immediately volunteered again, and became the Adjutant of 9th Battalion East Kent Regiment, (9th Buffs). He transferred to 14th York and Lancs as the 2IC in December 1915. Having been the temporary CO of the City Battalion he went to 13th York and Lancs as CO in January 1917, and remained there until June 1917 when he returned to the City Battalion as CO. During the course of the war he was awarded the DSO and was MID on three occasions.

The next trench tour from 5th to 9th December was uneventful. Having been relieved by 14th York and Lancs and two companies of 11th East Lancs the Battalion moved back to Rossignol Farm to rest. Maj Allen rejoined them there from hospital.

In the lead up to Christmas the Battalion was in the odd position of being split up while in the trenches. There was a staggered relief of 11th East Lancs, commencing on the evening of the 16th.

Maj Francis John Courtenay Hood DSO. CO of the City Battalion 5th December 1916-11th January 1917 and 1st June 1917-28th February 1918.

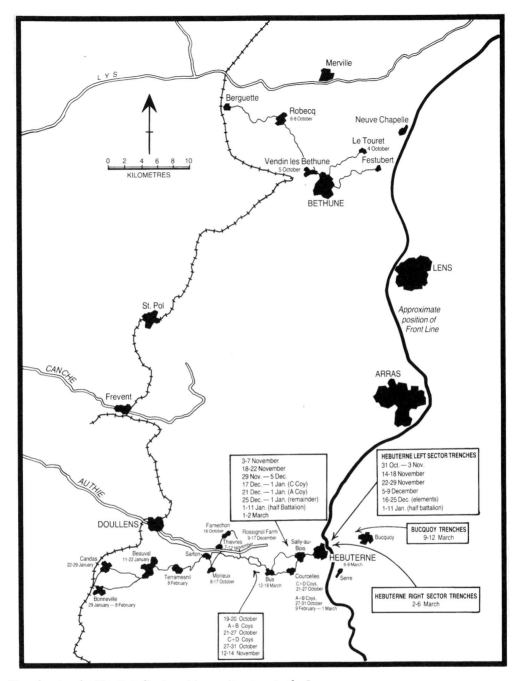

Map showing the City Battalion's position on its return to the Somme.

Detachments of B and D Companies took over the advanced posts in front of the left sector at Hebuterne, and next day the rest of the Battalion moved in. Almost immediately however, C Company was relieved by a company of 13th York and Lancs, and moved back to Sailly.

No specific details of this tour in the line are known save that 22260 Pte H. Garlick was killed on the 18th. He is buried in Sailly-au-Bois Military Cemetery. Relief began on 21st December, when A Company pulled out of the line to make way for A Company of 13th York and Lancs. On Christmas

Day the remainder of the Battalion were relieved by 14th York and Lancs, and made their way back to Sailly Dell.

Christmas celebrations were held on the 26th because of the moves on the previous day. As usual the rest was short lived. From the 27th onwards large work parties went out daily from the Dell, until it was time to go back into the line on New Year's Day. It was to be the same old trenches again, with the same grinding tedium of an inactive sector made worse by the weather. The Hebuterne area was very muddy, even by First World War standards.

At about this time some of the men wounded on 1st July 1916 were beginning to make a reappearance. Pte A. H. Hastings arrived at Etaples on the 4th and was warned off for drafting to the Battalion. On the 6th he and Pte T. C. Hunter were sent by train to Belle Eglise. There they were met by Lt C. C. Cloud who marched them, and the rest of the 99 strong draft, the 11 miles to Sailly.

Lt Cloud was one of only four officers not injured on 1st July 1916. When the QM fell ill in October 1916 he took over his duties, and those of the Transport Officer, until being taken ill himself later in the winter. He served for a period with 1/4th York and Lancs and at the end of the war was employed by the Ministry of Munitions.

When wounded officers were well on the way to recovery, they were sent to Crocken Hall at Leamside near Sunderland. This was the base of 3rd York and Lancs, a reserve battalion. In January 1917 Capt Middleton arrived there, and found Capt R. E. J. Moore and Lt G. J. H. Ingold there as well. They had both been wounded at Serre on 1st July 1916.

Meanwhile the Battalion had had a change round in the trenches. B and D Companies went out of the line and were replaced by A and C Companies. The troops out of the line had the usual round of fatigues to do, but there was some free time to visit the transport lines and listen to the band, or relax for an hour in the YMCA hut.

Maj Gurney returned from the Senior Officers' course in Aldershot, on the 10th, and resumed the post of 2IC. His stay with the Battalion did not last for long, for on 8th February he assumed command of 11th East Yorks on promotion to Lt Col.

On 11th January the two companies in the trenches came out of the line, and rejoined the rest of the Battalion in time for another move. The whole Division moved back into rest areas around Bernaville, and the Battalion was allocated billets in Beauval. On the same day the CO returned to the Battalion, and Maj Hood left for 13th York and Lancs.

Sparling described vividly the scene in the ruins of Sailly church that evening. The men rested in the church while waiting for buses to transport them to Beauval. The shattered building was lit by the eerie glow of coal braziers, and the snow fell in through holes in the roof. The heat from the braziers sent many of the soldiers to sleep. Those that could not sleep sang as shells screamed overhead on their way to destinations in the rear areas.

The men arrived in the early hours and were allocated to their billets. Pte A. H. Hastings slept in a pig sty, but made no comment about this in his diary. He had probably slept in worse places by then anyway.

Training began the same day with the emphasis being on battle drills at section up to company level. This went on until the 17th. As was normal during rest periods time was allocated to sports and recreation in the afternoons and evenings. The end of the training period culminated in a full inspection by the CO, held in the snow.

Over the next few days the men were subjected to a series of inspections, while the officers and the NCOs were lectured by the GOC of 31st Division. On the 18th the Commander of 94th Brigade had all his battalions on parade. According to Pte A. H. Hastings he then proceeded to mess them around and take them on a route march. Pte Hastings was convinced at the end of it all that the man was completely mad.

The same evening the officers were lectured by the GOC at the Mairie in Beauval. The subject is not known, but the NCOs had a similar lecture on the evening of the 20th. While the whole Division was out of the line it was an ideal opportunity for the GOC to instil his tactical ideas into his junior commanders. On the 19th the Commander of 5th Army, Gen Sir Hubert Gough, inspected the men while they were training.

On the morning of the 22nd the Battalion moved a short distance to Candas, and were inspected en route by the Brigade and Divisional Commanders. At Candas training continued, and more than the usual amount of sport was played. The weather was very severe and one morning Pte A. H. Hastings' water bottle was frozen solid, even though he had been sleeping inside a hut. The Commander of XIII Corps watched the companies carrying out practice attacks on the 26th, and the next day he addressed all the officers at Gezaincourt.

The character of the Battalion was gradually changed by the replacements. In A Company a friendly rivalry developed between the old hands and the new boys. On the 28th they played the first of a series of soccer matches in which Old A played against New A. On the first occasion Old A won 3-2. In the return match, on 5th February, the new arrivals had their revenge with a 3-1 win. However, the series went in favour of the old members of the Company when they won 3-2 in the third match on the 11th.

During the time these matches were being played the Battalion made another move, on 29th January, to Bonneville. Again there was plenty of training, but little else to report. After a week or so the Battalion had a two day march to Courcelles arriving on 9th February, after an overnight stop at Terramesnil. There had been considerable changes since the last time the Battalion had been at Courcelles. The place was in ruins and the remaining civilians had left. Shelling was almost continuous, and there was a constant danger of gas. The bell from the ruined church was used by the gas sentry as the village alarm.

After a few days resting the men began fatigues again, this time helping to build a railway. Many of the men had already done this kind of work in Egypt under 2Lt T. E. A. Grant. This time they were working for 2nd Canadian Railway Troops. Although the work made a change from the usual fatigues the men still had much to put up with. On the first day they reported for duty at 9.00 a.m., but did not get started until 2.15 p.m. In the meantime they were left in the freezing cold to wait. Such occurrences are commonplace in war, and are what lies behind the old adage that war is 90% waiting and 10% sheer terror.

The shelling in this area was heavy and eventually it found its mark. On the night of 15th-16th February two men were killed and five more injured. One of the A Company billets received a direct hit. These were the first fatalities in the Battalion since 18th December, although 12/1632 Pte J. T. Mitchell had died of wounds on 28th December.

At the end of February the Germans began their retirement to newly prepared positions on the Hindenburg Line. The Battle of the Somme had ground to a muddy halt in November with the British having little to show for some 500,000 casualties, save a few miles of devastated and almost impassable morass. The fighting had caused the Germans to adopt some awkward positions and during the winter they constructed new defences behind their front line system. When all was ready in the spring they began a steady and controlled withdrawal to these new positions.

The withdrawal initially caught the British unawares. Unlike the British commanders the German generals were prepared to give ground if it meant gaining a better defensive position. The onus after all was on the Allies to remove the Germans from their conquered territories, not vice versa. Not only did the withdrawal improve the German position, but it also shortened the length of the front and allowed them to withdraw some divisions from the line.

When news of the withdrawal was received at HQ V Corps, Gen Fanshawe ordered all units to regain contact with the enemy.

British troops in the old German front line following the retirement to the Hindenburg Line in early 1917. They look well pleased with their efforts, but the Hindenburg Line defences would be a costly nut to crack later on.

He was determined not to allow the Germans an easy time. A withdrawal is one of the most difficult operations of war, and is a great opportunity for the opposing army to catch the retiring force off balance. A full blooded follow up can have a disastrous effect and turn a withdrawal into a rout. However, the Germans were too wary to be easily caught out. They carefully planned the withdrawal in stages, allocating troops to cover the retirement of the main force.

94th Brigade was not initially involved in the follow up. 93rd Brigade was in action on the 23rd, but was stopped at Rossignol Wood. The Division then established itself along the Puisieux to Gommecourt road. On the 26th the Germans in front of Hebuterne fell back. As they did so 31st Division kept on their heels, but were unable to turn the retreat into a rout. The day before Serre had been taken by a battalion of the Warwickshire Regiment, without opposition.

At first the City Battalion was not involved but on 1st March orders were received for a short notice move to Sailly. On arrival the men went into Nissen hut billets to await developments, hopefully to follow up the Germans. This did not turn out to be the case and on the 2nd the Battalion took over the Hebuterne sector from 15 West Yorks. There was little need for extra security with the enemy retiring and 18th DLI were in front of the Battalion occupying the old German front line.

During the day of 3rd March the CO, company commanders and the Intelligence Officer (IO), went forward using the cover of the Sunken Road to recce the DLI positions. On the way back the road was being shelled so the recce party made their return over open ground. In the evening 14th York and Lancs relieved the Battalion, which then moved forward over the old NML, to take over from the DLI, north-west of Nameless Farm. During the day other elements of 31st Division captured Rossignol Wood and the Garde Stellung strong point. A few days later the Battalion moved into these positions.

Posts were established in the Garde Stellung-Rossignol Wood line. The position was consolidated and the area explored for information. This was a hazardous affair since the Germans had left behind booby traps, usually connected to attractive souvenirs such as binoculars and pistols. Soldiers were always on the look out for enemy equipment to take home on leave with them, and so they were favourite items for traps. The men also had to be on the look out for trip wires.

Hardly a stone left upon a stone in the village of Serre, 1917, after the Germans had withdrawn to the Hindenburg Line.

Sparling gave an impressive list of some of the types of traps found in these searches. There are no records of any casualties at this time, so we assume the Battalion were either very careful or very lucky. Some of the more ingenious traps are listed below.

1. A shovel stuck in between timbers in a dugout. When removed the shovel pulled a wire firing a mine.
2. A stove with its pipe left off. When picked up to put it back on a wire attached to it fired a hidden charge.
3. A thin wire stretched across the entrance of a dugout connected to a heavy window weight. When the wire was broken by a soldier entering the dugout, the weight fell into a box of detonators setting off a larger charge next to it.
4. One of the timbers lining the wall of a dugout was left sticking out at one end, with the nail protruding. Behind the nail was a cartridge percussion cap. When an unwitting soldier hit the nail to repair the wall it set off a large hidden charge.
5. A dozen stick grenades attached to a sandbag. The sandbag had to be removed to gain entry to a dugout. At the same time it set off the grenades.
6. A charge left up a chimney, with the fuse dangling down. When a good blaze was going, off would go the charge.
7. Lumps of coal had holes cut in them and detonators inserted. When put on a fire they exploded sending fragments of the coal into the men warming themselves.
8. A branch was placed over the entrance of a dugout as if to conceal it. When removed it started a two minute time delay fuse. This allowed the searchers time to get deep inside the dugout before exploding a huge charge, completely destroying it.

There were many variations on these examples. Almost anything could be made into a trap, with a little ingenuity.

As the Germans fell back the length of the front line was gradually shortened. This benefited both sides. On 6th March units of 46th Division took over the line and the Battalion made its way back to Hebuterne in daylight, suffering one casualty wounded on the way. For the next few days the men were tasked with salvaging useful and serviceable equipment from the old trenches around Hebuterne.

The Battalion was in for a very hot time over the period 9th-12th March. Orders were issued to take over the front line at Bucquoy near Puisieux. While the Battalion was moving up to the trenches the RSM won his MC, (see Appendix "Decorations 1916-18"). During the afternoon the Battalion relieved 14th York and Lancs, and took over the advanced posts after dark. During this phase a short sharp action was fought.

Men of 14th York & Lancs had been manning one of the advanced posts when they were surprised by a German fighting patrol. As the relieving patrol from the City Battalion came along they too were attacked by the Germans. Four men were missing and another five wounded. The CWGC record three deaths on the 9th and 10th, probably from this action. None of them have known graves, but strangely two are commemorated on the Thiepval Memorial and the other on the Arras Memorial. There is no explanation why a man killed on the Somme should be commemorated at Arras.

The pathetic remains of a British soldier on the Somme.

The Battalion's position was held in considerable depth. In front were eight posts in strengthened and consolidated shell holes, plus three more posts slightly behind them in support. Each post was held by an NCO and up to 12 soldiers, with a Lewis Gun. All the men were from two companies. Another company formed the support line and the last company was held back in Battalion reserve.

There was constant artillery activity by both sides, with the British concentrating on wire cutting. By night patrols and wiring parties were sent out, and much work was done to generally strengthen the position. The patrols were intended to find out if the Germans were to stand or continue their retirement.

On the evening of the 12th the Battalion was relieved and moved back to the White City, close to Serre. The Division went into General Headquarters (GHQ), and Army reserve and did not go back into the line until 1st May at Arras.

The Somme battlefields of 1916 were by then behind the British lines and the task of clearing up the gruesome remains of that dreadful conflict now began. At Serre V Corps began to establish cemeteries:

> *The Padre asked me if I would accompany him to visit our old front line and NML, which was littered with British dead. Ours were in lines where they had fallen. They were just skeletons in khaki rags and their equipment. We walked up to the old German wire. The Padre had brought a friend with him and the three of us turned back to look towards our lines. Then the Padre said a prayer for the dead, and we sang Hymn No 437 from Hymns Ancient and Modern, 'For all the Saints'. I've still got that hymn book, it holds a very poignant memory for me. Next morning the dead were buried by an overnight fall of snow. It was to be some weeks before NML was cleared when V Corps began to make new cemeteries to finally lay our pals to rest.'* 12/928 L/Cpl J. R. Glenn.

The Padre referred to by Reg Glenn was Frank Ford. He was a family friend of the Glenns' and continued to take a great interest in the Battalion post war. He took enormous risks to visit the men in the trenches. He also had a small organ which Reg played for him at services in the field.

On 14th March Padre Ford wrote to Reg Glenn's mother about the service in the old NML. He mentions singing Hymn No 499, 'On the Resurrection Morning' amongst the corpses. He also sent a copy of a poem written by the officer who accompanied them. We have tried to find who he was and if the poem was ever published, both to no avail. The poem's title is incomplete, probably as a security measure. The gap is probably a place name.

The Heroes of ————— Tree
  There they lay, as for months they had lain,
  In 'No Man's Land' of the Picardy Plain,
  Two long waves by the German wire
  Advancing, caught by machine gun fire.
  With bowed head and lips closed tight
  We passed, deep moved by the tragic sight,
  Then, voicing the wish of the rest, one said
  'Oh, Padre, pray for these heroes dead'.
  At break of dawn, to our surprise
  The world was white before our eyes;
  A Mighty Hand in answer spread
  A pure white mantle o'er the dead.

Some of the burials from this period are somewhat perplexing. For example, two soldiers of the City Battalion killed 1st July 1916 are buried some distance from the battlefield. Their resting place is in the Australian Imperial Force (AIF) Burial Ground at Grass Lane near Flers, famous as the site of the first tank attack. The cemetery contains the remains of many Australians killed in the later fighting on the Somme.

It is difficult to understand why they were buried so far away from where they fell, but there are a number of possible reasons why this is so. The first is that the remains were not identified until after the war, and they were subsequently buried in a cemetery with space. This is not plausible. Why take the bodies so far when other cemeteries near Serre have numerous late burials in them? Another theory is

Thiepval Military Cemetery at the end of the war. Gradually the CWGC replaced its temporary wooden crosses with the familiar white Portland gravestones.

that they were captured by the Germans, having been wounded in the fighting, but subsequently died and were buried. After the war the bodies were concentrated in the nearest British cemetery. Certainly after the war the CWGC did rationalise the hundreds of tiny battlefield burial grounds into proper cemeteries, and this entailed the wholesale exhumation and reburial of thousands of bodies. Perhaps the reason will never be known. The CWGC were not able to help with the rationale behind these burials.

Having rested in the White City dugouts for a short time the Battalion was soon moving again. Even the WD, normally a turgid and dry commentary, remarked that the men were very tired at this stage. They marched to Bus les Artois, where they were to stay for six days. There they were to train before starting the long march to the north, which eventually brought them to the battlefields around Arras.

The march was taken in reasonably easy stages, covering the 60 miles in six days, with a rest day in the middle. The route took them first to Beauval, then on to Bouret sur Canche via Doullens. Later they passed through St Pol and billeted at Valhoun, where they rested for a day. Merville was reached on the 25th having billeted at Ecquedecques the night before.

The Battalion remained at Merville to rest and train until the morning of 8th April. Battalion HQ was set up in Les Lauriers, a château-farmhouse on the Merville to Hazebrouck road. The morning after arriving Pte T. C. Hunter went for a bath before breakfast, and spent the rest of the day lazing around. There was also the chance to go out for evenings in Merville. Up to the end of March life was slow and easy, then training began once again.

The usual old subjects were rehearsed, such as route marches and bayonet fighting. There was also some organisational training in the war of movement, which it was hoped would soon return. Each section was given a specific task within its platoon, making the Battalion a more balanced and potent force.

It was at this time that the 1917 establishment was being introduced. Many practices that had crept into the infantry were now being formalised. A complete battalion organisation is given in the appendices at the end of the book, and a look at the organisation of a platoon will suffice here.

The infantry platoon retained its basic organisation of four sections, but each one now had a specialised role. There were two rifle sections to carry out assaults and to man defensive posts including one equipped with rifle grenades; a Lewis Gun section, to give covering fire; and a Bombing section.

The Lewis Gun section was 10 men strong, as were all the sections, and had one gun. It provided the immediate, intimate fire support for the platoon.

The Bombing section was the platoon's close range artillery, with hand thrown grenades. They were used to break up enemy attacks, or destroy difficult enemy posts in the attack.

With the Battalion's organisation on a surer footing, another move was made. The Battalion was in reserve to XI Corps and was moved up in readiness to exploit any success from the attack on Vimy Ridge by the Canadians.

On 8th April the main part of the Battalion moved to Oblinghem near Bethune, and a small party of four officers and 49 ORs were detached to the XIII Corps Reinforcement Camp at Robecq. Acting Capt E. L. Moxey was in command, and 2Lts S. Crawford, G. C. M. L. Pirkis and H. Booth accompanied him.

Eric Lawrence Moxey was born at Sao Paulo, Brazil in 1894. Before the war he was at Sheffield University, and was a well known Hallamshire motor-cyclist. He became the Battalion's Machine Gun Officer, and in July 1917 transferred to the RFC. In 1938 he was recalled into the Special Reserve of the Royal Air Force Volunteer Reserve as an Acting Squadron Leader. He served at the Air Ministry in the Special Branch as a Technical Intelligence Officer, dealing with unexploded bombs. On 27th August 1940 he volunteered to defuse two bombs at Biggin Hill, at the height of the Battle of Britain. Sadly one of the bombs exploded and he was killed. He was awarded a posthumous George Cross, the highest award for bravery out of contact with the enemy, and often referred to as the civilian Victoria Cross.

It was apparent that the standard of training of newer draftees was not as high as they had previously been. The detached party was sent to give the new arrivals an induction course prior to arriving in the Battalion. There was not the time to train them while other work was being carried out.

On 25th April the size of the instructional party was reduced, and 2Lt Pirkis plus 25 ORs returned to the Battalion. The remainder of the party moved to Pernes on the 26th.

On 9th April the Battalion stood by while the Arras offensive commenced, and Vimy Ridge was carried. But they were not called upon to go into action. On the 11th they moved again to La Bourse

Canadians on Vimy Ridge after its capture.

near Noeux les Mines. The next two days were spent in reconnaissance of the area around Bully Grenay, especially the assembly trenches. It seems an attack was being planned, but it never came to fruition. On the 14th the Battalion was on the march again, this time to Hermin. Here another period of intensive training was carried out, the emphasis being on open country fighting, with various tactical manoeuvres associated with the assault being practised.

RSM Polden was presented with his MC ribbon by the CO on the 16th. Otherwise the period was spent training, resting or in recreation. Following a searching kit inspection, on the 28th, the men began to move up to the front once again. The first stage was to Ecoivres, near Mont St Eloi, where they billeted in huts on the high ground outside the village. It was a very hot day and the men had a hard time of it on the march. On the 30th they marched on to Maroeuil and the hot weather continued. The area the Battalion moved into was also very hot, but it was not usually the sun that provided the heat.

Ruins of the Windmill at Gavrelle.

31st Division men in the trenches at Gavrelle.

Chapter Eleven

Arras

The peaceful time spent in GHQ and 1st Army Reserve came to an end on Sunday 29th April 1917. Under a blazing hot sun, unusual for the time of year, the Battalion marched from Hermin to Ecoivres. On arrival they were billeted in Nissen huts on high ground outside the village. Next morning the march continued to Maroeuil, and again the sun beat down onto the heavily laden troops. At least they had the luxury of sleeping in huts again that night.

31st Division was moved to the Gavrelle sector to take advantage of the capture of Vimy Ridge by the Canadians. It was to relieve 63rd (Royal Naval) Division and 2nd Division, on a total frontage of 2 miles. It was hoped that another advance would take place with fresh troops. However, the more experienced amongst the men could see that the ground was unsuitable. The effects of the winter, and the recent fighting, had made it all but impossible to move forward the heavy guns necessary for another successful attack. This however, did not deter the generals. The 2nd and 31st Divisions were ordered to attack on 3rd May in what was officially known as the Third Battle of the Scarpe.

The City Battalion played only a small part in the attack. It began to move into position on 1st May, into trenches that had been part of the old German third line beyond Roclincourt. The position was known as 'G6 Central' from its map reference, and was about 1,500 yards south-east of the village itself. After an uncomfortable night they spent the next day preparing to support the attack. The Battalion was under the command of 93rd Brigade. The Company commanders and their runners went forward during the day on a reconnaissance of the front line trenches at Gavrelle. At 5.00 p.m. the CO held a conference to discuss the next day's action, and announced that the Battalion were to hold themselves in readiness to support any part of the attack.

During the night of 2nd-3rd May the Battalion relieved 18th DLI and sent 7 Officers and 324 OR'S on working parties. The new position was only a mile away and the men were established by 1.30 a.m. For the rest of the night they sheltered in a railway cutting and a copse called Bois de la Maison Blanche.

The attack by both assaulting Divisions had limited success. 2nd Division made some progress, but exhausted itself to such an extent that it was useless as a fighting force thereafter. 31st Division had a mixture of success and failure. 92nd and 93rd Brigades attacked with 94th Brigade in support. A heavy preliminary bombardment had merely served to create more cover for the enemy. It had also reduced Oppy Wood to a tangled mass of smashed trees which was almost impassable to the assaulting troops. 93rd Brigade was partially successful, but 92nd Brigade had a very rough time of it, and even lost the famous Gavrelle Windmill for a time in a German counter attack. The enemy artillery fire was very heavy and casualties amongst the attacking Brigades were consequently high.

During the day the City Battalion had a tense and confusing time. From the very early hours the CO was in attendance at 93rd Brigade's Rear HQ, close to the Bois de la Maison Blanche. At 6.00 a.m. he issued his first orders of the day, to the Hotchkiss machine gun detachment from the Northumberland Hussars, temporarily under the Battalion's command. Four of the detachment's guns were sent forward to Hill 80, some 1,500 yards in front of Bailleul. An enemy counter attack had been observed developing from the Oppy direction, and a strong reserve position was urgently required in case of a breakthrough. This demonstrates just how quickly the Germans could recover from an attack, and even take advantage of a local failure, to launch an immediate counter attack. The Germans were certainly not foes to be underestimated.

No sooner had the orders to the Hussars gone out than instructions were sent for two companies also to proceed to Hill 80 at best speed. A Company under Capt V. S. Simpson was despatched at 6.08 a.m., followed two minutes later by C Company commanded by Capt R. W. Leamon. They had to travel 4,000 yards, but because of the urgency of the situation no attempt was made to conceal the advance. The two companies shook themselves out into artillery formation and moved across open ground in full view of the Germans. Soon afterwards the remaining Hotchkiss guns were brought up closer to the Bois de la Maison Blanche in readiness for rapid redeployment to any danger spots.

Scene of destruction at Ecurie, near Arras.

The next orders, issued at 7.45 a.m., were for Battalion HQ, B and D Companies to move into a reserve position near Brigade Forward HQ, about 2,000 yards away. They moved over open ground, but like A and C Companies they experienced little interference in spite of being in full view of the enemy. The Germans obviously had more pressing targets than the City Battalion. At the same time the CO moved to the Brigade Advanced HQ in order to keep in touch with the situation, and await further instructions. The Advanced HQ had been carefully sited to overlook the whole of the Oppy-Gavrelle sector.

There now followed a very confusing period in which orders and counterorders were issued for B and D Companies. They were firstly sent forward from their reserve position to support one of the front line battalions. On the way they were redirected because of urgent reports that the left wing of the attack was being turned by the enemy. The two companies were to support 16th West Yorks, but at 9.02 a.m. the order was cancelled because of the development of another threat. B Company was sent to support 15 West Yorks on the right, while D Company was sent to the centre to support 18th West Yorks and 18 DLL. While the two companies were being taken forward by guides, D Company was redirected yet again. It moved into trenches in front of Bailleul and stood by to reinforce any part of the centre of the attack.

Meanwhile back at Hill 80 the threat of the German counter attack had petered out. A and C Companies spent the rest of the day there under constant shellfire. The trenches had been constructed with typical German thoroughness and casualties were light. The Battalion lost only six men killed throughout the day, which is remarkable in view of the time the men were exposed to the enemy. It is, however, sad to reflect that these men died having achieved nothing towards the attack.

During 4th May the Battalion reverted to the command of 94th Brigade. That night C Company relieved 18th DLI in the front line south of the Arras-Gavrelle road, and Battalion HQ moved up to just behind Gavrelle. Another man was killed and three others wounded during the day.

That night the men watched a spectacular sight, as the ammunition dump at St Nicholas just north of Arras, caught fire and they were treated to an impromptu fireworks display of immense proportions. The dump was over five miles from the City Battalion men but it was still an awe inspiring sight even at that distance.

The next few days were spent at a spot known as 'RC2' in front of Bailleul. Extensive enquiries have failed to ascertain why this place got its strange name. It does not appear to be a map reference. The

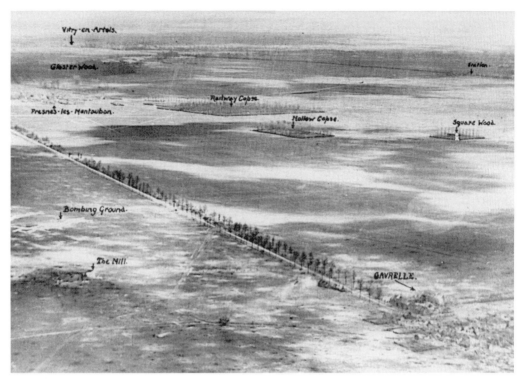

Air photo looking east showing the area around Gavrelle and the Windmill.

Battalion installed itself in some old German gun positions which proved to be of the usual high construction standards.

In this reserve position the men suffered from the intense daytime heat, but at least they could watch the antics of the duelling aircraft. A Company remained at Hill 80 until relieved by two platoons from 11th East Lancs on 7th May, and the same day the rest of the Battalion handed over their positions to 15 West Yorks.

Once again complete, the unit took over trenches to the north of the Bois de la Maison Blanche. A rest of sorts was taken in this area, but there was no escaping the confusing and alarming orders. On 8th May the Battalion was stood by to move from 8.40 a.m. onwards. At 8.00 p.m. the order to move eventually came; they were to close up behind Bailleul, and quickly set off. However, before reaching the destination the orders were cancelled and the Battalion returned to its trenches, remaining on 15 minutes notice to move throughout the night.

The evening of 9th May saw yet another move, this time back to the front line. At 8.15 p.m. they met guides and went forward to relieve 14th York and Lancs, in the right subsection of the 94th Brigade front at Gavrelle. This included the Windmill, a desperately held post important to both sides and which neither would easily relinquish. It was constantly fought over and claimed many lives. D Company drew the short straw on this occasion and was allocated the Windmill position. The Company had two platoons on the flanks of the Windmill itself, with the other two platoons in support to the south-east.

> *'Gavrelle Windmill, that was a horrible place. You dared not move or show yourself during the day. Everything had to be done at night. It was the worst place that I had ever been in, just like a charnel-house. There were bodies and bits of bodies all over the place, British and German. A butcher's shop. It stunk to high heaven.'* 12/1298 Pte D. C. Cameron.

Gavrelle proved to be one of the most unpleasant and unhealthy places in the entire British line. The entries in Pte T. C. Hunter's diary for the period 9th-13th May are monosyllabic. For each day there is the single word, 'Hell'. Both sides kept up constant fire and the artillery joined in. There was also the

A wiring party of 2/4 or 2/5 York and Lancs in the Oppy/Gavrelle area preparing to go out into NML after dark. The soldier on the right is wearing 1914 leather pattern equipment. On the left is the entrance to a dugout.

continual danger of gas attacks. The situation at night was even worse, with darkness hiding a multitude of unseen dangers.

Casualties steadily mounted. On the 9th 2Lt J. Thompson and eight ORs were gassed. Five men were wounded the next day, but the heaviest losses were sustained on 11th-12th May. On the 11th five men were killed, and 2Lts J. M. Sinclair and H. G. Mann plus 27 ORs were wounded. The next day 2Lt R. D. Berry and three men were killed, and 2Lt G. H. Jarvis and another 23 OR's were wounded.

The men hung on desperately waiting for the promised relief. An advance party left the trenches on 13th May to prepare to receive the men, but they returned when it was discovered that the neighbouring Brigade was also in relief that night. It was too dangerous to risk both Brigades being off balance at once so the Battalion had to wait another 24 hours.

The longed for relief by 14th York and Lancs arrived at dusk on 14th May. The City Battalion moved to what were described as 'rest trenches' to the north of the Arras-Bailleul road. The last two days in the front line had resulted in further additions to the lengthening casualty lists. Officer casualties were high; 2Lt F. A. Davies was killed, and he is commemorated on the Arras Memorial; 2Lt N. H. Malkin died of wounds, and was buried in Duisans Military Cemetery; and 2Lt A. R. Steven, attached to the Battalion from 5th Battalion Scottish Rifles (5 Cameronians) was wounded. In addition one OR was killed and another eight wounded. The high proportion of officer casualties is not surprising in view of their duties. They had to make frequent visits to isolated posts to check on their men, and consequently they were more frequently exposed to enemy fire than were their soldiers.

The Battalion WD describes the time spent in the rest trenches as being occupied with training and resting. There was however, a constant danger from long range artillery and casualties continued to be sustained. Because of this it was considered foolhardy to have the CO and 2IC in the line at the same time. So on 15th May the 2IC departed to await developments at the Transport lines. He did not have long to wait. On 18th May Lt Col Riall had to be evacuated. Having been under immense strain over the past few weeks his health had rapidly deteriorated, and he finally cracked under the pressure. Maj Allen returned to the Battalion in time to take it back into the front line that day.

The Battalion relieved 14th York and Lancs at Gavrelle in exactly the same position it had left only

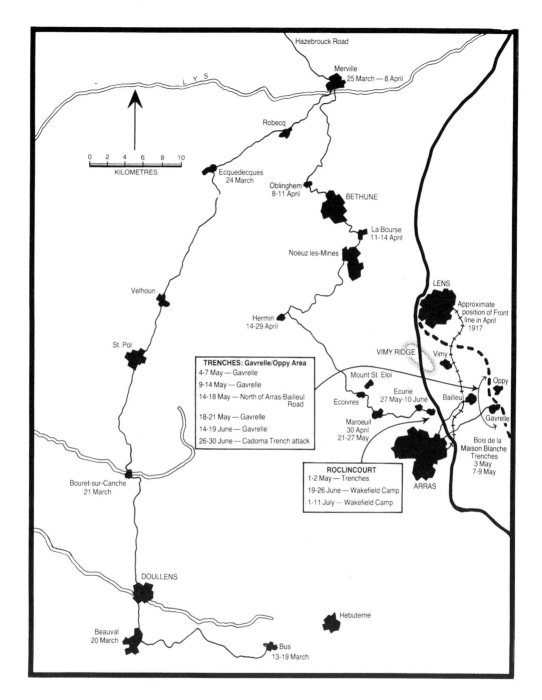

The map shows place names with dates:

Hazebrouck Road

Merville
25 March – 8 April

L Y S

Robecq

Ecquedecques
24 March

Oblinghem
8-11 April

BETHUNE

La Bourse
11-14 April

Noeuz les-Mines

0 2 4 6 8 10
KILOMETRES

Velhoun

Hermin
14-29 April

LENS

St. Pol

Approximate
position of Front
line in April
1917

VIMY RIDGE   Vimy

TRENCHES: Gavrelle/Oppy Area
4-7 May — Gavrelle
9-14 May — Gavrelle
14-18 May — North of Arras/Bailleul Road
18-21 May — Gavrelle
14-19 June — Gavrelle
26-30 June — Cadorna Trench attack

Mount St. Eloi

Oppy

Ecoivres

Ecurie
27 May-10 June

Bailleul

Gavrelle

Maroeuil
30 April
21-27 May

Bois de la
Maison Blanche
Trenches
3 May
7-9 May

ROCLINCOURT
1-2 May — Trenches
19-26 June — Wakefield Camp
1-11 July — Wakefield Camp

ARRAS

Bouret-sur-Canche
21 March

DOULLENS

Hebuterne

Beauval
20 March

Bus
13-19 March

four days before. The move up to the front line began at 8.30 a.m., and at midnight some men were still trying to reach their posts. Throughout the relief the German artillery was very effective, particularly at the Windmill.

The Windmill itself was occupied by 11 Platoon under 2Lt C. W. Pimm, who had only been in the Battalion for a month. He was assisted by his Platoon Sergeant, 12/656 Sgt J. W. Gould. They were heavily shelled and early on in the move 2Lt Pimm was killed. Sgt Gould however, kept his head and set about digging out the men buried by the shellfire, assisting the wounded and organising the position for defence in case of an attack. His Platoon's strength was steadily whittled away and a determined attack by the Germans would undoubtedly have overrun them. Following on behind 2Lt Pimm was Lt F. H. Westby's Platoon. When they arrived they found a scene of utter desolation. Sgt Gould had only three other men left standing; 2Lt Pimm and two others were dead and the rest were wounded. Sgt Gould was recommended for an award but received nothing in recognition of his splendid efforts that night. In January 1918 he was commissioned to 1/5th York and Lancs, and was killed on 13th October. Before the war he had been a teacher.

The relief of 14th York and Lancs cost the Battalion dearly. A total of seven men were killed and another 19 were wounded. The shelling and misery continued for two more days until the Battalion was itself relieved by 1st Battalion The Honourable Artillery Company (1 HAC), an infantry battalion in the Royal Naval Division.

Early on the morning of 21st May the Battalion came out of the line after 20 continuous days in the trenches. They took a very welcome hot breakfast from the field kitchens which had been set up behind the reserve lines, and then moved into billets at Maroeuil.

The casualties had been heavy. During May 1917 31st Division suffered 3,211 casualties killed, wounded, missing and POW. The City Battalion got away better than most other battalions. However,

Recommendation for a thoroughly well deserved medal that Sgt J. W. Gould never received. STAY in the signature block was the code name for the City Battalion on Field messages in case of capture by the enemy.

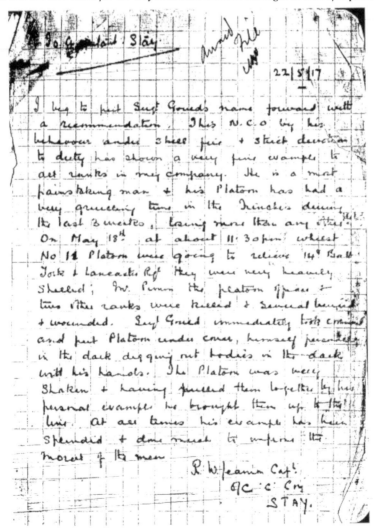

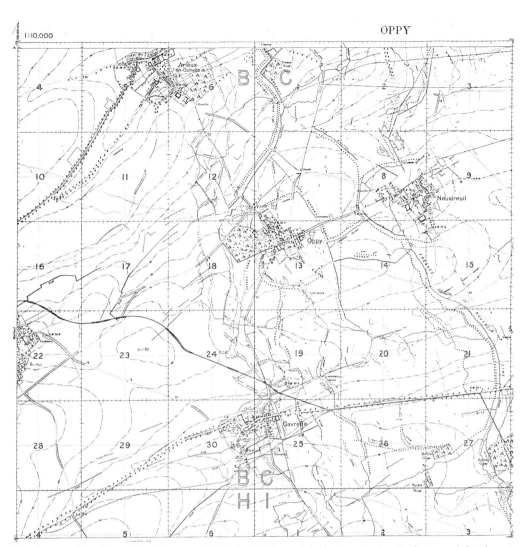

Trench map of the Oppy/Gavrelle sector in July 1917. Most of the features in the air photos and sketch maps in this chapter can be seen.

there are discrepancies between the WD and the CWGC records regarding the number of men killed. The WD records 21 men killed and one more died of wounds during May. For the same period the CWGC have records of 33 men killed and eight died of wounds, a difference of 19.

The most likely explanation is that seriously wounded men when evacuated from the Battalion would be recorded in the WD as wounded. If they subsequently died within a short time the CCSs or field hospitals would probably record them as killed in action. This would be the case if a man died in transit between the Regimental Aid Post (RAP) and the CCS. A man who died after being evacuated would not warrant another entry in the WD, hence the discrepancy between the WD and the CWGC records.

A German plane drops an aerial torpedo.

In addition to the men killed there were another 121 men recorded in the WD as being wounded. As mentioned above it is highly likely that 19 of these men later died of their wounds.

The Battalion had held the line for three weeks, during which time it took no direct part in any offensive operations, not even a raid, and had suffered almost 150 casualties. Such a wastage rate, averaging eight men per day, rapidly drained the unit's strength. A high percentage of the Army's losses were sustained in the unspectacular and unrewarding task of holding the line.

Following a few days of rest and continuation training it was back to work again. The Battalion moved to Ecurie on 27th May and that night began working in the Green Line, the name of the reserve line of defences at Gavrelle. Every night 300 men went into the Green Line and did four hours' work there before returning to Ecurie. The daily programme was:

> 7.45 p.m. March up to the trenches.
> 10.00 p.m. Commence work.
> 2.00 a.m. Finish work and march back to Ecurie.
> 4.00 a.m. Breakfast, followed by rest.
> 1.00 p.m. Lunch.
> 2.30 p.m. Company parades followed by training.
> 3.30 p.m. Recreation until tea-time then preparation for the night's work.

This went on until 10th June when the Battalion went back into the trenches again.

During this period a number of other notable incidents took place. On 1st June Maj F. J. C. Hood arrived to take command of the Battalion, and a few days later he was promoted to acting Lieutenant Colonel. Except for breaks for leave and courses he commanded the City Battalion until it was disbanded. He was well known to the men, having been in temporary command of the Battalion during December 1916 and January 1917.

Soldiers from various units in a camp in France 1917. On the left is 12/234 L/Cpl T. R. Slack, later commisioned to the East Yorks. 3rd from left in the front row is 12/218 Pte E. A. Reeve, also later commissioned to the East Lancs.

Work parties often had to contend with hostile fire, but at this time German aircraft proved to be the main hazard. Day and night the men were harassed by marauding bombers. At first the attacks were ineffective, even if they were somewhat unnerving. On 4th June however, three men were injured by a bomb. The Brigade Commander was not going to allow a few troublesome aircraft to bring a halt to normal military life, and the following afternoon the Brigade held a Sports Day to the south of Roclincourt. Teams were entered from all the divisions in the Corps, and the City Battalion only finished third overall. Obviously its sporting prowess was not what it had been!

After a fortnight of supplying working parties it was back to the trenches. The Battalion spent four days in Brigade reserve, taking over from the Hood Battalion of the Royal Naval Division. The main task was carrying parties up to the front line.

On 14th June the Battalion moved back into the front line at Gavrelle, taking over from 14th York and Lancs. The WD says very little about the next six days. The Brigade WD however, records that on 18th June the City Battalion established a post only yards from the enemy. This post was occupied day and night, and must have been a lonely and frightening place, especially at night when a sudden rush by the enemy could have overwhelmed it in seconds.

Although little is known of the operations during this tour, the Battalion lost five men killed and two more died of wounds. In addition another 17 men were wounded. One of those killed was 2Lt J. Buckland, on 16th June. He had joined the Battalion in February and commanded B Company for a period in May. He is buried in Bailleul Road East Military Cemetery.

One of the men that died of his wounds was 12/285 Pte E. Austin. He was hit by a shell on 19th June while on a ration carrying party. He was rushed to 8 CCS, but died there next day, and was buried in Duisans Military Cemetery. Soldiers often say that if a shell has your number on it there is nothing you can do to avoid it. The end result is inevitable so why worry about it? Back in October 1916, in Lansdowne Post at Neuve Chapelle, Pte Austin had been sheltering in a trench under heavy bombardment. A shell hit the parapet with a tremendous thud, but failed to detonate and slid to the bottom of the trench landing at his feet. When everyone had recovered slightly from the shock they examined the shell and saw it had the number 285 stamped into its base. The story went around the Battalion that Austin's 'number had come up' and he had survived. Because of this stroke of good fortune it was widely held that Austin would survive the war, but fate was not so kind to him on this occasion.

During the evening of 19th June the Battalion was relieved by 10th East Yorks. A short march took them to Wakefield Camp at Roclincourt, where they were billeted in Nissen huts. The whole of 94th Brigade was in the process of being withdrawn from the line to rehearse for a forthcoming attack in the Gavrelle-Oppy sector.

The Battalion's part in the attack was concerned with a section of the German front line called Cadorna Trench. The action has been referred to as the Cadorna Raid, but it had nothing in common with a raid at all. The operation was a carefully planned and prepared deliberate attack, with a defined objective to be taken and held. A raid was normally launched to disrupt the enemy, destroy his defences and take prisoners, but not to take and hold ground.

The attack was a small part of a much larger plan. In June 1917 the British were well advanced in their preparations for the forthcoming offensive in Flanders, which later became known as the Third Battle of Ypres, and culminated in the horrific struggle for Passchendaele. Before the offensive was launched the aim was to keep the Germans guessing where the blow would fall. Gen Horne, Commander of 1st Army, planned a series of small attacks to unsettle the Germans and divert their attention away from the Ypres area. He also decided to use these diversionary attacks to nibble away at the German defences around Lens until he could encircle the town. This aspect of his plan later had to be abandoned through a shortage of artillery. The Armies not directly involved in the Flanders offensive had given up much of their heavy artillery to strengthen the Ypres front, and without these resources it was pointless continuing with the side-show attacks.

When the Cadorna attack was launched, on 28th June, it was preceded by a bombardment fired by the whole of 1st Army's artillery on a frontage of 14 miles. This was to make the enemy think a general offensive on the Lens area was about to take place. The barrage also coincided with a violent thunderstorm, which must have added considerably to the noise and confusion.

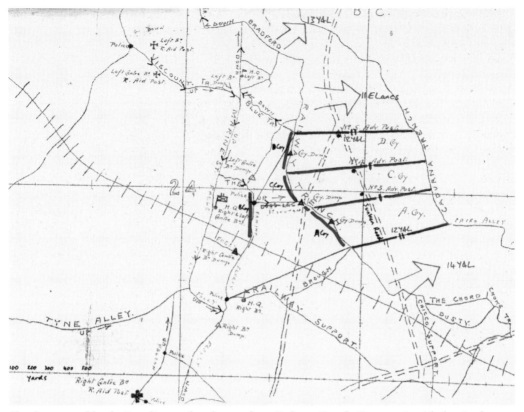

Sketch map used by the Battalion to plan the attack on Cadorna Trench. Compare it with the air photo on page 218.

The attack was to be carried out by two brigades. 94th Brigade, north of Gavrelle, was given a frontage of 1,000 yards, and 15 Brigade, opposite Oppy, had a frontage of 1,300 yards. 94th Brigade attacked with all four of its battalions in line, therefore each one had a frontage of about 250 yards.

The City Battalion was in the right centre of the Brigade. To the south was 14th York and Lancs and to the north were 11th East Lancs and 13th York and Lancs. Within the City Battalion three companies assaulted in line, with D on the left, C in the centre and A on the right. B Company was held in reserve. A Company of 13th East Yorks was attached as a carrying party, and was to follow up the successful attack with defensive stores to consolidate the newly won position.

Very careful rehearsals were carried out on model trenches at Brunehaut Farm, near Maroeuil. The Battalion practised its own part on 21st and 22nd June, and on 23rd and 24th the whole Brigade came together for a full scale rehearsal. The men were given the 25th off to rest before going back into the line during the night of 26th-27th June.

During the 26th, Maj Gen Wanless O'Gowan came to see the Battalion, and personally explained to them the reason for the attack and their part in it. At 9.35 p.m. that evening the men set off and took up their positions in the trenches by 11.15 p.m.

From the Operation Order it is known in detail what equipment the men carried. It is interesting to compare this with the kit taken into action on 1st July 1916. The assault troops wore basic fighting order, consisting of waist belt, shoulder straps, ammunition pouches, water bottle and entrenching tool. The haversack was worn on the back in place of the large pack, and inside it were rations, mess tins and solidified alcohol fuel blocks for cooking. The waterproof sheet was fastened under the flap of the haversack. Greatcoats were expressly forbidden to be taken. Respirators were worn on the front of the chest, where they could quickly be donned in the event of a gas attack.

A proper digging tool was carried by every man, in the ratio of 65 shovels to every 35 picks. They were secured to the men's backs in such a way that movement was not impeded. Three empty sandbags were carried by every man wrapped around the shafts of the digging tools. Although every man carried an entrenching tool as part of his basic fighting order, these were too small to dig a new position quickly. It was as essential to take a proper digging tool as it was to take a rifle.

Every rifleman carried 120 rounds of ammunition, with a few exceptions. Runners and signallers only carried 50 rounds each, presumably to leave an ammunition pouch free to carry messages in.

A system of coloured ribbons attached to the shoulder of every man, was used to denote each line and wave. Unfortunately the Operation order did not record the colour coding. As many pairs of wire cutters as possible were taken, attached by string to the shoulder straps and tucked into the waist belt. The overall weight was about 35 pounds, much less than they had carried on 1st July 1916, but still a heavy load to have to fight with.

Using a single trench periscope in the trenches in the Oppy/Gavrelle sector, 12th January 1918. The soldier is from an unidentified York & Lancs battalion. He is wearing 1914 Pattern equipment and a leather "body-warmer". On his chest is his respirator holder.

There were variations to the standard list of equipment, notably in the Lewis Gun teams, amongst the bombers and the officers and NCOs. The No. 1 in the Lewis Gun section, i.e. the man who carried and fired the gun, also had a revolver and 36 rounds. The section carried 20 ammunition pans, each filled with 47 rounds. An immediate reserve of another 22 pans was left in the front line trench. Bombers were ordered to carry their normal complement of grenades, but that was not specified. In practice they probably carried every bomb they could lay their hands on. In addition each bombing section was to carry four canvas bomb buckets each containing 15 grenades, and rifle grenadiers carried six rifle grenades each.

All officers and NCOs carried a notebook and pencil and report cards. Those with maps were to have an overlying trace showing the enemy trenches. No other documents were to be taken forward of the front line in case they were captured. Every NCO below the rank of Sgt carried two aircraft marker flares, and every Sgt and above carried a set of SOS flares. Each company had two Very pistols.

As part of the deception plan the assault troops were inserted into the line almost two days before the attack. It was hoped the Germans would think that the troop movements on the night of 26th-27th June were a routine relief in the line. For some reason they were not deceived, and at 5.00 p.m. on the 27th they shelled the British second line. C Company had a number of casualties as a result of this bombardment. Three men were killed with another dying of his wounds later, and another seven were wounded. During the night the troops occupied their assault positions and prepared for a long day waiting for Zero Hour, set for 7.10 p.m. on 28th June.

At 5.00 p.m. on the 28th the Germans repeated the previous day's bombardment of the assembly trenches. Some casualties were caused, but the well disciplined troops were not unduly affected. Even so the men's nerves must have been stretched almost to breaking point with the knowledge that the enemy appeared to know that the attack was coming, and presumably were fully prepared for it. By 6.15 p.m. it was quiet again and all the Companies reported that they were ready for the attack.

At 7.00 p.m. scaling ladders were fastened to the trench walls and bayonets were fixed silently at 7.05 p.m. Both actions were carried out very carefully to ensure that ladders and bayonets did not protrude over the trench top and alert the Germans. At 7.10 p.m. the artillery opened fire with an almost perfect barrage on the German front line. Simultaneously the first line of the first wave scrambled out of the front line trench, followed 20 yards behind by the second line. As the three assaulting companies moved

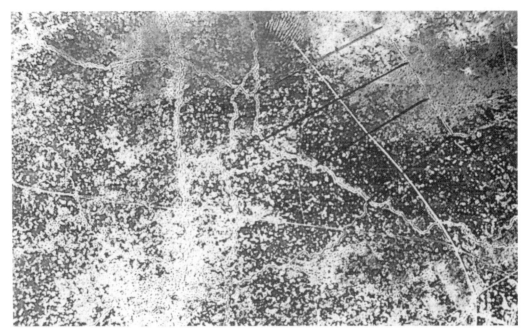

Air photo of the Cadorna Trench attack area. All the points marked on the Trench map can readily be seen on this photograph.

off, B Company left its reserve position in Famine Trench and advanced over open ground to occupy the now empty front line.

The assault troops moved rapidly over NML, pausing long enough in the Sunken Road to straighten their line and allow the artillery to lift off the German front line. Before the enemy could retaliate with their own artillery the City Battalion were in their trenches.

They had miraculously crossed NML without suffering a single casualty. The flanking battalions were also successful and the few Germans who could still fight were soon taken care of. In the 94th Brigade area 280 dead Germans were counted and over 200 POWs taken. The City Battalion took 28 POWs immediately and increased the bag to 50 before the night was out.

The second wave rapidly followed up behind the assault troops. Soon carrying parties were crossing NML, bringing in vital defence stores, including reserves of ammunition and concertina wire coils. Every load had been carefully made up to ensure that one man could comfortably carry it. By 7.17 p.m. when the Germans finally managed to fire their main barrage it was all over. Cadorna Trench was secured and nothing short of a major counter attack would retake it.

The work of consolidating the new line took all night. The British barrage had so badly battered Cadorna Trench that it was only 2–3 feet deep in most places. Work began almost immediately to deepen and reverse it. Over 7,000 sandbags were filled by the City Battalion to revet its 250 yards of the line.

A lot of the old German wire, now behind the front line, was moved forward of it and supplemented by the concertina wire brought up by the carrying parties. During the early hours of the next morning 14th York and Lancs took over some of the City Battalion posts in Cairo Alley. At 2.00 a.m. C Company pulled out of the front line, and at the same time A and D Companies shuffled inwards to fill the gap.

Each company put out two Lewis Guns teams 50-60 yards forward of their positions, and the front was held with five posts. Behind the posts a strong point was constructed at the junction of Cadorna Trench and Cairo Alley.

During the night of 30th June-1st July the Battalion was relieved by 14th York and Lancs and 11th East Lancs. After spending some hours in support the men moved back to Wakefield Camp. The Battalion's casualties for the period 27th-30th June were ten killed and wounded, although the WD only records nine deaths. Another man later died of his wounds.

German prisoners being searched for documents.

In part the disaster of 1st July 1916 had been avenged, almost a year to the day later. On 3rd July the GOC again visited the Battalion to congratulate the men on their outstanding success. The whole Division was taken out of the line for a well deserved rest.

The manpower crisis that would eventually cause the disbandment of the City Battalion began to be felt at this time. The Flanders offensive took all available reinforcements, and consequently other areas went short as a result. The City Battalion was so badly undermanned that D Company was disbanded, and the remaining three companies reduced to only two platoons each. A conference at Brigade HQ on 9th July concluded that battalions could not expect to rise above 700 men again. Each battalion was to form an HQ Company and reform its fighting element into three rifle companies, each of three platoons.

Apart from the reorganisation the troops mainly rested and undertook some night training. During the day sports were played and concerts were held in the evenings. On 9th July some men were sent to line the road at the Madagascar crossroads on the Arras-Souchez road, when the King drove past. He was on one of his periodic visits to the front.

31st Division was next moved to the infamous Vimy Ridge, captured by the Canadians in April.

OVER THE TOP
Preparations

Pte H. E. Bertaut.

I will now... explain to you the part played by a mere Tommy in an attack. We start about two days beforehand and draw extra iron rations, (consisting of bully beef, tea and sugar and very hard biscuits) and also a pick or shovel and two bombs.

Then there are various inspections of ammunition, rifles, field ambulance dressings and steel helmets etc. As the "day" approaches the platoon officer . . . parades all his men and speaks to them something like this. "Now men in a day or two's time I shall have the somewhat doubtful pleasure of leading you over the lid. I shall do my best to act as an officer should, and if anything happens to me I want you to take command in order of seniority. Each section commander knows what to do and I want you fellows to back him up and help him to do it. .." There are murmers from the irrepressible ones of "ear, ear" (sic), and then a list of the next of kin of each man is taken just in case. Then the order comes round, "packs in the QM's stores at 5 p.m., fall in at 7 p.m. ... at 7 p.m. you fall in, in "fighting order". .. You then proceed to march up to the trenches and when you get to the first of these the order is silence. .. and no smoking. By 3 a.m. you arrive like a lot of shadows at the assembly trenches from where you are to start the stunt and catch old Fritz unawares.

Der Tag

Previous to all this happening plans have been made at GHQ for the whole affair and a certain time is fixed and called "zero". That minute is the one in which the first wave mounts the parapet.. . we will call ours 4.10 a.m. At about 4 a.m. a desultory shelling by our artillery is converted into an intense bombardment and is carried on until 4.10 a.m. At 4.05 a.m. the platoon, already divided into a complete fighting unit (about 40 strong) of bombers, rifle grenade men and rifle men begin to get excited as the moment draws near. The last few minutes is (sic) the windiest... of the whole affair, the suspense makes it feel like an hour. A hissing whisper comes from the officer, although if he shouted he would not be heard owing to the rattle and crash of shells and machine guns, but like everybody else he is feeling the suspense and no doubt thinking of his girl somewhere in Blighty. He says 5 minutes to go, 4, 3, 2, 1, now boys . . .

Over

With that simple little word all feelings are banished and you scramble out of the trench and walk on towards a yellow glare, like a great bonfire which is really the flash of the shells comprising of our barrage. These barrages are a terrible curtain of fire poured into Fritz's front line by our guns of all calibres and our gallant Machine Gun Corps and their cheeky chatter. . . The idea (and it usually works all right) is to make him seek shelter of course, he is then at our mercy. That accounts for the large number of prisoners being taken. When a dugout is captured there are generally between 50 and 60 in one haul. Three or four of our men act as escorts for this lot to the rear of our lines... Although I have recently taken part in five attacks I cannot really analyse my feelings, while actually crossing "no man's land". One sees all his pals dropping around him and unconsciously says to himself "poor devils" and the next second is splitting his sides with laughing at a man who has been wounded and whose only object is to get to the shelter of our lines before the hubbub ceases and the snipers get to work. While all this is going on you never think of stopping but walk on as unconcerned as if walking down High Street. No doubt if a thought of danger entered one's head he would get down into one of the numerous shell holes knocking about which afford excellent shelter. As soon as Fritz gets it into his thick square head that trouble is approaching in big numbers he starts to retaliate and then the noise is deafening. . . When the objective has been captured the first feeling is of thirst and a desire for a smoke and the next of pleasure at having taken part in a successful stunt. Then comes the nerve trying time when you have to dig a trench under fire and prepare to receive any counter attack . . . After that comes a tedious waiting for the party who are to relieve those who have been "over the top".
12/1357 Pte H. E. Bertaut

Author's note:
Pte Bertaut was serving in the City Battalion on 1st July 1916, although he did not take part in the attack. He later served for a period in 10 York and Lancs before returning to the City Battalion. In February 1918 he transferred to 13th York and Lancs. As to when he took part in the five attacks mentioned in the text is not known. The original script is dated 20th June 1917, i.e. before the City Battalion attack on Cadorna trench. It is therefore likely that the attacks he refers to took place while he served with 10 York and Lancs. The account gives a vivid description of the soldiers' attitudes, and the sense of humour that kept them going.

Chapter Twelve

Vimy Ridge

In April the Canadian Corps had wrested Vimy Ridge from the Germans, and on 11th July they handed over the sector to XIII Corps. The same day the City Battalion began to move forward to take up positions on the Ridge, and that night they halted at Paisley Camp north of St Vaast. At 10.00 p.m. on 12th July the Battalion took over a section of the front line from 14th Battalion Canadian Infantry (14 Canadians).

For the next seven months the Battalion would be in and out of this area of the line. The period was characterised by high casualties, many of them due to gas attacks. There was also a noticeable change in tactics, with greater emphasis being placed on patrolling. The manner in which the patrols were carried out was very aggressive, and they were even conducted in broad daylight.

This was only possible because NML in this area was very wide, and allowed space for manoeuvre. It was a complete contrast to the Somme where only a very brave, or stupid, man peered over the parapet in daylight. To wander about in NML, except at night, was unthinkable.

94th Brigade established a six day cycle of reliefs. After six days in the front line a battalion spent the next six days in the close support trenches, known as the Red Line. The battalion would then spend another six days in rest either in depth support in the Brown Line or in one of the hutted camps in the area (called Roberts, Springvale and Cubitt). While resting in the last six days of the cycle battalions were usually tasked with work and carrying parties.

The camps in the rear areas were not particularly pleasant places. They were on land that had been battlefields during the previous three years. In addition to the old trenches, barbed wire, water filled shell holes and mud, there were also numerous corpses.

The dead of all nations were constantly being uncovered in all stages of decomposition. A number of the men commented in their diaries and letters about the human remains lying around, and the Graves Registration units exhuming remains around the camps.

The first spell in the front line was quiet with nothing to report, except for the presentation of the MC to Capt V. S. Simpson by Gen Haig at a ceremony on 16th July.

The Battalion was relieved on the 18th by 14th York and Lancs, and moved back to occupy the Railway embankment and Ridge line positions. After three uneventful days they were relieved by 18th DLI and moved back to a camp at Neuville St Vaast. It seems that the 94th Brigade six day cycle of trench reliefs had already broken down.

With two days rest behind them the Battalion formed nightly work parties from the 24th onwards. Each night a party of at least company strength went out at about 9.00 p.m., returning the following morning at 5.00 a.m.

The British had at last woken up to the idea of preparing for the effects of winter on their trenches. The work parties that the men were engaged on were geared towards preparations for the coming winter, and they had some success. Although it was still wet in the trenches they were at least passable, and although life in them was not pleasant it was at least bearable. Trenches were revetted and drainage systems installed. In front of the lines thick belts of barbed wire were erected, and to the rear hutted camps were erected for the men out of the line. In addition proper winter standing was provided for the many draft animals.

On the 29th the Battalion moved back into Brigade support, but the work parties continued every night until 3rd August, when they again took over the front line. During the relief of 14th York and Lancs a man was wounded. Amazingly this was the first casualty since going into the line on 11th July. The happy situation regarding casualties however, did not last for much longer.

The Battalion had just settled back into the routine of the front line when the Germans launched a surprise gas attack. This was the first of a series of gas attacks affecting the Battalion in this area. The men had experienced gas before but not in such heavy concentrations. They were also unprepared for the suddenness of the attack.

German gas shells laid out ready for firing.

At 1.30 a.m. on 6th August a heavy bombardment fell on the Battalion's trenches. Gas and smoke shells were fired by the German artillery, and their trench mortars and machine guns joined in to add to the general disruption and confusion. By 1.45 a.m. the barrage had ended. In this short space of time two officers and 58 ORs had been gassed and five other men were wounded. Later in the day two men were found to be missing. The attack came with no warning in what had been until then a quiet period. Many of those gassed were caught unawares as they slept in their dugouts.

The two gassed officers were 2Lts F. B. Wilson and J. Thompson. Frederick Brookfield Wilson was 25 years old, and had been a laboratory assistant at Sheffield University. He enlisted in the ranks of the City Battalion and he was commissioned on 7th July 1915. He went to the Reserve Battalion at Silkstone and rejoined the City Battalion on 15th August 1916. He died from the effects of the gas on 7th August, and is buried in Aubigny Communal Cemetery Extension.

The other officer, J. Thompson, presents us with one of the mysteries that First World War records often produce. Sparling lists a 2Lt J. T. Thompson dying of wounds on 6th August 1917. The CWGC have no trace of a J. or J. T. Thompson. It is likely that Sparling was confusing him with 2Lt Wilson, who died that day. According to the Army List, 2Lt. J. Thompson joined the Battalion on being commissioned on 8th July 1915. The 1917 Army List shows him under 8 York and Lancs, so it is likely that having recovered from the gassing he was transferred to that battalion.

On 9th August the tour in the front line ended and the Battalion moved into support at a position called the Beehive. The next day they went into Brigade reserve at Thelus, and the nightly work parties began again going on until the 16th. Having been relieved by 18th West Yorks the Battalion marched to Winnipeg Camp, at Mont St Eloi.

After the heavy casualties on 6th August there were only two others in the tours in the front line and support trenches. Both were officers. 2Lt H. Booth, who had joined the Battalion on 21st February 1917, was wounded on 13th August, and 2Lt G. C. Buzzacott was wounded on the 16th. He had only been in the Battalion since 12th June.

The trench strength, (i.e. the men who actually went into the line), of the Battalion had by this stage been reduced to 21 officers and 427 ORs, although on paper its total strength was 31 officers and 559 ORs. The other ten officers and 132 ORs were detached on other duties. Once again it was necessary to reduce the three rifle companies to two platoons each.

Following the tour in the trenches the men had two days' rest to clean up and to take part in some sports. There then followed an intensive period of refresher training. Riflemen and snipers fired their weapons on improvised ranges and courses were run for all the specialists. There were also night exercises in respirators, to overcome the problems of disorientation that this apparatus often caused.

The Sappers gave instruction in methods of revetting trenches to prevent the walls from collapsing. At the same time rehearsals for a raid began, using live Bangalore torpedoes.

Training went on until the afternoon of the 23rd, when the whole Battalion hitched a lift on a light railway to Neuville St. Vaast. At 7.30 p.m. they began to move forward to relieve 15 West Yorks in the Acheville sector of the line.

An innovation, the camouflaged suit, was introduced on 25th August to be used on daylight patrols. They proved to be very effective. At the same time active night patrolling began. The aim of the increased patrol activity was to keep in contact with the enemy and to dominate NML, which in this area was 1,000 yards wide and more in places. There was therefore plenty of scope for patrols to range widely, and for the junior commanders to use their initiative.

At first the patrols were very adept at making contact with the enemy, but initially the Germans seem to have come off best. Later the Battalion were to have a number of notable successes, but at first it suffered some losses.

On 28th August a C Company patrol encountered some Germans in NML and in the ensuing battle was driven back. One man failed to return. The next night a strong patrol of an officer and 16 men went out on another contact patrol, as they were called. They were seen by the Germans leaving the trenches, and before they got far into NML were heavily engaged by a machine gun and rifle fire. When everyone had scrambled back to the front line trench it was discovered that 19187 Sgt P. Footit was missing. A soldier from the front line saw him fall as if he had been hit. Later a search party failed to locate him, and next morning a camouflaged daylight patrol went out and also returned having found no trace of him. The CWGC make no mention of a man of this name. We can only assume the Germans followed up the engagement and took the wounded Sergeant prisoner.

During the night of 30th-31st August the Battalion was relieved by 14th York and Lancs, and moved back into Brigade support at the Beehive and Canada Trench. Apart from the usual work parties it was a reasonably quiet time until 5th September, when the Germans launched another massive gas attack. In a bombardment lasting two and a half hours they poured 5,000 gas shells into the Vimy area.

The Battalion were lucky on this occasion and avoided any casualties. That evening they relieved 14th York and Lancs in the front line at Acheville, and patrols went out almost immediately.

Daylight patrolling techniques were quickly perfected. On one occasion a patrol from the Battalion got to within 50 yards of the enemy front line. From there they could see the Germans' shoulder titles, and were therefore able to report that the 6th Bavarian Division had been relieved by the 11th Reserve Guards Division. The daylight patrols were also able to bring back valuable information on the locations of wire obstacles, defended posts, snipers and guard positions.

It was discovered the hard way that our own gas was every bit as dangerous as the Germans'.

On 10th September 2Lt D. O. Browning and three ORs in C Company were overcome when a gas cylinder in the front line was perforated by enemy trench shellfire. 2Lt Browning had been commissioned on 30th May and joined the Battalion on 3rd July. Even by the standards of the First World War his was not a long military career.

Apart from these four gas cases there were no other casualties on this tour in the line. The following day 13th York and Lancs relieved them

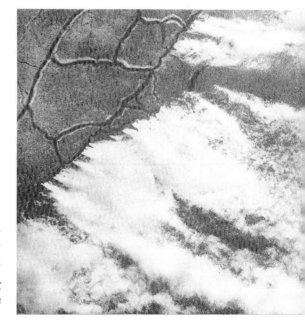

An air photo captures the moment when ORs in C Company were overcome when gas is released from a front line.

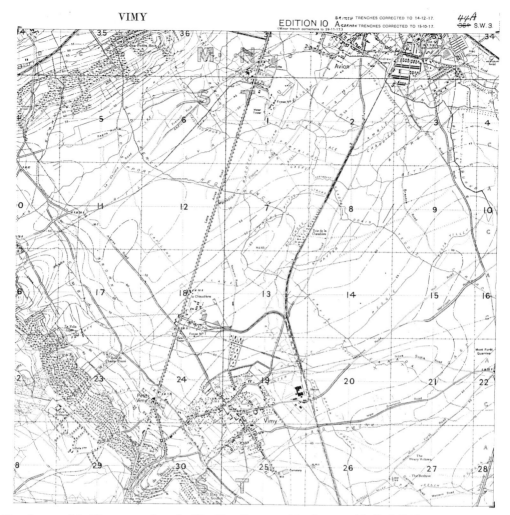

Trench map of the Vimy area where the City Battalion served in the second half of 1917.

and they moved back to Springvale Camp at Roclincourt. Here they were to undertake another period of intensive training. The emphasis this time was on patrolling techniques, and rehearsals began for a raid to be carried out during the next tour in the trenches.

During this rest period the Battalion was once again reorganised. A draft of 132 ORs arrived from 1/6th Battalion Norfolk Regiment (1/6 Norfolks), originally a cyclist battalion. This allowed the rifle companies to be increased to three platoons once again. The trench strength of the Battalion then rose to 475 ORs with an overall total, including those detached, of 595. The establishment of an infantry battalion in 1917 was 884 ORs. The Battalion was thus a third understrength, and this is typical of all battalions at this time.

The short rest ended on 18th September, and the Battalion went into Brigade support in the Brown Line. The same pattern of work parties undertaken on the last tour began again.

Reconnaissance patrols went into NML to observe the precise points of entry for the forthcoming raid. A Company had been selected to carry out the raid. On the second of these patrols Capt V. S. Simpson commanding A Company, went out to see for himself.

During the patrol he was wounded by a bullet in the arm, and although it was not very serious he still had to be evacuated. Capt Simpson was a very experienced, brave and competent officer. He had also been made responsible for the planning and execution of the raid. His loss left a void, which the CO

An officer checking his soldiers' gas masks.

himself chose to fill. For a week, (22nd–29th September), the raiding party went out of the trenches to live at the Transport lines, to train under the CO's personal supervision.

While the raiding party were training, the rest of the Battalion moved forward into the Red Line in front of Willerval, to relieve 11th East Lancs. At 12.00 noon the next day, 25th September, the Germans shelled the Battalion positions and B Company had three killed and three wounded. Except for one of the wounded all of these men were from a recent draft. Those killed were 235619 Pte W. F. Clarke, 235622 Pte E. J. Dicks and 235639 Pte W. E. Lake. They were all buried in Roclincourt Military Cemetery. It is sad to reflect on the workings of fate. Some men went through the whole war without a scratch, while these poor fellows were struck down almost on their first day in the trenches.

The rest of the time in the Red Line was taken up with more work parties, and the routine was only broken by the heavy aerial activity during the day. If the troops were bored at this time it was far preferable to what was to come. On 30th September the Battalion moved forward again and relieved 11th East Lancs in the front line.

The same evening that they took over the front line the Germans launched another large gas attack. From 8.00 p.m. to 9.30 p.m. at approximately 10 minute intervals, they fired salvoes of five gas shells from trench mortars. The gas was a mixture of Phosgene and lachrymatory gas.

Phosgene is an acute lung irritant, which even in fairly low concentrations causes serious debility and death. Lachrymatory gases came in many forms, but the most common types were akin to the modern tear gas. They could be fatal but only in massive doses. By and large they were a nuisance forcing troops to don their respirators, and thus reducing their fighting effectiveness.

The salvoes first of all landed in the northern part of the Battalion's position, but began to work southwards. As darkness fell the men could clearly see the burning fuses of the shells as they arced through the night sky towards them.

Casualties were caused by the suddenness of the salvoes, which hit a different portion of the line on each occasion. The salvoes were also very accurate, and many men were gassed almost by direct hits. 2Lt R. Marsden and 74 ORs were evacuated, plus 24 more from 13th York and Lancs and 16 from other units.

2Lt Rowland Marsden had been in the Battalion since 3rd September. Sparling says he died on 1st October 1917, presumably as a result of this gas attack. The CWGC have no record of him. According to the Army List he was alive in 1918 serving in 5 York and Lancs, and was promoted to Lt on 27th December 1918.

During the next day the men who were only slightly affected were allowed to rest and recover. However, some of the delayed effects were not felt until 2nd October when another 34 men were evacuated, bringing the total casualties to 109 all ranks. In one short attack almost a quarter of the trench strength of the Battalion had been knocked out. To make matters worse the raiding party had returned to the trenches on 29th September their training completed, and many of them were amongst the casualties.

Victims of a gas attack. Many have their eyes bandaged indicating mustard gas which especially affected wet areas on the body surface and the lungs.

Of those gassed only one man is known to have died. He was 235617 Pte S. Catlyn, who passed away on 1st October and was buried in Roclincourt Military Cemetery. He had only just joined the Battalion in the last draft.

The use of gas was, and still is, very controversial. Casualties in a gas attack were normally high, but the percentage of deaths was comparatively low. During the war British Empire forces suffered 190,000 gas casualties that were serious enough to be evacuated to the CCSs and beyond. Of these some 8,000 died. More men probably died on the battlefield and were not recorded as gas victims, but it is impossible to assess their numbers. They were certainly not great. The total number of deaths due to gas poisoning were a drop in the ocean when compared with the 996,000 Empire soldiers killed in action or died of wounds.

In a big attack the sheer volume of gas cases overloaded the CCSs and field hospitals, and imposed a severe burden on the logistic chain of the Army. Gas was a cheap and effective way to inflict casualties on the enemy, disrupt his medical services, and undermine the morale of his troops.

During the war gas was not the great killer that it has been purported to be. However, what cannot be fully assessed is its long term effects, but it is certain that men died of gas related illnesses for many years after the war ended.

In response to the German attack a massive retaliatory bombardment was organised for the night of 3rd-4th October. 31st Division's artillery fired over 50 tons of gas shells into the German positions. The various WDs consulted estimated that the enemy suffered heavy casualties, although it is not known on what evidence the assessments were based.

In addition to the retaliatory gas attack, orders were issued to respond much more aggressively to any type of German fire. Any fire was to be countered tenfold, using the next heaviest category of weapons. For example, if the enemy sent over one trench mortar round, the Division's artillery was to send back 10 shells. Similarly German rifle and machine gun fire was to be countered by trench mortar fire. Clearly the Divisional Commander had had enough of the Germans' harassing fire. He was going to give back as good as he got, and more.

We do not know how successful this new policy was, because the Battalion withdrew from the line on the morning of 6th October. They were relieved by 13th York and Lancs, and marched to Springvale Camp at Roclincourt.

Despite the fact that a large proportion of the raiding party had been gassed, the decision was taken that the raid was to go ahead. On 30th September a major reorganisation of the raiding party was carried out. Whereas A Company had previously being providing the whole party it did not have sufficient strength left to do this. To compensate, 20 volunteers were withdrawn from each company, and left the trenches on 3rd October to begin a crash training programme.

The raid was scheduled for 5th October as planned, leaving very little time to achieve the same level of competence that the original party had reached. Capt G. C. M. L. Pirkis was put in command, with 2Lts A. C. Ridlington and C. V. Burgess in charge of the two assault groups.

A 2Lt (who appears to be wearing a soldier's tunic) inspecting a Lewis gun team of 6 York & Lancs at Cambrin 6th Feburary 1918. The soldier on the left is sitting on the firestep. The walls at this trench are strongly revetted with sandbags, timber, chicken wire and wickerwork screens.

Capt Pirkis was born in 1878, and was therefore older than the average junior officer. He was commissioned on 2nd June 1915, and joined the Battalion on 27th July 1916. Before the war he had been a well known Barnsley solicitor. The two subalterns had very little experience. Both had been commissioned in March and had served in the Battalion for only a short time.

Fortunately there was heavy rain on 5th October and a 24 hour postponement was ordered, which allowed an extra day in which to train. However, the rain continued to fall throughout the next day, but it was decided to go ahead that night regardless.

The aims of the raid were threefold: to inflict casualties on the enemy; to seek information as to his dispositions; and to discover the identity of the unit in the line. There were two specific targets so the raiding party was split into two groups, each under one of the subalterns.

The left group's point of entry into the German lines was at a rifle and bombing post, whereas the right group were to enter at a machine gun post. Fire support had been arranged to cover the attack. 165 Brigade and 170 Brigade RFA were to fire a standing barrage on Turmeric Trench, with the 4.5″ Howitzers allocated to blocking access trenches at various points, and to engage a machine gun post which could cause the raiders problems. In addition to the RFA, four trench mortars were detailed to block a junction of Tortoise Trench, and also to neutralise another machine gun.

The indirect fire of the artillery and trench mortars was to be supplemented by traversing machine gun fire, to make the Germans keep their heads down. In addition extra fire support was to be given by 92nd Brigade's trench mortars and Lewis guns, on the northern edge of Fresnoy Park. In total there was a formidable range of firepower available.

The raiders assembled in Hudson Trench at 6.00 p.m. on 6th October. The front line was found to be too wet for them to fill the Bangalore torpedoes with explosives, and so this was done further back in Winnipeg Road instead. The torpedoes when filled and assembled were 40 feet long and could not be carried along the zig-zag communication trenches. For this reason it had been intended to fill them in the front line. They would have to be taken forward overland.

The type of torpedoes used were electronically detonated from the end of 30 yards of cable. It was while they were being moved forward to the front line that the problems began. At 10.00 p.m. the supporting artillery, trench mortars and machine guns opened fire. This was far too early. Brigade HQ soon halted the fire, but no explanation is given in any of the WDs as to why they should have opened fire at that time.

It is assumed that 10.00 p.m. was the appointed time for the supporting fire to begin. It is too much of a coincidence for all the elements to have opened fire together, for it to have been a mistake. It is likely that the filling and moving forward of the torpedoes had caused a delay and someone had failed to rearrange the time for the fire support. Such an omission could have resulted in heavy casualties.

As soon as the British barrage started the Germans sent up a shower of flares, and the right party was spotted and engaged with rifle fire and grenades. Meanwhile the left party had been able to proceed unobserved. By 10.35 p.m. their Bangalore torpedo was in position, a few yards to the left of the machine gun post.

By 11.30 p.m. the Germans had quietened down and NML was quiet. The right party reported that they would soon be ready, but at midnight there had been no further news from them. The CO was becoming increasingly concerned about the left party, who had been lying in the open for over two hours by then. They would be very cold and getting too stiff to move quickly when the time came to launch the attack. He decided to go and find out for himself what was going on.

He quickly realised that the right party had gone too far to the right to be able to link up with the left party in the enemy trench. However, it was too late to do anything about it. At 1.00 a.m. all was finally ready and five minutes later the artillery again opened fire. When the torpedoes were fired to breach the enemy wire, only the one on the right exploded and even this one failed to completely clear a path through the wire. Without a cleared route into the enemy trenches both parties had no choice but to withdraw. They reassembled in the front line trench with four men wounded. They were lucky to get away so lightly.

This story illustrates just how difficult even the smallest operation could be. The original leader of the raid had been wounded, and most of the raiding party gassed on 30th September. The replacements had very little time to master the operation, but despite the problems they tried their best.

Most of the survivors of the original A Company party were in the left group, and this was borne out by the way they quickly got into the correct position. The right party were hampered by the early firing of the supporting barrage which resulted in them being fired on for some time before they could move into position. It is hardly surprising that they failed to find the right place.

The Bangalore torpedoes had been filled behind the front line because of the wet conditions. However, it is most likely that while filling them with ammonal they still got wet. The torpedo with the left party was lying in the mud in NML for some hours, and it is possible that water seeped in during this time. Although the right torpedo exploded it did not breach the wire. It is possible that the wire was too thick, but it is much more likely that this torpedo also got damp, and it only partially detonated.

The raiders rejoined the Battalion at Springvale Camp later on the 7th, but there was no time to rest with a full programme of refresher training to undertake. This included bayonet fighting, musketry, and ranges for the riflemen and Lewis gunners. There were also periods allocated to revetting practice trenches and wiring.

Day and night tactical exercises were held, especially for the newly formed patrol platoons. It was difficult to maintain an acceptable level of expertise in patrolling duties. For this reason B and C Companies trained one of their platoons as Special Fighting Patrols. There were also Battalion night marches in respirators. The only let up in the routine was when some officers and men were allowed to go to Bethune on a pleasure trip, on 11th October.

94th Brigade instituted a new system of reliefs at this time. The six day pattern of the early days in the Vimy area quickly broke down, as we saw earlier. The new system was for units to follow each other in strict rotation. They therefore always took over from the same Battalion. In this way they got to know each other's operating methods better, and it made for a quicker hand over in the line. The City Battalion moved into the Brown Line on 12th October to relieve 11th East Lancs. Over the next few weeks the Battalion made its way forward to the front line in stages, always relieving 11th East Lancs and in turn always being relieved by York and Lancs.

Bethune, prior to its destruction.

Reliefs took place at 10.00 a.m., which is unusual, since they would normally occur at night. If one side got to know a relief was in progress they would do anything possible to take advantage of the other side being off-balance. It was also an ideal time to bombard the enemy trenches, since there were twice the number of troops in them, and therefore a better chance of inflicting casualties on the enemy.

The relief was completed without incident and that evening the inevitable work parties began again. During the day the men had been busy constructing concertina barbed wire coils, and after dark they went out to erect them. In a six day period the Battalion constructed and put up 600 rolls of barbed wire, which gives some idea of just how much wire there was lying around.

The tour produced only one incident of note. On 15th October, at 5.10 a.m., approximately 250 men of the 6th Sturm Battalion (Bavarians), attempted a raid on the section of front line occupied by 14th York and Lancs. The City Battalion was stood by to assist if necessary. Despite a heavy bombardment the German attack failed and was driven off. The City Battalion was not called upon.

On 18th October, after six days in the Brown Line, (also known as the Brigade B Support Line), the Battalion moved forward into the Red Line, (Brigade A support). A Company was detached to 11th East Lancs in the front line, and C Company joined them on the 20th, having relieved a company of 6th Battalion Warwickshire Regiment (Warwicks). Nothing happened apart from the usual work parties, and on 24th October the rest of the Battalion moved forward into the front line.

This relief was carried out when the British artillery was very active, which is unusual, since it would have attracted retaliatory fire from the German artillery. At 4.15 p.m. a bombardment by 10 cm and 77 mm artillery plus trench mortars, fell on the British trenches. A Company, on the right of the Battalion, had its front line trench blown in at four separate places. B Company in the centre, also had a direct hit.

Despite the weight of enemy fire only two men were wounded, which is remarkably light in the circumstances. However, the WD reveals that the shells consistently fell 20-50 yards behind the front line trench. The Battalion had been lucky.

Soon after arrival patrols from the Battalion noticed the Germans taking more than the usual amount of interest to one particular stretch of the line. It was apparent that they were preparing for a raid. In an attempt to nab a prisoner to find out what was going on, enterprise patrols were concentrated on this area. Enterprise patrols are another example of the change in tactics at this time, to suit the conditions of modern warfare. A patrol was sent out with an area to work in, but within it the patrol leader worked on his own initiative and took whatever action he thought appropriate.

Over the period 25th to 28th October the German trench mortars were more aggressive than normal, and on the 27th the British artillery made a concentrated reply. Known trench mortar positions were bombarded, but the fire continued. A circling German plane was suspected of spotting for the trench mortars and it was driven off by Lewis Gun fire.

A number of measures were taken as precautions against the possible raid. All SOS flare sets were checked and spare ammunition cleaned. At night each front line company sent out two listening posts into NML, to give advanced warning of an approaching raiding party. The artillery continued harassing fire on the 28th, and on the night of the 28th-29th Lewis Guns periodically opening fire at known gaps in the German parapet. They were supported by trench mortars and on two occasions by the artillery as well. Whether or not this activity dissuaded the Germans from carrying out the raid is not known. Neither is it known for certain if a raid was planned at all, but all the indications were there. No raid ever came to fruition.

While all this activity was going on three American officers were attached to the Battalion, to gain experience in the trenches. By 30th October the Battalion had completed an 18 day cycle of trench duty, with six days each in Brigade B Support, Brigade A Support and the front line. Having been relieved by 13th York and Lancs they marched to Springvale Camp for a well earned rest.

This rest period was not as energetic as previous ones had been. There was the usual clean up of equipment followed by inspections on the first day. Training and sports occupied most of the time up to 4th November when there was a Battalion tactical exercise. On the 5th the Battalion began the process of moving up towards the front line again. They moved into the Brown Line and commenced the usual round of work parties, with the emphasis again on wiring.

Brigade HQ were aware that spending 18 days in the trenches in winter, without a break, was too long. A new pattern of reliefs was therefore instituted. Six days in the forward area, either the front line or the Red Line, was to be followed by six days in the rear area, the Brown Line, and then six days resting. The Battalion moved into the Red Line on the 11th.

The period was quiet except for a minor gas attack at 11.15 p.m. on the 12th. 2Lt G. H. Wood was the only man affected and he was evacuated. He had been in the Battalion since 12th February, having received his commission on 19th December 1916.

Relief by 14th York and Lancs took place on the morning of 17th November, and the Battalion marched to Roberts Camp in Ecurie Wood. The men were expecting to have six days out of the line in accordance with the new system of reliefs, but were to be disappointed. The Division was moved a few miles south to take over the front of 47th Division at Oppy. This area was familiar to the men, and they did not relish going back to it.

There was a short break before the move took place, and the men made the most of it. The newly formed Brigade Concert Party held its first show on the 19th, in an old cinema at Ecurie. Known as the 'Nissen Nuts', the Concert Party drew its talent from all the Brigade units, and many of the artists came from the City Battalion together with the scenery painter. The CO was the President of the Concert Committee. The standard of performance was very high, and when 94th Brigade disbanded, 31st Division took over the concert party complete.

At 7.30 a.m. next morning the Battalion relieved 22nd Battalion London Regiment (22 Londons) of 47th Division, opposite Oppy Wood. The next day they moved into the front line relieving 13th East Yorks. The term from line is very misleading, since there was no continuous line as in other areas. Instead the front was held by a series of strongly defended posts, with a company in support behind. The area had been neglected by previous units, and the men were set to work constructing firesteps and widening and deepening the trenches. New shelters were built and sumps sunk for drainage. Trench boards were laid, and at night the wire defences were improved.

The German positions in this area were uncharacteristically weak, and it was a possibility that they might try to withdraw to a better line of defence. The British commanders, having been caught unawares by the German withdrawal in the spring, were determined not to let them get away so lightly if they attempted it again. Patrols were sent out regularly, and were ordered to keep in constant contact with the Germans, day and night.

The continuous patrols and work parties left little time for rest, but despite being so busy there was little to report. The only incident in the WD was Capt Pirkis being wounded in the nose and cheek by a sniper on 22nd November. The Battalion went into reserve on the morning of the 27th at Bailleul, and remained there until 2nd December when it moved back into the same stretch of front line.

The first few days in the trenches were calm, but the rest of the tour was livelier than the last one. Just before midnight on 3rd December the sentries in two bombing posts on the Arleux to Oppy road saw six Germans close to the road. They fired on them and the Germans disappeared. Shortly afterwards however, about 50 enemy appeared, moving forward in small groups. They too were driven off by Lewis Gun and rifle fire, helped along with a liberal sprinkling of rifle grenades. After dawn a patrol found a new section of communication trench, about 20 yards long, had been dug to a post midway between the two British bombing posts. The Germans had been trying to improve their position by infiltrating between the British outer posts.

On the 5th gas shells were fired into both flanks of the Battalion front, but the concentration was not very thick, and there were no casualties. Next day a few men were injured by a heavy artillery bombardment.

On the 7th Capt Cousin was killed having been shot in the throat by a sniper. He is buried in Roclincourt Military Cemetery. He had taken over as the Adjutant on 1st December from Capt Tunbridge, who had departed to take over a staff job.

The new Adjutant was Lt John Clifford Cowen, an ex-City Battalion OR commissioned on 15th July 1915. On 16th February 1918 he transferred to the 4th Entrenching Battalion. In April he went to 13th York and Lancs, and won the MC at Veux Berquin on 31st July 1918.

31st Division was relieved from the Oppy area by the 56th (London) Division. On 8th December the City Battalion handed over its section of the line to 1/4th Londons, and then marched to Lancaster Camp at Mont St Eloi. The same day a new draft arrived, consisting of seven officers from the East Lancs and Duke of Wellington's Regiments, and 53 ORs from the 2nd Westminster Dragoons, 3rd Hussars and the RFA.

Training began again on the 9th with the emphasis on platoon and company tactics. Most afternoons were devoted to sports. The period culminated in a battalion exercise on 17th December. On the 22nd they moved back to familiar ground at Springvale Camp, Roclincourt. Because they were under orders for the trenches on Christmas Day, the Battalion held its seasonal festivities on the 23rd.

The Battalion relieved 14th York and Lancs at Hudson Post, on the 25th. By now the ground was covered in snow, and daylight patrols went out in white over-suits to camouflage themselves. In spite of the intense cold most men were glad to see the snow settling. Freezing conditions at least meant that the ground would be hard and the worst of the mud would be solid. On the other hand when the snow melted it brought even more misery.

From now on patrols were organised in a different way. Instead of battalions running their own schedules and sending out patrols as they saw fit, Brigade HQ now drew up a proper patrol programme.

Patrol routes were planned so they could not accidentally meet another friendly patrol, with disastrous consequences. They were also planned to give full coverage of NML. The patrols, given the grandiose title of lateral enterprise patrols, generally consisted of an officer and 20 ORs, and including a Lewis Gun team. On entering NML they all moved in the same direction and returned to the lines through pre-arranged entry points, thus cutting down the risk of being mistaken as an enemy patrol.

Despite a change in the organisation the aim of individual patrols remained unchanged. They were to locate enemy patrols and inflict casualties on them, take prisoners if possible, gather information and generally to observe the Germans' habits. A great deal of information was thus gleaned and a number of the enemy were sniped. However, the new arrangements failed to produce contact with German patrols in NML.

Relief by 13th York and Lancs arrived on New Year's Eve, and the Battalion went to Cubitt Camp at Neuville St Vaast. The first day of 1918 was spent resting, followed by four days of refresher training. Another tour in the trenches followed, this time in close support at Vancouver Road. The period was uneventful, and A Company was detached to 11th East Lancs in the front line. They were relieved by 13th York and Lancs on 12th January, and moved to Springvale Camp.

Another period of refresher training should have followed, but the winter weather was at its worst, and most of the outdoor activities were cancelled. Foul weather or not it was back to the trenches again on the 18th, to relieve 14th York and Lancs at Hudson Post. The journey had to be made overland, because the communications trenches were so full of water they were impassable to heavily laden troops. The hard preparatory work for winter had by now been largely negated in the forward areas by the atrocious weather.

The front was more active than it had been in previous tours. On the 19th two soldiers in a camouflaged post in NML observed an enemy work party. They opened fire and accounted for three of them. Their sharpness and quick reaction brought congratulations from the Brigade Commander himself. The two soldiers, 235720 L/Cpl J. Poole and 235212 Pte W. A. Clarke, were part of the Special Patrol Party which had been established in HQ Company.

After dark on 20th and 21st January enemy patrols were engaged in NML, but no visible results were noticed. At 2.45 a.m. on the 22nd 2Lt C. V. Burgess and a patrol of 16 men were in NML, when they observed a German patrol of about 60 men approaching the Battalion's lines near Alberta Road. When the Germans reached the British wire, about 100 yards

31st Division Christmas Card 1917.

A York & Lancs Lewis gun team in the Oppy/Gavrelle sector, 13th January, 1918.

from the front line, they began to take up positions. 2Lt Burgess then realised that this was not a patrol but the prelude to some form of attack. Burgess was in a bad position to engage the enemy, so he withdrew his patrol to the front line to raise the alarm. Lewis gun fire soon drove the Germans off.

After daybreak a patrol went out to investigate what the Germans had been up to. Two grenatwerfen, demolition charges and other equipment were recovered. 2Lt Burgess's quick action had averted an enemy raid, without the loss of a single man. Again the value of enterprise patrols was proven.

In the early hours of the 24th patrols reported an increase in the level of enemy activity, and at 4.40 a.m. one of them was fired on by the Germans. They returned the fire and withdrew with no casualties. In daylight a patrol followed up the action and found fresh blood in the area.

Although the WD records no casualties as a result of this action in NML, the CWGC record the names of two City Battalion soldiers killed on 24th January.

A Vickers MG in an anti-aircraft mounting on the Oppy/Gavrelle sector.

They are 12/2075 Pte J. H. Bagshaw and 28715 Pte J. J. Graham. Both are buried in Roclincourt Military Cemetery.

The same afternoon the Battalion was relieved by 13th York and Lancs, and moved to Cubitt Camp at Neuville St Vaast. B Company, however, was left behind and moved into the Red Line in support of 11th East Lancs.

This final rest period was taken up with work parties in the communications trenches in the forward areas, and therefore there was precious little rest to be had. On 29th January Brig Gen Carter-Campbell sent out a special order of the day as he handed over 94th Brigade. He had commanded it since September 1915, except for a short break from May to July 1916. A major reorganisation of the BEF was about to take place and one of the measures would be the disbandment of 94th Brigade and the City Battalion.

Before the Battalion was disbanded it completed one last trench tour. At 8.00 a.m. on the 30th the Battalion relieved 14th York and Lancs in the Red Line, and C Company was detached to 11th East Lancs in the front line as a carrying party. On 2nd February the formal order to disband was received. In the dispassionate language of the WD there is no hint as to how this news was greeted. For the older hands it was a severe blow, but to many of the conscripts it probably meant very little. On 5th February they handed over to 13th York and Lancs, and the bulk of the Battalion moved to Cubitt Camp to complete the disbandment arrangements. A Company was left behind with 13th York and Lancs in Ottawa Trench. It is not known when, or even if, the Company ever rejoined the Battalion. Most of its members were transferred to 13th York and Lancs anyway.

British troops belonging to the 13th Battalion York and Lancaster Regiment take up positions to meet advancing Germans during the German Spring offensive 1918. Sheffield City men were serving with this composite battalion after the 12th Battalion was disbanded.

Chapter Thirteen

Disbandment and Post War

In the early days of 1918 the BEF faced a severe manpower crisis. The horrific casualties suffered in 1917, at Arras, Cambrai, and most particularly at Ypres and Passchendaele, had far exceeded the replacements sent out from the training units at home. The men needed by the BEF did exist in England, but they were not released for service in France and Belgium.

Lloyd-George's War Cabinet wanted to get rid of Haig, because of his run of wasteful and, so far, unsuccessful offensives. However, Haig was a man of considerable influence, and even had connections within the Royal Family itself. To dismiss him outright would have caused a scandal, and a crisis of confidence which the War Cabinet was not prepared to accept. Instead they looked for ways to curb Haig's insatiable appetite for more troops.

The BEF was deliberately kept short of men by sending out fewer replacements than were required to replace the casualties. The aim was to keep Haig so short of men that he would not be able to amass sufficient reserves to launch any more offensives. When he wanted to attack Haig would have to go cap in hand to the Cabinet. If it did not approve of his plan then the troops would not be forthcoming.

To get around the manpower shortage the BEF underwent a major reorganisation in the early part of 1918. The aim was to create a reserve of troops for future offensive operations, or to stem a German offensive if one occurred. As it turned out keeping the BEF short of men was counter productive. When the German spring offensive opened in March, there were insufficient troops to halt it and a complete disaster was only just averted. Indeed the war was almost lost.

To achieve the desired result the organisation of divisions was drastically changed. Some brigades were disbanded altogether, including 94th Brigade, and those that remained were reduced to three battalions. The end result was to keep about the same number of divisions and brigades but at reduced strengths. This allowed for units to be rotated for periodic withdrawal from the line to rest and to undertake other tasks. Those units selected for disbandment were generally numerically the weakest. Their remaining manpower was allocated to other units, normally in the same brigade.

In 31st Division, 94th Brigade was disbanded and replaced by 4th Guards Brigade, which had been created from the excess units of the Guards Division. Later in 1918 a reformed 94th Brigade rejoined the Division. Being the junior brigade in the Division, and the weakest, 94th Brigade was inevitably chosen for disbandment. Its battalions were disposed of as shown below:

11th East Lancs - To 92nd Brigade.
12th York and Lancs - Disbanded, men to 13th York and Lancs and excess to other units.
13th York and Lancs - To 93rd Brigade.
14th York and Lancs - Disbanded, men to 13th York and Lancs and excess to other units.

DATE	OFFRS	ORS	UNIT	REMARKS
10 Feb 18	13	280	7 Y & L	7 Y & L WD records 10+223 arriving on 11 Feb 18. 7 Y & L history says 260 were transferred.
12 Feb 18	15	300	13 Y & L	
12 Feb 18	1	34	3 Gren Gds	The transport
14 Feb 18	–	19	2/4 Y & L	The band
16 Feb 18	2	27	4 Entrench Battalion	Via XIII Corps Reinforcement Camp on 15 Feb 18.
25 Feb 18	1	8	7 Y & L	
? Feb 18	7	–	XIII Corps Rft Camp	Includes CO who left for UK on 2 Mar 18

13th York and Lancs was the strongest battalion left in 94th Brigade, and was therefore chosen to carry on, having been reinforced by men from 12 and 14th York and Lancs. It was still a blow to the City Battalion to be disbanded in favour of a junior battalion.

The order to disband was received on 2nd February, and the next week or so was spent in preparation. Every man was individually selected to go to a particular unit, depending on his specialist training. 13th York and Lancs had priority call on them and the remaining men were sent to a number of other units.

From 5th to 10th February the Battalion was based at Cubitt Camp, Neuville St Vaast. A large contingent for 7 York and Lancs left on the 10th and then the remainder of the Battalion moved to Lancaster Camp at Mont St Eloi. From there the rest of the men were transferred to their allotted units.

By 15th February only a handful were left and they were sent to XIII Corps Reinforcement Camp to await disposal.

That was the end of the City Battalion. During the Second World War the Regiment only raised 10 battalions, and therefore the 12th was not reformed. For the rest of the First War the old boys of the Battalion continued to give a good account of themselves. 13th York and Lancs were in the thick of the fighting in the German spring offensive, and many old 12th Battalion men fell. Their adventures after February 1918, however, are not the subject of this book and so here the wartime story ends.

The men retained their loyalty to the City Battalion and with the Armistice less than six weeks old the first Reunion Dinner was held. The venue was the Grand Hotel in Sheffield on 21st December 1918. About 100 ex-Battalion men attended, with Lt Col Crosthwaite presiding.

The men still serving in the Army were not left out either. A '12th Battalion

28th November 1920. Colours are presented to the Service Battalions of the York & Lancs at Sheffield Cathedral.

Overseas Club' was formed, mainly from the men in the 13th Battalion. The Sheffield Daily Telegraph of 30th January 1919 reports a dinner held at the Hotel Site De St Catherine in Arques, attended by 45 ex-members of the Battalion. Capt T. G. Berry was in the chair.

As demobilisation proceeded the Overseas Branch broke up, but most of them returned to swell the ranks of the Sheffield based 'Twelfth Club'. Regular 'smokers' and other social events were held in the early days after the war.

The Club was open to all men who had served in the City Battalion on or before 1st July 1916. Other men who had joined the Battalion later had to be elected by a two-thirds majority of the members.

The programme of events for 1919 included monthly 'Smoking Concerts' from January to June, held at the Sergeants' Mess, Olympia, Bramall Lane. In July a Memorial Service was held at the Cathedral, followed by the Annual General Meeting in Church House.

By September the Club was using the Imperial Rooms on Pinstone Street for its meetings. However, by then the style of entertainment had changed. Out went the all male 'smokers', to be replaced by whist drives and informal dances. This was probably due to protests from the wives of the married men!

The first President of the Club was Maj Gen Carter-Campbell, who had commanded 94th Brigade for most of the war. The Vice-Presidents were Lt Cols Crosthwaite, Hood and Gurney, and Majs Riall, Clough, Plackett, Hoette and Allen. The Treasurer was Mr S. J. P. Ellin, who had been a Cpl in B Company. The Secretary was CSM H. R. F. Coates, who had served in C Company. A committee was formed to organise the social events chaired by Capt F. C. Earl. He was assisted by 11 members, including RSM F. E. M. Chambers.

Although monthly meetings became less frequent annual functions continued up to the Second World War. Each July, as close to the 1st as possible, a Memorial Service was held and in December there was a Reunion Dinner. The Dinners were usually held at one of three venues; the Grand Hotel, the Royal Victoria Hotel or the King's Head Hotel, where D Company had held its concerts in 1914.

The Second Reunion Dinner, on 20th December 1919, was preceded by the dedication of the City Battalion Memorial in Sheffield Cathedral. The memorial is mounted on the wall on the left as you enter the York and Lancaster Regiment Chapel, and was unveiled by Col Mainwaring, with Archdeacon Gresford-Jones performing the dedication. It was designed by Mr F. Ratcliffe, who had himself served in the Battalion, being wounded on 1st July 1916. On the Memorial is the York and Lancaster Regiment badge and the crest of the City of Sheffield, together with the following inscription:

'1914-1919. To the Glory of God, and to the ever glorious memory of Officers, NCOs and Men of the 12th Battalion York and Lancaster Regiment (Sheffield City Battalion), who at the call of Duty and in the cause of freedom nobly made the supreme sacrifice. The tablet is erected by the surviving members of the Battalion and dedicated on 20th December, 1919.'

In common with most Service battalions the City Battalion was never presented with Colours during the war. In bygone days Colours had been the rallying point for battalions in battle, but in modern times they only served ceremonial purposes. However, to this day a battalion's Colours are still treated with the greatest reverence. On Sunday 28th November 1920 King's Colours were presented to all the local

Col Wedgewood unveils the City Battalion memorial at Serre on 24th May 1923, after its dedication by Archdeacon Gresford-Jones.

Reg Glenn, on the right, and a friend on the Serre battlefield following the unveiling of the memorial in 1923. Just in front of the other man's right foot is the handle of a German stick grenade.

battalions of the York and Lancaster Regiment. Although belated, this was a fitting end to the Battalion's history.

The presentation ceremony took place in the Cathedral Yard, with Capt Tunbridge accepting the Colour for the City Battalion. After the presentation the Colour was marched into the Cathedral and given to the Regimental Chapel for safe custody, along with those of the other battalions. It is still there. On entering the Chapel if you look up on the right hand side it is the Colour closest to the entrance.

In addition to the Memorial in Sheffield it was thought fitting to erect another memorial at Serre, where so many men had died on 1st July 1916. The villagers of Serre donated a piece of ground for the purpose. Ironically the memorial site is behind the old German lines,

Ex RSM Charles Polden MC poses at the memorial after the unveiling ceremony.

A reunion in the 1930s.

at the highest point in the village. This area was not reached by the Battalion, save for the odd man who may have passed by as a prisoner. It was erected on the main road where passers-by were more likely to see it, rather than on the battlefield itself some 1,000 yards away.

The design was chosen from entries in a competition held for the purpose. The winning entry was by an ex-City Battalion soldier, Mr J. S. Brown of 258 Barnsley Road. He had studied architecture before the war at the University. His name does not appear on the nominal roll of 5th May 1916. It is assumed that he had been transferred, and possibly commissioned by the time of the Somme battle.

A sculptor in Paris was commissioned to produce the Memorial. When it was ready a large contingent went from Sheffield for the unveiling ceremony, which took place on 24th May 1923. The area around Serre at that time was still devastated from the war, and the Memorial stood in open country. It is now surrounded by trees and the small houses of the village, and little can be seen of the battlefield from its site. Archdeacon Gresford-Jones, who was by then the Bishop of Kampala, dedicated the Memorial. It was unveiled by Col Wedgewood, serving with one of the Regular battalions of the Regiment in Germany.

After the ceremony there was time to look over the battlefield. The evidence of war was still everywhere to be seen. Some of those attending took back souvenirs, including bayonets and oil bottles.

One man did go a bit too far. He took home a German jawbone full of fillings, as his grisly reminder of the journey. Hopefully by now it has been laid to rest. It was known to be German because the rest of the skull was still contained in a rusty German helmet.

The 'Twelfth Club' went into decline after 1939, but interest in the Battalion was rekindled in the early 1960s. An ex-Sheffield Telegraph reporter, John Harris, wrote a novel based on the City Battalion's experiences up to and including 1st July 1916. The book entitled 'Covenant With Death' was launched at a reception at the Grand Hotel at which many of the survivors were present.

The annual dinners picked up again. On 9th July 1961 80 members attended, but the years gradually took their toll. On the 60th Anniversary of the Battle of the Somme in 1976, 26 members of the 'Twelfth Club' held the last reunion and went into voluntary liquidation. There were too few survivors to carry on the annual meetings.

Appendix One

Decorations 1916–1918

Honours and Awards to men serving with the Sheffield City Battalion.

ARRIDGE, H.C., 12/24 Pte, Military Medal. On 1st July 1916 Pte Arridge was a member of a five man Lewis Gun team, and advanced in the first wave of the attack. Two men were wounded almost immediately. Pte Arridge and the other two, 12/1164 L/Cpl Burnby and 12/923 Pte Garbutt, could not get far and took cover in a shell hole. They engaged an enemy machine gun post with their Lewis Gun and some bombs, until they ran out of ammunition. This action relieved the pressure on other men trapped in No Man's Land. They were heavily engaged themselves. They withdrew at night, bringing the gun with them. London Gazette 16th November 1916.

BREATHWICK, J., 13/147 L/Sgt, Military Medal. The Battalion was holding the Gavrelle area, including the Windmill, over the period 9th-20th May 1917. L/Sgt Breathwick was particularly brave in bringing in wounded men under fire. The medal was presented on 20th July 1917. London Gazette 29th August 1917.

BRIGGS, J., 14/1464 Pte, Military Medal. Pte Briggs was a company runner during the attack on Cadorna Trench on 28th June 1917. He made several crossings of No Man's Land to deliver important reports and messages. The day before he had been blown up by a shell which wounded other men. When not running he helped to consolidate the new position. The medal was presented on 20th July 1917. The Army Medal Office have no trace of this award even though it is well documented in the Battalion War Diary.

BURNBY, M.B., 12/1164 L/Cpl, Military Medal. See details for Pte Arridge above.

BURRELL, W., 17/385 A/Cpl, Military Medal. No details are known. The medal was presented on 20th July, 1917, presumably for actions in the Gavrelle area or the Cadorna attack. London Gazette 29th August 1917.

CLARKE, J.W., 24251 Pte, Military Medal. On 28th June 1917, during the attack on Cadorna trench, Pte Clarke was in an advanced Lewis Gun post with L/Cpl Manterfield. They were able to inflict heavy losses on the enemy as they retired. When the gun was knocked out by a shell they went to the rear for another, returned and continued to fire on the enemy. Throughout this action they were under heavy shellfire. Pte Clarke also gave valuable assistance to his section commander. London Gazette 21st August 1917.

Pte B. Corthorn wearing his DCM.

CORTHORN, B., 12/338 Pte, Distinguished Conduct Medal. On 1st July 1916 Pte Corthorn was in a six man Lewis Gun team. At zero hour they advanced, but within the first 50 yards three of them had been hit. After 15 minutes Pte Corthorn was left to work the gun on his own. This he did until it was knocked out, but he continued to fight with a rifle which became red hot from use. When the advance petered out he crawled into a shell hole, where 12/1125 Pte R. F. Brookes lay mortally wounded. This was at 7.50 a.m. He remained in the shell hole until 10.30 p.m. the next day, almost 40 hours later. He took great risks to get water for Pte Brookes and to make him as comfortable as possible. Pte Corthorn could have escaped on the first night but he would not leave his wounded comrade behind. Neither could he drag Pte Brookes back with him as he was wounded himself. He hoped that the medics would find them but alas they did not. On the afternoon of the second day Pte Brookes died. Pte Corthorn wrapped the body in some groundsheets and after dark made his way back to our own lines, bringing back the damaged Lewis Gun. London Gazette 22nd September 1916.

CROZIER, H.C., 12/628 Sgt, Military Medal. On the night of 15th-16th May 1916 the Battalion position opposite Serre was very heavily bombarded as part of a German raid on the unit to the north. Some trenches were completely obliterated in the shelling which lasted for over two hours. Sgt Crozier helped to dig out some of the men who had been buried by the shellfire in a dugout. He did this with no consideration for his own safety and at the height of the bombardment. London Gazette 19th February 1917.

CUNNINGTON, E.C., Capt, Mentioned in Despatches. On 1st July 1916 Capt Cunnington was the Battalion MO. He did not take part in the attack but spent the next three days and nights helping the wounded. He made numerous trips into NML at night to assist those evacuating the wounded. He exposed himself to great risks and at the end of the period was totally exhausted.

DALE, A., 12/631 L/Cpl, Military Medal. On 3rd May 1917 in the Gavrelle sector L/Cpl Dale went forward in front of Hill 80 to observe enemy movements. The situation was very uncertain and the exact whereabouts of our own troops was not known. The enemy were firing a lot of smoke shells as if to mask an attack. L/Cpl Dale went forward of the smoked off area and sent back a steady stream of reliable information. During the whole time he was under heavy fire and had a number of near disasters. London Gazette 18th July 1917.

DOWNING, A., 12/354 Pte, Military Medal. On 1st July 1916 Pte Downing was a Battalion runner. On two occasions he carried messages from Battalion HQ, in John Copse, to Brigade HQ near Observation Wood. He was under very heavy fire but got the messages through. London Gazette 16th November 1916.

GARBUTT, C.S., 12/923 Pte, Military Medal. See details for Pte Arridge above.

GRANT, T.E.A., 2Lt, Mentioned in Despatches. This officer had commanded the railway construction party in Egypt. On arrival in France he became the 94th Brigade Pioneer Officer for the period 20th May-19th August 1916. His work was consistently good and often performed under arduous and dangerous conditions.

HANSON, G., 12/1358 Pte, Military Medal. On the night of 15th-16th May 1916 Pte Hanson was buried by shellfire in a dugout with some other men. He kept calm and managed to get them all out. Once freed himself he casually lit a cigarette and went back to digging out the rest. All this was under very heavy shellfire. London Gazette 28th July 1917.

HEADEACH, M.C.P., 12/392 Cpl, Military Medal. On the night of 15th-16th May 1916 Cpl Headeach was repeatedly blown over by the concussion of exploding shells. Despite the bombardment he visited a number of destroyed posts and displayed coolness and courage. He helped many wounded and assisted in the extraction of the dead.

HOOD, F.J.C., Lt Col, Distinguished Service Order, Mentioned in Despatches. For services while commanding the City Battalion, London Gazette 1st January 1918. Lt Col Hood was also MID for actions with the City Battalion. London Gazette 21st December 1917.

JARVIS, R.A., 18582 Sgt, Military Medal. On 28th June 1917 during the attack on Cadorna Trench Sgt Jarvis led his section forward with great dash and determination. He personally bayoneted several of the enemy and generally set an excellent example. The medal was presented on 20th July 1917. London Gazette 21st August 1917.

MANTERFIELD, B., 235226 L/Cpl, Military Medal. For details see entry for Pte Clarke above.

MARSDEN, R., 12/443 Pte, Military Medal. On 1st July 1916 Pte Marsden was a Battalion runner. On one occasion while taking a message he was knocked flat and partially buried by heavy shellfire. He extracted himself and got his message through. London Gazette 16th November 1916.

MATTHEWS, S., 12/727 Pte, Distinguished Conduct Medal. On 1st July 1916 Pte Matthews was working as a stretcher bearer. After the attack had failed he spent the next three days and nights working in a sap in John Copse, tending the wounded. During this time one man in his team was killed and two others wounded. He was under constant shellfire. London Gazette 20th October 1916.

OTTAWAY, W.T., 9489 RSM, Mentioned in Despatches. On the Cadorna attack on 28th June 1917 RSM Ottaway issued ammunition and other stores from the Battalion dump under constant heavy shellfire and difficult circumstances. He set an excellent example with complete disregard for his own safety.

Capt Vivian Sumner Simpson, MC. He was killed on 13th April, 1918 while serving 13th York & Lancs, and is buried in Outtersteene Communal Cemetery.

OWEN, R.T., 12/742 Pte, Military Medal. On the night of 15th-16th May 1916 Pte Owen was wounded during a German attack. Despite this he continued to fire his rifle, until his own blood clogged the working parts so badly that it would no longer work. London Gazette 9th November 1916.

POLDEN, C., 12/481 RSM, Military Cross. On 9th March 1917 RSM Polden preceded the Battalion on the move to Puisieux. He was waiting for them to catch up with him in the town, when the area he was in came under heavy shellfire. Many men and horses of other units were killed and wounded and there was great confusion. RSM Polden organised the remaining men and aided the wounded. He set a fine example of conduct under fire. London Gazette 11th May 1917.

RIALL, C.P.B., Lt Col, Mentioned in Despatches. Awarded for services while CO of the City Battalion. London Gazette 4th January 1917.

SIMPSON, V.S., Capt, Military Cross, Mentioned in Despatches. On 28th June 1917 Capt Simpson played a leading part in the attack on Cadorna Trench. He had also been heavily involved in the planning for this attack. He was the first man into the enemy trench and was involved in hand to hand combat with the defenders. Later he brilliantly organised the consolidation and protection of the newly won position. London Gazette 17 September 1917. At some time he was also MID, the gazette date is not known but it may have been in connection with the preparatory work for this attack.

SPARLING, R.A., 12/1058 Sgt, Meritorious Service Medal. As the Orderly Room Clerk he consistently produced good work and displayed a high degree of reliability in difficult circumstances. London Gazette 1st January 1918.

SPENCER, E., 12/785 Pte, Military Medal. On the night of 15th-16th May 1916 Pte Spencer and Pte B. C. Wilkinson brought up more ammunition from their company's reserve in Rob Roy Trench. They were under heavy fire. In a number of places the trenches were so badly blown in that they had to cross open ground. At one stage Pte Wilkinson was stunned by shrapnel hitting his helmet. However, he recovered and they continued. They eventually delivered the ammunition which was desperately needed. London Gazette 28th July 1917.

SQUIRES, E.F., 12/520 Cpl, Mentioned in Despatches. On an unknown date in December 1916 or January 1917 Cpl Squires was in charge of a post which received a direct hit by a shell. All his men except one were buried or wounded. He set the one remaining fit man on digging out those who were trapped. He himself took over the guard duties, and remained at his post even after he had sent the others to the rear.

STORRY, F.W.S., Lt, Mentioned in Despatches. On the night of 27th-28th June 1916 Lt Storry was out in NML with a patrol cutting the enemy wire. He came under heavy artillery and trench mortar fire, but remained cool and brought his patrol back after completing their task.

VICKERS, S., 12/1118 Pte, Military Medal. No details are known other than the award was for actions on 1st July 1916. London Gazette 16th November 1916.

WATKINS, F.E., 12/548 L/Cpl, Military Medal. On the night of 15th-16th May 1916 L/Cpl Watkins was the only man in his post uninjured. Several times he was knocked to the ground by shells exploding nearby. He doggedly refused to leave his place of duty until Cpl Headeach reached him and told him to go to the rear. See also the entry for Cpl Headeach above. London Gazette 19th February 1917.

WILKINSON, B.C., 12/822 Pte, Military Medal. For details see the entry for Pte Spencer above.

WILSON, R., 12/825 Pte, Military Medal. On the night of 15th-16th May 1916 Pte Wilson was severely wounded in the back during the German attack. He assisted the defenders of his post, despite his wounds, by filling ammunition clips for them. London Gazette 9th November 1916.

WRIGHT, G.C., 12/275 Pte, Distinguished Conduct Medal. On 1st July 1916 Pte Wright was a Battalion runner. He was given a message to take to Brigade HQ, in Dunmow Trench, from the Battalion's HQ in John Copse. The distance was about half a mile. He was under heavy fire throughout the journey and was blown up three times and partially buried. Despite being very shaken he delivered the message just before collapsing. London Gazette 22nd September 1916.

Honours and Awards to Sheffield City Battalion men won with other units.

ATKINSON C., 12/2042 Cpl, Military Medal. Won the MM with 19 MGC after transferring to that unit. No other details known.

BAKER, A., Capt, Military Cross. On 9th October 1917 while serving with 1/5 Y&L Capt Baker was commanding a reserve company in an attack near Passchendaele, Belgium. All other company commanders had become casualties. He pushed his own company forward of the Battalion's objective and reorganised the bulk of the unit in consolidating the gains made. He also went forward on a risky reconnaissance for his CO. London Gazette 17th December 1917.

BAMFORTH B., 12/1392 Cpl, 1918. Meritorious Service Medal. For services while in 13 Y&L some time after 12th February. Exact details unknown. London Gazette 18th January 1919.

BOURNE, W.K., ASgt 31348 Mentioned in Despatches. Date and other details unknown.

BUCKLEY, A., 12/883, Pte, Mentioned in Despatches. Won with 2/4 Y&L for unknown deeds after 12th February 1918.

CAHILL, E., 12/883 Sgt, Military Medal. No other details known.

CHAPMAN, S.W., 12/2157 Pte, Military Medal. Details unknown but likely to have been won with 1 Y&L in Salonica, on or before 11th October 1916 on which date he was killed.

CLARKE, N.W.B., 12/71 Cpl, Meritorious Service Medal. For services in 13 Y&L after 12th February 1918. Exact details unknown. London Gazette 18th January 1919.

COLES, S., 7587 A/Cpl, Distinguished Conduct Medal. On 23rd October 1918 A/Cpl Coles was commanding a trench mortar crew at Pecq. He was attached to 93 Light Trench Mortar Battery from 13 Y&L. A heavy German trench mortar was firing on the Battalion's advanced positions. A/Cpl Coles took his mortar forward to an advanced position under the direct observation of the enemy. He succeeded in silencing the enemy mortar after firing 30 rounds at it. All the while he was under heavy machine gun and artillery fire. He acted with great audacity and with total disregard for his own safety. London Gazette 2nd February 1919.

COLQUHOUN, J.F., Military Cross. As the 31st Division Chaplain he displayed gallantry and devotion to duty near Ayette in the period 22nd-31st March 1918. Daily he was in the front line during heavy fighting, cheering up the men and generally looking after their comforts. London Gazette 26th July 1918.

COWEN, J.C., Capt, Military Cross. On 31st July 1918 Capt Cowen was serving with 13 Y&L near Veux Berquin. He went forward with another officer and three men to investigate an unusual occurence in front of our wire. He penetrated the line of German posts and took some prisoners. These he brought back to our lines under heavy machine gun fire. Much valuable identification was thus gained. He set a fine example of courage and initiative. London Gazette 15th October 1918.

CROSTHWAITE, J.A., Lt Col, Mentioned in Despatches. Lt Col Crosthwaite was awarded two MIDs with London Gazette dates of 17th February and 22nd June 1915. These were for actions while serving with a battalion of the DLI at Ypres.

DE LANDRE, GROGAN, L.V.St.P., Lt, Military Cross. Won with 1/5 Y&L after 12th February 1918, for unknown actions. London Gazette 15th February 1919.

GELDERT, S., 12/111 Pte, Military Medal. Won with 1/5 Y&L for deeds unknown, after 1st July 1916.

GURNEY, C.H., Lt Col, Distinguished Service Order and Bar. For services with 13 Y&L before joining the City Battalion. London Gazette 1st January 1917. The bar was awarded when he was CO of 11 EY on 24th-25th March 1918 at Ervillers. The troops on his right flank gave way. He personally went to restore the situation and took several prisoners. That night he organised a very difficult withdrawal. Throughout the whole of the fighting he visited all parts of the front displaying considerable gallantry and setting a splendid example. London Gazette 26th July 1918.

HAWLEY, D.D., 2Lt, Military Cross. In November 1916 2Lt Hawley was serving with 10 Y&L as a 2Lt at Beaucourt. He displayed conspicuous gallantry in action. Some of his men were buried by shellfire. He set to work, despite the intense shellfire to dig them out. Later he established a strong point in broad daylight. London Gazette 3rd March 1917.

HIPKINS, F.W., A/Capt, Military Cross. The details of the action are not known. He was serving with 1/6 N&D at the time in France. The action was on or before 3rd October 1918, the day he was killed. London Gazette 1st January 1919.

HOOD, F.J.C., Lt Col, Mentioned in Despatches. In addition to the MID with the City Battalion, Lt Col Hood was MID on another two occasions. The actions are unknown. One was gazetted on 25th May 1917, the other date is not known.

HOPE, C.R., 2Lt, Military Cross. Serving with an unknown Y&L battalion, at Kemmel, on 26 April he displayed conspicuous gallantry and devotion to duty. During an attack all officers senior to him became casualties and he took over command of three companies. He moved about regardless of personal safety in the open. He was under heavy rifle and machine gun fire and continued to encourage and direct his men. He produced excellent results by his leadership and energy. London Gazette 16th September 1918.

HOWE, P., 2Lt., Military Cross. On 1st July 1916 he was serving with 10 WY. He was in the first wave of the attack north of Fricourt. During the day he crossed NML four times, was wounded and eventually passed out. His unit suffered 710 casualties, the heaviest suffered by any battalion on the worst day ever for the British Army. 2Lt Howe was the only officer left standing at the end of the day.

LEAMAN, R.W., Mentioned in Despatches. No details are known.

LONGDEN, G. 12/718, Pte, Military Medal. No other details known

LOCKWOOD, AP, Pte Military Cross. Won with a N&D Battalion in 1917. No other details known.

MALKIN, T., 13/611 Pte, Military Medal. London Gazette 16th August 1918. No other details known.

MARSHALL, J.F., Lt, Military Cross. On 9th October 1917 Lt Marshall was serving with 1/5 Y&L, attached to HQ 148th Infantry Brigade near Passchendaele, Belgium. He displayed conspicuous gallantry and devotion to duty. For 48 hours during an attack, he moved forward ammunition and ration dumps. He was under constant shellfire and on one occasion led pack animals through a heavy barrage. London Gazette 17th December 1917.

MCNAMARA, J., 10525 Pte, Distinguished Conduct Medal. On 9th May 1915 serving with 2 East Lancs, near Rouges, he assisted in bringing in a wounded officer under heavy shell fire. Later the same evening he helped to bring in more wounded, again under heavy fire. London Gazette 5th August 1915.

MIDDLETON, J.L., Distinguished Flying Cross. Details are unknown. He transferred to the RFC in 1917.

OTTAWAY, W.T., 9489 RSM, Distinguished Conduct Medal. On 24th-25th September 1918 serving with 2 Y&L near Gricourt, RSM Ottaway displayed courage and devotion to duty. He did splendid work marshalling the wounded and POWs in the valley by Trout Copse. He was subjected to heavy and constant shelling. He also created a forward dump of bombs and ammunition, and in doing so had to pass over a ridge swept by heavy machine gun and shell fire. His coolness and courage were a fine example to all ranks. London Gazette 2nd February 1919.

PITT, E.H.P., Capt, Military Cross. Won with 14 Y&L for unknown actions in 1918. London Gazette 2nd April 1919.

REID, T.R., Lt, Military Cross, Mentioned in Depatches. Details for the MC are unknown. It was won with a battalion of KRRC, possibly in September 1915 when he was gassed and wounded at Loos. The MID was for actions on 30th November 1915.

SHEMELD, E., 25023 Pte, Military Medal. Won with 31 MGC in March 1918. Other details unknown.

SIMPKIN, A.L., 2Lt, Military Cross. On 2nd September 1918, serving with 2/4 Y&L at Vaulx Vraucourt, he led his company unassisted until wounded. All his officers and all but one of his NCOs were casualties. His position was heavily counter attacked. He went up and down his line until he was eventually severely wounded.

SLEIGH, H.R., S4/199050 Sgt, Meritorious Service Medal, Mentioned in Despatches. Both awards are for service with HQ 94th Brigade after transferring from 12 Y&L to the ASC. The MSM was Gazetted on 1st January 1918, the MID on 29th May 1917.

STANSER, J.R., Lt, Military Cross. The actions for this award are unknown. Lt Stanser was serving with 2/5 Y&L at the time, possibly as the Brigade Signals Officer. London Gazette 1st January 1918.

STONES, F.D., Capt, Military Cross. Won while serving with 2/6 N&D, on or before 28th September, 1917 on which date he was killed.

TALBOT, F.S., 31273 Pte, Military Medal. Won with 13 Y&L after 12th February 1918. Other details are unknown. London Gazette 14th May 1919.

THOMPSON, S. 2Lt, Military Cross. Won while serving with 2 Y&L, attached to a MGCoy. Other details unknown. London Gazette 1st January 1917.

TONGE, F., 2Lt, Military Medal. Won with an unknown battalion of the Manchesters serving as a L/Cpl (number 10047) some time in 1915.

TUNBRIDGE, N.L., Capt, Mentioned in Despatches. Awarded for unknown actions, but likely to have been while serving as a Staff Officer with HQ 75th Brigade in 1917. London Gazette 1 st January 1918.

WEVER, P.O., Capt, Military Cross, Mentioned in Despatches. Both awards were won serving with the West Riding Division Signal Coy. The MC was for laying cables under heavy fire. The reason for the MID is not known.

WILLOUGHBY, J.A., 12/1246 Sgt, Distinguished Conduct Medal. On an unknown date in 1918, while serving with 9 Y&L, he displayed a complete disregard for danger during a German attack. He led several parties to their battle positions through gas and heavy shell fire. He also brought in a wounded man from a patrol under heavy machine gun fire. London Gazette 30th October 1918.

COMMANDING OFFICERS – SHEFFIELD CITY BATTALION 10th SEPTEMBER 1914-28th FEBRUARY 1918

NAME	DATES	OTHER INFORMATION
Col. H. Hughes CB CMG	10 Sep–10 Oct 14	Acted as Commandant until a younger man was found. Ex-CO of 4 Y&L and Sheffield Lord Mayor
Lt Col C.V. Mainwaring	10 Oct 14–27 Sep 15	Too ill to serve abroad due to time spent in Far East in the Indian Army
Lt Col J. A. Crosthwaite	28 Sep 15–30 Jun 16	Fell ill as a result of wounds received at Ypres in 1915 serving with DLI
Maj A. Plackett	30 Jun–1 Jul 16	At 31st Division School as Chief Instructor, recalled as acting CO. Wounded Jul 16
Capt E. G. G. Woolhouse	2–4 Jul 16	Left out of Jul 16 attack
Capt D. C. Allen	4–31 Jul 16	Recalled from 4th Army School

Maj C. H. Gurney	31 Jul–18 Aug 16	From 13 Y&L, possibly took over on 25 Jul
Lt Col H.B. Fisher	18 Aug–3 Oct 16	Ex Wilts Regt. Killed on 3 Oct 16
Maj C. H. Gurney	3–12 Oct 16	City Battalion 2IC
Lt Col C. P. B. Riall	12 Oct 16–18 May 17	Transferred from 13th York and Lancs. Maj Hood stood in 5 Dec 16–11 Jan 17, while he was on leave
Maj D. C. Allen	18 May–1 Jun 17	City Battalion 2IC
Lt Col F.J.C. Hood DSO	1 Jun 17–28 Feb 18	Transferred from 13th York and Lancs. He was on leave 15 Dec 17–17 Jan 18, during which time Maj Allen stood in until 31 Dec 16. Maj J. V. Kershaw of 11th East Lancs, stood in for the balance.

Notes:
1. Ranks and decorations are as at the dates shown.
2. Names underlined are proper COs, the others were acting only.

Appendix Two

The Reserve Companies

The Battalion was recruited to its establishment strength in September 1914. At first there were hopes of forming a second battalion, but they were dashed on 1st October when the War Office announced it would not sanction the raising of any more local battalions. The War Office did however recognize that the existing battalions would need replacements for men lost due to natural wastage, and so in December announced that all New Army battalions were to raise a reserve company. The City Battalion therefore began to recruit what was to became E Company.

Advertisements calling for 250 volunteers were posted in the local newspapers in the third week of December. Recruiting was carried out in much the same way as for the original Battalion.

Capt G. Beley was the officer in command of the reserves, and he was based at the Town Hall. Once they had signed on the volunteers were sent home, since it was not practical to start training before Christmas.

George Beley had been a subaltern in D Company, and had figured largely in the Company concerts at the King's Head Hotel during the autumn. He remained with the reserves until being replaced by Capt Jarrard the following June. He then rejoined the Battalion, which by then had moved to Cannock Chase. E Company had a similar start to their army lives as the volunteers of the previous September. They drilled in Norfolk Park and on wet days used the Jungle on Hawley Street, a disused ice rink. It was demolished between the wars and was a Sheffield Transport garage for a time. The site is now covered by office blocks.

The Company was based at Hyde Park Barracks, but the men had to live at home until extra accommodation could be provided at Redmires Camp. The camp was reorganised and extra huts provided. On 10th April 1915 all was ready and the Company marched up to Redmires, with a strength of 224 ORs. By the end of May the Company was recruited to its full establishment.

Capt Beley had four other officers to assist him. His 2IC was Capt J Kenner, who was also commanding. 18 Platoon, (E Company's platoons were numbered 17 to 20). Capt Kenner remained with E Company until being transferred to the General List later in the year. The other platoon commanders were: OC 17 Platoon - 2Lt J. S. Cooper OC 19 Platoon - 2Lt N. 0. Lucas, OC 20 Platoon - 2Lt V. S. Simpson. John Cooper later transferred to the RFC and was killed serving with 70 Squadron on 25th March 1917, aged 25.

Neville Lucas had been a Sheffield University student before the war. He joined the City Battalion as an OR and was commissioned in December 1914.

Vivian Simpson was even later receiving his commission, having to wait until January 1915. He stayed with the reserves until August 1916 when he rejoined the Battalion in France. He proved to be a brilliant officer and at various times filling the posts of Adjutant and OC A Company. He won the MC in June 1917. In February 1918 he transferred to 13th York and Lancs, and was killed in action on 13th April 1918 at the age of 33.

The Battalion left Redmires on 13th May 1915, leaving E Company behind. The next day authority was received to raise yet another reserve company, which became F Company.

At the end of June 1915 Capt W. J. Jarrard left the Battalion at Penkridge Bank Camp on Cannock Chase, and returned to Redmires to take command of both reserve companies. Capt Jarrard had been OC A Company, and was destined to become the Adjutant of the future 15th (Reserve) Battalion of the York and Lancs. He brought Capt C. F. Ellwood with him as his 2IC, who later transferred to 10 York and Lancs.

By now it had been realised by Northern Command that the system of reserve companies was a very inefficient way of utilising the available reserve manpower. Order No. 1228 was therefore issued which decreed that reserve battalions were to be formed by amalgamating the various reserve companies of each regiment. In addition reserve companies were not to accompany the parent battalion when it moved from their recruiting areas to join their brigades.

E and F Companies joined 15 York and Lancs, the Reserve Battalion already mentioned, at Silkstone Camp near Barnsley. The camp had been origionally built for 13th York and Lancs, who were by this stage on Cannock Chase with the City Battalion and the rest of 94th Brigade. 15 York and Lancs were to train recruits for all York and Lancs Battalions.

An advance party of 40 ORs left Redmires on 20th July 1915 under the command of 2Lt Cooper. They marched into town and caught the train from Victoria Station to Barnsley. The main body, however, did not have it quite so easy. On 23rd July the remaining 290 men left Redmires and marched the 17 miles to Silkstone, via Stannington, Deepcar and Wortley.

Lt Col W. G. Raley, who had previously served with 14th York and Lancs, was appointed CO of the new 15th Battalion. He could not be released immediately and in the interim Capt Jarrard acted as CO.

By all accounts he had a very hard time of it, and was extremely busy sorting out the thousand and one details involved in setting up a new unit. He eventually became Lt Col Raley's Adjutant.

When E and F Companies left Redmires, Capt Ellwood was left behind with a small recruiting party. However, this party also moved to Silkstone, on 6th September, thus severing the last link between the City Battalion and Redmires Camp. Volunteers for the City Battalion then joined the Army at the Central Recruiting Office in East Parade. However, from December 1915 to April 1916 a City Battalion recruiting depot was kept open at Hyde Park Barracks. The agent was Sergeant Major Waddington of the 3rd West Riding Royal Field Artillery.

Capt Ellwood kept up a steady recruiting drive. On 16th September 1915 he returned to Sheffield from Silkstone and held a concert at the Victoria Hall, in the hope of attracting more volunteers.

Another recruiting stunt was recorded in the Sheffield Daily Telegraph, of 4th October. The paper carries a photograph of Sgt Mower and other City Battalion men on the streets of Sheffield, attempting to entice more volunteers.

It is not known how successful these enterprises were. 12th Battalion numbers up to 12/2157 are known, but many of the men with numbers over 12/1150 were destined never to serve with the Battalion. Even though they were recruited into the Battalion initially, once recruits were sent to 15 York and Lancs they could be sent to any battalion of the Regiment.

Many letters of complaint were received by the Sheffield Daily Telegraph from men who had enlisted in the City Battalion, but after training had been sent to other battalions. The newspaper ran an article on 31st January 1916 about these men. The recruiters promised thereafter that if it was possible men would be put in battalions of their choice.

The reserves were not idle tor long. Fifty of them joined the Battalion on 4th August 1915, and a further 200 were still needed at that stage to replace men who had taken commissions. Eventually the volunteers were all committed, and as the war went on more and more conscripts replaced the original volunteers. When the Battalion disbanded in February 1918, only a third of the men had 12 prefix numbers, and only 1 in 6 had been in the original four companies in September 1914.

Recruiting for the Battalion went on until April 1916. From then on conscription was in force and no more volunteers were taken into the Army.

The system of reserve battalions underwent reform during the war, because they were unable to cope with the influx of conscripts. On 1 st September 1916 the Training Reserve was formed, with battalions numbered from 1 to 112. Regiments continued to draw reinforcements from their own reserve battalions, but when more men were needed they drew on the Training Reserve establishment strength.

Appendix Three

Biographical List

Abbreviations used in the list

UNIT TITLES

ACC – Army Cyclist Corps
ASC – Army Service Corps
Buffs – East Kent Regiment
DLI – Durham Light Infantry
ELanes – East Lancashire Regiment
Entr Bn – Entrenching Battalion
Essex – Essex Regiment
EY – East Yorkshire Regiment
HAC – Honourable Artillery Company
Hamps – Hampshire Regiment
KOYLI – King's Own Yorkshire Light Infantry
KRRC – King's Royal Rifle Corps
KSLI – King's Shropshire Light Infantry
Leies – Leicestershire Regiment
LFus – Lancashire Fusiliers
Lincs – Lincolnshire Regiment
London – London Regiment
London Yeo – City of London Yeomanry
LNLanes – Loyal North Lancashire Regiment
Manes – Manchester Regiment
MGC – Machine Gun Company
MGCorps – Machine Gun Corps
M'Sex – Middlesex Regiment (Duke of
  Cambridges's Own)
N&D – Nottinghamshire and Derbyshire
  Regiment (The Sherwood Foresters)
Notts Yeo – Nottinghamshire Yeomanry
  (Sherwood Rangers)
NFus – Northumberland Fusiliers
Norfolks – Norfolk Regiment
Northants – Northamptonshire Regiment
NStaffs – North Staffordshire Regiment (The
  Prince of Wales's)

RAF – Royal Air Force
RAMC – Royal Army Medical Corps
RDubFus – Royal Dublin Fusiliers
RE – Royal Engineers
RFC – Royal Flying Corps
RFus – Royal Fusiliers (City of London
  Regiment)
RinnisFus – Royal Inniskilling Fusiliers
RIR – Royal Irish Rifles
RLanc – Royal Lancaster Regiment (The King's
  Own)
RND – Royal Naval Division
RSFus – Royal Scots Fusiliers
RWFus – Royal Welsh Fusiliers
RWKent – Royal West Kent Regiment (The
  Queen's Own)
Scot Rfls – Scottish Rifles (The Cameronians)
SLancs – South Lancashire Regiment (The
  Prince of Wales's Volunteers)
SStaffs – South Staffordshire Regiment
Suffolk – Suffolk Regiment
TMB – Trench Mortar Battery
Wilts – Wiltshire Regiment (The Duke of
  Edinburgh's)
WRiding – West Riding Regiment (Duke of
  Wellington's)
WY – West Yorkshire Regiment (The Prince of
  Wales's Own)
Y&L – York and Lancaster Regiment
Yorks – Yorkshire Regiment (Alexandra,
  Princess of Wales's Own) (Green Howards)

OTHER ABBREVIATIONS (INCLUDING SYMBOLS)

Admin – Administration
Amb – Ambulance
APM – Assistant Provost Marshal
Arty – Artillery
Asst – Assistant
Attd – Attached
Ave – Avenue
Bde – Brigade
BM – Brigade Major
Bn – Battalion

BSM – Battery Sergeant Major
C – Cemetery
CC – Communal Cemetery
Chyd – Churchyard
CI – Chief Instructor
Clk – Clerk
Comm – Commissioned
Con – Control
CWGC – Commonwealth War Graves
  Commission

D – Died
DCM – Distinguished Conduct Medal
Demob – Demobilized
Div – Division
Dmr – Drummer
Dow – Died of Wounds
DSO – Distinguished Service Order
Empl – Employed / ment
Engr – Engineer
Enl – Enlisted
Ext – Extension
Fd – Field
FGCM – Field General Court Martial
Fm – Farm
FM – Field Mar shal
G – Gassed
Garr – Garrison
GC – George Cross
Gds – Guards
Gen – General
Gnr – Gunner
Hon – Honorary
IC – In Command / Charge
Instr – Instructor
Kia – Killed in Action
Lab – Labour
Lived – Lived at (address)
Ln – Lane
Lt – Light
MC – Military Cross / Cemetery
Med – Medium / Medical
Mem – Memorial
MG – Machine Gun
MID – Mentioned in Dispatches
Mil – Military
Min – Ministry

MM – Military Medal
MO – Medical Officer
Mob – Mobilized
MSM – Meritorious Service Medal
NCO – Non-Commissioned Officer
Offr – Officer
Ord – Orderly
OU-Other Unitls (served in)
PI – Platoon
Pie – Place
POW – Prisoner of War
PTI – Physical Training Instructor
Ptl – Patrol
Pty – Party
Reg – Regular
Regt – Regiment
Res – Reserve
Rft – Reinforcement
Rlwy – Railway
Rm – Room
SB – Stretcher Bearer
See – Secretary
Sect – Section
Sqn – Squadron
SS – Shell Shock
Stmn – Storeman
Sve – Service
Tee – Terrace
TF – Territorial Force
Tfc – Traffic
Tpt – Transport
Trans – Transfer / red
Univ – University
Vet – Veterinary
W – Wounded
Wksp – Workshop

SYMBOLS
* = Serving in 12 Y&L on 1 Jul 16
+ = Took part in 1 Jul 16 attack
– = Left out of 1 Jul 16 attack

1. Sequence. Information is set out as far as possible in the following order:
SURNAME
Initials:
Rank:
Number:
Company:
 Dec orations:
Birthplace / date:
Injuries / date: Memorial:
Occupation-civilian and military:
Address:
Other units served in:
Status on 1 Jul 16:
Commissioning details:
Other items of interest.

Often very little is known about a man. In such cases an explanation is given why it is known he was in the Battalion, e.g. member of the 12th Club.

2. Rank. The highest rank held is shown with one exception. If a soldier was commissioned from the ranks of 12 Y&L to another unit. then his highest rank in 12 Y&L is given.

3. Company. Soldiers often changed companies. The following companies existed: A, B and C Rifle Companies – Formed throughout the Battalion's existence.

D Rifle Company – Disbanded on a number of occasions in 1917.
E and F Companies – Reserve Companies, never part of the fighting element of the Battalion, remained in UK.

HQ Company – Shown as H in the list. It formed in 1917 to centralize all the administrative elements of the Battalion.

4. Decorations. Only those won in the First World War or before are shown. For details of the awards see the section on 'Honours and Awards'.

5. Birthplace and Date. Sadly incomplete, but as accurate as possible.

6. Injuries and Date. Details of deaths are fairly comprehensive, thanks to the CWGC. Details of non-fatal wounds are incomplete and have been compiled from a number of sources. Injuries sustained with other units are shown as such.

Often only a month is shown, because newspaper casualty lists did not give the actual date of wounding.

7. Memorial. These refer only to burial places and memorials from wartime deaths. All cemeteries and memorials are in France unless otherwise stated.

Memorials are where those with no known graves are recorded.

8. Occupation. Sadly incomplete. Military specialisations are shown where known. Often a man's civilian firm will be shown when his actual occupation is unknown.

9. Address. Addresses during the war only are shown.

10. Other Units. Units served with before and after 12 Y&L. They are not necessarily in chronological order.

11. Status on 1 Jul 16. The symbol ' *' denotes a man on the Battalion strength on 1 Jul 16.

The symbol* +' denotes he took part in the attack, or was in the forward trenches. The symbol '–' denotes he was left out of battle, but May have been in range of enemy guns or moved up to the trenches later in the day.

12. Sources. The information given has been compiled from many varied sources.

Sadly the details given in different sources often vary. In such cases the majority case has been taken, or official records given preference. Relatives, friends or old comrades May spot some mistakes or omissions. We would be delighted to hear of them through the offices of the publishers, so that a fuller record than is possible in this book can be deposited in the York and Lancaster Regiment Museum in Rotherham.

ABERSHAW, H: Pte: 34167: OU-2, 1/5, 10 & 14 Y&L

ABRAHAM, GG: Pte: 12/573: C: Bank Clk

ACKROYD, TE: Pte: 46368: OU-1/4 & 2/5 Y&L

ADAMSON, F: Pte: 20491: OU-2/4 & 6 Y&L

ADAMSON, WH: Pte: 33538: OU-7 Y&L

ADDEY, RC: Pte: 12/1293: B: Signaller: * +

ADKIN, CH: Pte: 37970: OU-2, 2/4 & 6 Y&L

ADUNGTON, S: Pte: 31752: OU-1eics, 2, 6 & 13 Y&L

AGER, HV: Pte: 33551: OU-2/4 & 6 Y&L

AHERN, R: Pte: 12/280: B: W 1 Jul 16: * +: Comm WY 12 Apr 17

ALDIS, H: Pte: 235599: B: OU-94 MGC

ALFLAT, WG: Pte: 12/847: D: Born Sheffield 1895: SS Jun 16: Lived 32 Andover St, Pitsmoor

ALLATT, NH: Pte: 12/848: D: * +

ALLCARD, JW: Pte: 12/1443: B: Born Bakewell 1897: Runner: * -: OU-DLI

ALLCARD, J: Pte: 12/1530: Born Walkley, Sheffield 1895: OU-2, 7, 9 & 14 Y&L

ALLEN, DC: Maj: OU-Tank Corps

ALLEN, JH: Pte: 12/282: B: * –

ALLEN, L: 12th Club member

ALLEN, R: Pte: 12/1974: D: W 1 Jul 16: * +

ALLEN, T: Pte: 31555

ALLEN, W: Pte: 37613: OU-2 Y&L

ALLEN, WV: Pte: 12/20: A: * +

ALLISON, JF: Pte: 31961: B: OU-41 Mob Vet Sect & 10 NFus

ALLOTT, WW: Pte: 12/21: A: Batman: * –

ALLOTT, M: LCpl: 13020: A: OU-211 Fd Coy RE: Bomber

ALLSOP, H: Pte *12/575: C: W 1 Jul 16: * +: 12th Club Treasurer

ALLSOPP, R: Pte: 12/576: C: * +

ALPIN, JC: Pte: 14/1453: Born 1890: Kia 2 Jul 18 with 2 Y&L: Nine Elms MC, Poperinghe, Belgium: OU-2, 7 & 8 Y&L

ALVEY, T: Pte: 12/1984: D: W 1 Jul 16: * +

AMBLER, JH: Pte: 12/849: D: Born Bishop Aukland: Kia 1 Jul 16: Thiepvai Mem: * +

AMBLER, H: Pte: 12/1958: Born Hillsboro, Sheffield 1885: Kia 9 Jul 17 with 13 Y&L: Coxyde MC, Belgium

ANCOATS, J: Pte: 12/2006: OU-14 Y&L

ANDERSON, T: Attended 1918 Reunion Dinner

ANDREW, J: LCpl: 12/577: C: Born Walkley, Sheffield: Kia 1 Jul 16: Thiepval Mem: * +: Lived 69 Walkley Rd

ANTHONY, LA: Pte: 12/1340: A: * –: OU-1 15 & 13 Y&L

APPLEBY, FO: Pte: 12/851: D: Born All Saints, Sheffield 1893: Kia 1 Jul 16 Thiepval Mem: Bank Clk: Lived 163 Ellesmere Rd: * +

APPLETON, C: LCpl: 40185: C: Born Driffield 1894: Kia 16 Feb 17: Courcelleo MC Ext: Lived Driffield: OU-EY & 7 Y&L

APPLEYARD, A: Pte: 12/1903: OU-13 Y&L

ARDERN, S: Pte: 12/1172: A: * –

ARMITAGE, LE: Pte: 12/1749: C: W 1 Jul 16: * +: OU-6 & 8 Y&L

ARMITAGE, LJ: Pte: 13/1307: OU-1 Y&L

ARMITAGE, WJ: Maj: Ex TF: Left Bn Oct 14

ARMSTRONG, E: Pte: 31353: OU-Northants, 2 & 7 Y&L

ARNOLD, F: Pte: 12/283: B: * +

ARNOLD, TC: Pte: 41102: A: Born Doncaster 1884: OU-94 MGC & 13- Y&L: Lewis gnr: Labourer

ARRIDGE, SE: Pte: 12/23: A: * +: Comm KOYLI25 Sep 17

ARRIDGE, HC: Pte: 12/24: MM: * +: Comm KOYL129 Sep 17

ARROWSMITH, AE: Pte: 12/25: A: Born Walkley, Sheffield 1895: Kia 16 May 16 Sucrerie MC, Colincamps: Empl William Huttons: Lived Harcourt Rd

ASH, T: Pte: 28783: OU-2 Y&L

ASHBOURNE, J: Pte: 31589: OU-3/5 NStaffs & 7 Y&L

ASHMORE, H: Pte: 39100: OU-1 O Y&L

ASHTON, A: Pte: 12/1893: B: Born Grimesthorpe: Kia 1 Jul 16: Queens MC, Serre

ASHTON, CH: Pte: 12/850: D: * –: OU-13 Y&L

ASHTON, GA: Pte: 12/2000: A: Signaller: * +

ASHTON, WH: Pte: 12/2001: A: Signaller: OU-7 & 13 Y&L

ASHWORTH, S: Pte: 12/1349: B: * –: Discharged underage

ASKEW, CL: Pte: 12/852: D: W 1 Jul 16: Lived 8 Stanley Rd, Meersbrook: * +

ASKEW, H: Cpl: 12/578: C: Born Sheffield: Dow 25 Oct 18 with 7 Y&L: Awoingt MC: * +

ASPINALL, R: Pte: 12/1527: Born Leigh: Kia 21 May 16 with 2 Y&L: Essex Fm MC, Boesinghe, Belgium: Lived Rotherham

ASPINALL, S: Pte: 38579: OU-2, 7 & 13 Y&L

ASPLAND, SE: Pte: 12/284: B: Born Handsworth, Sheffield 1896: Kia 1 Jul 16: Queens MC, Serre: Lived Fitzallan Rd, Handsworth: * +

ASQUITH, T: Pte: 31960: OU-10 NFus & 7 Y&L

ASTILL, A: Pte: 41080: Dow 19 Sep 17 with 8 Y&L

ATHERTON, JT: Pte: 12/1631: A: Cook: * +

ATKIN, C: Cpl: 12/1526: D: * –

ATKIN, GE: Pte: 34053: Kia 18 Mar 18 with 1/4 Y&L: Duhaliow Advance Dressing Station MC, Ypres, Belgium: OU-1/4, 2/4, 2, 10 & 14 Y&L

ATKIN, GR: Pte: 12/853: D: * +

ATKIN, H: Pte: 12/1353: C: W Jun 16: Empl City Flour Mills

ATKIN, WJ: Sgt: 12/840: + –

ATKINS, A: Pte: 12/579: C: * +

ATKINS, WE: Pte: 40064: OU-9 Y&L

ATKINSON, AE: ASgt: 12/580: C: * –: OU-13 Y&L

ATKINSON, C: Pte: 12/1381: C: Born St Mar ys, Sheffield 1894: Kia 1 Jul 16: Thiepval Mem: Sheffield Univ Student: * +

ATKINSON, C: 12/2042: MM: Born Sheffield 1875: Kia 30 May 18 with 19 MGC: Soissons Mem

ATKINSON, E: Pte: 41758: OU-6 Y&L

ATKINSON, HA: ACSM: 12/838: AD: Born Skegness 1-882: Dow 9 Jul 16: St Clements Chyd, Skegness: Lived Grantham: * +

ATKINSON, JSB: Pte: 12/27: A: W 1 Jul 16: * +

ATKINSON, M: Pte: 37824: OU-10 Y&L

ATKINSON, SJ: Lt: Tpt Offr Jan – Oct 16

AUSTIN, E: Pte: 12/285: B: Born Ecclesfield 1884: Dow 20 Jun 17: Duisans MC, Etrun: * –

AYLING, F: Pte: 235675: C: 94 Bde concert pty

BACKHOUSE, W: Pte: 19347: OU-2 & 6 Y&L

BADGER, G: Sgt: 12/29: A: W 1 Jul 16: QM storeman: * +

BADGER, H: CSgt/CQMS: Sheff Univ Lab Asst

BAGGALAY, W: Pte: 12/854: D: SS Jul 16: Observer: * +

BAGOT, CH: ASgt: 235678: HQ

BAGSHAW, A: Pte: 2375: A: * –

BAGSHAW, A: LCpl: 18673: OU-9 Y&L

BAGSHAW, E: Pte: 12/287: B: W 1 Jul 16

BAGSHAW, GW: Pte: 12/855: D: Sheffield Univ Student * +

BAGSHAW, JH: Pte: 12/2075: Born St Georges, Sheffield 1895: Kia 24 Jan 18: Roclincourt MC

BAGSHAW, WH: Pte: 12/288: Born Sheffield 1887: Kia 1 Jul 16: Queens MC, Serre: Lived 4 Maple Rd, Kiveton Park: * +

BAGSHAWE, WW: Pte: 12/1163: A: Born Netheredge, Sheffield: Kia 1 Jul 16: Thiepval Mem: Lived 32 Wostenholm Rd: * +

BAILEY, BE: Pte: 12/30: A: Born Tipton, Staffs 1892: Dow 26 Jul 16: Abbeville CC: * +

BAILEY, G: Pte: 12/1928: C: * –

BAILEY, H: Pte: 12/1746: Born Eckington. Kia 1 Jul 16 with 8 Y&L: Thiepval Mem: Lived Rotherham

BAILEY, HE: Pte: 12/31: A: W 1 Jul 16: Sheffield Univ Student * +

BAILEY, J: Pte: 241497: OU-2 & 2/5 Y&L

BAILEY, J: Pte: 12/289: B: Born Penistone: Kia 1 Jul 16: Thiepval Mem: Rlwy Platelayer: * +

BAILEY, JM: Pte: 14/964: Born 1890: Kia 29 Jul 18 with 7 Y&L: Harponville CC Ext: OU-7, 13 & 14 Y&L

BAILEY, JS: Pte: 39098: OU-7 & 10 Y&L

BAILEY, M: Pte: 12/1444: D: * –: OU-7 Y&L

BAILEY, NO: Cpl: 21880: D: * +

BAILEY, PT: LCpl: 12/581: C: Released for Munitions work Jun 16

BAILEY, W: ASgt: 16326: OU-2 & 8 Y&L

BAKER, A: Pte: MC: Sheffield Univ Student: Comm 1/5 Y&L 17 Nov 14

BAKER, EG: Pte: 235677: OU-7 Y&L

BAKER, G: Pte: 235678: OU-7 Y&L

BAKER, G: Pte: 33552: A: Born Milton Bryant, Bedfordshire: Kia 28 Mar 18 with 13 Y&L: Bucquoy Rd MC, Ficheux

BAKER, RT: LCpl: 12/1587: C: Born Cambridge 1880: Kia 1 Jul 16: Railway Hollow MC Serre: * +

BAKER, T: Pte: 18502: OU-2 & 6 Y&L

BAKER, WE: Engineer: Lived Thornsett Rd: Comm 3/5 RLancs Sep 15

BALL, WH: Pte: 27574: A: OU-2, 10 & 13 Y&L

BALLARD, E: Pte: 12/582: C: * +

BALLINGER, H: Pte: 17821: OU-2, 7 & 10 Y&L

BAMENT, CF: 2Lt: Comm 12 Y&L 26 Sep 17

BAMFORD, J: LCpl: 3/2486: Born Wakefield 1894: Dow 28 Jul 17: Aubigny CC Ext Lived Wakefield: OU-2 Y&L

BAMFORTH, B: Cpl: 12/1392: B: MSM: Regt Police: * –

BANHAM, E: Pte: 12/33: A: Kia 28 Sep 16 with 10EY: Underhili Fm MC, Belgium: Comm 13 Y&L 28 May 18, attd 10EY

BANNER, F: Pte: 12/1232: B: W 1 Jul 16: * +

BANNISTER, J: Pte: 15907: OU-7, 9 & 10 Y&L

BANTON, W: Pte: 31603: A: OU-3/5 NStaffs & 211 Fd Coy RE

BARBER, B: ASgt: 12/1162: B: Born Wales, Sheffield: W May 16 with 12 Y&L and Kia 28 Jun 18 with 13 Y&L: Cinq Rues MC, Hazebrouck: OU-2 & 13 Y&L

BARBER, H: Pte: 31354: Born Southery, Norfolk: Kia 12 May 17: Albuera MC, Bailleul: Lived Downham, Norfolk: OU-Northants

BARBER, H: ACpl: 46458: OU-7 Y&L

BARBER, J: Pte: 16982: D: * +: OU-7 & 9 Y&L

BARBER, JH: Pte: 235604: OU-7 Y&L

BARDSLEY, D: LCpl: 12/34: A: * –: Comm SStaffs 29 May 17

BARDSLEY, JCG: Lt: Sheffield Univ Student Comm 12 Y&L 15 May 15: Ex 12 Y&L OR: Signals Offr

BARKER, A: Pte: 12/859: D: * +: OU-13 Y&L

BARKER, A: Pte: 39040: OU-1/5, 9 & 10 Y&L

BARKER, AW: LCpl: 12/290: D: Born Sheffield 1897: W 1 Jul 16: Sniper: * +: OU: DLI

BARKER, D: Pte: 12/860: D: * +

BARKER, FF: Pte: 12/86: D: * –

BARKER, GJ: Dte: 12/585: C: W 1 Jul 16: Lived Tinsley: * +

BARKER, EE: ACpl: 12/35: A: * –

BARKWELL, WH: LCpl: 12/36: A: Ord Rm Clk: * –

BARLOW, J: Pte: 31558: Born Madeley, Staffs 1881: Kia 15 Nov 16: Sally au Bois MC: Lived Newcastle, Staffs: OU-NStafis

BARLOW, W: Pte: 12/291: B: Born Thurlestone, Penistone: Kia 16 May 16: Sucrene MG, Colincamps: Half brother of EF Squires

BARNABY, WG: Kia 23 Aug 16 with 7KOYLI: Thiepval Mem: Sheffield Univ Student: Comm 7KOYLI

BARNABY, F: Pte: 12/1201: C: * –

BARNES, A: Pte: 14/1534: C: Shoemaker: OU-13 & 14 Y&L

BARNES, A: Sgt: A: * +

BARNHAM, F: Pte: 241785: OU-1/4, 2/5 & 9 Y&L

BARNISH, H: Pte: 31562: OU-7 Y&L

BARNSLEY, F: LCpl: 12/862: D: Born Crookes, Sheffield 1895: Kia 1 Jul 16: Thiepval Mem: Lived 168 Channing St, Walkley: * +

BARNSLEY, H: Pte: 12/1909: OU-14 Y&L

BARNSLEY, WR: Pte: 12/863: W Apr 16 and Kia 25 Sep 16 with 10 N Fus: Thiepval Mem

BARON, E: Pte: 12/1960: A: * –

BARRACLOUGH, H: Pte: 12/1338: D: * –

BARRACLOUGH, JH: Pte: 27969: OU-2 & 7 Y&L

BARRACLOUGH, WA: Pte: 12/1483: B: * +: OU-2 & 8 Y&L

BARRAS, JH: Pte: 12/864: D: * –

BARRASS, G: Pte: 33540: OU-7 Y&L

BARRETT, R: Pte: 31563: OU-NStaffs, 2 & 2/4 Y&L

BARRON, A: Pte: 12/1799: Born Sheffield 1891: Kia 28 Mar 18 with 13 Y&L: Bienvillers MC

BARRETT, J: Pte: 235602: OU-7 Y&L

BARROTT, JH: Pte: 12/865: D: Born Portsmouth 1895: Kia 1 Jul 16: Thiepval Mem: Lived 93 Tadeaster Rd, Woodseats: * +

BARROW, T: Pte: 12/1035: A: * +

BARSTOW, E: Cpl: 12/866: D: Born Sheffield 1885: W 1 Jul 16: Lived 21 Berkeley St: * +

BARSTOW, HP: Pte: 12/1901: OU-13 Y&L

BARTEL, F: Pte: 28425: OU-2 Y&L

BARTHOLOMEW, H: Sgt: 12/293: BC: * –: Comm 6 Y&L 29 Aug 17

BARTLETT, LP: Pte: 12/586: C: W 16 May 16

BARTON, A: Pte: 12/587: C: * +

BARTON, BB: Pte: 203001: OU-1/5 & 7 Y&L

BARTON, H: Pte: 12/1575: D: Born Sharrow, Sheffield 1886: Kia 9 Sep 17 with 1/4 Y&L: Tyne Cot Mem, Belgium: * –: OU-1/4 & 9 Y&L

BARTON, J: Pte: 24034: A: Signaller: OU-10 & 13 Y&L

BARTON, JA: Pte: 12/867: D: Born Sharrow, Sheffield 1894: Kia 1 Jul – 16: Euston Rd MC, Colincamps: Lived 6 Upper Hannover St & 34 South View Rd: * +

BASS, J: Pte: 37982: OU-2 Y&L

BASSINDER, L: Pte: 12/1471: 8: Born Attercliffe, Sheffield: Kia 1 Jul 16: Thiepval Mem: Lived Barnsley: * +

BASTOW, J: Pte: 31964: OU-1 0 NFus

BATEMAN, J: Pte: 12/1810: B: W 1 Jul 16: * +

BATES, J: Pte: 31560: A: Batman

BATLEY, A: Pte: A: W 1 Jul 16

BATLEY, AG: Kia 27 Sep 18 with 11 Mancs: Quarry MC, Marquion: Comm. 4 Mancs

BATLEY, E: Pte: 12/294: A: Born Stainboro, Barnsley 1893: Kia 1 Jul 16: AIF Burial Gd, Flers: Lived Barnsley: * +

BATLEY, J: Pte: 12/38: A: Runner: * +

BATLEY, JW: Bank Clk

BATTY, E: Pte: 12/1861: C: * –

BAYLIS, LS: Pte: 12/295: B

BAYLIS, L: Pte: 12/296: B.Born Selby: Kia 1 Jul 16: Thlepval Mem: Lived Stainfoot, Barnsley: * +

BAYUS, R: Cpl: 12/1849: Born Selby 1895: Dow 22 Mar 18 with 2 Y&L Dernancourt CC Ext: OU, 2, 1 15 & 13 Y&L

BAYNES, AC: ACSM: 12/589: C: Teacher: W Aug 16: OU-7 & 13 Y&L: Stainless Stepnen-radio comic

BEACHER, PK: ASgt: 24131: OU-7 Y&L.

BEACH, NH: Pte: Sheffield Univ Student

BEAL, M: Pte: 12/1433: D

BEAL, AJ: 2Lt: B: Born 1894: Kia 1. Jul 16: Queens MC, Serre: Sheffield Univ Student: Lived Ivy Park Rd: * +: OC 16 PL and MG Sect

BEAL, FA: Lt: SS 1 Jul 16: Empl family firm J&J Beal: Lived Red Hill, Shefiield: Ex Mancs, trans 12 Y&L Sep 15: OU-94 TMB

BEALL, WR: ASgt: 12/39: AC: Born Christ Ch, Doncaster 1892: Kia 1 Jul 16: Thiepval Mem: Bank Clk: Lived Harrogate: * +

BEARD, I: Pte: 31564: OU-3/5 NStaffs, 2 & 2/4 Y&L

BEARDSHAW, B: Pte: 12/590: C: * –

BEARSHAW, W: Pte: 13/127: OU-2, 1 0 & 13 Y&L

BEAUMONT, A: Pte: 31965: Born Leeds: Kia 11 May 17: Arras Mem: Lived Leeds: OU-WY & 10 NFus

BEAUMONT, D: Pte: 12/1448: B: Born Sheffield 1892: Kia 1 Jul 16: Queens MC, Serre: Lived 21 Brookfield Rd, Sharrow: * +

BEAUMONT, E: Pte: 37965: OU-2 Y&L

BEAUMONT, F: Pte: 12/1732: OU-1 Y&L

BEAUMONT, JG: 2Lt: OU-7 Y&L

BEAUMONT, WS: Pte: 12/42: A: W 1 Jul 16: Sheffield Univ Student: * +

BECKETT, JW: Pte: 12/2038: A: * –

BECKETT, R: Pte: 21994: O: Born 1891: Kia 12 Apr 18 with 1I4 Y&L: Tyne Cot Mem, Passchendaele, Belgium: OU-1/4 & 14 Y&L: * –

BECKETT, W: ASSgt: 12/2008: Armourer

BEDFORD, AH: Pte: 39089: OU-2/4, 6 & 10 Y&L

BEDFORD, J: D: Born 1894: Tailor

BEDFORD, N: Pte: 12/591: C: Born Sheffield: Kia 1 Jul 16: Thiepval Mem: Sheffield Univ Student: * +

BEDFORD, W: Pte: 12/868: D: * –

BEE, A: Pte: 40076: OU-9 Y&L

BEECH, L: Pte: 12/1385: B: * –: OU-7 Y&L

BEELEY, FW: Pte: 12/1919: C: 31 Div carpenter: * –

BEENY, HH: Pte: 12/43: A: * –: OU-RAF

BEIGHTON, H: Pte: 12/1731: OU-13 Y&L

BEIGHTON, J: Pte: 13/152: Kia 12 Apr 18 with 13 Y&L: Tyne Cot Mem, Passchendaele, Belgium: OU-1/4, 2/5 & 13 Y&L: CWGC say he died with 1/4 Y&L

BELEY, G: Capt: DE: Comm 23 Sep 14

BELK, J: LCpl: 12/44: A: W 1 Jul 16: * +

BELK, WG: Pte: 37589: OU-2, 1/5, 8 & 10 Y&L

BELL, F: Pte: 40086: Born Austerfield, Yorkshire: Kia 18 Jul 17: Aubigny CC Ext Lived Doncater: OU-KOYLI

BELL, F: Pte: 31968: HQ: Regt Police: OU-10 NFus, 2 & 13 Y&L

BELL, GG: Pte: 12i1591: 0: * +

BELL, MW: LCpl: 12/297: B: Bank Clk: Signaller: * –

BELL, R: Pte: 36258: OU-7 & 10 Y&L

BELLAMY, F: Pte: 12/1759: OU-13 Y&L

BELLIS, R: Pte: 21677: OU-2, 6 & 13 Y&L

BELTON, FE: Pte: 12/869: O: W 1 Jul 16: Lived 97 Cemetery Rd: * +

BENHAM, A: Pte: 46456: OU-7 Y&L

BENNETT, EH: Pte: 12/298: W 1 Jul 16: Lived Mexboro: * +

BENNETT, F: Pte: 12/2165

BENNETT, JA: Pte: 12/870: D: Born Sharrow, Sheffield 1892: Kia 1 Jul 16: Euston Rd MC, Coiincamps: Lived 135 South View Rd: * +

BENNETT, JW: Pte: 13/68: O: * –: OU-7 & 13 Y&L

BENNETT, RRB: Pte: 41 042: OU-8 Y&L

BENNETT, SF: Pte: 12/592: C: W 1 Jul 16: * +

BENNISTON, A: Pte: 12/593: C: Born Sheffield: Kia 1 Jul 16: Thiepval Mem: –Bank Clk: Lived Western Bank: * +

BENSON, BJ: Sheffield Univ Student

BENTLEY, GE: Pte: 31557: OU-2 & 2/4 Y&L

BENTLEY, J: Pte: 12/1501: B: W 1 Jul 16: * +

BENTON, A: Pte: 12/1468: B: Born Sheffield: Kia 24 Oct 18 with 2 Y&L: St Souplet MC: * –: OU-2 & 13 Y&L

BERRIDGE, H: Pte: 13/99: OU-2 & 13 Y&L

BERRY, RD: Lt: Born 1895: Kia 12 May 17: A/buera MC, Bailleul: Lived 3 Endcliffe Grove Ave: Comm 20 Nov 14: 0C 12 Pl

BERRY, TG: 2Lt: Comm 20 Nov 14: 0C 13 PL: OU-13 Y&L

BERRY, G: Pte: 235603: HQ: Pioneer: OU-2/4 & 13 Y&L

BERRY, G: Pte: 235679: HQ: Specia/ Patrol Pty: OU-2/4 & 13 Y&L

BERTANT, HE: Pte: 12/1357: O: Signailer: * –;OU-10 & 13 Y&L

BERTAUT, H: Pte: 12/1813: O: Born Sheffield 1896: Kia 15 Apr 18 with 13 Y&L: Ploegsteert Mem, Belgiurn: Signaller: * –

BESCOBY, AJ: Pte: 12/594: C: Born Sheffield 1893: W date not known: – Lived Ryda/hurst, Wadsiey

BEST, SJ: Pte: 235680: OU-9 Y&L

BETHELL, LR: 2Lt: Comm 25 Jan 16 3 Y&L12 Y&L from 8 Jan 17: OU-4 Y&L

BETTERIDGE, J: Pte: 235681: OU-7 Y&L

BEVINGTON, TE: CSM: 12/299: 0: * –: OU-9 Y&L

BIDWELL, GT: Pte: 39036: OU-10 Y&L

BIGGIN, A: Cpl: 12/1160: A: * –

BILBEY, AT: CSM: 12/4: AC: Born Haliam, Sheffield: Kia 1 Jul 16: Thiepval Mem: Ex Regular: * +

BILLAM, FD: Pte: 12/595: C: W 16 May 16: Empl TW Ward: Lived 124 Gram Mar St, Walkley

BILLS, V: Cpl: 31369: OU-2, 1/4, 1/5, 6 & 14 Y&L

BILTCLIFFE, E: Pte: 26821: Born 1895: Kia 21 Jul 18 with 1/5 Y&L: Courmas MC: OU-1/5 & 13 Y&L

BINDER, WB: LCpl: 12/871: D: Born Kimberworth: Kia 1 Jul 16: Thiepval Mem: Lived Red House, Thorpe Hesley: * +

BINGHAM, A: Pte: 203724: C: OU-94 TMB, 1/4 & 13 Y&L

BINGHAM, JE: Pte: 21763: A: * –: Bandsman: OU-13 Y&L

BINGHAM, RA: Pte: 27446: Kia 13 Nov 16 with 5 MGC: Thiepval Mem

BINGHAM, T: W02/RQMS: 12/300: D: Teacher: Ex TF: OU-9, 13 & 18 Y&L

BINNS, F: Pte: 12/1139: D: Cook: * +

BIRCH, F: Pte: 31556: OU- 7 & 8 Y&L

BIRCH, GE: Pte: 12/1619: OU-2, 10 & 14 Y&L

BIRD, R: Pte: 12/48: A: W May 16: Comm Y&L 26 Jun 17

BISATT, GN: Pte: 12/301: Comm WY 26 Jun 17

BISHOP, H: Pte: 12/1441: B: W 1 Jul 16: Lived Rotherham: * +

BISHTON, AJ: Pte: 18692: OU-1/4, 6 & 10 Y&L

BLACK, SS: Pte: 12/1116: A: Born Sheffield: Kia 1 Jul 16: Thiepval Mem: * +

BLACKBOURN, WI: Pte: 39084: OU-1 O Y&L

BLACKNELL, W: Pte: 37963: Born 1893: Kia 6 Apr 17 with 2 Y&L: Mar oc MC, Grenay

BLACKTIN, SC: Pte: 12/596: C

BLAD, CE: 2Lt: W 28 May 18 with 7 Y&L: Comm 31 Jan 17: 12 Y&L from 11 Sep 17: Lived Guernsey

BLAKE, JH: Pte: 12/872: OU-2 Y&L

BLAKE, LA: Pte: 46455: OU-13 Y&L

BLAKEMORE, T: Pte: 12/2049: A: * –: OU-7 & 10 Y&L

BLAKESLEY, JH: Pte: 12/873: 0: W Jul 16: * +

BLAND, E: LCpl: 12/874: 0: Born Liandudno 1894: Kia 1 Jul 16: Thiepval Mem: Lived Liandudno: * +

BLANK, FW: Sgt: 12/50: A: Born Milford, Oerbyshire: W May 16: Teacher: Lived Ashbourne: * –

BLENKARN, W: LCpl: 12/597: C: Born Burngreave, Sheffield 1891: Kia 10 Sep 16: Loos Mem: * –

BLOOR, JH: Pte: 31561: OU-3/5 NStaffs, 2, 6 & 13 Y&L

BOCKING, F: Pte: 235200: OU-1/4 Y&L

BOLSOVER, GF: LCpl: 12/1292: A: Netheredge, Sheffield 1899: W May 16 with 12 Y&L and Kia 23 Jul 18 with 2/4 Y&L: Courmas MC: OU-2/4 & 6 Y&L

BOND, F: Pte: 12/598: C: SS May / Jun 16: Lived 192 Crookesmoor Rd

BOND, I: Pte: 12/599: C: * +: OU-2 & 13 Y&L

BOND, SG: Pte: 12/1 060: A

BONNELL, J: Pte: 39483: Kia 28 Jun 18 with 13 Y&L: Ploegsteert Mem, Belgium: OU-7, 13 & 14 Y&L

BONNER, A: Pte: 12/302: B: * +: OU-13 Y&L

BONSER, PJ: Pte: 31966: OU-3/5 NStaffs, 2, 6 & 10 Y&L

BOOCOCK, J: Pte: 16166: Born Wakefield: Kia 1 O May 17: Arras Mem: Lived Wakefield

BOOKER, F: Pte: 12/2011: A: OU-6 Y&L

BOOT, WH: Sgt: 12/304: 8: * –

BOOTH, CA: Pte: 12/1171: A: Bugler: * –: OU-8 & 13 Y&L

BOOTH, E: Pte: 22237: OU-8 & 10 Y&L

BOOTH, H: 2Lt: W 13 Aug 17: Served 12 Y&L 21 Feb ·8 Apr 17

BOOTH, S: Pte: 12239: C

BOSTOCK, HL: Pte: 235682

BOSTON, GA: Pte: 39052: 0ow 29 Mar 18: OU-2 & 10 Y&L

BOSWELL, HJ: Pte: 235605

BOTTOMLEY, J: Pte: 13/145: OU-2 & 13 Y&L

BOURN, AA: Pte: 12/305: B: SS 1 Jul i 6: * +

BOURNE, WK: ASgt: 31348: MID: OU-1 Northants & 7 Y&L

BOUTLAND, A: PteA0205: OU-6 & 7 Y&L

BOWEN, HR: 2Lt: Served 12 Y&L from 80se17

BOWES, F: Pte: 12/600: D: Born Drypool, Huil: Kia 1 Jul 16: Thiepval Mem: Lived Hull: * +

BOWNS, H: Pte: 12/2005: A: * –

BOWSKILL, I: Pte: 12/1710 Born Hollinsend, Shefiield: Kia 1 Jul 16: Thiepval 227 Mem

BOWYER, A: Pte: 13334: RunNOJner

BOYCE, HW: Sgt12/601: ABC: ABCcf3: Comm Essex 31 Oct 17: * +

BOYD, JM: LCpl: 12/53: A: Born Clapham, M'sex: Kia 1 Jul 16: Thiepval Mem: Sheffield Univ Student: * +

BOYD, F: Pte: 12/2117: B: * –

BRAACK, JW: Pte: 12/1707: OU-1/5, 10 & 14 Y&L

BRACK, HM: Pte: 12/54: A: W 1 Jul 16: Sheffield Univ Student: * +

BRADLEY, JW: Pte: 38965: OU-2 & 8 Y&L

BRADLEY, W: Pte: 12/1650: D: W 1 Jul 16: * +

BRADSHAW, JE: LCpl: 12/602: C: W May 16: lived 271 Western Rd

BRADSHAW, O: ASgt12/877: D: G date not known: Sheffield Daily Telegraph cartoonist: * +: OU-13 Y&L

BRADWELL, CH: Pte: 12/878: D: W 1 Jul 16: lived 17 Pexton Rd: * +

BRAHAM, A: Pte: 12/1128: OU-9 Y&L

BRAHAM, G: Cpl: 12/307: B: Born Hoyland 1888: Kia 1 Jul 16: Thiepval Mem: Teacher: Lived The Briars, Sheffield Rd, Birdwell: * +

BRAHAM, WH: Pte: 27865: OU-13 Y&L

BRAITHWAITE, T: Pte: 12/603: C: * +

BRAMELD, RO: Pte: 22381: A: Born Pitsmoor, Sheffield 1888: Dow 14 Dec 16: Burngreave C, Sheffield * –

BRAMHAM, G: Pte: 12/31 O: Born St Philips, Sheffield: Dow 13 Oct 18 with 6 Y&L: Abbey lane C, Sheffield: Released for Munitions work 26 Sep 15: OU-2 & 6 Y&L

BRAMHAM, GH: Pte: 12/1668: C: Born St Philips, Sheffield 1887: Kia 14 Nov 16: Sailly au Bois MC: * +

BRAMMALL, P: Pte: 12/1259: C: * +: OU-2 & 14 Y&L

BRAMMER, A: Pte: 12/879: D: Born Walkley, Sheffield 1894: Kia 1 Jul 16: Railway Hollow MC, Serre: Lived 91 Carr Bank Rd, Walkley: Signaller: * +

BRAMMER, W: Pte: 12/1946: OU-1, 2, 8 & 13 Y&L

BRAMPTON, CBE: Pte: 22375: C: * –

BRASSINGTON, C: Pte: 12/1694

BRATLEY, CW: Pte: 12/604: C: Born Pontefract Kia 11 Apr 18 with 13 Y&L: Ploegsteert Mem, Belgium: * –

BRATLEY, JW: Pte: 12/1461: B: Born Sheffield 1895: Kia 1 Jul 16: Thiepval Mem: Lived 26 Wate Rd, Sharrow: * +

BRAZIER, G: Pte: 28207: OU-2, 2/4 & 6 Y&L

BREAM, H: LCpl: 12/2155: Born Sheffield: Kia 11 Oct 16 with 1 Y&L: Struma MC, Greece

BREATHWICK, J: LSgt13/147: D: MM: OU-2 & 13 Y&L

BREWER, A: Pte: 12/55: A: W 1 Jul 16: * +

BRIDGENS, FH: Pte: 12/1305: C: Cook: * +

BRIDGERS, HC: Pte: 235606: OU-7 Y&L

BRIDGEWATER, SE: SgtBorn 1874: Kia 29 Mar 16 with 15N&D: Royal Irish Rifles MC, Laventie: Comm N&D 1915: lived Middlewood Rd

BRIGGS, G: Sgt23155: OU-2 Y&L: Deserted 13 Oct 17

BRIGGS, H: Pte: 37994: OU-1 & 2 Y&L

BRIGGS, HF: Pte: 31962: OU-2 & 2/4 Y&L

BRIGGS, J: Pte: 14/1464: C: MM: Runner: OU-2, 8 & 9 Y&L

BRIGGS, R: Pte: 12/1881: C: Born Heeley, Sheffield 1891: Kia 1 Jul 16-: Luke Copse MC, Serre: Empl Sheffield Tramways: Lived 79 Lancing Rd: * +

BRIGGS, WAH: Pte: 12/1834: C: W 1 Jul 16: * +

BRIGHT, AW: CSM: 12/314: B: Born Eccleshail, Sheffield 1891: Kia 12 Apr 18 with 13 Y&L: Outtersteene CC Ext: * –

BRIGHT, S: Pte: 12/315: B: W 23 Mar 18 with 7 Y&L: * –

BRINDLEY, CW: Pte: 12/606: B: Born Sheffield 1897: W 1 Jul 16 with 12 Y&L and D 14 May 17 with 8 Y&L: Etaples MC: * +: OU-2 & 8 Y&L

BRINING, B: Pte: 12/56: A: * –

BRINNEN, CH: Pte: 12/1545: W Jul 16: OU-8 Y&L

BROADHURST, F: Pte: 203004: OU-1/5 & 7 Y&L

BROADHURST, G: Pte: 14/406: Dow 12 Apr 18 with 1/5 Y&L: Aire CC: OU-2, 1/5, 2/5 & 14 Y&L

BROADHURST, T: Pte: 13/148: A: * –: OU-13 Y&L

BROCKLESBY, GW: Pte: 235224: OU-2/4, 1/5 & 2/5 Y&L

BROCKLESBY, P: Comm 13 Y&L 1915

BRODIE, DS: 2Lt: Kia 15 Jun 18: Comm 29 Aug 17

BROGAN, W: Pte: 12/316: B: W 1 Jul 16: Empl GC Rlwy: Lived Don St, Pitsmoor: * +: OU-2 11 10 Y&L

BROMLEY H: Pte: 12/880: D: Cook: OU-1 0 & 13 Y&L

BROOK, J: Pte: 13/95: OU-1 /5, 2/5, 6, 10 & 13 Y&L

BROOKE, FW: Pte: 12/57: A: * +

BROOKE, HW: 2Lt: Comm 8 Jul 15

BROOKE, L: Sgt12/317: AB: * –: Comm WY 30 Oct 17

BROOKES, C: Pte: 24434: OU-13 Y&L

BROOKES, LW: LCpl: 12/1199: Born Rotherham 1889: Kia 20 Jul 16 with 2 Y&L: Ypres (Reservoir) MC, Belgium: Lived Rotherham

BROOKES, RF: Pte: 12/1125: B: Born Knighton, Leicester 1893: Kia 1 Jul 16: Thiepval Mem: lived 23 Change Alley: * +

BROOKFIELD, FH: Pte: 12/318: B: Kia 1 Jul 16: Thiepval Mem: lived Royal Hotel, Walkley St * +

BROOKS, GRE: Pte: 12/609: C: * +: OU-13 Y&L

BROOKS, H: Pte: 19873: OU-1.2 & 8 Y&L

BROOKS, JE: Pte: 12/1195: A: Born Kirton in Lindsey 1893: W 1 Jul 16 with 12 Y&L and Kia 20 Jul 18 with 2/4 Y&L: Soissons Mem: * +: OU-2/4 & 6 Y&L

BROOMHEAD, J: Pte: 21882: C: * +: OU-2 & 8 Y&L

BROOMHEAD, J: Pte: 12/31 9: B: * –: Comm Y&L 26 Jun 17

BROWETT, H: Pte: 28836: OU-2 Y&L

BROWLEE, W: Pte: 28417: OU-2 Y&L

BROWN, A: Pte: 12/607: C: Born Parkgate, Rotherham: Kia 1 Jul 16: Thiepval Mem: * +

BROWN, C: Pte: 12/320: B: * +

BROWN, CC: Pte: Sheff Univ Student

BROWN, CH: Pte: 235227: HQ: lewis gnr: OU-1 /4, 2/4, 1 /5 & 13 Y&L

BROWN, F: Pte: 12/1383: B: Born Hillsboro, Sheffield: Kia 1 Jul 16: Thiepval Mem: Lived 10 Tennyson Rd, Walkley: * +

BROWN, FK: Lived 38 Herries Rd: Member of 12th Club

BROWN, GA: Pte: 46460: OU-7 Y&L

BROWN, HS: Pte: 235607: Born Mancroft, Norwich: Dow 28 Oct 17: Duisans MC, Etrun: OU-Norfolks: lived Norwich

BROWN, J: 2Lt: Comm 29 Aug 17: Served 12 Y&L from 20 Oct 17

BROWN, JA: Pte: 12/1180: B: Born Walkley, Sheffield 1895: Kia 9 Oct 17 with 1/4 Y&L: Tyne Cot MC, Passchendaele, Belgium: OU-2, 1/4, 9 & 14 Y&L

BROWN, R: Pte: 12/2040: A: OU-33 Corps Wksp: Bomber: * –

BROWN, RB: Pte: 12/881: Born Ecclesall, Sheffield: Kia 20 Jul 16 with 2/4 Y&L: Soissons Mem: Sheffield Univ StudentOU-2/4 & 6 Y&L

BROWN, RH: Cpl: 191 00: OU-7 Y&L

BROWN, S: Pte: 12/608: Born Sheffield: D 6 Dec 17: Rociincourt MC: * –

BROWN, S: Pte: 12/882: D: Born Sharrow, Sheffield 1892: Kia 1 Jul 16 Thiepval Mem: lived Sharrow Lane: * +

BROWN, W: Pte: 39148: OU-2, 7 & 10 Y&L

BROWN, WH: Pte: 12/1904: C: W 1 Jul 16: * +

BROWN, WJ: Sgt: 12/12: B: SS Jul 16: lived Sharrow: * –: Comm WRiding 30 Apr 18

BROWNE, F: Pte: 12/1430: D: W 1 Jul 16: * +

BROWNHILL, JB: Pte: 12/1674: OU-14 Y&L

BROWNING, DO: 2Lt: C: G 1 O Sep 17: Comm 30 May 17: Served 12 Y&L from 3 Jul 17

BROWNLEES, TA: Pte: 37976: OU-2, 6 & ? Y&L

BRYAN, TJ: Pte: 29158: OU-2, 10, 13 & 14 Y&L

BRYANT, BG: 2Lt: Comm 16 Jan 15

BUCKLAND, J: 2Lt: Kia 16 Jun 17: Bailleul Rd East MC: Served 12 Y&L from 9 Feb 17

BUCKLE, Sgt: Served 12 Y&L Dec 14

BUCKLEY, A: Sgt: 12/883: D: MID: Bandsman: * +: OU-2/4 Y&L

BUCKLEY, G: Pte: 25570: D: OU-2 & 6 Y&L

BUCKLEY, G: Pte: 18468: A: OU-211 Fd Coy RE, ? & 13 Y&L

BUCKLEY, TL: Pte: 31457: OU-2, 2/4 & 6 Y&L

BUCKNALL, GS: Pte: 31590: OU-3/5 NStaffs & 7 Y&L

BUDDS, CW: Pte: 12/885: D: Born 1896: Kia 8 Sep 18 with 5 KOYU: Gouzeaucourt New MC: Bank Clk: Comm KOYL128 May 18

BULL, AE: Pte: 12/1831: C: Born Sheff 1896: Kia 1 Jul 16: Serre Rd No. 2 Me: * +

BULLAS, A: Pte: 28077: OU-2 Y&L

BULLIVANT, A: Pte: 3/4845: Born Birmingham 1898: Kia 12 May 17: Arras Mem: OU-NStaffs & 2 Y&L: Lived Hanley, Staffs

BUNTING, J: Pte: OU-2/4, 1/5 & 2/5 Y&L

BUNTING, R: Pte: 12/1758: A: * –: OU-2, 6 & 10 Y&L

BUNTING, WT: Pte: 12/60: A: Bandsman: * +: Lived Manor, Sheffield

BURCH, P: Pte: 12/1267: C: Born St Georges, Sheffield: Kia 16 May – 16: Sucrerie MC, Colincamps: Lived Bridge Inn, Hereford St

BURDETT, S: Pte: 12/1693: Born Walkley, Sheffield: Kia 1 Jul 16 with 14 Y&L: Thiepval Mem

BURDIN, H: Sgt: 18900: A: Bomber: OU-9, 10 & 13 Y&L

BURGESS, CV: 2Lt: Comm 28 Mar 17

BURGIN, RC: Pte: 12/321: B: * –: OU-2 & 8 Y&L

BURGON, JW: Pte: 12/1149: B: Born St Silas, Sheffield 1892: Kia 1 Jul 16: Thiepval Mem: Empllsaac Burgin & Co: Lived Endcliffe Vale Rd: * +

BURKETT, H: D: Born 1893: W 1 Jul 16 and Kia 5 Jun 17with 10 KSLI: Henin CC Ext: Sheffield Univ Student: Comm KSLI: Lived Junction Rd

BURKETT, RN: Member of 12th Club

BURMAN, PL: Sgt: 8139: MM: OU-2 Y&L

BURNBY, MB: Sgt: 12/1164: A: MM: * +: Comm MGC 30 Oct 17

BURNLEY, JW: Pte: 12/886: D: * –

BURNSIDE, F: Pte: 28565: OU-2, 13 & 18 Y&L: Deserted 23 Dec 18

BURRELL, J: Pte: 235608: OU-7 Y&L

BURRELL, NP: Pte: 12/1991: Born Broomhill, Sheffield 1897: Kia 20 Jul 16 with 2 Y&L: Authuilie MC: Empl Edgar Allen: Lived Byron Rd, Netheredge

BURRELL, W: ACpl: 17/385: MM

BURRIDGE, S: Pte: 12/276

BURTT, HN: Pte: 12/610: C: Waterman: * +

BURWELL, TF: Pte: 12/63: A: * +: Comm Y&L 26 Jun 17

BUSFIELD, HC: Pte: 12/611: A: Born Whitby 1882: W 1 Jul 16 and Kia 18 May 17: Arras Mem: Lived Scarboro: * +: OU-2 Y&L

BUSH, CH: Pte: 15306: OU-2 & 9 Y&L

BUSH, GP: Pte: 12/323: HQ: Batman in HQ 94 Bde

BUSSEY, L: Pte: 12/1243: A: Born Park, Sheffield: Kia 1 Jul 16: Thiepval Mem: * +

BUSWICK, CSgt/CQMS: OU-13 Y&L

BUTLER, AE: Pte: 12/1936: Born Sheffield 1893: Dow 2 Nov 16 with 13 Y&L: Hebuterne MC

BUTLER, RH: Cpl: 22357: OU-13 Y&L

BUTLER, W: Pte: 3235: HQ: Special Patrol Pty

BUTTERWORTH, ENM: 2Lt: Comm 20 Oct 15: Served 12 Y&L Jun 16–1 Jul 17

BUTTERY, JA: Pte: 12/887: D: Born St Philips, Sheffield 1890: SS Jun 16 and Kia 1 Jul 16: Rlwy Hollow MC, Serre: * +

BUTTON, W: Pte: 31565: OU-3/5 NStaffs & 7 Y&L

BUXTON, HA: LCpl: 12/64: A: Born Meersbrook, Sheffield: D 26 Mar 17-: Norton C, Sheffield: * +

BUZZACOTT, GC: 2Lt: W 16 Aug 17: Comm 26 Apr 17: Served 12 Y&L from 12 Jun 17

BYRD, H: Sgt: 12614: OU-8 Y&L

CADMAN, WB: Pte: 12/2009: A: Born Nr Manchester 1897: Kia 10 Sep 16: St Vaast MC, Richebourg: * –

CAHILL, EA: Pte: 12/1277: MM: OU-2, 1/4 & 14 Y&L

CAHILL, JJ: Pte: 31938: OU-64 Bn MGC, 56 Coy MGC, 2, 11 & 17 N&D, 1/4, 1/5, 2/5& 10 Y&L

CAMBE, JR: Pte: 12/1322: A: * +

CAMERON, DC: Pte: 12/1298: A: Signaller: * –

CAMPBELL, W: Pte: 12/1782: Born Lincoln: Kia 1 Jul 16 with 8 Y&L: Thiepva Mem

CANNELL, H: Pte: 235609

CAPPER, J: Pte: 12/1963: OU-13 Y&L

CARDING-WELLS, JR: Pte: 12/65: A: Born Whitwell, Mansfield 1895: Kia 1 Jul–16: Luke Copse MC, Serre: Bomber: Lived 219 Shirebrook Rd, Heeley: * +

CARLING, WA: Pte: 12/324: B: Bde canteen: * +

CARLISLE, R: Born 1895: Kia 3 May 17 with 1 OEY: Arras Mem: Sheffield Univ Student: Comm EY

CARLISLE, CA: Pte: Sheffield Univ Student

CARNEY, FK: Pte: 12/1926: Born Sheffield 1895 Kia 14 Aug 16 with 13 Y&L: St Vaast MC, Richebourg

CARNEY, W: LCpl: 15813: OU-2 & 8 Y&L

CARPENTER, FE: Pte: 12/325: Comm N&D 30 Oct 17

CARPENTER, FH: Pte: A: Signaller: * –

CARR, EM: 2Lt: D: Born 1896: Kia 1 Jul 16: Thiepval Mem: Lived 120 Millhouses Lane: Ex 12 Y&L OR: Comm 27 Jun 15: * +

CARR, JE: Pte: 12/888: D: Born Wadsley, Sheffield 1894: Dow 3 Jul–16: Beauval CC: Lived 69 Marlboro Rd: * +

CARR, JW: ACpl: 28073: Born 1884: Kia 27 Jun 18 with 13 Y&L: Cinq Rues MC: OU-13 Y&L

CARTER, A: Pte: 12/1716: Born Brighton: Kia 1 Jul 16 with 8 Y&L: Thiepval Mem

CARTER, R: Pte: 235614: B: UO-211 Fd Coy RE, 7 & 13 Y&L

CARTER, WR: Pte: 12/1323: A: Batman to Comd 94 Bde until Sep 15 then Pioneer sadler: * –

CARTWRIGHT, E: Pte: 12/326: B: * –

CARTWRIGHT, F: Pte: 12/68: C: Born Tickhill, Sheffield: Kia 1 Jul 16: Thiepval Mem: * +: Lived Tickhill

CARVER, R: Pte: 40172: OU-8 EY, 2 & 7 Y&L

CASEY, AA: Pte: 12/69: A: Born Hannesley, Mansfield 1895: Kia 1 Jul 16: Thiepval Mem: Sheffield Univ Student: * +

CASSIDY, T: Sgt: 20424: OU-2 & 7 Y&L

CASTLEDINE, S: Pte: 23187: OU-2, 1/5 & 7 Y&L

CATCHPOLE, H: LSgt: 12/1387: A: W 1 Jul 16: * –

CATLYN, S: Pte: 235615: Born Wymandham, Norfolk 1896: Dow 1 Oct 17: Roclincourt MC: OU-Norfolks: Lived Wymandham

CATTELL, DE: Sgt: 12/70: A: Born 1890: Teacher: * +

CAUNT, J: Pte: 12/613: W Apr 16

CAUNT, W: Sgt: 12/327: OU-2/4 Y&L

CAVANAGH, CSM: D: 1914 only

CAVE, LFS: Pte: 12/1989: Born Ripley, Derbyshire: Kia 18 May 17: Arras Mem: OU-2 Y&L

CAVILL, A: Pte: 12/1190: D: Born Attercliffe, Sheffield 1893: Dow 30 Aug 16: Merville CC Ext: Brother of C Cavill: * +

CAVILL, C: Pte: 12/1189: D: Born Attercliffe, Sheffield 1896: W 1 Jul–16: Lived Dransfield Rd, Crosspool: Brother of A Cavill: * +

CHADBURN, T: Sgt: 201768: HO: Kia 12 Apr 18 with 13 Y&L: OU-1/5 & 13 – Y&L: Musketry Instr-31 Div School

CHADDOCK, WM: ACpl: 12/1337: D: Born Hanley, Staffs 1894: Kia 12 Apr 18 with 13 Y&L: Outtersteene CC Ext: Grocers asst: Stretcher bearer: Lived Rotherham: * –

CHADWICK, JH: LCpl: 38013: Born Clitheroe, Lancashire 1884: D 18 Feb 18: Gt Harwood C, Lancashire: OU-1Fus: Lived Clitheroe

CHAFFER, WH: Pte: 12/1317: B: SS Apr 16 and W 1 Jul 16: * +

CHALLINOR, GW: Pte: 31583: Born 1890: Kia 2 Sep 18 with 2/4 Y&L: Vaulx Hill MC, Vaulx-Vraucourt: OU-3/5 NStaffs, 2 & 2/4 Y&L: CWGC give number as 58189

CHAMBERLAIN, CF: Pte: 12/889: D: Born Sheffield 1889: Kia 2 Nov 16: Hebuterne MC: * –

CHAMBERS, C: Pte: 13/1178: A: Lewis gnr

CHAMBERS, C: LCpl: 14/1178: OU-2, 13 & 14 Y&L

CHAMBERS, FEM: W01: 12/1133: 0: * –

CHAMBERS, FJ: Pte: 12/1159: B: * –: OU-2/4 & 6 Y&L

CHAMBERS, H: Pte: 12/1456: D: Born Handsworth, Sheffield 1897: Dow 4 Apr 18 with 13 Y&L: Woodhouse C, Sheffield: * –

CHAMBERS, RW: Pte: 25160: OU-2, 1 14 & 9 Y&L

CHANDLER, CH: Attended 1st Reunion Dinner

CHANDLER, G: Pte: 235616: OU-13 Y&L

CHANDLER, NWG: LCpl: 12/615: C: Born Cardiff 1885: Kia 1 Jul 16: Thiepval Mem: * +

CHAPMAN, GW: Pte: 12/616: C: OU-2, 8 &1 4 Y&L

CHAPMAN, H: Pte: 235617: Dow 30 Jun 18 with 7 Y&L

CHAPMAN, H: Pte: 31580: A: Batman: OU-3/5 NStaffs & 211 Fd Coy RE

CHAPMAN, H: LCpl: 12/i 140: A: W 1 Jul i6

CHAPMAN, W: Pte: 12/1516: B: * +

CHAPMAN, S: Pte: 12/2157: MM: Born Sittingbourne, Kent 1891: Kia 11 Oct 16 with 1 Y&L: Doiran Mem, Greece

CHAPMAN, T: Pte: 22258: Born Sleaford, Lincs: Kia 4 May 17: Arras Mern: OU-2 & 10 Y&L

CHARLES, JR: Pie: 12/1235: C: Born Nr Chesterfield 1892: W Sep 16 & Kia 18 Jun 17: Bailleul MC, SI Laurent: * –: Lived Chesterfield

CHARLES, WH: Pte: 31581: OU-3/5 NStaffs

CHARLESWORTH, F: CSgt/CQMS: 12/561: C: * –: Comm WRiding 31 Jul 17

CHARLESWORTH, G: Pte: 38012

CHARLESWORTH, JJ: Pte: 12/1645: Attercliffe, Sheffield: Kia 1 Jul 16 with 14 Y&L: Thiepval Mem

CHARLTON, J: Pte: 34875: A: Born Newcastle u T: Kia 12 Apr 18 with 13 Y&L: Ploegsteert Mem, Belgium: Batman: OU-11 DLI, 7 & 13 Y&L

CHATTERTON, R: Pte: 12/890: D: Bandsman and Bde Concert Pty: * –

CHILDS, A: Pte: 40065: Born 1898: Dow 13 Jul 17 with 9 Y&L: Etaples MC: OU-9 Y&L

CHING, JL: Pte: 12/1649: OU-2 & 14 Y&L

CHISHOLM, W: LCpl: 17688: OU-6 & 13 Y&L

CLAPHAM, AG: Pte: 12/1147: D: * –: W Sep 16: Lived Rotherham

CLARK, CF: Pte 12/1536: C: * –: OU-13 Y&L

CLARK, EJW: te: 235618: OU-7 Y&L

CLARK, G: Pte: 9950: A

CLARK, G: Pte: 3119: A

CLARK, GE: Pte: 12/1747: Convicted deserter 26 Oct 18: OU-2, 1/4, 9 & 13 Y&L

CLARK, GW: LCpl: 12/329: B: * –

CLARK, H: Pte: 12/1606: W Jul 16: OU-8 Y&L

CLARK, JP: Pte: 12/330: B: W 1 Jul 16: Lived Mexboro: * +: OU-2 & 14 – Y&L: Comm Y&L 25 Sep 17

CLARK, PW: Cpl: 20726: OU-2 & 7 Y&L

CLARK, S: Pte: 33553: A: Born 1899: Kia 13 Apr 18 with 13 Y&L: Ploegsteer Mem, Belgium: OU-94 TMB

CLARK, S: Pte: 28416: Born Newcastle u T 1881: Dow 27 Jul 17: AII Sts Chyd, Newcastle u T

CLARK, TH: Pte: 12/1859: Born Attercliffe, Sheffield 1897: Kia 13 Oct 181 with 1 15 Y&L: Vis en Artois Mem: Lived Attercliffe: OU-2, 1 15 & 13 Y&L

CLARK, WA: Pte: 235212: HO: Special Patrol Pty: OU-2/4, 1/5 & 13 Y&L

CLARK, WH: Pte: 21523: OU-2.6 6 7 Y&L

CLARK, WH: Dmr: 12/617: C: Born Hathersage 1893: Dow 27 Oct 18 with 1/4 Y&L: Boussu CC: * +: OU-1/4, 7 & 10 Y&L

CLARK, WS: CaptA: Born 1892: Kia 1 Jul 16: Serre Rd NO.2 MC: Lived Whiteley Wood Hall: Comm 23 Sep 14: * +

CLARKE, A: Pte: 39118: C: OU-94 MGC, 10 & 13 Y&L

CLARKE, AF: Pte: 12/73: A: Born Hucknall, Notts 1895: Kia 1 Jul 16: Thiepval Mem: Sheffield Univ Student * +: Lived Relford

CLARKE, C: Pte: 14112: OU-2, 6 & 8 Y&L

CLARKE, E: Pte: 12/1563: W 1 Jul 16: Lived Platts Common, Barnsley: * +

CLARKE, EW: Pte: 47546: OU-9 Norfolks & 7 Y&L

CLARKE, F: Pte: 30952: Kia 21 Mar 18 with 61 MGC: Pozieres Mem

CLARKE, JW: LCpl: 24251: MM: Kia 21 Mar 18 with 7 Y&L: OU-2 & 7 Y&L

CLARKE, NWB: Cpl: 12/71: A: MSM: Born Sheffield: Sheffield Univ Student * –: OU-13 Y&L

CLARKE, TW: Pte/12/331: B: W 1 Jul 16: Lived 33 Nelherthorpe St: * +

CLARKE, WC: Pte: 235685: OU-7 Y&L

CLARKE, WF: Pte: 235619: B: Kia 24 Sep 17: Roclincourt MC: Lived Gt Yarmouth: OU-Norfolks

CLARKSON, A: Pte: 12/332: B: Clk HO 31 Div: * +

CLARKSON, J: Pte: 38053: OU-13 Y&L

CLAY, HC: Sgt12/1388: A: MID?: Born Nottingharn: Kia 17 Jun 16: Bertrancourt MC: Sheffield Policernan: Served in S Africa War

CLAY, S: Pte: 39050: Born Sheffield: Kia 19 Jun 17: Bailleul Rd MC, Blangy: OU-10 Y&L

CLAY, W: Pte: 37996: OU-2 Y&L

CLAYDON, W: ACpl: 12/1343: C: W 1 Jul 16: Pioneer: * +

CLAYTON, A: LCpl: 235206: C: OU-94 MGC

CLAYTON, A: Pte: 12/1902: W Jul 16: OU-13 Y&L

CLAYTON, F: Pte: 12/1616: W 1 Jul 16: * +: OU-2 & 8 Y&L

CLAYTON, JR: Pte: 31579: OU-3/5 NStaffs

CLEAREY, J: Pte: 32258: Kia 26 Apr 18 with 1 15 Y&L: Tyne Cot Mem, Passchendaele, Belgium: OU-1/4, 1/5, 215 & 6 Y&L

CLEGG, CJ: Pte: 40096: Born 1893: Kia 7 Jun 17 with 9 Y&L: Menin Gate Mem, Ypres, Beigium: OU-9 Y&L

CLEMENTS, FR: Pte: 235611: OU-7Y &L

CLIFFE, F: Pte: 3/2625: Born Nr Rotherham: Kia 30 Jun 17: Arras Mem: Lived Rotherham

CLIFTON, B: LCpl: 12/72: A

CLIFTON, E: ACpl: 12/74: A: Born Lenton, Notts 1888: Kia 1 Jul 16: Thiepval Mem: Lived 8 Blair Athol Rd: * +

CLIXBY, CC: Pte: 12/1249: D: Born St Marys, Sheffield: Kia 1 Jul 16: Oueens MC, Serre: Bank Clk: * +

CLOUD, CC: Lt: B: OU-1 14 Y&L: * +: Comm 22 Jul 15: Served 12 Y&L from 31 Mar 16

CLOUGH, TC: Maj: B: Ex TF: 1st 2IC: Left 12 Y&L in Jun 16

CLOUGH, HH: Pte: 12/1320: Born Walkley, Sheffield: Kia 22 Jul 16 with 14 Y&L: Lived 163 Paradise Rd, Walkley

COATES, S: Pte: 28426: Born Middlesboro 1886: Dow 25 Aug 17: Aubigny CC Ext: Lived Middlesboro: OU-2 Y&L

COATES, HRF: CSM: 12/619: C: W 1 Jul 16: * +: 1st Sec 12th Club 1918

COATES, W: Pte: 40092: Kia 1 Oct 17 with 9 Y&L: Hooge Crater MC, Zillebeke, Belgiurn: OU-9 Y&L

COATS, W: Pte: 12/620: C: W 1 Jul 16: * +

COCKERILL, FH: Pte: 40085: OU-9 Y&L

COCKEY, JEL: Pte: 12/621: C: Sheffield Univ Student

COFFEY, H: Pte: 38014

COGGAN, HF: Pte: 12/1466: B: * –

COGGON, AH: Pte: 21950: A: Born Walkley, Sheffield 1892: Dow 1 Jul–17: Duisans MC, Etrun: Bandsman: * –

COLBRIDGE, R: Pte: 12/334: B: * +: OU-13 Y&L

COLCLOUGH, W: Pte: 3/4903: OU-1, 2, 6 & 13 Y&L

COLE, A: Pte: 31971: A: Lewis gnr

COLE, AE: 2Lt: Comm 14 Jul 16: Served City Bn from 8 Jan 17

COLE, W: Pte: 12/891: C: Born Nr Birkenhead: Kia 1 Jul 16: Thiepval Mem: Clerk: Lived 15 Goddard Hall Rd: * +

COLE, W: AW02: 12/1393: Attached AGS France

COLEMAN, WG: Pte: 12/75: W 1 Jul 16: * +

COLES, S: ACpl: 7587: HO: DCM: Sanitary man: OU-13 Y&L & 93 TMB

COLLEY, G: Pte: 21762: Born 1895: Kia 11 Mar 18 with 7 Y&L: Rocquigny MC, Manancourt: OU-2, 1/5 & 7 Y&L

COLLEY, J: Pte: 15455: OU-2, 7 & 9 Y&L

COLLEY, WA: Capt: C: Born Sheffield 1869: Kia 1 Jul 16: Thiepval Mem: Sheffield businessman and Councillor: Ex TF RE Maj: * +

COLLIER, GH: Pte: 12/1925: A: * –

COLLINS, E: Pte: 38060

COLQUHOUN, JF: Capt: MC: Padre: Served 12 Y&L from 14 Dec 14, later 31 Div Chaplain

COLVER, J: Pte: 12/1828: C: W 1 Jul 16: * +

CONNELL, JW: Sgt: Teacher

CONSTABLE, H: Pte: 12/1541: Born Upperthorpe, Sheffield 1897: Dow 16 Sep 16 with 2 Y&L: Corbie CC Ext: OU-2 & 14 Y&L

CONWAY, G: Pte: 22702: OU-2 Y&L

COOK, A: Pte: 31578: OU-3/5 NStaffs

COOK, AE: Pte: 12/2007: A: * –

COOK, F: Pte: 12/622: C: W 1 Jul 16: Bank Clk: Lived 54 Clarence Rd, Hillsboro: * +: OU-1 O Y&L: Comm Indian Army 11 Sep 18

COOK, F: Pte: 31571: A: Lewis gnr: OU-13 Y&L

COOK, GG: Pte: 12/1469: B: Born Churchill, Oxfordshire 1885: Kia 16 May 16: Sucrerie MC, Colincamps

COOK, H: Pte: 12/2168: OU-1 Y&L

COOK, J: Pte: 16696: Born 1897: Dow 30 Sep 18 with 13 Y&L: Dranoutre MC, Belgium: OU-2, 9 & 13 Y&L

COOKE, J: Pte: 31570: HQ: Runner: OU-3/5 NStaffs & 13 Y&L

COOKE, WJ: Pte: 12/335: B: W Jun 16: OU-173 Coy RE

COOPER, F: Pte: 18538: B

COOPER, FO: Sgt: 9863: OU-2 & 8 Y&L

COOPER, JS: 2Lt: E: Born 1892: Kia 25 Mar 17 with 70 Sqn RFC: HAC MC, Ecoust – St Mein: Served 12 Y&L 22 Nov 14 – May 15: OC 17 PI

COOPER, R: Sgt: 12/336: B: Born Grindleford, Derbyshire 1896: Kia 1 Jul 16: Queens MC, Serre: Sheffield Univ Student: Lived Derwent House, Grindieford: * +

COOPER, S: Pte: 12/1276: A: W 1 Jul 16: Lived Abbey Lane: * +

COOPLAND, C: LCpl: 12/337: C: W 1 Jul 16: * +

COPE, WT: Ptel 31567: OU-3/5 NStaffs

COPLEY, B: Pte: 235201: Born 1896: Dow 25 May 17: Aubigny CC Ext: Lived Hoyland: OU-2/4 & 1/5

COPLEY, C: Pte: 17917: OU-2 & 6 Y&L

COPPING, VS: LCpl: 12/623: C: W 1 Jul 16: * +: OU-10 Y&L: Comm Indian Army 11 Sep 18

COPPLESTONE, J: Pte: 12/76: A: Born Pitsmoor, Sheffield1894: Kia 1 Jul 16: Thiepval Mem: Sheffield Univ Student * +

CORBETT, T: Pte: 37661: OU-7, 9 & 14 Y&L

CORBYN, GS: ASgt: 12/1174: D: Born Norwich 1883: Kia 1 Jul 16: Thiepval Mem: Empl Walsh's Store: * +

CORCORAN, JA: Pte: 13/1484: OU-7 Y&L

CORNE, E: Pte: 33561

CORTHORN, B: Pte: 12/338: B: DCM: W 1 Jul 16: Lived 36 Florence Rd: * +

COTTAM, RH: Pte: 12/340: B: W 1 Jul 16: Bank Clk: * +: OU-2 & 14 Y&L

COTTAM, RW: Pte: 12/339: B: W 1 Jul 16: Lived 13 Wood Rd, Hillsboro: * +

COTTERILL, P: Pte: 36054: OU-34 Pigeon Svc RE

COTTERILL, SW: Pte: 12/625: C: * +

COULTISH, CH: ACpl: 40066: OU-9 Y&L

COURT, GH: Sgtl211144: OU-2 & 13 Y&L

COURTS, JH: Pte: 46462: D 22 Nov 18: OU-7 Y&L

COUSIN, AN: CaptKia 7 Dec 17: Roclincourt MC: Sheffield Univ Student: OU-HQ 94 Bde 7 Apr–20 Aug 16

COVERDALE, L: ACpl: 12/626: C: Born Cathedral Ch, Sheffield 1891: Kia 1 Jul 16: Thiepval Mem: * +

COWELL, BN: Sgt: 12/1112: B: W 1 Jul 16: * +

COWEN, C: Pte: Sheffield Univ Student

COWEN, H: Pte: 12/78: A: * –NOJ: OU-RAF

COWEN, JC: Cap JCcf3: MC: W 28 Jun 16: Ex 12 Y&L OR: Gomm 15 Jul–15: Bombing and Lewis gun offr: Adjt Dec 17

COWLISHAW, C: LCpl: 12/892: D: Born Intake, Sheffield 1892: Kia 18 Feb 17 with 14 Y&L: Gezaincourt MC: * +: OU-2 & 14 Y&L

COWLISHAW, GD: Pte: Sheff Univ Student

COX, FL: Pte: 12/894: D: W 1 Jul 16: * +

COX, T: Pte: 12/1179: C: SS May 16 & W Sep 16: Pioneer: * –

COX, W: Pte: 12/1765: OU-8 Y&L

CRABTREE, W: Pte: 37936: Born Morley: Kia 1 O May 17: Arras Mem: Lived Morley: OU-10 Y&L

CRACKNELL, W: Pte: 31575: OU-3/5 NStaffs

CRAGGS, P: 2Lt: Born 1893: Kia 30 Sep 18 with 13 Y&L: Strand MG, Ploegsteert, Belgium: Gomm 29 Aug 17: Served 12 Y&L 25 Oct 17 – 12 Feb 18: Lived Shrewsbury

CRAMMOND, C: GSgt: 12/80: A: * +: Tried By FGCM 17 Jan 16 and reduced to Pte: OU-2 Y&L

CRAPPER, F: Pte: 12/1513: OU-2, 1/4, 9, 13 & 14 Y&L

CRATCHLEY, JT: Pte: 12/1391: A: * –: OU-214 Y&L

CRAVEN 12 Y&L in Feb 15

CRAVEN, W: Pte: 31972: OU-10 NFus

CRAWFORD, S: Capt: Comm 26 Sep 16: Served 12 Y&L from 25 Nov 16: OU-7 Y&L

CRAWSHAW, JH: Pte: 24164: OU-7 & 10 Y&L

CRAWSHAW, Pte: 12/895: OU-94 TMB

CREAGHAN, MW: LCpl: 17001: OU-2, 7 & 8 Y&L

CRESSEY, AS: Pte: A: SS Jun 16

CRIMES, LG: Pte: 12/82: A: Talkel Hill, Staffs 1892: Kia 1 Jul 16: Thiepval Mem: Bank Clk: Lived Kidsgrove, Starrs: * +

CRISP, PJ: Pte: 205350: OU-2/2 London Yeo, 2 & 14 Y&L

CROFT, HA: Pte: 12/83: A: W 1 Jul 16: Sheffield Univ Student: * +

CROFT, A: Pte: 12/1702: G: Born Ecclesall, Sheffield: Kia 10 Sep 16: St Vaast MG, Richebourg: * +

CROLL, FE: Cpl: 12i2123: OU-2 & 1 15 Y&L

CROMPTON, JW: Pte: 12/1537: C: * +: OU-6 & 7 Y&L

CROOKES, A: Pte: 12/1721: W Jul 16: OU-6 Y&L

CROOKES, H: Pte: 12/1820: D: W 1 Jul 16: * +

CROOKS, A: Pte: 12/1596: G: W 1 Jul 16: Empl Newton & Chambers: * – +: OU-10 Y&L

CROSBY, TM: Pte: 12/1552: W Jul 16: OU-8, 10 & 13 Y&L

CROSS, FJ: Pte: 235620: Kia 27 May 18 with 7 Y&L

CROSSLAND, H: Pte: 12/84: A: Born Woodhouse, Leeds: Kia 1 Jul 16: Thiepvai Mem: Lived Leeds: * +

CROSSLAND, J: Pte: 13/1411: OU-2 & 13 Y&L

CROSTHWAITE, JA: Lt Col: MID: Regular offr DLI: CO 28 Sep 15–30 Jun 16

CROUFIER, LSgt: 12 Y&L Dec 14

CROWTHER, C: Cpl: 12/896: D: Waterman

CROZIER, HC: Sgt: 12/628: C: MM: Born Nr Preston: Kia 1 Jul 16: Thiepval Mem: Teacher: * +

CRUTCHLEY, JT: Pte: Bandsman

CULF, FC: Pte: 12/1316: C: Walkley, Sheffield 1893: Kia 1 Jul 16: Thiepval Mem: Lived 357 London Rd: * +

CUMMINS, TC: 2Lt Born 1899: Kia 25 Mar 18 with 7 Y&L: Warlencourt MC: Comm 29 Aug 17

CUMPER, G: Pte: 235613: OU-7 Y&L

CUNDALL, J: Pte: 31969: OU-10 NFus

CUNDLIFFE, C: Sgt: 12/897: D: Born Nr Hyde, Cheshire 1892: Kia 1 Jul – 16: Rlwy Hollow MC, Serre: Teacher: Lived 128 Doncater Rd, Rotherham: * +

CUNDY, JH: Pte: 22830: HQ: Observer: OU-2, 10 & 13 Y&L

CUNNINGHAM, FH: Pte: 12/629: A: * –

CUNNINGHAM, R: Pte: 31582: OU-3/5 NStaffs

CUNNINGTON, EC: CaptMID: Born 1890: Kia 23 Mar 18 with 95 Fd Amb: Cabaret Rouge MC: * +

CURRIER, JF: Pte: 12/1154: D: Born Nr Rotherham: Kia 1 Jul 16: Thiepvai Mem: Lived Queen St, Swinton, Rotherham: * +

CURTIS, CW: Pte: 12/1951: W Jul 16: OU-13 Y&L

CURWEN, ES: LCpl: 12/85: A: Born Plumbland, Cumberland 1879: Kia 1 Jul 16: Thiepval Mem: Teacher Rotherham Gram Mar : * +

CUST, HI: Sgt: 12/343: A: W 1 Jul 16: Lived Westholm Rd: * +: OU-13 Y&L

CUSWORTH, C: Cpl: 13/220: OU-13 Y&L

CUTHBERT, E: Pte: 12/344: A: D 12 Oct 14: St Hibald Chyd, Lincs

CUTHILL, W: ACpl: 12/345: A: * +

CUTTRILL, AO: Sheffield Univ Student

CUTTS, M: Pte: 12/1202: B: 31 Div carpenter: * –

CUTTS, G: Pte: 3/2194: OU-2, 1/4 & 6 Y&L

CUTTS, GC: LCpl: 12/1455: B: * –

DAINTY, WM: Pte: 31592: B: 31 Div gardener: OU-3/5 NStaffs

DALE, A: ASgt: 12/631: C: MM: SS Jul 16: Lived Wadsley: * –

DALE, WB: Pte: 12/2114: C: * –

DALE, L: 12th Club member

DALTON, W: Pte: 12/1414: B: Storeman: * +

DAMMS, W: Pte: 24468: A: Bomber: OU-7, 10, 13 & 14 Y&L

DAMMS, WH: Pte: 202850: A: Born Sheffield 1895: Dow 28 Mar 18 with 13 Y&L: St Pol MC: Bomber: OU-2/4 & 13 Y&L

DAMMS, WO: Pte: 38901: OU-7 & 8 Y&L

DANDISON, J: Pte: 12/1228: B: * +

DARLOW, FM: Pte: 12/86: A: * –

DAVENPORT, L: Pte: 12/1722: C: Born St Marys, Sheff 1897: Thiepval Mem: * +

DAVEY, A: Pte: 12/1957: OU-7 & 13 Y&L

DAVEY, AF: Pte: C

DAVEY, W: Pte: 12/899: D: Lived 3 Falding St, Rotherham: POW: * –

DAVIES, FA: 2U: Kia 14 May 17: Arras Mem: Comm 12 Dec 14 to 14 – Y&L: Served 12 Y&L from 15 Aug 16

DAVIES, G: Pte: 12/633: C: Pigeonman: * –

DAVIES, HE: Pte: 12/1345: D: Born Crookes, Shefiield: Kia 1 Jul 16: Thiepval Mem: * +

DAVIES, HG: LCpl: 39129: HQ: Special Patrol Ply

DAVIES, JA: Pte: 12/1742: B: Born Darnall, Sheffield: Kia 1 Jul 16: Thiepval Mem: * –: –

DAVIES, KR: Capt: C: Served 12 Y&L 8 Jul–27 Sep 17

DAVIES, L: Pte: 14/916: OU-13 & 14 Y&L

DAVIES, T: Pte: 205358: OU-2 London Yeo, 1/5 & 2/5 Y&L

DAVIES, W: Pte: 12/1825: C: Born Nr Parkgate: Kia 1 Jul 16: Thiepval Mem: Lived 244 Wortley Rd, Rotherham: * +

DAVIS, E: Pte: 21532: OU-2 & 10 Y&L

DAVIS, FT: ACp/: 12/634: C: * +: Comm NFus 31 Jul 17

DAVIS, JH: Pte: OU-214 Y&L

DAVIS, JW: Pte: 235621: A: OU-211 Fd Coy RE

DAVIS, R: LSgt: 14/587: OU-2 & 14 Y&L

DAVIS, RG: Pte: 39126: OU-2, 10 & 13 Y&L

DAVISON, BJ: Pte: 12/902: D: * –: W Sep 16: OU-2, 2/4 & 2/5 Y&L

DAVY, RM: Pte: W May 16: Sheffield Univ Student: Lived Sharrow Head House: Comm 15WY

DAWSON, A: Pte: W 1 Jul 16: Empl Sheff Tramways: Lived Taptonville Rd

DAWSON, A: Pte: 31975: OU-10 NFus & 13 Y&L

DAWSON, CW: Pte: 12/1415: B: Born Doncaster 1898: Kia 1 Jul 16: Thiepval Mem: Empl Great N Rlwys: Lived 64 Copley Rd, Doncaster: * +

DAWSON, F: Pte: 12/1918: D: W 1 Jul 16: * +

DAWSON, FG: Pte: 31588: HO: Born Burton 0 T: Kia 26 Mar 18: Batman: OU-3/5 NStaffs & 13 Y&L

DAWSON, FS: Pte: 12/635: C: * +: OU-2/4 & 6 Y&L

DAWSON, H: Pte: 31594: Born Stafford: Kia 29 Jun 17: Arras Mem: OU-3/5 NStaffs: Lived Stafford

DAWSON, H: Pte: 31974: Born Huddersfield 1878: Dow 26 Nov 16: Bovin MC: OU-WY & 1 a NFus: Lived Leeds

DAWSON, J: Pte: 15652: A: OU-2, 1 0& 13 Y&L

DAY, H: Pte: 40067: OU-9 Y&L

DE LANDRE GROGAN LVSP: Lt: MC: Kia 13 Oct 18: Comm 28 Mar 17: OU-1 /5 Y&L

DEAKIN, E: Pte: 28659: OU-2 & 2/4 Y&L

DEAKIN, G: CSgt: 12/1600: MSM?: OU-8 Y&L

DEAKIN, GH: Pte: 205068: OU-7 Y&L

DEAN, F: Pte: 22177: OU-2 & 10 Y&L

DEAN, G: Cpl: 15611: OU-9 & 10 Y&L

DEAN, WH: Pie: 12/636: C: W 14 May 16

DEARDEN, HF: Pte: 12/2004: OU-2, 1 0& 14 Y&L

DEARLOVE, JW: Pte: 12/341: 8: * +

DEBNEY, J: Cpl: 13/244: MM: OU-13 Y&L

DEBY, JTH: Pte: 12/90: A: * –: Comm RE 16 Aug 18: Attended 1919 Reunion: Sheffield Univ Student

DENNER, H: Pte: 12/1595: OU-1 Y&L

DENNEY, H: Pte: 31306: OU-1 Northants

DERNIE, LH: Pte: 12/1885: Born Blythe, Kent 1897: Kia 24 Mar 18 with 13 Y&L: Arras Mem: Lived Sheffield

DERRY, DAL: Lt: B: Born 1896: Dow 9 Oct 16 with 2 Y&L: Guards MC, Les Boeufs: Sheffield Univ Student: Comm 21, Jun 15

DESMOND, J: Interviewed by J Harris for 'Covenant With Death'

DEVEY, AF: Pte: 12/1336: C: Born St Peters, Sheffield 1896: Kia 1 Jul 16: Thiepval Mem: * +

DEVILLE, PR: Pte: 31587: Born Burton 0 T 1876: Kia 4 May 17: Bailleul Rd Me, Blangy: OU-3/5 NStaffs: Lived Burton 0 T

DEVLIN, B: Pte: 31593: OU-3/5 NStaffs

DICKINSON, L: 2Lt: Born 1886: Kia 11 Apr 18 with 13 Y&L: Ploegsteert Mem, Belgium: Comm 27 Jul 17

DICKINSON, RB: Sgt: Empl British Wagon Co: Comm 28 Dec 14, later Staff Capt HQ 94 Bde

DICKMAN, E: Pte: 33554: A: Lewis gnr: OU-94MGC

DICKS, AW: Pte: 235684: HQ: W Feb 18

DICKS, EJ: Pte: 235622: B: Born Twickenham, M'Sex 1878: Dow 25 Sep 17: Roclincourt MC: OU-Norfolks: Lived Wandsworth, M'Sex

DIMMER, R: LCpl: 29904: HQ: OU-6 Wilts

DINSDALE, F: 2Lt: Born 1893: Kia 1 Jul 16: Queens MC, Serre: * +: Comm 21 Sep 15 to 11 Y&L: Served 12 Y&L from May / Jun 16

DIPPLE, JA: LCpl: 12/349: B: OU-13 Y&L

DIXON, C: Pte: 12/1130: D

DIXON, FT: Pte: Sheffield Univ Student

DIXON, J: Cpl: 12/1137: 0rd Rm Cpl: * –: Lived 93 Tillotson Rd

DIXON, RA: Pte: 12/351: B: Comm 1 Mar 17 to 1/4 Y&L

DOBB, C: LSgt: 3/2495: OU-2 & 6 Y&L

DOBB, L: Pte: 25638: OU-6 & 7 Y&L

DOBSON, C: Pte: 18889: OU-2 & 9 Y&L

DOCKERTY, H: Pte: 31585: Born 1896: Kia 9 Oct 17 with 6 Y&L: Tyne Cot Mem, Passchendaele, Belgium: OU-3/5 NStaffs, 2 & 6 Y&L

DODDS, WP: Pte: OU-2 Y&L

DODGSON, J: Pte: 31973: OU-10 NFus

DODWORTH, FE: LCpl: 12/637: C: * +: OU-2& 13 Y&L

DOMAN, W: Pte: 21 020: OU-2 & 6 Y&L

DONCASTER, P: ROMS: 12/834: D: * –: Ex Regular: Gymnastic Instr: Comrr 9 Aug 17

DONOGHUE, F: ALSgt: 12/352: B: Born Colchester 1894: Kia I Jul 16: Rlwy Hollow MC, Serre: Lived Maxwell Tce, New Rd, Belper: * +

DORMAN, P: Pte: 14/267: OU-2, 13 & 14 Y&L

DORRELL, HGH: 2Lt: Comm 180ec14

DOUGLAS, TW: Pte: 12/904: C: * –: OU-2 & 6 Y&L

DOWNES, W: Pte: 37575: Kia 12 Apr 18 with 13 Y&L: OU-13 Y&L: Details not confirmed by CWGC

DOWNING, A: LCpl: 12/354: A: MM: * +: Runner: Comm Leics 29 May 17

DOWTY, HB: Pte: 12/638: C: Born Totland Bay, I of W: Kia 16 May – 16: Sucrerie MC, Colincamps: Lived I of W

DRABBLE, HS: Sheffield Univ Student: Lived The Rise, Endcliffe Vale: – Comm 2/4 Y&L

DRANSFIELD, F: Pte: 28887: OU-13 Y&L

DRANSFIELD, GH: LSgt: 12/640: C: Comm LFus 29 Jan 18

DRAPER, JR: Pte: 12/93: A: * +: Comm 26 Sep 17 to 2/4 Y&L

DRAYCOTT, CD: Pte: 12/94: A: Sheffield Univ Student: * +: Comm Y&L 26 Sep 17

DRINKALL, JG: Photo Y&L Museum

DRINKWATER, AT: Pte: 20727: A: Bde Concert Pty: OU-6 & 13 Y&L

DRIVER, H: Pte: 12/641: C: Born Meersbrook, Sheffield: Kia 1 Jul 16: Luke Copse MC, Serre: Lived 682 Abbeydale Rd: * +

DRURY, A: 2Lt: Comm 29 Aug 17: Served 12 Y&L from 26 Oct 17: W 30 Sep 18 with 13 Y&L

DUFFY, JD: Pte: 12/1517: B: * –

DUFFY, M: Pte: 37977: 80rn 1884: Dow 1 Jul 18 with 2 Y&L: Esquelbecq MC: OU-2 Y&L

DUGGAN, T: Pte: 1 9572: OU-2 & 9 Y&L

DUGGAN, WV: Pte: 39117: OU-7 & lo Y&L

DUKE, L: LCpl: 12/96: A: W unknown date: Comm 8 Y&L 19 Mar 16

DUMMER, FO: Pte: 235686: OU-9 & 13Y&L

DUNGWORTH, F: ALCpl: 12/355: A: Born Owlerton, Sheffield 1890: W 1 Jul 16 With 12 Y&L and Dow 23 Oct 17 with 8 Y&L: Godewaersvelde MC, Belgium: * +: OU-2 & 8 Y&L

DUNGWORTH, HC: Pte: 12/1457: 0: * –: Comm EY 10 Sep 18

DUNKLEY, J: Pte: 33555: A

DUNN, J: Pte: 12/1889: Born Barnsley 1878: 0 4 Dec :: 15 with 15 Y&L: St Pauls Chyd, Heeley, Sheffield: Fought in S African War

DUNN, JE: Pte: 38015: Born Pendleton, Lancs: Dow 7 Nov 16: Warlincourt Halte MC: Ex 34749 Lanc Fus: Brother of 39016 T Dunn: Lived Manchester

DUNN, T: LCpl: 38016: Born St Michael, Manchester 1888: Kia 16 May 17: Bailleul Rd MC, Blangy: Ex 34755 Lanc Fus: Brother of JE Dunn

DUNNINGTON, G: Pte: 31977: OU-1 a NFus, 2 & 8 Y&L

DYE, CR: ASgt: 235687: OU-7 Y&L

DYSON, A: Pte: 23373: C: * –

DYSON, H: Pte: 12/2012: C: * –: OU-7 Y&L

DYSON, H: Bank Clk: Comm Y&L 20 Dec 14: Lived Cowiishaw Rd

EADON, JW: Pte: 12/1542: B: Born Sheffield 1897: W Jul 16 with 12 Y&L. and Dow 19 Apr 18 with 1 /5 Y&L: Lijssenthoek MC, Belgium: OU-1/5, 2/5, 7 & 13 Y&L

EAGLING, JW: Pte: 37487: C: OU-2 Y&L

EALEY, J: Pte: 33556: OU-7 Y&L

EARL, FC: Lt: A: W 1 Jul 16: Bank Clk: * +: Comm 28 Nov 14: 0C 2 Pl: OU-Home Defence Bn of Y&L

EARLE, E: Pte: 31396: HQ: Shoemaker

EARLE, FG: W01: 12/906: D: Lived 284 Wickersley Rd, Rotherham: * +

EARLE, GJ: Member of 12th Club

EARLS, E: Pte: 31596: OU-3/5 NStaffs & 13 Y&L

EARNSHAW, E: Pte: 12/1639: C: * –: OU-13 Y&L

EARNSHAW, F: Pte: 12/1397: B: Born Doncaster 1898: Dow 20 May 16: Etaples MC

EARNSHAW, NC: Pte: 37960: OU-2 & 6 Y&L

EASTELL, W: Pte: 235725: A: Born Attleboro, Norfolk: Kia 12 Apr 18 with 13 Y&L: Lewis gnr: Ex 2704 Norfolks

EDLEY, B: Cpl: 17187: OU-7 Y&L

EDWARD, R: Pte: 14/1184: D: W I Jul 16: * –: Rotherham

EDWARDS, FR: Pte: 16421: OU-7 Y&L

EDWARDS, GAC: Pte: 12/642: C: * +

EDWARDS, HE: Pte: 31599: Born 1895: Kia 1 Jun 18 with 7 Y&L: Aeheux MC: OU-3/5 NStaffs and 7 Y&L

EDWARDS, JR: Pte: 31601: OU-3/5 NStaffs

EDWARDS, SW: Pte: 31847: OU-1 Leics, 6 & 13 Y&L

EGLEN, HG: Pte: 12/97: A: 12/97: SS 1 Jul 16 and W 16 Feb 17: * +

ELAM, C: Lt: AD: Born 1895: Kia 1 Jul 16: AIF Burial Gd, Flers: Sheffield Univ Student: Ex 12 Y&L OR: Comm 12 Y&L 11 Nov 14: 0C 6 Pl: Lived Endeliffe Cres

ELBURN, A: Pte: 58428

ELDER, TH: Pte: 31979: Born 1893: Kia 17 Jul 17 with 10 Y&L: Pondfarm MC, Wulverghem, Belgium: OU-10 NFus, 10 & 14 Y&L

ELLENDER, A: Pte: 31600: OU-3/5 NStaffs and 7 Y&L

ELLIN, SJP: Cpl: 12/356: B: * –: W Sep 16: Lived 143 Crimicar Ln: Early 12th Club Treasurer

ELLIOTT, FM: Pte: 12/907: W Apr 16

ELLIOTT, WG: Pte: 12/1781: C: Born Pitsmoor, Sheffield 1889: Kia 1 Jul–16: Serre Rd No.2 MC, Serre: * +: Lived 35 Hadfield St or 544 Langsett Rd

ELLIS, A: Pte: 22262: Born Attereliffe, Sheffield 1892: Dow

ELLIS, EB: Pte: 12/2154: OU-1 Y&L

ELLIS, EW: Pte: 12/151 O: B: Born Liverpool 1892: Kia 1 Jul 16: Thiepval Mem: * +

ELLIS, HC: Cpl: 21891: C: Born Huddersfield 1893: Kia 18 May 17: Arras Mem: * –20 May 17: Etaples MC: * –

ELLIS, HV: Pte: 12/357: B: Born Handsworth, Sheffield 1893: Kia 1 Jul 16: Thiepval Mem: Bank Clk: * +: Lived Woodthorpe Common, Handsworth

ELLIS, JS: Pte: 12/644: C

ELLIS, JTP: Pte: 12/2033: Born Whitwell, Derbyshire 1880: Kia 20 Jul 16 with 2 Y&L: Authuilie MC

ELLIS, JW: CSM: 12/560: B: Born Eeeleshall, Sheffield 1872: Kia 4 May 16: Suererie MC, Colineamps: Walsh's Commissionaire: Ex Regular & TF, retired 1911: Lived Crosspool.

ELLIS, S: Pte: 14/554: OU-14 Y&L.

ELLIS, SW: LCpl: 12/908: D: * +: Comm 4 Lines 29 Jan 18.

ELLIS, WJ: Pte: 34480: OU-11 EY, 2/4, 2/5, 7 & 9 Y&L. 0 & 14 Y&L.

ELLISON, C: Sgt: 12/91 6: AcD: * –

ELLWOOD, CF: Maj: EF: OU-15 & 10 Y&L

ELLYARD, E: ASgt: 46473

ELSTON, JR: Pte: 12/1806: Born Brightside, Sheffield: Kia 1 Jul 16 with 8 Y&L: Thiepval Mem

ELWELL, JJ: Pte: 31598: OU-3/5 NStaffs

EMERY, H: Pte: 12/1884: OU-1/5, 8 & 13 Y&L

EMERY, JC: Cpl: 3/4354: OU-2, 2/4 & 6 Y&L

EMMERSON, AE: LCpl: 25088: A: OU-94MGC

EMMERSON, E: LCpl: 12/1247: B: Born Nr Rotherham: Kia 1 Jul 16: Serre Rd No. 2 MC, Serre: * +: Lived Norton

EMMERSON, WA: Pte: 12/358: Born Wales, Sheffield: Kia 8 Apr 16: Suererie MC, Colincamps

EMMOTT, WP: Pte: 24293: OU-10 Y&L

ENEVER, H: Pte: 235624: OU-7 Y&L

ENGLAND, C: ACpl: 21831: OU-1 15, 2/5 & 10 Y&L

ENGLAND, R: Pte: 12/1132: B: * +

ENGLISH, E: Pte: 12/1663: D: * –

ENRIGHT, FP: Interviewed by J Harris for Covenant With Death

ETESON, H: Cpl: 12/645: C: Born Nr Bradford: Kia 1 Jul 16: Thiepval Mem: * +

EVANS, CC: ASgt: 12/912: A: * –: Lived 242 Wickersley Rd, Rotherham

EVANS, F: Pte: 12/646: C: W 1 Jul 16: * +: Batman

EVANS, J: Pte: 12/359: OU-2 Y&L

EVANS, TLT: Pte: 37990: Kia 19 Apr 17 with 2 Y&L: St Patrieks MC, Loos: OU-2 Y&L

EVANS, W: Pte: 12/1733: Born Attercliffe, Sheff: Kia 1 Jul i6 with 8 Y&L Thiepval Mem

EVERATT, T: ACSM: 12/842: D: Sheffield Univ Student: * –: Comm Y&L 29 May 17

EVERETT, HA: Sgt: 3/3915: OU-1, 2, 7 & 8 Y&L

EVERITT, R: Pte: 24270: OU-2 & 9 Y&L

EXLEY, A: CQMS: 240775: HQ: OU-9 Y&L
EYRE, GW: Pte: 12/362: B: * –: Bandsman: OU-2/4 Y&L
EYRE, HC: Pte: 12/1371: B: W 1 Jul 16: * +: Lived Chesterfield
EYRE, J: Pte: 44856: OU-2 & 14 Y&L
EYRE, L: Pte: 12/1301: B: Kia 1 Jul 16: Queens MC, Serre. * +: Lived Sharrow

FAIR, EE: Pte: 12/1329: C: * +: OU-1/4, 10 & 14 Y&L
FAIRCLOUGH, JS: Pte: 12/2047: A: Born Neepsend, Sheffield: Kia 24 Sep 16: Le Touret MC,
   Richebourg: * –
FAIRHURST, C: Pte: 15825: OU-1/5, 2/5, 8 & 10 Y&L
FAIRWEATHER, A: Pte: 22423: D
FAKER, FL: ACSM: 12/647: C: Born Sheffield 1892: Kia 13 Nov 16 with 12EY: Thiepval Mem: * –
   ?Comm EY l Oct 16
FALCK, CW: Pte: 203739
FANSHAW, WA: Cpl: 12/14: A: Sheffield Univ Student: * –: Comm Y&L 29 Oct 18
FARMERY, G: Pte: 12/648: W Apr 16: Cabinet maker
FARMERY, G: Sgt: 21518: A: Special Patrol Pty: OU-2 & 13 Y&L
FARRAND, HP: LCpl: 12/649: C: Born Nr Wakefield 1892: Kia 1 Jul 16: Luke Copse MC, Serre: * +:
   Lived 22 Clevedon Rd, North Shore, Blackpool
FARRER, WD: Pte: 12/2030: Comm RAF 28 Aug 17
FAULKNER, AJ: Pte: 31606: OU-3/5 NStaffs
FAVELL, L: LSgt: 22173: OU-7 Y&L
FAWLEY, WE: Pte: 12/913: D: W 1 Jul 16: Bank Clk: * +: Lived 82 Grove Rd, Millhouses: Comm
   N&D 17 Dec 17
FEARN, H: Pte: 13/1232: OU-2 & 13 Y&L
FEARN, H: Pte: 38019: Dow 20 Apr 18 with 1/5 Y&L: Longuenesse (St Omer) Souvenir MC: OU-
   1/5 & 10 Y&L
FEARN, JW: Pte: 12/363: B: W 1 Jul 16: * +: OU-2 & 14 Y&L
FEARNEYHOUGH, A: Pte: 31607: A: OU-3/5 NStaffs & Army Tramways
FEARNLEY, F: Pte: 12/364: Born Penistone 1893: Kia 15 Sep 16 with 2 Y&L: Thiepval Mem
FEARNSHAW Cpl: IC SBs on Nestor: Left 12 Y&L by May 16
FELL, JW: Pte: 14/1 052: B: Born Wombwell, Barnsley: Kia 12 May – 17: Arras Mem: * –: Lived
   Barnsley
FELTON, G: Pte: 45940: OU-2 Suffolk & 7 Y&L
FENNELL, E: Pte: 12/365: B: Born Penistone 1882: Kia 1 Jul 16: Thiepval Mem: * +: Lived Union St,
   Penistone
FIDDES, FA: Cpl: 24490: OU-1/5 & 13 Y&L
FIDLER, C: 2Lt: Comm 26 Sep 17
FIELD, A: LCpl: 12/914: D: * –
FIELD, R: Pte: 235730: A: Batman: OU-13 Y&L
FIELDING, W: Pte: 38021: OU-7 & 10 Y&L
FIELD, GA: Pte: 12/915: D: Born Pitsmoor, Sheffield: Kia 1 Jul 16: Thiepval Mem: * +
FIELDSEND, B: Pte: 12/366: B: Born Penistone 1894: Dow 5 Apr 18 with 42MGC: Etaples MC: * +:
   Lived Penistone
FIRTH, CH: Pte: 25484: OU-26 NFus, 6 & 13 Y&L
FIRTH, H: Pte: 13/301: OU-13 Y&L
FIRTH, J: Pte: 13/298: W 31 Mar 18 with 7 Y&L: OU-2, 7 & 13 Y&L
FISH, G: Pte: 12/1691: Born Burngreave, Sheffield: Kia 22 Jul 16 with 14 Y&L: Ploegsteert Mem,
   Belgium: Lived Woodseats
FISHER, WW: Pte: 13/315: B: * –: OU-13 Y&L
FISHER, HB: Lt Col: Born 1878: Kia 3 Oct 16: Le Touret MC, Richebourg: Reg offr Wilts, served in S
   African War: Ex 8M 92 Bde: Served 12 Y&Lfrom 18 Aug 16
FLATHER, R: Pte: 12/1252: D: OU-94 TMB
FLATHER, WH: Pte: 12/1168: A: W May 16: Lived Mexboro: OU-9 Y&L
FLATHERS, WG: 12th Club Member
FLETCHER, A: Pte: 12/1407: Born Rotherham 1895: Kia 1 Jul 16: Euston Rd MC, Colincamps: * +:
   Lived Rotherham

FLETCHER, A: Pte: B: OU-Coldstream Gds

FLETCHER, A: Pte: 12/1853: OU-2 & 13Y&.L

FLETCHER, AE: Pte: 12/916: D: Born Sharrow, Sheffield 1893: Kia 1 Jul 16: Thiepval Mem: * +

FLETCHER, C: Pte: 12/1297: A: Born Ripley, Derbyshire: Dow 2 Jul 16: Doullens MC Ext No.1: * +: Lived St Marys Gate, Chesterfield

FLETCHER, JH: Pte: 40078: Born 1884: Kia 13 Oct 17 with 1 O Y&L: Tyne Cot Mem, Belgium: OU-8 & 10 Y&L

FLETCHER, SS: Cpl: 12/1291: C: Born Ecclesall, Sheffield: Kia 13 Oct 18 with 1 /5 Y&L: York MC, Haspres: * +: Lived 13 Wath Rd, Netheredge: OU-2, 1/5, 8 & 10 Y&L 233

FLETCHER, W: Pte: 31981: Born York 1893: Kia 27 Jun 17: Arras Mem: OUWY & 10 NFus: Lived York

FLETCHER, W: Sgt: 15513: OU-2 & 9 Y&L

FLINT, W: Pte: 12/1375: D: W May 16 with 12 Y&L and W 28 May 18 with 7 Y&L: * +

FLOOD, W: Sgt: 12/367: B: * –

FLOUNDERS, JW: Pte: 31983: OU-10 NFus & 13 Y&L

FLOWER, WJ: LCpl: 12/1382: A: Born Sheffield 1892: Kia 18 Aug 17 with 117 Worcs: Mendinghem MC, Belgium: * +: Comm 117 Worcs after Jul 16

FLOWER, HC: Pte: 33557: A: Bomber: OU-2/4 & 13 Y&L

FOLLOW, H: Pte: 3161 O: HQ: Born Christs Ch Stafford 1883: Kia 12 Apr 18 with 13 Y&L: Le Grand Beau Mar t MC, Steenwerck: Regt Police: OU-3/5 NStaffs & 13 Y&L

FOOTIT, P: Sgt: 19187: OU-2 & 9 Y&L

FORD, F: ASgt: 12/2110: A: * –: OU-6 Y&L

FORD, F: CaptPadre: Served 12 Y&L 1916-18

FORD, WE: Cpl: 12/1 OO: A: Born Chesterfield: Kia 15 Nov 16: Sailly au Bois MC: Bank Clk: * +: Lived NOJ Chesterfield

FORREST, C: Pte: 12/2031: A: * –

FORREST, P: Pte: 38020: OU-2 Y&L

FORSHAW, AW: Pte: 31608: HQ: Observer: OU-3/5 NStaffs & 13 Y&L

FORSTER, SH: Pte: Sheffield Univ Student

FOSTER, G: Interviewed by J Harris for Covenant With Death

FOSTER, H: LCpl: 9/2236: B: OU-2, 7 & 9 Y&L

FOSTER, SS: Pte: 12/650: A: * +

FOSTON, T: Pte: 12/917: D: * +

FOULSTONE, WA: Pte: 12/369: B: Sheffield Univ Student* +

FOUNTAIN, JA: Pte: 12/1265: OU-2 Y&L

FOWELL, AE: Pte: 3/2631: OU-1, 2 & 7 Y&L: Deserted 16 Nov 18

FOWLER, RD: Pte: 20581: B: OU-2 Y&L

FOWLSTONE, F: Pte: 12/1 03: A: W 1 Jul 16: Sheffield Univ Student* +: Lived 172 Crookesmoor Rd

FOX, AE: Pte: 12/1588: W Oct 16: OU-2, 8 & 14 Y&L

FOX, CA: Pte: 33549: OU-7 Y&L

FOX, TH: Pte: 12/370: B: * +: Postman

FOXON, AH: Pte: 12/1 05: A: Born Ecclesall, Sheffield: Kia 16 Sep 16: Le Touret MC: Sheffield Univ Student: * +: Lived 10 Sheldon Rd, Netheredge

FOXON, DH: Pte: 12/1 04: A

FOXON, S: Pte: 12/1505: A: W 1 Jul 16: * +: Lived Crookesmoor

FRANK, A: Pte: 21601: OU-2, 9 & 13 Y&L

FRANK, AH: Pte: 12/1964: A: Born Gainsboro 1897: Kia 1 Jul 16: Rlwy Hollow MC, Serre: * +: Lived 39 St Marys Rd

FREAK, JM: Pte: 31602: OU-3/5 NStaffs & 7 Y&L

FREAR, R: Sgt: 7897: HQ: Lewis gnr

FREEDMAN, A: Pte: 12/2161: OU-1 Y&L

FREEMAN, H: Pte: 31982: Born Studholme, Bedford: Kia 9 Oct 17: Arras Mem: OU-WY, 10 NFus, 328 Quarry Coy RE & 109 Rlwy Coy RE: Lived Leeds

FREESTONE, FW: CSMI: Bayonet Instr: Attached 12 Y&L from 23 Oct 16

FRENCH, J: Pte: 12/1408: C: * –: OU-1 & 10 Y&L

FRENCH, S: Pte: 12/2032: D: Born Keighley 1883: Dow 1 O Sep 16: St Vaast MC, Richebourg: * –

FRETWELL, A: Pte: 12/371: B: * –: OU-7 Y&L

FRIEND, JF: Pte: 235689: OU-13 Y&L

FRITH, H: Pte: 12/1482: OU-2, 8 & 9 Y&L

FRITH, JW: Pte: 12/1453: B: Born Darnell: Kia 1 Jul 16: Thiepval Mem: * +: Lived 56 Frederick St, Darnell

FROBISHER, G: LCpl: 31984: HQ: Born Lofthouse, Leeds 1890: Kia 18 Sep 18 with 13 Y&L: Ploegsteert Mem, Belgium: Special Patrol Pty: OU-WY, 10 NFus& 13 Y&L

FROGGATT, GF: Pte: 11194: A

FROGGATT, J: LCpl: 12/920: D: Born Nr Chesterfield: Kia 1 Jul 16: Thiepval Mem: * +: Lived 63 Cobnar Rd

FROGGATT, JA: Pte: 19484: OU-6 & 13 Y&L

FROGGATT, JAS: LCpl: 12/373: A: Town Hall Licensing Dept* +: OU-2 & 9 Y&L

FROGGATT, JS: Sgt12/372: B: Born Sheffield 1885: Kia 12 Apr 18 with 13 Y&L: Ploegsteert Mem, Belgium: * –: Observer

FROST, AD: Pte: 12/1238: C: Born Dore, Sheffield 1895: Kia 4 May–16: Sucrerie MC, Colincamps

FROST, GA: Pte: 12/1802: OU-6, 8 & 13 Y&L

FRY, JA: Pte: 12/921: D: * –: QM Storeman

FRYER, GF: Pte: 28444: OU-2 Y&L

FRYER, OCW: WO2: 235731: OU-2/4, 7 & 13 Y&L

FRYER, W: Pte: 39862: HQ: Born Birtley, Durham: Kia 26 Mar 18 with 13 Y&L: Arras Mem: Signaller: OU-DLI, 10 & 13 Y&L

FULCHER, J: Pte: 31605: OU-3/5 NStaffs

FULFORD, W: Pte: 12/106: A: * +

FULLER, F: Pte: 235626: A: Lewis gnr

FULWOOD, C: Pte: 12/374: B: W 1 Jul 16: * +: Lived Doncaster

FURNISS, CF: Pte: 12/107: A: Born l896: W 1 Jul 16 with 12 Y&L and Kia l6 Apr 18 with 10 NStaffs: Haringhe MC, Belgium: Sheffield Univ Student: * +: Brother of EV Furniss: Lived 35 Conduit Rd: Comm 4 Y&L 29 Aug 17

FURNISS, E: Pte: 12/651: C: Kia 16 May 16: Sucrerie MC, Colincamps: Lived 63 Harleston St

FURNISS, EV: Pte: 12/1548: A: Born Broomhill, Sheffield 1897: Kia 1 Jul 16: Thiepval Mem: * +: Lived 35 Conduit Rd: Brother of CF Furniss

FURNISS, H: Pte: 12/2140: A: * +: Runner

FURNISS, S: Pte: 12/1222: C: * +

FYFFE, AE: Pte: 12/108: A: * –: Waterman

FYFFE, RW: Sheffield Univ Student: Comm 4 Y&L 18 Aug 15, attd MGC

GALE, JW: Pte: 37992: Kia 24 Mar 18 with 2 Y&L: Achiet-le-Grand CC Ext

GALLIMORE, R: Sgt 12/1123: A: W 1 Ju/16: Bank Clk: * +: Lived Ilkestone

GAMBLE, W: Pte: 1 0346: OU-2 Y&L. & Labour Corps

GAMBLE, F: ACpl: 39135: OU-7 & 10 Y&L

GAMBLE, TE: Pte: 12/375: B: Born Sharrow, Sheffield 1891: Dow 1 Jul – 16: Couin MC: * –

GAMSTON, J: Pte: 26804: OU-2 & 6 Y&L

GAPES, RE: Pte: 12/922: D: Born Feltwell, Norfolk 1894: Kia 1 Jul 16-: Thiepval Mem: Apprentice Electrician: * +: Lived 268 Barnsley Rd

GARBUTT, CS: LCpl: 12/923: A: MM: Sheffield Univ Student: * +

GARDINER, E: Interviewed by J Harris for Covenant With Death

GARDINER, J: ASgt 11013: Born Royston 1896: Dow 25 Nov 17: Duisans MC, Etrun: Lived Pontefract

GARDINER, E: Pte: 12/924: D: Born Castleford 1891: Kia 1 Jul 16: Thiepval Mem: * +: Lived 6 The Terrace, Canklow, Chesterfield

GARFIELD, S: Pte: 12/1910: A: * –

GARFITT, L: Pte: 12/652: C: W 1 Jul 16: * +: Lived Cresswell: OU-14 Y&L: Comm NStaffs Jun 17

GARLICK, H: Pte: 22260: B: Born St Georges, Sheffield 1889: Kia 18 Dec 16: Sailly au Bois: * –

GARRETT, E: Pte: 21645: OU-8, 10 & 13 Y&L

GARRETT, GF: Pte: 18671: OU-2 & 6 Y&L

GARRY, T: LCpl: 12/376: B: MM?: W Sep 16: * –NOJ: Runner

GARSIDE, E: Sgt: 12/2037: C: * +: * +:

GARSIDE, E: Pte: 12/1952: W Aug 16: OU-13 Y&L

GARVEY, FJ: Pte: 12/653: C: * +: OU-2/4 & 13 Y&L

GARWOOD, C: CSgt: 12/377: NOJB: * –

GAUNT, R: Pte: 3198cf3: 3198cf3: OU-13 Corps

GAYNOR, F: Pte: 203989: HQ: Special Patrol Pty: OU-1/4, 7 & 13 Y&L

GEE, F: LCpl: 12/1l O: A: Kia 4 May 16: Sucrerie MC, Colincamps

GELDERT, S: Pte: 12/111: A: MM: * –: Batman: OU-2 & 1/5 Y&L

GENT, HS: Pte: 12/112: B: Born Sheffield 1892: Lived Burngreave Rd: Comm 11 SStaffs Mar 15, served at Gallipoli

GENT, JC: Sheffield Univ Student: Comm KOYLI 1915

GENT, PE: Pte: 235627: OU-7 Y&L

GIBBS, J: Pte: 235691: OU-7 Y&L

GIBSON, EN: Pte: W 1 Jul 16: Left 12 Y&L before May 16

GIBSON, F: Pte: 235628: HQ: Mess waiter: OU-1/4 & 9 Y&L

GIBSON, H: 2Lt Born 1885: Kia 30 Sep 18 with 13 Y&L: Strand MC, Ploegsteert, Belgium: Comm 26 Sep 17: Served 12 Y&L from 21 Dec 17: Lived Kingston on Thames

GILBERT, D: Pte: 12/115: A: W 1 Jul 16: * +: OU-2 & 13 Y&L

GILBERT, WS: Pte: 12/113: A: Born 1894: W 1 Jul 16: * +: Sheffield University Student Comm LFus 28 Aug 17: Lived 1 Havelock St: Empl Cammell Laird

GILBERTHORPE, W: Pte: 13/1 059: Born Barnsley 1888: Kia 27 Jun 17: Arras Mem: Lived Barnsley: OU-2 & 13 Y&L

GILDING, JT: Pte 13388: Born Chesterfield: W 1 Jul 16 and Kia 27 Jun 17: Arras Mem: Lived Dalton Parva

GILL, A: Pte: 31989: OU-10 NFus

GILL, JL: Pte: 12/1360: B: W May 16: Bank Clk: Comm 29 Aug 17 to 13 Y&L: Lived Doncaster

GILL, JW: Pte: 12/1923: D: Born Heeley, Sheffield 1895: Kia 1 Jul 16: Thiepval Mem: * +

GILL, S: Pte: 12/114: A: Born Mosboro 1896: Kia 1 Jul 16: Thiepval Mem: * +: Lived Grimethorpe

GILL, WC: LCpl: 12/378: B: Born Doncaster 1886: Kia 1 Jul 16: Thiepval Mem: * +: Lived Doncaster

GILLAM, WH: Pte: 12/116: A: W 1 Jul 16: * +: Pioneer: OU-10 & 13 Y&L

GILLATT, F: Pte: 12/1809: OU-Cyclist Corps & 13 Y&L

GILSON, C: Pte: 12/925: D: * –

GILSON, EN: Pte: 12/118: A: W 1 Jul 16 with 12 Y&L and D 5 Nov 18 as POW: Niederzwehren MC, Kassel, West Germany: Sheffield Univ Student '+: Lived 125 Whitham Rd: Comm 2 Y&L 29 Aug 17

GILSON, EL: Pte: Sheffield Univ Student

GINNS, J: Pte: 23532: OU-2, 7 & 8 Y&L

GIRAUD, WH: Pte: 12/927: D: Born Lowestoft 1881: W Aug 16 & Kia 7 May 17 with 14 Y&L: Arras Mem: Sheff Telegraph Reporter: * –: OU-10 & 14 Y&L

GLADMAN, G: Pte: 31286: Dow 23 Mar 18 with 7 Y&L: Dernancourt CC Ext OU-1 Northants & 7 Y&L

GLADWELL, F: Pte: 12/1569: OU-2 Y&L

GLASS, JS: ACaptW 16 Oct 17 with 14 Y&L: OU-14 Y&L, 4 Entr Bn & 2 RSFus

GLEAVE, F: Pte: 12/1354: C: Born Carbrook, Sheffield 1879: Kia 14 Jun 16: Bertrancourt MC

GLENN, JR: LCpl: 12/928: AD: Born Pitsmoor, Sheffield 1893: Empl Education Dept* +: Lived 107 Nottingham St, Pitsmoor: · Signaller: Comm NStaffs 29 Jan 18

GLEW, J: Left 12 Y&L early on

GLOSSOP, ER: Pte: 12/655: C: Born Ecclesfield: Kia 1 Jul 16: Queens MC, Serre: * +: Lived 82 Holme Ln

GLOSSOP, H: Pte: 12/119: A: W 1 Jul 16: * +: Lived 133 Walkley St Bde Canteen

GLOVER, JA: Sgt15519: OU-10& 13 Y&L

GODWIN, CH: 2Lt: Born 1894: Kia 1 Jul 16 with 1 O Y&L: Thiepval Mem: Sheffield Univ Student Ex 12 Y&L OR: Comm 10 Y&L

GOFF, DL: Pte: 235694: OU-7 Y&L

GOLBY, JJ: Pte: 31284: OU-1 Northants

GOLDSMITH, O: Pte: 235629

GOOD, A: Pte: 2921 O: OU-2 Y&L

GOODALL, C: Pte: 3D90: A: Born Killinghall, Harrogate: Kia 15 Sep 18 with 13 Y&L: Ploegsteert Mem, Belgium: Offrs Mess cook: OU-1 0 NFus & 13 Y&L

GOODALL, JC: Cpl: 12/930: D: * – : OU-13 Y&L

GOODFELLOW, M: Pte: 12/379: A: * –

GOODLAD, A: Pte: 12/929: D: Born Sheffield 1894: Kia 1 Jul 16: Rlwy Hollow MC, Serre: * +: Lived 36 Mar shall Rd, Woodseats

GOODRICH, JEC: LCpl: 12/122: A: * –

GOODWIN, JW: Pte: 27522: Born 1S97: Kia S Feb 17 with 115 Coy MG Corps: Ferme: Olivier MC, Elverdinghe, Belgium: OU: MG Corps

GOODWIN, T: Pte: 11660: A

GOODYEAR, W: Cpl: 12/121: A: * –

GORRILL, R: Pte: 12/1376: Born Sheffield 1899: Kia 27 May 18 with 25 MGC: Soissons Mem: * +: Lived 97 Blair Athol Rd

GOSLING, GB: Pte: 14/655: OU-2, 1/5, 10 & 14 Y&L

GOSLING, L: Pte: 31985: OU-10 NFus & 13 Y&L

GOTHARD, F: Pte: 39119: OU-1/4, 9 & 10 Y&L

GOULD, JW: Sgt12/656: C: Born Pontefract 1887: Kia 13 Oct 18 with 1/5 Y&L: York MC, Haspres: Teacher: * +: 11 Pl Sgt Comm 30 Jan 18

GOULD, WH: Pte: W 1 Jul 16 with MG Corps: Empl Davy Bros: Lived Holmcliffe, Brincliffe Edge Rd: Comm 1/5 Y&L 21 Aug 15: OU- MG Corps & RFC

GOULDING, A: Pte: 27315: OU-2 & 7 Y&L

GRAHAM, AE: Pte: 8/2980: B: W Jul 16: * – : Lived Rotherham: OU-7, 8 & 13 Y&L

GRAHAM, JJ: Pte: 28715: Born Hexham, Nothumberland: Kia 24 Mar 18: Roclincourt MC: Lived Newcastle u T: OU-2 Y&L

GRANT, DE: Capt: Served City Bn until 11 May 17, later empl in Min of Munitions

GRANT, TEA: Capt: C: MID: W 24 Sep 16: Comm 27 Apr 15: OC 9 Pl: 94 Bde Pioneer Offr 20 May–19 Aug 16

GRATION, FA: Pte: 12/380: B: D 25 Jan 18: * +: Lived Alfreton: Discharged 10 May 17

GRAY, AH: Pte: 12/931: D: * +: Comm EY 27 Nov 17

GRAY, AE: Pte: 235638: A

GRAY, G: Pte: 39090: Born 1891: Kia 27 May 18 with 2 Y&L: Nine Elms MC, Poperinghe, Belgium: OU-2 & 10 Y&L

GRAY, GH: Pte: 12/1522: B: W 1 Jul 16 with 12 Y&L and W 6 May 18 with 7 Y&L: * +

GRAY, GH: Pte: 241154: OU-2 & 2/5 Y&L

GRAYNON, J: Pte: 3/3042: OU-2, 7 & 13 Y&L

GRAYSON, RB: Solicitor

GRAYSON, W: Pte: 12/1403: D: Born Sheffield 1892: D 24 Dec 18 with 1 Y&L: Taranto Town C Ext, Italy: * +

GREAVES, D: Cpl: 38059: Comm WRiding 26 Jun 18

GREAVES, EF: Pte: 12/1406: C: * +

GREAVES, EL: Pte: 12/126: A

GREAVES, T: Pte: 14318: OU-8 Y&L

GREAVES, TA: Pte: 12/385: A: W 1 Jul 16: * +: Lived Goldthorpe

GREEN, C: Pte: 37988: OU-2 Y&L

GREEN, G: Pte: 37821: OU-7 & 8 Y&L

GREEN, G: Pte: 14/146: B: OU-7 & 14 Y&L

GREEN, H: Pte: 235233: Born Rotherham 1895: Kia 30 Jun 17: Arras Mem: OU-2/4 & 1/5 Y&L

GREEN, J: Cpl: 27649: OU-13 Y&L

GREEN, OH: 2Lt: B: Comm 30 May 17: Served 12 Y&L from 31 Jul 17: OU-7 Y&L

GREEN, SS: Pte: Sheffield Univ Student

GREENAWAY, A: Pte: 12/1521: B: Born Bermondsey, Surrey 1880: Kia 1 Jul 16: Thiepval Mem: * +

GREENFIELD, PW: Pte: 31285: A: Born Chichester: Kia 16 Apr 18 with 13 – Y&L: Sailly sur la Lys Chyd: Lewis gnr: OU-1 Northants & 13 Y&L

GREEN SMITH, AC: Pte: 12/934: D: Born Sheffield 1894: Kia 1 Jul 16: Thiepval Mem: Mining Engineer Student: * +: Lived Hughenden House, Sharrow or 4 Kenwood Park Rd

GREENWOOD, A: Pte: 12/658: C: W May 16: * +: OU-13 Rlwy Tpt Sect RE & 1/5 Y&L

GREENWOOD, W: Pte: 12/935: D: W 1 Jul 16: * +: OU-2 & 2/4 Y&L: Comm Indian Army 24 Sep 18

GREENWOOD, WH: Pte: 38022: OU-7 Y&L

GREGORY, E: Pte: 12/1485: B: Born St Philips, Sheffield 1896: Kia 1 Jul 16: Thiepval Mem: * +: Lived 44 Roebuck Rd, Crookesmoor

GREGORY, H: Cpl: 1874 7: OU-2, 1 0 & 14 Y&L

GREGORY, EG: Bank Clk

GREGORY, F: Pte: 12/936: D: * +: SB

GREGORY, G: Sgt: 12/381: B: W 1 Jul 16: * +: Comm 25 Jan 177

GREGORY, JD: Pte: 12/382: B: * +

GREGORY, T: Pte: 31988: OU-10 NFus

GRIFFITHS, E: Pte: 12/383: B: Born Castleford 1890: Kia 1 Jul 16: Euston Rd MC, Colincamps: * +: Lived Leeds End Rd, Glasshoughton, Castleford

GRIFFITHS, J: Pte: 40095: OU-9 & 13 Y&L

GRIFFITHS, R: LCpl: 11172: A: Lewis gnr

GRIFFITHS, ST: Pte: 235207: OU-1/4, 2/4 & 7 Y&L

GRIMES, FT: Pte: 235696: OU-7 Y&L

GOULD, JW: Sgt12/656: C: Born Pontefract 1887: Kia 13 Oct 18 with 1/5 Y&L: York MC, Haspres: Teacher: * +: 11 Pl SgtComm 30 Jan 18

GOULD, WH: Pte: W 1 Jul 16 with MG Corps: Empl Davy Bros: Lived Holmcliffe, Brinciiffe Edge Rd: Comm 1/5 Y&L 21 Aug 15: OU- MG Corps & RFC

GOULDING, A: Pte: 27315: OU-2 & 7 Y&L

GRAHAM, AE: Pte: 8/2980: B: W Jul 16: * –: Lived Rotherham: OU-7, 8 & 13 Y&L

GRAHAM, JJ: Pte: 28715: Born Hexham, Nothumberland: Kia 24 Mar 18: Roclincourt MC: Lived Newcastle u T: OU-2 Y&L

GRANT, DE: Capt: Served City Bn until11 May 17, later empl in Min of Munitions

GRANT, TEA: CaptC: MID: W 24 Sep 16: Comm 27 Apr 15: 0C 9 Pl: 94 Bde Pioneer Offr 20 May– 19 Aug 16

GRATION, FA: Pte: 12/380: B: D 25 Jan 18: * +: Lived Alfreton: Discharged

GRAY, AH: Pte: 12/931: D: * +: Comm EY 27 Nov 17

GRAY, AE: Pte: 235638: A

GRAY, G: Pte: 39090: Born 1891: Kia 27 May 18 with 2 Y&L: Nine Elms MC, Poperinghe, Belgium: OU-2 & 10 Y&L

GRAY, GH: Pte: 12/1522: B: W 1 Jul 16 with 12 Y&L and W 6 May 18 with 7 Y&L: * +

GRAY, GH: Pte: 241154: OU-2 & 2/5 Y&L

GRAYNON, J: Pte: 3/3042: OU-2, 7 & 13 Y&L

GRAYSON, RB: Solicitor

GRAYSON, W: Pte: 12/1403: D: Born Sheffield 1892: D 24 Dec 18 with 1 Y&L: Taranto Town C Ext, Italy: * +

GREAVES, D: Cpl: 38059: Comm WRiding 26 Jun 18

GREAVES, EF: Pte: 12/1406: C: * +

GREAVES, EL: Pte: 12/126: A

GREAVES, T: Pte: 14318: OU-8 Y&L

GREAVES, TA: Pte: 12/385: A: W 1 Jul 16: * +: Lived Goldthorpe

GREEN, C: Pte: 37988: OU-2 Y&L

GREEN, G: Pte: 37821: OU-7 & 8 Y&L

GREEN, G: Pte: 14/146: B: OU-7 & 14 Y&L

GREEN, H: Pte: 235233: Born Rotherham 1895: Kia 30 Jun 17: Arras Mem: OU-2/4 & 1/5 Y&L

GREEN, J: Cpl: 27649: OU-13 Y&L

GREEN, OH: 2Lt: B: Comm 30 May 17: Served 12 Y&L from 31 Jul 17: OU-7 Y&L

GREEN, SS: Pte: Sheffield Univ Student

GREENAWAY, A: Pte: 12/1521: B: Born Bermondsey, Surrey 1880: Kia 1 Jul 16: Thiepval Mem: * +

GREENFIELD, PW: Pte: 31285: A: Born Chichester: Kia 16 Apr 18 with 13 – Y&L: Sailly sur la Lys Chyd: Lewis gnr: OU-1 Northants & 13 Y&L

GREEN SMITH, AC: Pte: 12/934: D: Born Sheffield 1894: Kia 1 Jul 16: Thiepval Mem: Mining Engineer Student * +: Lived Hughenden House, Sharrow or 4 Kenwood Park Rd

GREENWOOD, A: Pte: 12/658: C: W May 16: * +: OU-13 Rlwy Tpt Sect RE & 1/5 Y&L

GREENWOOD, W: Pte: 12/935: D: W 1 Jul 16: * +: OU-2 & 2/4 Y&L: Comm Indian Army 24 Sep 18

GREENWOOD, WH: Pte: 38022: OU-7 Y&L

GREGORY, E: Pte: 12/1485: B: Born St Philips, Sheffield 1896: Kia 1 Jul 16: Thiepval Mem: * +: Lived 44 Roebuck Rd, Crookesmoor

GREGORY, H: Cpl: 1874 7: OU-2, 1 0 & 14 Y&L

GREGORY, EG: Bank Clk

GREGORY, F: Pte: 12/936: D: * +: SB

GREGORY, G: Sgt: 12/381: B: W 1 Jul 16: * +: Comm 25 Jan 177

GREGORY, JD: Pte: 12/382: B: * +

GREGORY, T: Pte: 31988: OU-10 NFus

GRIFFITHS, E: Pte: 12/383: B: Born Castleford 1890: Kia 1 Jul 16: Euston Rd MC, Colincamps: * +: Lived Leeds End Rd, Glasshoughton, Castleford

GRIFFITHS, J: Pte: 40095: OU-9 & 13 Y&L

GRIFFITHS, R: LCpl: 11172: A: Lewis gnr

GRIFFITHS, ST: Pte: 235207: OU-1/4, 2/4 & 7 Y&L

GRIMES, FT: Pte: 235696: OU- 7 Y&L

GROOCOCK, AW: Pte: 12/384: A: W 1 Jul 16: * +

GROOM, J: Pte: 235692

GROVE, A: Pte: 12/1535: C: Born Horncastle, Lines 1890: Kia 1 Jul 16-: Serre Rd No.2 MC, Serre: * +

GRUNDY, W: Pte: 12/386: B: W 1 Jul 16: Empl Guests, Stocksbridge: * – +: Lived Penistone

GUEST, B: Pte: 24267: Kia 24 Mar 18 with 13 Y&L: Arras Mem

GUEST, E: Pte: 12/1657: OU-1 & 18 Y&L

GUEST, F: Pte: 12/1188: A: W 1 Jul 16: * +: OU-2/4, 6 & 14 Y&L

GUEST, FR: Pte: 12/1839: OU-13 Y&L

GUEST, J: Cpl: 1 1975: OU-7 & 14 Y&L

GUIREY, J: Pte: 2937: B: OU-41 Mob Vet Sect

GUMMER, H: Pte: Sheffield Univ Student: Comm 2/5 Y&L 17 Nov 14, later attd ACC

GUMMER, S: Pte: Kia 9 Oct 17 with 5 Y&L: Tyne Cot Mem, Belgium: Solicitor: Comm 1 /5 Y&L 7 Feb 15

GUNSON, EE: LCpl: 12/926: D: Sheffield Telegraph Reporter: * –: Comm N&D 29 May 17

GUNSTONE, FR: LCpl: 12/660: C: Born Nr Liverpool 1891: Kia 1 Jul 16: Luke Copse MC, Serre: * +: Lived 11 Ashland Rd, Netheredge: Brother of WW Gunstone

GUNSTONE, WW: Pte: 12/661: C: Born Nr Liverpool 1892: Kia 1 Jul 16: Luke Copse MC, Serre: * +: Lived 11 Ashland Rd, Netheredge: Brother of FR Gunstone

GURNEY, CH: Lt Col: DSO and Bar: Served 12 Y&L from 25 Jul 16: 2IC: CO 11 EY from 8 Feb 17

GUY, C: Pte: 12/1924: C: * –

GYTE, W: Pte: 25369: Born 1890: Dow 3 Oct 18 with 6 Y&L: Bucquoy Road MC, Ficheux: OU-2, 6 & 8 Y&L

HACKETT, R: Pte: 12/939: D: Born Atley, Kildare 1891: Kia 1 Jul 16: Thiepval Mem: * +

HACKING, W: Sgt38057: Born Blackburn: Dow 11 May 17: Duisans MC: OU-1 Fus: Lived Blackburn

HADDOCK, JA: Pte: 7595: B: Born 1884: Executed 16 Sep 16: Vielle-Chapelle MC, Lacoutre: FGCM 24 Aug 16 for desertion: OU-2 Y&L

HADDOCK, Pte: HM: 38025: OU-2 & 6 Y&L

HADEN, E: Pte: 45942: OU-2 Suffolk, 7 & 18 Y&L

HADFIELD, JW: Pte: 41090: OU-8 Y&L

HAGON, R: Pte: Born Sheffield 1892: Sheffield Univ Student Lived 38 Main Rd, Hilisboro: Recalied to Munitions work 1915

HAGUE, EA: Pte: 200670: OU-1/5 & 7 Y&L

HAGUE, GRT: Pte: 12/129: A: * +: SS Aug 16: Comm EY 10 Sep 16

HAGUE, H: Pte: 13/1337: B: Born 1893: Kia 21 Apr 18 with 7 Y&L: Forceville CC & Ext

HAGUE, H: Sgt: 12/666: C: W 1 Jul 16: * +: Comm RDubFus 17 Dec 17

HAGUE, W: Sgt: B: Served in S African War: Drililnstr: Discharged Mar 15

HAGUE, W: Pte: 14/303: Kia 1 Jul 16 with 14 Y&L: Tilloy MC: Sheffield Univ Student

HAIGH, J: Pte: 37895: OU-7 & 14 Y&L

HAINES, CH: Sgt31298: MM: OU-1 Northants, 6 & 9 Y&L

HALCROW, WG: Pte: 37989: Born 1897: Kia 15 Dec 17 with 1/4 Y&L: Duhallow Advanced Dressing Station MC, Ypres, Belgium: OU-2, 1/4 & 9 Y&L

HALE, HT: Pte: 12/663: C: Born Todmorden, Lancs 1890: Kia 1 Jul 16: Queens Me, Serre: * +: Lived 5 Devonshire Tee

HALL, AG: Pte: 40206: A: OU-APM, 6 & 13 Y&L

HALL, CH: Pte: 31991: OU-10 NFus, 8 & 10 Y&L

HALL, EL: Sheffield Univ Student

HALL, EP: Sheffield Univ StudentComm 13 Hamps 1915

HALL, H: Pte: 12/664: C: * +: Sniper and Lewis gnr: Comm KOYL

HALL, P: Pte: 12/1546: Born Renishaw, Derbyshire 1896: Dow 28 Mar 17 with 2 Y&L: Mar oc MC: Lived Renishaw

HALL, W: Sgt: 22158: OU-2 Y&L

HALL, W: Pte: 12/1755: OU-2, 13 & 14 Y&L

HALLAM, AE: Pte: 12/1306: A: W 1 Jul 16: * +: Lived Aughton

HALLAM, L: Pte: 12/2026: B: W 30 Aug 18 with 7 Y&L

HALLAM, WO: Pte: 12/1719: A: * –: Lewis gnr

HALLAS, W: Pte: 1 0166: Kia 21 Mar 18 with 2 Y&L: Queant Road MC, Buissy: OU-2 & 10 Y&L

HALLER, E: Pte: 41111: OU-2/4.6 & 8 Y&L

HALPIN, EG: Lt: Served 12 Y&L from 25 Nov 16: Tpt Offr after Atkinson

HALSEY, FW: Pte: 31294: OU-1 Northants & 10 Y&L

HAMBLIN, P: Pte: 28793: OU-2 Y&L

HAMMOND, JA: Pte: 24439: Born Broomhill, Sheffield 1896: Dow 25 May 17: Duisans MC: OU-2 & 9 Y&L

HAMPSHIRE, H: Pte: 38748: Born 1898: Kia 19 Jul 18 with 7 Y&L: Harponvilie CC Ext: OU-7 & 8 Y&L

HAMPTON, FB: Cpl: 12/667: B: Born Nr Waisall, Staffs 1895: Kia 1 Jul · 16: Rlwy Hollow MC, Serre: Bank Clk: * +: Lived 63 Clarendon Rd, Fulwood

HAMPTON, HP: Pte: 12/940: D: * +

HANBIDGE, TG: Pte: 12'1196: A: W 16 Feb 17: * –: Signaller: Lived Fargate

HANCOCK, A: Pte: 12/1499: A: * –: OU-2 & 9 Y&L

HANCOCK, TW: Pte: 12/1763: Born Ringinglow, Sheffield: Kia 1 Jul 16 with 13 Y&L: Thiepval Mem

HANCOLE, E: Pte: 12/1795: OU-2, 2/4 & 13 Y&L

HANDBURY, H: Pte: 12/388: B: Born Handley, Derbyshire 1895: Kia 8 Apr 16: Sucrerie MC, Colincamps

HANDLEY, F: Cpl: 12/1720: OU-8 Y&L

HANDLEY, W: Pte: 39042: Born Badsworth, Yorks 1896: Kia 12 May 17-: Arras Mem: Lived Barnsley: OU-10 Y&L

HANFORTH, CH: Pte: 12/133: A: Born St Georges, Sheffield 1895: D 9 Feb 15: Christ Ch Chyd, Fulwood: Oxford Univ Student: Lived Hillside, Carsick

HANKINS, AJ: Pte: 12/1167: A: SS 1 Jul 16: * +: Lived Brighton

HANNAH, WH: Pte: 12/1543: OU-14 Y&L

HANSFORD, RWD: 2Lt: W 24 Mar 18 with 13 Y&L

HANSFORD, WHITE T: lnterviewed by J Hariis for Covenant With Death

HANSON, FC: LCpl: 12/1413: A: Dow 27 Jul 16: Rue du Bacquerot MC No 1, Leventie: * +: OU-1 0, 13 & 14 Y&L

HANSON, G: Pte: 12/1358: C: MM: Born Bradford: Kia 1 Jul 16: Euston Rd MC, Colincamps: * +

HANSON, JT: Pte: 31998: OU-1 ONFus

HARAN, F: Pte: 14/234: A: Bomber

HARBORD, CG: Kia 1 Sep 16 with 14 Y&L: St Vaast MC, Richebourg: Comm 14 Y&L31 Mar 15

HARCOURT, EA: Pte: 235631: OU-7 Y&L

HARDCASTLE, T: Pte: 14/519: OU-2, 9 & 14 Y&L

HARDING, AW: Pte: 235630: A: Water Police

HARDMAN, E: Pte: 12/2002

HARDWICK, S: LCpl: 12/668: C: Kia 4 May 16: Sucrerie MC, Coiincamps: Lived 35 Maltravers Rd

HARDY, C: Pte: 41 036: OU-8 Y&L

HARDY, HE: Cpl: 31297: OU-1 Northants

HARGREAVES, R: Pte: 31992: OU-10 NFus, 2 & 7 Y&L

HARKIS, M: Pte: 38024: A: Born Manchester 1887: Kia 13 Jul 18 with 13 Y&L: Le Grand Hasard MC, Morbecque: Lewis gnr: OULFus & 13 Y&L

HARLING, HH: Pte: 33550: OU-7 Y&L

HARLOW, H: Pte: 12/941: D: Born Audenshaw, Lancs 1889: SS Jun 16: + – : Lived 121 Middlewood Rd: Batman

HARPER, G: Pte: 12/1969: OU-14 Y&L

HARPER, JA: Pte: 25129: OU-2, 1/5, 8 & 10 Y&L

HARPER, TH: Sgt: 13074: B: W Jul 16: Lived Truro Place, Rotherham

HARRINGTON, AJ: Attended 1918 Reunion Dinner

HARRINGTON, C: Pte: 12/943: O: MM: W 1 Jul 16: * +: OU-2 & 2/4 Y&L: Lived Penistone Rd

HARRINGTON, HW: Pte: 12/389: B: Born Worksop: Kia 11 Apr 18 with 13 Y&L: Le Grande Beaumont MC: * –: Waterman: Lived Worksop

HARRIS, C: Pte: 31822: OU-1 Leics, 1 /5, 2, 5 & 6 Y&L

HARRIS, F: Pte: 31290: A: OU-1 Northants & 13 Y&L

HARRIS, H: Pte: 12/944: D: W 1 Jul 16: Sheffield Univ Student: * – Lived Dalton: Comm 3 Y&L 25 Jun 18

HARRIS, L: Pte: 26590: OU-2/4, 10 & 13 Y&L

HARRIS, M: Sheffield Univ Student

HARRISON, A: Pte: 202291: OU-1/5 & 7 Y&L

HARRISON, AJ: **Pte**: 12/1244: B: * –: OU-7 & 10 Y&L

HARRISON, C: ASgt: 36099: OU-2, 7 & 10 Y&L

HARRISON, CE: Pte: 12/1170: A: W 1 Jul 16: * +: Lived Byron Lea, Byron Rd, Netheredge: OU-2 & 2/4 Y&L

HARRISON, CJ: Pte: 12/1325: A: Born Dronfield 1898: Kia 1 Jul 16: Thiepval Mem: * +: Lived Packington Vicarage

HARRISON, D: 2Lt: C: Comm 27 Jun 17: Served 12 Y&L from 11 Sep 17

HARRISON, F: Pte: 13/460: OU-1/5, 2/5, 1 0, 13 & 14 Y&L

HARRISON, G: Ptel12/1479: A: W 1 Jul 16: * +: Comm 8 Y&L 30 May 17?

HARRISON, H: Pte: 31622: A: Bomber: OU-3/5 NStaffs & 13 Y&L

HARRISON, H: Pte: 3834: HQ: Special Patrol Ply

HARRISON, HS: Pte: 45365: OU-2/4 & 2/5 Y&L

HARRISON, J: Joined 12 Y&L with JL Middleton

HARRISON, J: Pte: 31997: A: Bomber: OU-10 NFus & 13 Y&L

HARRISON, L: Pte: 27794: Born Nr Barnsley 1892: Kia 10 May 17: Canadian C No.2, St Vaast: Lived Barnsley: OU-2 Y&L

HARRISON, N: Pte: 12/1473: B: * +

HARRISON, RH: Pte: 31994: HQ: Batman: OU-10 NFus & 13 Y&L

HARRISON, WG: Pte: 12/2041: Born St Silas, Sheffield 1888: Dow 20 Jul 16 with 14 Y&L: Dartmoor MC: Estate Manager: Lived 404 Glossop Rd

HARROP, J: Pte: 40068: OU-9 Y&L

HARTLEY, A: Pte: 22069: OU-2 & 8 Y&L

HARTLEY, F: Pte: 12/1206: A: Born Heeley, Sheffield 1894: Kia 1 Jul 16-: Thiepval Mem: * +

HARTLEY, FD: Pte: 38828: Born 1882: D 31 Mar 18 with 7 Y&L: Doullens CC Ext N01: OU-7 & 10 Y&L

HARTLEY, PH: Pte: 12/1711: OU-2 & 8 Y&L

HARTLEY, WC: Pte: 12/945: D: * +

HARVEY, WP: Pte: 12/1858: OU-13 Y&L

HASKEY ,GH: LCpl: 12/1377: AB: Born Nr Peterboro: Kia 1 Jul 16: Queens MC, Serre: * +: Lived Chesterfield

HASLAM, EA: Pte: 12/1334: B: W 1 Jul 16: * +

HASTINGS, AH: Pte: 12/1299: A: Born Sheffield 1896: W 1 Jul 16: Auctioneer: * +: Lived 126 Abbey Ln: OU-1ab Corps

HASTINGS, J: Sgt: 12/946: AD: Born 1889: W 1 Jul 16: * +: Lived 40 Collegiate Cres

HASSALL, F: Pte: 31617: OU-3/5 NStaffs & 7 Y&L

HATTON, GC: Pte: 12/2023: A: * –

HATTON, JH: Pte: 27758: OU-1/5, 2/5 & 2 Y&L

HATTON, S: Pte: 12/1994: C: * –: OU-7 Y&L

HATTON, WH: Pte: 23231: OU-2, 8 & 14 Y&L

HAUGHTON, CS: Pte: 12/963: D: OU-94 TMB & 9 Y&L

HAWDON, A: Pte: 37991: OU-2 Y&L

HAWES, R: ACpl: 12/390: B: * –

HAWLEY, DD: MC: Sheffield Univ Sludent: Comm 1 OVal 29 Apr 15: Later attd Min of Lab

HAWLEY, HW: Pte: 12/1135: D: W 1 Jul 16: * +: Lewis gnr

HAWORTH, GE: Pte: 12/670: C: * +: OU-13 Y&L

HAWSON, G: Pte: 12/671: C: Born St Georges, Sheffield 1888: Kia 1 Jul 16: Thiepval Mem: * +

HAYCOCK, I: Pte: 12/672: C: Born Walkley, Sheffield 1893: Kia 1 Jul 16-: Thiepval Mem: * +

HAYDOCK, JW: LCpl: 12/673: C: Born Hindley, Wigan: Kia 1 Jul 16: Thiepval Mem: * +

HAYES, W: Pte: 205001

HAYWOOD, AH: Pte: 12/391: B: W 25 Mar 18 wilh 7 Y&L: * +

HAZELWOOD, IP: Pte: 12/136: A: W 1 Jul 16: * +: Comm Y&L 26 Jun 17

HEADEACH, MCP: ASgt: 12/392: B: MM: Born Todmorden, Lancs 1874: Kia 1 Jul 16: Rlwy Hollow MC, Serre: * +

HEADING, RJ: Pte: 31291: Born SI Albans, Kent: Kia 29 Nov 16: Sailly au Bois MC: OU-Northants

HEADWORTH, J: ASgt: 12/949: D: * +

HEATH, AB Coys: Left 12 Y&L early on

HEATH, F: Cpl: 25128: OU-2 Y&L: Comm Y&L 28 May 18

HEATLEY, H: Sgt: 13/515: B: OU-2 & 13 Y&L

HECKINGBOTTOM, FMP: Pte: 12/1577

HEDLEY, A: Pte: 12/1977: B: * –

HEELEY, D: Pte: 17364: OU-2 & 6 Y&L

HELLIWELL, J: Pte: 171 01: OU-2, 6 & 9 Y&L

HEMSWORTH, F: Pte: 18912: OU-2, 1/5, 2/5 & 9 Y&L

HENDERSON, KA: Pte: 12/137: OU-9 Y&L

HENDERSON, RB: Sgt: 12/1141: D: Born Nr Middlesboro 1877: Dow 30 Jun 16: Bertrancourt MC: Lived 291 Sharrow Vale Rd: Served in S African War

HENN, FM: Pte: 12/951: D: * –: OU-13 Y&L

HENSBY, WI: Pte: 44815: Kia 22 Sep 18: OU-1/5 & 2/5 Y&L

HENSER, A: Pte: 12/1507: B: W 1 Jul 16: * +

HENTON, H: Pte: 31618: Born Atherstone, Warwicks 1887: Kia 12 May 17: Arras Mem: OU-3/5 NStaffs: Lived Tamworth

HEPPENSTALL, F: Pte: 21836: OU-2 & 10 Y&L

HEPPENSTALL, PG: Sgt: B: W 1 Jul 16: Sheffield Univ Student

HERBERT, EG: Pte: 235632: OU-7 Y&L

HERN, H: Pte: 43898: Born Nr Sunderland: Kia 12 May 17: Albuera MC, Bailleul: OU-6 Yorks: Lived Sunderland

HERON, G: Pte: 28739: A: Batman

HERRING, GS: Pte: 12/674: C

HESLING, A: Pte: 40098: Born 1888: Kia 1 O Apr 17 with 9 Y&L: Railway Dugouts Burial Ground (Transport Farm), Zillebeke, Belgium

HESLINGTON, FH: LCpl: 12/395: B: * –

HESLINGTON, TP: ACpl12/397: B: * –: Comm RE 27 Nov 16

HEWITT, HD: Pte: 12/675: C: W 1 Jul 16: Sheffield Univ Student: * +: Comm MGC29 Oct 18

HEWSON, W: Pte: 12/2084: Born Heeley, Sheffield 1893: Dow 27 Aug 16: Warloy – Baillon CC Ext

HIBBARD, AE: Pte: 39125: OU-7 & 10 Y&L

HIBBERD, WT: Pte: 31302: Born Battersea, Surrey 1889: Dow 21 May 17: St Nicholas Chyd, Tooting: OU-Northants

HIBBERSON, GS: Pte: 12/952: D: Battle Police

HIBBERT, FH: Pte: 39032: OU-1 Oval

HIBBERT, O: Pte: 29133: OU-2 & 9 Y&L

HICKIN, E: Pte: 31625: OU-3/5 NStaffs

HICKS, C: Dmr: 13/453: OU-2 & 13 Y&L

HICKS, C: Pte: 12/139: A: SS Sep 16: Lived 70 William St: OU-2 Y&L

HICKS, WH: Pte: 12/1593: A: * –: OU-1/4 & 9 Y&L

HICKSON, H: Pte: 12/953: D: * –: OU-7 Y&L

HICKSON, S: Pte: 12/1967: C: * +

HICKSON, J: Sgt: 31615: A: OU-211 Fd Coy RE, 3/5 NStaffs & 13 Y&L

HIDES, AM: Pte: 12/954: OU-2 Y&L

HIDES, CE: Pte: 12/1754: OU-2, 6, 8 & 13 Y&L

HIGHAM, JW: Pte: 40427: OU-2/4, 2/5 & 9 Y&L

HIGHFIELD, W: Pte: 12/140: A: * –: SB: OU-2 & 9 Y&L

HILL, F: Pte: 12/398: D: * –

HILL, J: Pte: 14/1353: B

HILL, J: Cpl: 12/676: C

HILL, J: Pte: 37644: A: Bomber

HILL, LA: Pte: 12/141: A: Born Sheffield 1893: Gardener: Lived 34 Bramwith Rd: Batman & Signaller

HILL, SJ: Pte: 12/20: B

HILL, TW: Cpl: 12/677: C: W 1 Jul 16: * +: Comm MGC 25 May 17

HILLIARD, H: Pte: 31293: OU-1 Northants, 2 & 2/4 Y&L

HILLIARD, P: Cpl: 31292: OU-1 Northants, 2 & 7 Y&L

HILLS, AJ: Pte: 234697: C: HQ 94 Bde Waiter

HILLS, AJ: Pte: 12/678: C: * +: OU-13 Y&L

HILSDEN, GW: Pte: 31307: OU-1 Northants, 6 & 10 Y&L

HILTON, C: Pte: 31303: HQ: HQ 94 Bde Batman

HILTON, J: Pte: 35023: A: lewis gnr

HILTON, JA: Pte: 38023: Born 1893: Kia 28 Mar 18 with 13 Y&L: Bucquoy Road MC, Ficheux

HINCHCLIFFE, A: Pte: 12/1878: D: * –: OU-7 Y&L

HINCHCLIFFE, AE: Pte: 12/142: A: W 1 Jul 16: Empl Hibernia Works: * +: Lived 34 Crescent Rd: OU-10 & 14 Y&L: Comm MGC 29 Oct 18

HINCHCLIFFE, W: Pte: 12/679: C: Born Wombwell: Kia 1 Jul 16: Thiepval Mem: * – +: Lived 34 Wombwell Main, Barnsley

HINCHLIFFE, CH: Pte: 12/1890: W Jul 16 with 8 Y&L

HINCHLIFFE, T: Pte: 12/1766: W Jul 16 with 8 Y&L

HINCKLEY, DR: 2Lt: Born 1896: Kia 13 Jan 17 with 5 Sqn RFC: Douchy les Ayette MC: Accountant: Lived Cobnar Rd, Woodseats: Comm 11 May 15: Served 12 Y&L after Oct 16

HIND, B: Pte: 37987: Born 1891: Kia 15 Apr 17 with 2 Y&L: Mar oc MC, Grenay

HIPKINS, FW: MC: Kia 3 Oct 18 with 6N&D: Bellicourt MC

HIPKISS, T: Pte: 12/1888: W Jul 16 with 8 Y&L 237

HIRST, H: Pte: 37962: Kia 18 May 18 with 2 Y&L: Arras Mem

HIRST, H: Pte: interviewed by J Harris for Covenant With Death

HOARE, E: Pte: 1 2/143: A: W 1 Jul 16: * +

HOBBS, FJ: Pte: 33558: HQ: Runner: OU-2 & 13 Y&L

HOBBS, AJ: Pte: 31614: Born 1890: Kia 2 Sep 18 with 2/4 Y&L: Vaulx Hill MC, Vaulx-Vraucourt: OU-3/5 NStaffs, 2/4 & 10 Y&L

HOBBS, JW: Pte: 26599: B: OU-7 Y&L

HOBBS, W: Pte: 31299: OU-1 Northants, 1/5& 13 Y&L

HOBSON, A: Pte: 12/400: B: W May 16

HOBSON, A: Pte: 12/956: D: * +: OU-2 & 13 Y&L

HOBSON, FH: Pte: 12/957: D: Born Heeley, Sheffield 1895: * +: Kia 1 Jul – 16: Rlwy Hollow MC, Serre: Bank Clk: Lived 82 Machon Bank Rd, Netheredge

HOBSON, HG: Pte: 12/1215: A: OU-94 UTMB

HOBSON, HN: ASgt: 12/681: C: Born Sheffield 1895: * +: Bomber: Comm LNLancs 31 Jul 17

HOBSON, HW: Pte: 12/682: C: W Jul 16:

HOBSON, JC: Pte: 12/1398: C: Born St Philips, Sheffield: W 1 Jul 16 with i2 Y&L and Dow 19 Apr 17 with 2 Y&L: Bethune Town MC: * +

HOBSON, P: LCpl: 12/401: B: Born Crookesmoor, Sheffield: Kia 1 Jul 16–: Thiepval Mem: * +

HOBSON, R: Cpl: 12/958: A: Born Abbeydale, Sheffield: Kia 26 Mar 18 with 13 Y&L: Arras Mem: * –: Signailer

HOBSON, S: Pte: Sheffield Univ Student

HODDER, CG: Pte: 31304: OU-1 Northants & 13 Y&L

HODDLE, ED: Pte: 12/402: B: W 1 Jul 16 with 12 Y&L and W 19 Sep 17 with 7 Y&L: * +: OU-2/4, 6, 7 & 10 Y&L

HODGINS, T: Pte: 39120: A: Lewis gnr: OU-1/4, 9 & 10 Y&L

HODGSON, F: Pte: 39133: OU-10& 13 Y&L

HODSON, A: Pte: 31619: Kia 28 Mar 18 with 2/4 Y&L: Arras Mem: OU-3/5 NStaffs, 2 & 2/4 Y&L

HODSON, JB: Pte: 31616: A: Lewis gnr: OU-3/5 NStaffs & 13 Y&L

HOETTE, AR: Maj: D: W 1 Jul 16: * +: OC 0 Coy

HOGARTH, R: Pte: 37995: Dow i 3 Apr 17 with 2 Y&L: Bethune Town C

HOGG, AC: Pte: 12/683: C: Born St Mar ys, Beverley 1893: Kia 1 Jul 16: Thiepval Mem: * +: Lived 2 Hamilton Park Rd, Firth Park: Brother of C & E Hogg

HOGG, C: Pte: 12/684: C: W Jul 16: * +: Lived 2 Hamilton Park Rd, Firth Park: Brother of AC & E Hogg: Bde Canteen

HOGG, E: ALCpl: 12/685: C: * –: Brother of AC & C Hogg: Lived 2 Hamilton Park Rd, Firth Park: OU-2 Y&L

HOGG, F: Pte: 12/1318: A: Born Anston, Sheffield 1891: Dow 7 Aug 16: St James Chyd, South Anston: * +

HOGG, FM: Pte: 235635: B: 94 Bde canteen

HOGG, S: 12th Club Member

HOGG, TS: Sgt: 12/960: D: * –: Butcher

HOLDSWORTH, DC: Pte: 41098: OU-8 Y&L

HOLLAND, A: Pte: 12/1647: D: Born Carbrook, Sheffield 1892: Kia 18 May 18 with 2 Y&L: Brandhoek New MC: * +

HOLLAND, D: Pte: 39145: OU-1 /5, 2/5 & 10 Y&L

HOLLAND, G: Pte: 13/1133: D: * +

HOLLAND, J: Pte: 20113: OU-1 & 2 Y&L

HOLLING, GW: ACpl: 37866: OU-2, 7, 13 & 14 Y&L

HOLLING, H: Pte: 12/404: B: W 1 Jul 16: * +

HOLLING, JW: Pte: 37830: HO: Lewis gnr

HOLLINGSWORTH, H: Pte: 12/686: C: Boen Ecc/esali, Sheifie/d: Kia 1 Jul 16: Thiepval Mem: * +

HOLLINWORTH, FJE: Pte: 31349: HO: Bde Runner: OU-Northants & 13 Y&L

HOLLIS, AJ: Pte: 12i687: C: Born Coventry 1895: Kia 1 Jul 16: Luke Copse MC, Serre: * +: Lived 25 Pinner Rd

HOLLIS, J: Pte: 12/688: C: * +: MO asst

HOLLIS, PW: Pte: 31629: A: Born Burton 0 T 1893: Kiil 28 Jun 17: Bailleu Rd MC, Blangy: OU-3/5 NStaffs: Lived Burton o T

HOLMES, C: Pte: 12/1605: W Sep 16 with 2 Y&L: OU-2, 1- & 14 Y&L

HOLMES, H: ACSM: 12/405: B: * –: Musketry Instr: OU-2, 6 & 13 Y&L

HOLMES, JH: Pte: 12/961: A: * +

HOLMES, JH: Pte: 12/1689: B: * –: OU-13 Y&L

HOLMES, TW: Pte: 12/144: A: Sheffield Univ Student: * –

HOLT, GC: Pte: 38030: OU-6 & 9 Y&L

HOLT, H: Sgt: 12/406: A: W 1 Jul 16: * +: Lived Hebden Bridge

HONER, DJ: D 4 Jun 17 with RFC: Arras Mem: Comm RFA, attd RFC

HOOD, FH: Pte: 235635: OU-13 Y&L

HOOD, FJC: Lt Col: DSO and MID: Served in S Africa War: Adjt 9 Buffs 1914: 21C 14 Y&L 1915: CO 13 Y&L 1916: CO 12 Y&L 1 Jun 17 onwards

HOODLESS, HR: Pte: 12/407: A: Born Wigton, Carlisle 1893: Kia 1 Jul 16: Thiepval Mem: * +: Bank Clk: Lived Doncaster

HOOPER, AW: Pte: 31295: Born We/lingboro, Northants 1885Dow 7 Jun 17: Etaples MC: OU-Northants: Lived Wellingboro

HOOTON, W: Pte: 31626: Born Hanley, Staffs: Kia 6 May 17: Bailleul Rd MC, Blangy: OU-3/5 NStaffs: Lived Stoke o T

HOPE, CR: Pte: 12/145: A: MC: W 1 Jul 16: * + Comm 15 Y&L 29 Aug 17: Lived 9 Barleywood Rd, Darnall

HOPKINS, F: Pte: 2031 07: OU-1/S & 7 Y&L

HOPKINS, J: Pte: 38031: OU-6 Y&L

HOPKINS, RH: Pte: 31287: C: OU-94 MGC (Sigs)

HOPKINSON, J: Pte: 21545: D: OU-9 & 10 Y&L

HOPKINSON, W: Pte: 31623: OU-3/5 NStaffs, 2, 2/4 & 8 Y&L

HOPWOOD, H: Pte: 38029

HORBURY, G: Pte: 14/56: D: W 1 Jul 16: Lived Barnsley

HORNBUCKLE, LC: ACpl: 221 51: Kia 23 Mar 18 with 13 Y&L: Arras Mem

HORNCASTLE, EH: Sgt: 12/408: B: * +: Comm Manes 4 Aug 16

HORNER, H: Pte: 12/1773: B: * +: OU-7 Y&L

HORRABIN, AE: Pte: 12/151 A * –: Signaller

HORRAX, LA: Dmr: 12/152: A: Born Sheffield 1893: * – : Signaller and Bandsman: Brother of OJ Horrax: Lived Joan Ln, Bamford·: OU-2/4 Y&L

HORRAX, OJ: LCpl: 12/153: A: Regt Police: Comm unknown unit, connected with intelligence

HORRIDGE, H: Sgt: 12/99: A: Signaller

HORROCK, W: Pte: 15910: B: W 1 Jul 16: * –: Lived Barnsley

HORSFALL, H: Pte: 31996: OU-10 NFus & 7 Y&L

HORSFIELD, EL: LCpl: 12/409A * +

HORSFIELD, RB: Pte: 12/154: A: Born St Barnabus, Sheffield 1893: Kia 1 Jul 16: Thiepvai Mem: * + –

HORSLEY, AJ: Pte: 31300: OU-1 Northants & 8 Y&L

HORSLEY, CW: Pte: 12/2128

HORTON, E: Pte: 12/23: D: W 1 Jul 16: Lived Rotherham

HORTON, JW: Sgt: 13968: MM: Kia 7 Jun 17 with 8 Y&L: Menin Gate Mem, Ypres, Belgium: OU-2 & 8 Y&L

HORTON, PC: 2Lt: Served 12 Y&L from 8 Dec 17

HOUGH, E: Pte: 12/691: C: Born Sharrow, Sheffield: Kia 1 Jul 16: Thiepval Mem: * +: Lived 17 Tasker Rd, Crookes

HOUGHTON, J: Pte: 63706: OU-967 Area Empi Coy Labour Corps, 2 & 8 Y&L

HOUSEMAN, D: 2Lt: Comm 10 Mar IS: OU-7 Y&L

HOUSLEY, C: Pte: 39073: Born Nr Woodhouse, Nottingharn: Kia 4 May 17: Arras Mem: Lived Doncaster: OU-1 O Y&L

HOVERS, CW: Pte: 31621: HQ: Balman: OU-3/S NStaffs & 13 Y&L

HOWARD, ES: Pte: Kia 9 Aug 18 with 6 Tank Corps: Vis en Artois Mem: Sheffield Univ Student: Comm unknown date

HOWARD, RN: Pte: 12/147: A: * –: OU-B Y&L

HOWDEN, CH: Pte: 12/410: B: * +

HOWE, FL: Pte: 12/149A * –: OU-7 Y&L

HOWE, JW: Pte: 22068: OU-2.7.8 & 9 Y&L: Deserted 5 Sep 18

HOWE, P: Pte: MC: Born 1894", 'v Aug 15 and l, Ju/~ S with 10 WY: – Sheffield Univ Student: Comm 10 WY Oct 14

HOWLETT, C: Pte: 31995: A: Sanitary Man: OU-10 NFus & 13 Y&L

HOWSON, TW: Pte: 12/2119: A: * –: Bandsman: Bde Concert Pty

HOYLAND, S: Pte: 12/964 D: * –

HOYLAND, WH: Pte: 12/1886: C: * +: OU-6 Y&L

HOYLE, AE: Pte: 12/692: Bor Thurgoland 1890: D 8 Nov 18 with 1 Y&L: Mikra MC, Salonika, Greece: Lived Sheffield

HOYLE, T: Pte: 12/1496: B: W May 16: Lived 56 Oxford St: OU-2 & 7 Y&L

HUDSON, A: Pte: 12/1308: C: Born Pitsmoor, Sheffield: Kia 1 Jul 16: Thiepval Mem: * +

HUDSON, CO: Cpl: Sheffield Univ Student: Ex TF RAMC Sgt: Comm RFA Nov 14

HUDSON, E: Pte: 10624: A: OU-211 Fd Coy RE

HUDSON, EC: Pte: 12/1369: A: Born Walkley, Sheffield 1892: Kia 1 Jul–16: Queens MC, Serre: * +: Lived 50 Rivelin St, Walkley

HUGHES, H: Col: 1 st CO until 1 O Oct 14: Ex CO 4 Y&L: Member Sheffield Univ Council

HULLEY, F: Pte: 12/1370: C: Born W Melton, Yorks: Kia 1 Jul 16: Thiepval Mem: * +: Lived Rotherham

HULLEY, G: Pte: 12/693: B: W Apr 16: Lived Rotherham

HULLEY, JR: Pte: 235202: OU-1/4.2/4 & 7 Y&L

HULLEY, W: Pte: 39030: OU-2/4, 8 & 10 Y&L

HUMPHREY, BP: ASgt: 12/412: 8ank Clk: OU-2 Y&L

HUMPHREY, JA: Pte: 12/413: B: 8orn Worsboro, Barsley 1888: Kia 12 May 17: Arras Mem: Lived Barnsley: OU-2 & 10 Y&L

HUNT, FM: LCpl: 12/966: D: * –

HUNT, G: Pte: 235214: HQ: Dow 17 Sep 18 with 13 Y&L: RSM's Batman: OU-2/4, 1/5, 10 & 13 Y&L

HUNTER, TC: Pte: 12/156: A: Born Walkley, Sheffield 1896: W 1 Jul 16 – Draper: * +: Lived 4 Harrington Rd, Millhouses: OU-2 Y&L: Comm 3 WY 1 Nov 17

HUTCHINSON, A: Pte: 12/1714: W Aug 16 with 2 Y&L: OU-2.6 & 14 Y&L

HUTCHINSON, E: Pte: 41 024: OU-13 Y&L

HUTT, M: Pte: 12/695: C

HUTTON, B: Pte: 12/1339: B: * +: OU-1/4 & 9 Y&L

HUTTON, R: Sgt: 12/839D: * –

HUTTON, W: Pte: 12/965: D: * +: OU-2 & 2/4 Y&L

HUXLEY, JB: LCpl: 12/415: B: OU-2 & 14 Y&L: Comm ASC 17 Mar 18

HYDE, CLW: Pte: 12/1396: A: Born Ledbury, Warwicks 1896: W 1 Jul 16: Chauffeur: Brother of FB Hyde: Sniper and observer: Lived 15b Botanical Rd: OU-2 & 13 Y&L

HYDE, E: Pte: 12/157: A: Sheffield Univ Student: * T

HYDE, FB: Pte: 12/158: A: * +: Brother of CLW Hyde: Observer and runner: OU-94 MGC

HYDE, TJ: Sgt: 26737: OU-13 Y&L

IBBOTSON CG: Pte: 12/416: B: Born Heeley. Sheffield: Kia 21 Jun 16: Bertrancourt MC: Empl Beardman's, Glossop: Lived Grove Rd, Totley

IBBOTSON EC: Pte: 12/696: C: W 1 Jul 16: * +: Comm 1 Mar 17

IBBOTSON EE: Pte: 12/1121: C: W 1 Jul 16: * +

IBBOTSON F: Pte: 12/417: B: Comm N&D 26 Apr 17

IBBOTSON GH: Pte: 11317: Born Hillsboro, Sheffield: Kia 14 May 17: Arras Mem

IBBOTSON L: ACSgt: 38746: OU-7 & 8 Y&L

IBBOTSON M: Pte: 12/1409: B: W 1 Jul 16: * +

IBBOTSON M: Pte: 16742: Born Leeds: Kia 9 Mar 17: Thiepval Mem: OU-WY: Lived Leeds

ILES J: Sgt: 12/418: B: * +

ILLINGWORTH E: Pte: 31308: OU-1 Northants

ILLINGWORTH W: Pte: 19428: OU-2 & 6 Y&L

INGHAM TH: LCpl: 40178: Born Skid by, Hull 1889: Kia 11 May 17: Arras Mem: OU-EY & 7 Y&L: Lived Hull

INGLE CW: Pte: 241 01

INGOLD GJH: U: D: W 1 Jul 16: Sheffield Univ Student: * +: Comm 18 Sep–14: Lived Wooley House, Wincobank

INGRAM CI: Pte: 12/967: D: Born Sherwood, Nottingham: Kia 1 Jul 16– : Thiepval Mem: * +

INMAN E: Pte: 13/1492

INNESS PC: Cpl: 37974: OU-2 Y&L

IRELAND J: Pte: 37492: OU-13 Y&L

IRONS PW: Pte: 391 05: Born Bradford 1893: Kia 12 Apr 18 with 13 Y&L Ploegsteert Mem, Belgium: Lewis gnr: OU-10 & 13 Y&L

IRONS RJ: Pte: 31630: OU-3/5 NStaffs

IRONSIDE I: Pte: 12/1303: C: W 1 Jul 16: * +

JACKMAN, F: Pte: 12/1775: C: Born St Philips, Sheffield 1898: Kia 1 Jul 16 Thiepval Mem: * +

JACKSON, A: Pte: 12/1285: A: W 1 Jul 16: * +: OU-10 N Fus

JACKSON, CA: U: Born 1894: 0 5 Nov 17 with RFC: Christchurch Chyd. Dore: Ex Cpl in BCoy: Comm 28 May 15: 94 Bde Pioneer Offr from 29 Jul 17

JACKSON, EE: Cpl: 12/419: B: Born Penistone 1892: Kia 18 Sep 18 with 2 Y&L: Vis – en-Artois Mem: * +: OU-2 & 13 Y&L

JACKSON, G: Pte: 17535: OU-2/4, 1/5, 6 & 10 Y&L

JACKSON, J: Pte: 12/1862: A: * –

JACKSON, SA: Pte: Sheffield Univ Student

JACOBS, T: Pte: 31315: OU-1 Northants & 13 Y&L

JAGO, JW: Pte: 12i968: A: * +: Comm N&D 27 Jun 17

JAMES, LE: LCpl: 12/969: D: * –

JAMESON, F: LCpl: 12/697: CA: Born Sheffield 1882: W 1 Jul 16 with 12 Y&L and Mar 18 with 6 KOYLI: * +: Signaiier: Comrn 6 KOYLI 1 Mar 17: Lived 257 Glossop Rd

JAQUE, J: Pte: 39076: OU-1;4.9 & 10 Y&L

JARRARD, WJ: CaptAEF: Sheffield Univ Staff: OU-15 & 10 Y&L

JARVIS, EA: Pte: 12/1833: C: Born Pilsmoor. Sheffield: Kia 1 Jul 16: Thiepval Mem: * +: Lived Walkley

JARVIS, GH: 2U: W 12 May 17: Comm 25 Oct 16 to 5 Y&L: Served 12 Y&L from 8 Jan 17

JARVIS, JH: Pte: 43564: OU-2 & 14 Y&L

JARVIS, RA: Sgt18582: 0: MM: W 1 Jul 16: * –?: Lived Conisboro: OU-9 Y&L

JEALOUS, HF: LCpl: 12/1982: Born Tupton. Derbys: Kia 27 Sep 16 with 14 Y&L

JEBSON, E: Pte: 12/1344: D: Born St Philips, Sheff: Dow 3 Jul 16: Etretat Chyd: * +

JEFFCOCK, E: LCpl: 12/698: C: Born 1890: Kia 25 Mar 18 with 7 Y&L: Arras Mem: Pioneer and cold shoer

JEFFCOCK, F: LCpl: 12/699: A * +: OU-1/4 & 13 Y&L

JEFFERSON, GL: U: Comm 29 Aug 15: OU-2/4 Y&L

JEFFERY, G: Pte: 31314: OU-1 Northants

JEFFREY, H: Pte: 203495: OU-I/5 Yorks.1/4.2/4.15 & 2/5 Y&L

JENKINS, GG: Pte: 12/422: B: Bank Clk: * +

JENKINS, LA: Pte: 235636

JENKINSON, TH: Pte: 235221: OU-2/4, 1/5 & 7 Y&L

JENKINSON, WC: Pte12/1965: D: * +

JENNINGS, CH: Pte: 12/162: A: * –

JENNINGS, T: Pte: 12/1821: C: * –

JEPSON W: Pte: 12/2015: Born Heeley, Sheffield 1892: Kia 11 Oct 16 with 1 Y&L: Struma MC, Greece

JERRY, GS: Pte: 235699: OU-7 Y&L

JESS, AB: Pte: 12/21 09: OU-7 & 10 Y&L

JESSOP, AH: Cpl: 41082: OU-8 Y&L

JEWITT, H: Pte: 41104: OU-8 Y&L

JOHNSON, A: Pte: 27427: OU-2, 2/4, 9 & 10 Y&L

JOHNSON, A: Pte: 31312: D 25 Mar 18 with 7 Y&L

JOHNSON, C: Pte: 12/2022: Born Hucknall, Notts 1895: Dow 19 Dec 17 with 2 Y&L: St Sever MC, Rouen: * –: OU-94 TMB, 2 & 6 Y&L

JOHNSON, C: Pte: 40200: OU-2 & 12 NFus & 6 Y&L

JOHNSON, C: Pte: 12/700: C: Born St Georges, Sheffield: Kia 16 May 16: Sucrerie MC, Colincamps: Lived Sportsman Inn, Cambridge St

JOHNSON, F: Cpl: 24496: Born Sheffield 1893: Kia 27 Jun 17: Arras Mem – : OU-2 Y&L

JOHNSON, G: Pte: 12/701: A: * –

JOHNSON, GE: Pte: 41 099: OU-8 Y&L

JOHNSON, H: Pte: 12/1585: Born Swallownest, Sheffield: Kia 17 May 16-: Sucrerie MC, Colincamps

JOHNSON, HD: Pte: 31309: OU-1 Northants, 6 & 7 Y&L

JOHNSON, JS: Pte: 32002: Born Shiptonthorpe, York: Kia 12 May 17: Arras Mem: OU-WY & 10 NFus: Lived York

JOHNSON, R: Sgt: 12/974: D: * –: Comm DLI 30 Oct 17

JOHNSON, SB: Pte: 12/1304: A: W 1 Jul 16: * +: OU-2 Y&L

JOHNSON, T: Pte: 31631: OU-3/5 NStaffs & 13 Y&L

JOHNSON, W: Pte: 19419: OU-2 & 6 Y&L

JOHNSTON, A: Pte: 12/972: D: Born Burngreave, Sheffield: W 1 Jul 16 with 12 Y&L and D 4 Nov 18 at Depot Burngreave C, Sheffield: * +: OU-8 & 10 Y&L

JOHNSTON, FR: Pte: 12/702: C: Born Battersea. London: Kia 10 Jul 16: Caudry Old CC: Lived Battersea

JOHNSTON, JE: Pte: 15937: HQ: Special Patrol Ply

JONES, AR: Sgt: 8633: OU-1 & 2 Y&L

JONES, D: Pte: 12/163: A: Born Heeley, Sheffield 1884: Kia 1 Jul 16 – : Queens MC, Serre: * +: Lived 73 Staveley Rd

JONES, ED: Pte: 12/164: AW 1 Jul 16: * +: Sheffield Univ Student

JONES, H: Cpl: 29082: Kia 6 Jun 17: CWGC have no details

JONES, EE: Pte: 12/703: C

JONES, F: Pte: 12/1625: 0: Born Birmingham: Kia 25 Mar 18 with 7 Y&L: Arras Mem: * +

JONES, F: Pte: 27655: OU-7 & 10 Y&L

JONES, FC: Pte: 31311: OU-1 Northants.2/4 & 8 Y&L

JONES, FS: Sgt: 12/971: B

JONES, GE: Sgt: 1811 0: OU-1, 2 & 9 Y&L

JONES, GF: ACpl: 12/1175: D: W 1 Jul 16: Chemist: * +: Lived Wentwor – Arms Hotel. Penistone

JONES, GW: ASgt: 12/970: D: Kia 12 Apr 18 with 13 Y&L: Ploegsteert Mem, Belgium: Sheffield
Univ Lab Asst: * –: Comm 30 May – 17: Served 12 Y&L as offr from 24 Jul 17

JONES, HL: Pte: 235637: OU-7 Y&L

JONES, JW: Pte: 13/1245: OU-2 & 13 Y&L

JONES, JW: Pte: 32000: OU-10 NFus, 2, 7 & 13 Y&L

JONES, R: Pte: 12/1249: A: SS Jul 16: * –

JONES, SH: Pte: 8332: B: * –

JONES, W: Pte: 34074: OU-1/410 & 13 Y&L

JORDAN, HG: 2Lt: Comm 7 Jan 15 unknown unit

JOWETT, A: Pte: 31632: HQ: Sanitary Man: OU-3/5 NStaffs & 13 Y&L

JOWETT, H: Pte: 32001: OU-1 0 NFus.2/4 & 2/5 Y&L

JUBB, F: Pte: 12/1922: B: * +

JUDD, HL: 2Lt Comm 26 Apr 17: Served 12 Y&L from 12 Jun 17

JUDGE, A: Pte: 235211: Born 1897: Kia 18 May 17: Arras Mem: OU-2, 1/4 & 2/4 Y&L

JUDGE, JWS: CSgtlCQMS: 12/165: A * +: Comm 7 Y&L 29 Aug 17

JUKES, A: Pte: 12/1254: C: * –

JUSTICE, A: ACSgt: 12/1220: OU-1 Y&L

JUTSON, WH: Pte: 21890: C: * –OU-1 Y&L

KAY, A: Pte: 12/704

KAY, W: Pte: 12/1988: Born Rotherham: D 15 Oct 16 at sea with 1 Y&L: Doiran Mem, Greece: Lived
45 Manningham Rd, Attercliffe

KEETON, WJ: Pte: 26753: OU-6 & 13 Y&L

KELK, JH: Pte: 12/1481: D: Born Sheffield 1892: Kia 1 Jul 16: Thiepval Mem: * + : Lived 33
Goddard Hail Rd, Pitsmoor

KELLINGTON, FW: Pte: 12/1193: D: W 1 Jul 16: * +

KELLY, JVP: Pte: 12/424: B: * –

KELLY, T: Pte: 53191: OU-122 & 797 Area Empl Coy Labour Corps & 2 Y&L

KEMP, A: Pte: 31638: OU-3/5 NStaffs & 7 Y&L

KENCH, FJ: Pte: 31318: OU-1 Northants & 7 Y&L

KENNER, J: Capt: E: Sheffield Univ Staff: OC 18 PI: OU-15 Y&L & Gen List

KENNERLEY, AW: Cpl: 26718: OU-13 Y&L

KENWORTHY, S: Pte: 37959: OU-2 Y&L

KENWORTHY, W: Pte: 12/1798: OU-13 Y&L

KENYON, R: 2U: Served 12 Y&L from 8 Dec 17

KERR, A: Pte: D: Born 1883: Kia 3 Nov 18 with 10N&D: Forest CC Nord: Sheffield Telegraph
Reporter: Comm 17 N&D Sep – 15: Lived 67 Hastings Rd, Millhouses

KERR, CF: Pte: 12/425: B: SS 8 Apr 16: * –: Lived 36 Victoria St: Comm 27 Jun 17 to 6 Y&L: OU-Min
of Lab

KERR, WS: Capt: Sheffield Univ Student: 1st MO: OU-3 West Riding Fd Amb

KERRIGAN, P: Pte: 28737: HQ: Bn Tailor: OU-2 & 13 Y&L

KERSHAW, JV: Maj: ACO 1-17 Jun 17: From 11 ELancs

KERSHAW, LH: Pte: 12/1739: C: * –: OU-9 Y&L

KERVEIN, E: Pte: 40087: OU-NOJ9 Y&L

KETTELL, CH: Pte: 12/14cf3: 12/14cf3: Born St Marys, Sheffield: Kia 1 Jul–16: Thiepval Mem: * +:
Lived 53 Fieldhead Rd

KETTLE, WH: Pte: 12/706: C: * +: Comm DLI 17 Dec 17

KETTLEWELL, M: Pte: 32003: Born Whixley, Yorks: Kia 29 Jun 17: Orcharc Dump MC, Arleux:
OU-WY & 10 NFus: Lived York

KEYWORTH ,S: Pte: 14126: OU-2, 115 & 9 Y&L

KIDNEY, BL: Member of 12th Club: Lived 289 Abbey Ln

KIDNEY, HG: Pte: 12/976: W 1 Jul 16: * +: Lived 54 Wolseley Rd: OU-9 Y&L

KILGRASS, C: Pte: 38032: A: OU-211 Fd Coy RE

KILLINGSWORTH, J: Pte: 12/1528: A: * +: Bn Tailor: OU-2 & 13 Y&L

KILVINGTON, EJ: Pte: 32004: OU-10 NFus

KING, JJ: ACpl: 12/1648: OU-1/5 & 14 Y&L

KING, T: Pte: 31319: C: Batman: OU-Northants & 13 Corps Rft Camp

KING, W: Pte: 12/977: D

KINGWELL, LW: Pte: 12/1361: B: Born Accrington, Lancs 1895: Dow 6 Jul 16: Wimereux CC: Draughtsman: * +: Lived Rutland Rd. Chesterfield

KINMAN, GA: Sgt: B: Teacher

KINMAN, HB: Attended 1918 Reunion Dinner

KIRBY, H: Pte: 22487: OU-13 Y&L

KIRK, JH: Sgt: Regt Police SgtEx Regular

KIRKBY, L: Pte: 21754: A: * +: Bandsman

KIRKHAM, W: Pte: 12A27: B: Born Bootie, Liverpool 1888: Dow 3 Jul 16: Bertrancourt MC: * + : Lived Upperthorpe

KIRKHAM, G: Pte: 31635: OU-35 NStaffs & 2 Y&L

KITCHING, E: Pte: 3/2482: B: OU-2, 10 & 13 Y&L.

KITCHING, WJ: Pte: 3/1689: OU-2, 10 & 13 Y&L: Convicted of desertion 30 Sep 18

KNIGHT, H: Member of 12th Club

KNIGHTON, GH: Comm 3/4 Y&L 27 Sep 15

KNIGHTON, J: Pte: 12/709: A: Born Ilkestone, Derbys 1892: Kia 1 Jul 16–: Queens MC, Serre: * +: Teacher: Lived Salterwood House, Smithy Houses, Alfreton, Derbys

KNIGHTON, T: Pte: 31635: OU-3/5 NStaffs

KNOTT, W: Pte: 31637: OU-3/5 NStaffs & 7 Y&L

KNOWLES, CR: Pte: 12i167: C: W May 16: Sheffield Univ Student Lived Manningham

KNOWLES, CR: LCpl: 12/1242: OU-1/4 & 2/5 Y&L

KNOWLES, FK: Pte: 12/71 O: C: Born Crookesmoor. Sheffield: Kia 1 Jul–15: Thiepval Mem: * +

KNOWLES, J: LCpl: 12/428: B: * –: Comm 27 Mar 18 unknown unit?

LACEY, JR: Sgt: 14221: Dow 6 May 18: Gezaincourt CC Ext: OU-8 Y&L

LACK, H: Pte: 12/429: B: Born St Thomas, Chesterfield 1895: Dow 6 Jul 16: St Sever MC, Rouen: * + : Draughtsman: Lived Poplar Ave, Chesterfield

LAIDLAW, AW: 2Lt: Comm 4 Y&L 25 Oct 16: Served 12 Y&L from 8 Jan 17

LAISTER, H: Pte: 12/1966: Born St Marys, Sheffield 1894: Kia 1 Jul 16 with 14 Y&L: Thiepval Mem: Lived 16 Lancing Rd

LAIT, A: Pte: 16956: OU-2, 7 & 8 Y&L

LAIT, M: Pte: 12/430: C: Born Leicester: Kia 1 Jul 16: Thiepval Mem: * – + Lived Oakfield, Sylvan Cliff, Buxton, Derbys

LAKE, LA: Pte: 46455: A

LAKE ,SJ: Pte: 235640: HQ: Observer: OU-13Y&L

LAKE, WE: Pte: 235639: B: Born Lakenham, Norfolk 1891: Kia 24 Sep 17: Roclincourt MC: OU-Norfolks: Lived Norwich

LAKIN, RW: Pte: 26427: A: Batman

LAMB, A: Pte: 40207: OU-6 Y&L

LAMB, S: Pte: 12/1780: C: Born St Johns, Sheffield: Kia 1 Jul 16: Thiepval Mem: * +

LAMBERT, A: Pte: 12/711: C: * – : Runner

LAMBERT, CW: Pte: 29275: OU-2 Y&L

LAMBOURNE, AJ: Pte: 205455: A: Kia 28 Mar 18 with 13 Y&L: Lewis gnr: OU-2 London Yeo & 13 Y&L

LAMIN, FB: Pte: 31640: OU-3/5 NStaffs, 6 & 9 Y&L

LAMONT, D: Pte: 20641: OU-2, 1/4 & 2/5 Y&L

LANCASHIRE, F: LCpl: 24148: Born 1893: Kia 13 0ct 18 with 1 AY&L: York MC, Haspres: OU-1/4, 6 & 13 Y&L

LANCASTER, C: Pte: 12/1284: A: W May 16: * –

LANCASTER, H: Pte: 12/1283: A: W May 16: * – :OU-2 & 6 Y&L

LANDER, WD: Pte: 12/1841: OU-1 Y&L

LANE, HJ: Pte: 31323: OU-1 Northants & 7 Y&L

LANE, WD: Sheffield Univ Student: Comm 10 WY 1915

LANFEAR, AS: Pte: 12/341: B: Born Sleaford, Lincs 1896: Kia 1 Jul 16–: Euston Rd MC, Colincamps: Bank Clk: * + : Lived 46 Highfield Ad, Doncaster

LANG, T: Cpl: 40179: OU-8 EY & 7 Y&L

LANGLEY, B: LCpl: 12/168: A: * +

LANGLEY, CH: Pte: 12/1156: D: Born Park, Sheffield: Kia 1 Jul 16: Thiepvs Mem: * +: Sheffield Univ Student

LANGLEY, FT: Pte: Sheffield Univ Student

LANK, GW: Pte: 22036: OU-2 & 8 Y&L

LATHAM, A: Pte: 12/1699: Born Highfield, She Jul 16: Thiepval: Mem: * –

LAWTON, S: Pte: 12/714: C: * +: Cook: OU-7 Y&L

LAYCOCK, CF: Pte: 40080: Kia 21 Jan 17 with 9 Y&L: Railway Dugouts Burial: Ground (Transport Farm), Zillebeke, Belgium

LAYCOCK, CW: Pte: 12/1761: Born Barnsley: Kia 22 Jul 16 with 13 Y&L: Pioegsteert: Mem, Belgium

LAYCOCK, HR: 2U: Comm 28 Mar 17: Served 12 Y&L from 17 Sep 17

LAYTE, F: Pte: 15492: OU-2, 7 8: 9 Y&L

LEACH, JE: Pte: 12/1241: A: W 1 Jul 16: * +: Lived Barnsley

LEADBETIER, E: Pte: 31641: Born Stafford: Kia 16 Feb 17: Courcelles au Bois CC: Ext: OU-3/5 NStaffs: Lived Stafford

LEAK, L: Pte: 23521 9: OU-1, 2/4, 1/5, 8 & 9 Y&L

LEAMAN, RW: Capt: MID: Comm 3 Y&L 15 Aug 14: Served 12 Y&L Feb 15–Sep 17

LEASK, FC: Pte: 25829: OU-10 Y&L

LEATHER, C: Pte: 12/1727: Born Wombwell 1897: Dow 17 Jul 16 with 3 Y&L Wimereux CC: Lived Wombwell

LEAVESLEY, S: Pte: 12/715: C: Born Sheff: Kia 4 Jul 16: Thieoval Mem: Empl Cole Bros: * +: Lived 210 Alexander Rd, Heeley

LEDGER, JF: Pte: 12/1328: D: SS May 16: Lived 45 Upperthorpe

LEE, AR: LCpl: 12/433: B: W 1 Jul 16: * + : Lived Tennyson Ave, Chesterfield

LEE, LC: Pte: 31321: OU-1 Northants & 7 Y&L

LEE-DUNHAM, L: Sheffield Univ Student: Comm 2/4 Y&L 29 Apr 15

LEEFE, TO: Pte: 12/171: A: * + : Lived Malton: Repatriated 2/4 Y&L 29 Apr 15

LEES, F: Pte: 24246: Born 1895: D 31 Jan 18 with 3 Y&L: Anzin-St-Aubin MC

LEES, JG: Pte: 15630: A: OU-13 Y&L

LEES, T: LCpl: 12/980: D: Born Sheffield: Kia 1 Jul 16: Euston Rd MC, Colincamps: * +

LEES, TS: Pte: 205459: A: Kia 25 Mar 18 with 13 Y&L: OU-2 London Yeo & 13 Y&L

LEESON, AE: Pte: Sheffieid Univ Student

LEESONS, GA: Pte: Sheffieid Univ Student

LEGGOTT, W: Pte: 41021: OU-8 Y&L

LEIGH, R: Pte: 12/716: B: Born Sheffield: Kia 1 Jul 16: Thiepval Mem: * +

LE MASURIER, AG: Pte: 31352: OU-1 Northants

LENGTHORN, W: Pte: 32007: Born 1877: Kia 20 Jan 18 with 2/5 Y&L: Roclincourt MC OU-10 NFus & 2/5 Y&L

LESITER, EG: Pte: 24390: D

LEVER, C: Pte: 37883: OU-7 & 13 Y&L

LEVERETT, J: Pte: 31324: A: Born Balham, M'Sex: D 7 Jun 18 with 13-Y&L: Vis-en-Artois MC: OU-Northants & 13 Y&L: Bomber

LEVICK, A: Pte: 12/1186: A: Born Aston, Sheffield: Kia 1 Jul 16: Queens MC, Serre: * +

LEVICK, H: Pte: 12/1227: A: Born Swallownest, Sheffield: Dow 15 Oct 18 with 2 Y&L: Tincourt New MC: * +

LEWIS, B: Pte: 12/434: B: W 1 Jul 16: * +: Res Signaller

LEWIS, HG: Pte: 205454: HQ: Ord Rm Clk

LEWIS T: Pte: 12/435: B: Born Ecclesfield, Sheffield 1891: Kia 1 Jul 16 Thiepval Mem:*+

LEWIS, TW: 2Lt: Comm 29 Aug 17: Served 12 Y&L from 25 Oct 17

LIGHTWOOD, CE: Pte: 32295: Kia 29 Sep 18 with ¼ Y&L: Le Cateau MC

LIMB, HE: Pte: 12/173: A: * –: Comm Indain Army Res 29 May 18

LINDLEY, H: Pte: 12/1192: B: * +: W Aug 16

LINDLEY, W: Pte: 12/214: C: * + : OU-31 Div APM Tfc Con

LINES, CW: Pte: 12/174: A: W May 16: Lived 37 Tylney Rd

LINFOOT, MW: Pte: 235642: OU-1/5 Y&L

LINLEY, H: Pte: 12/1262: B: W 1 Jul 16: * + :Silversmith

LINNEY, CA: Pte: 41914

LINSLEY, JA: LCpl: 12/436: B: W 1 Ju1 16: Empl Midland Rlwy: * +: Lived 79 Roe Ln, Pitsmoor

LISTER, B: Pte: 12/2057: OU-13 Y&L

LISTER, J: A: SB

LISTER, R: Pte: 12/175: A: Born Eccleshall, Sheffield 1892: Kia 1 Jul 16 Thiepval Mem: * +: 26 Grove Rd: Sheffield Univ Student

LISTER, W: Pte: 12/1659: Born Darnall, Sheffield 1880: Kia 1 Jul 16 with 14 Y&L: Thiepval Mem

LISTER, WG: Pte: 12/176: A: W Jun 16: Sheffield Univ Student: * +

LITCHFIELD, P: Pte: 19686: Kia 31Ocl18 with 1/S Y&L: York MC, Haspres: OU-2, 1/5, 10& 14 Y&L

LITTLEWOOD, H: Pte: 12/1309: B: W 1 Jul 16: * +: OU-2 Y&L

LITTLEWORTH, AJ: Cpl: 31322: A: Lewis gnr: OU-Northants & 13 Y&L

LOCKETT, G: Pte: 12/717: C: * +: OU-9 Y&L

LOCKWOOD, AP: Pte: Sheffield Univ Student

LOCKWOOD, F: Pte: 12.A37: BC: W 1, Jul 16: * –* –: Lived White Hart Hotel, Penistone OU-10 Y&L

LOCKWOOD, T: Pte: 12/1644: C: * –

LOMAS, JJ: Pte: 201606: HQ: OU-13 Y&L

LONG, R: Pte: 25666: OU-2 & 8 Y&L

LONG, WC: Pte: 12/982: D: W 1 Jul 16: * +: Empl Lee & Sons: Lived 79 Roe Ln: SB OU-2.2/4 & 13 Y&L

LONGBOTTOM, H: Pte: 38814: OU-8.9 & 10 Y&L

LONGDEN, A: Pte: 12/697: OU-1 Y&L

LONGDEN, G: Pte: 12/718: C: W May 16: * +: Comm 2/4 Y&L 30 Jan 18

LONGDEN, WS: ACpl: 12/719: BC: W 1 Jul 16: * + : Empl Don Cutlery Works: Comm: 5 Y&L 29 Aug 17: Lived 263 School Rd

LOVEDAY, CJ: Pte: 235643: OU-7 Y&L

LOVELL, A: Pte: 12/1207: D: Born Sandygate, Sheffield 1595: * + : Kia 1 Jul 16 Thiepval Mem: Empl WK & C Peace, Eagle Works: Lived Mowbray St

LOWCOCK, H: Pte: 12/438: Born Dronfield: Kia 15 Sep 16 with 2 Y&L: Thiepval Mem

LOWE, S: Pte: 57616: A

LOWE, V: Pte: 27618: Kia 12 Apr 18 with 13 Y&L: Ploegsteert Mem, Belgium OU-1 & 13 Y&L

LOXLEY, CW: ASgt: 12/983: D: W 1 Jul 16: * +

LOXLEY, WH: CSM: 12/562: B: Born St Georges, Sheffield 1876: Kia 1 Jul 16: Rlwy Hollow MC, Serre: * + : Lived 64 Hammerton Rd, Hillsboro: Ex KRRC: Regular: Served in S African War

LUCAS, RH: Pte: 205461: A: OU-2 London Yeo & 13 Y&L

LUDBROOK, G: Pte: 12/720: C: W May 16

LUMB, H: Pte: 40069: OU-9 Y&L

LUMB, HS: 2Lt: W 17 Jun 16: Comm 11 Y&L 2 Apr 15: Served 12 Y&L from 23 Apr 16

LUMLEY, W: Pte: 32006: Born Leeds: Kia 9 Oct 17: Arras Mem: OU-WY, 10 NFus & 113 Rlwy Coy RE: Lived Leeds

LUND, JH: Pte: 40070: OU-9 Y&L

LUNN, WH: Pte: 25445: Dow 17 Sep 17 with 9 Y&L: OU-2, 6 & 9 Y&L

LYCHETT, S: Pte: 12/1971: C: * –

MACHON, EA: Pte: 12/1280: D: Born 1898: W 1 Jul 16 & 20 Aug 16: * + : Empl John Brown: Lived 116 Abbeyfield Rd

MACKAY, WV: Pte: 12/1350: A: SS Jun 16: * +

MACKINTOSH, J: Pte: 40079: OU-1/5, 8 & 9 Y&L

MACLAURIN, E: LCpl: 12/985: D: Born Sheffield 1893: Kia 1 Jul 16: Euston Rd MC, Colincamps: * + : Poor Law Admin Clk: Lived 112 South View Rd

MACQUADE, WH: LCpl: 12/722: C: Born St Barnabus, Sheffield: Kia 1 Jul 16: Luke Copse MC, Serre: * +

MADDOCK, A: Pte: 12/1519: OU-1 V&L

MAGUIRE, T: Pte: 41006: OU-8 Y&L

MAHONEY, E: Pte: 205466: A: OU-2 London Yeo & 13 Y&L

MAINWARING, CV: Lt Col: Born 1862: Regular orrr: Comm RinnisF 1883: Comm N&D 1917

MALES, SJ: Pte: 205467: OU-2 London Yeo & 7 Y&L

MALKIN, T: Pte: 13/611: MM: SB: OU-2, 8 & 13 Y&L

MALKIN, NH: 2Lt: Born 1892: Dow 14 May 17: Duisans MC: Comm 26 Sep 16: Served 12 Y&L from 26 Feb 17

MALLINDER, GW: Pte: 12/724: D: W 1 Jul 16: * +

MALLOWS, H: Pte: 19226: A: OU-Army Tramways, 9.1 0 &, 13 Y&L

MALTBY, JE: Pte: 12/441: Born Eyam. Nr Sheffield 1896: Kia 20 Jul 16 with 2 Y&L: Phiio Sep he MC

MANN, HG: 2Lt: W 12 May 17: Comm 3 Y&L 26 Aug 15: Served 12 Y&L from 15 Apr 17 OU-2 Y&L

MANSON, J: Sgt: 34608: HQ: Cook: OU-94 Fd Amb, 11 EL & 13 Y&L: MANTERFIELD B: LCpl: 235226: MM: Lewis gnr

MANTERFIELD, F: Pte: 12/2028: B: * −

MANTON, T: Bom 1890: Dow 22 Oct 17 with 7 Y&L: Solferino Fm MC, Belgium: Comm to 7 Y&L date unknown: Lived Walkley

MAPPIN, FT: Pte: 12/2100: OU-1/4, 9 & 14 Y&L

MARCH, J: Pte: 13/640: OU-2.13 & 14 Y&L

MARCHINGTON, JH: Pte: 12/178: W 1 Jul 16: * +

MARJORAM, S: Pte: 12/442: B: * −: OU-10 Y&L: Comm RLancs 26 Mar 18

MARK, RW: ACpl: 33539: A: Born Newcastle u T: Kia 12 Apr 18 with 13 Y&L Ploegsteert Mem. Belgium

MARPLES, EA: Capt: OU-13 NFus: Served in S African War

MARPLES, G: Pte: Sheffield Univ Student

MARSDEN, JH: Cpl: 12/180: C: W 1 Jul 16: Sheffield Univ Student: * +: Lived Huddersfield

MARSDEN, JW: Pte: 40088: Bom 1891: Kia 1 Oct 17 with 9 Y&L: Tyne Cot Mem, Passchendaele, Belgium

MARSDEN, R: Pte: 12/443: B: MM: SS Apr 16, W 1 Jul 16 & G 30 Sep 17: * − +: Runner: OU-2 & 14 Y&L: Comm Y&L 26 Jun 17: Served 12 Y&L from 3 Sep 17: Lived Duffield, Derbys

MARSDEN, WH: CSM: 12/2: A: Born Sheffield 1878: Kia 17 Jun 16: Thiepval Mem Lived 13 Marion Rd, Hillsboro

MARSH, B: Sgt: 9453: OU-7 & 14 Y&L

MARSH, JT: Pte: 29259: OU-2, 7 & 13 Y&L

MARSH, JW: Pte: 12/1331: A: * +

MARSH, JW: Pte: 12/1341: B: * +

MARSHALL, AW: CSgtlCQMS: 12/572: AC: * −: Lived 167 Springvale Rd

MARSHALL, C: Pte: 12/1921: D: Born Sheffield 1891: Kia 1 0 Oct 17 with 9 Y&L: Tyne Cot Mem. Passchendaele, Belgium: * −: OU-6 & 9 Y&L: Lived Sheffield

MARSHALL, EA: Pte: 21949: C: * +

MARSHALL, EC: Bank Clk

MARSHALL, FA: Pte: 12/986: D: Born Sharrow, Sheffield: Kia 8 Aug 16: St Vaast MC, Richebourg: * −

MARSHALL, G: Pte: 41022: OU-8 Y&L

MARSHALL, GB: Pte: 12/201 0: A: * −: OU-2 & 10 Y&L

MARSHALL, H: Pte: 12/987: 0: Born Conisboro 1893: 0 17 Mar 16: Port Said MC, Egypt Sheff Telegraph Reporter

MARSHALL, H: Pte: 12/1379: Born Walkley, Sheffield 1895: Kia 25 Jul 16 with 14 Y&L: Rue du Bacquerot MC: Signaller: Lived 251 School Rd Crookes

MARSHALL, J: Pte: 203744: Kia 13 Oct 18 with 1 /4 Y&L: OU-1 14 & 1/5 Y&L

MARSHALL, JF: MC: Teacher: Comm 1 /5 Y&L 24 Mar 15: OU-HQ 148 Inf Bd

MARSHALL, W: Pte: 13/1516: B: OU-2, 6, 13 & 14 Y&L

MARSHALL, W: Pte: 31332: OU-1 Northants & 6 Y&L

MARSLAND, SW: 12th Club Member

MARTIN, H: Pte: B: OU-RE

MARTIN, H: Pte: 19224: Born Nottingham: Kia 14 Nov 16: Sailly au Bois MC: Lived Nottingham: OU-2 & 9 Y&L

MARTIN, J: Pte: 41 069: OU-8 Y&L

MARTIN, JW: Pte: 31326: Born Wooton, Northants 1889: Kia 27 Nov 16 Puchevillers MC: OU-Northants: Lived Northampton

MARTIN, W: Pte: 31327: Born Thunderidge, Herts: Kia 30Dec17: Roclincourt MC OU-Northants: Lived Hertford

MARTIN, WA: Pte: 235726: OU-1 /4 London

MASDIN, T: Pte: 12/1614: B: * –: 31 Div Photographer: Lived 183 Fox St and 515 Abbeydale Rd

MASON, C: Pte: 12/1511: C: Born Sheffield 1894: Dow 4 Jul 16: Doullens CC Ext No1: * +: Lived 74 Boisover Rd, Pitsmoor

MASON, CS: Pte: 12/181: A: Born Sheffield 1896: Kia 1 Jul 16: Thiepval Mem: * + Lived 1 Briar Rd, Netheredge

MASON, OP: Pte: 12/1752: OU-2/4, 2/5 & 13 Y&L

MASSEY, S: Pte: 37993: OU-2 Y&L

MASSIE, AJL: LCpl: 12/447: B: * –: OU-1 Y&L

MASSON, JM: Pte: 205395: A: Kia 27 Mar 18 with 13 Y&L: OU-2 London Yeo & 13 Y&L

MASTERTON, B: Pte: 12/989: D: * –

MASTERTON, W: Pte: 12/1920: D: * +: OU-2I4 & 13 Y&L

MATE, F: Pte: 31647: HQ: Waterman: OU-3/5 NStaffs & 13 Y&L

MATHER, F: Cpl: 12/990: CD: Born St Mar ys, Sheffield 1889: Kia 1 Jul 16 Thiepval Mem: * +: Lived 17 Rampton Rd, Sharrow

MATTHEWMAN, W: Pte: 12/1607: C: Born Park, Sheffield: Kia 1 Jul 16: Serre Rd No2 MC: * +: Lived 111 Brookhouse Hill, Fulwood

MATTHEWS, E: Pte: 12/726: C: * +

MATTHEWS, EH: Pte: 3/4868: OU-1.2/4 & 2I5 Y&L

MATTHEWS, RHB: Pte: 12/568: C: Born Sheffield 1896: Kia 16 May 16: Sucrerie MC Colincamps: Sheffield Univ Student: Lived London Rd

MATTHEWS, S: Pte: 12/727: C: DCM: * +: Lived 30 Verdon St, Spital St: Accountant

MATTHEWSON, W: LCpl: 40209: A: Kia 18 Sep 18 with 13 Y&L: Lewis gnr: OU-6 & 13 Y&L

MAUNDER, SW: Hon Lt: Quartermaster: Comm 14 Sep 14

MAWE, E: Pte: 12/449: B: Batman HQ 94 Bde

MAWER, W: W02: 12/1194: CE: Sheffield Daily Telegraph Reporter: * –: Bn Ord RmClk

MAWSON, AW: Pte: Sheffield Univ Student

MAXFIELD, G: Pte: 12/182: A: W 1 Jul 16: * +: Lived Hartington Rd, Millhouses **MAY, HO:** Pte: 22435: OU-7 Y&L May W: Pte: 12/1954: Born St Barnabus, Sheffield 1897: Kia 29 Jun 18 with 8 Y&L: Granezza MC, Italy: OU-8 & 13 Y&L

MAY, ESP: Pte: 12/451: B: W 1 Jul 16: * +: OU-2 Y&L: Comm WY 28 May 18

MCBRIDE, P: Pte: 12/183: A: Born Melbourne, Australia 1895: Kia 1 Jul 16 Thiepval Mem: * +: Lived London

MCCANN, H: Pte: 40203: OU-12 NFus & 6 Y&L

MCDONALD, F: Pte: 235197: OU-1/6 NFus, 2/4, 1/5 & 7 Y&L

MCDONALD, J: Sgt: 40197: OU-9 NFus, 6 & 7 Y&L

MCDONOUGH, M: Sgt: 40201: A: D 14 Jan 19 with 1 15 Y&L: OU-13 NFus, 1 15, 6 & 13 Y&L

MCIVOR, L: Pte: 12/1434: C: Born Walkley, Sheffield 1892: SS May 16 and Kia 1 Jul 16: Thiepval Mem: * +: Lived 133 Channing St

MCKENZIE, A: Pte: 12/991: D: Born St Mar ys, Sheffield 1895: Kia 4 Apr 16 Sucrerie MC. Colincamps: Empl Moss & Gamble: Lived 47 Southgrove Ad

MCLACHLAN, D: Pte: 205064: HQ: Special Patrol Pty: OU-13 Y&L

MCLEOD, AJ: Pte: 33545: HQ: D 24 May 18 with 13 Y&L: Glasgow Eastwood C Scotiand: Observer

MCNAMARA, J: 2UDCM: Comm 28 Mar 17: Served 12 Y&L mid 1917–8 Jan 18: OU-RFC

MCNEILL, SA: Pte: 12/184: A: Born Antrim, N Ireland 1896: Kia 27 Jul 16: Rue du Bacquerot MC No1: Sheffield Univ Student: * –: Lived 16 Bowood Ad

MCNIELLIE, E: Pte: 2841 O: Born KirkcudbrightKia 18 May 17: Arras Mem: Lived Newcastle u T: OU-2 Y&L

MEAKIN, B: ACpl: 24055: OU-7 & 10 Y&L

MEAKIN, F: LCpl: 12/729U: Served 12 Y&L from late 1916

MEARS, H: Pte: 205397: OU-2 London Yeo & 7 Y&L

MEDLEY, H: Pte: 12/992: D: Born Rotherham: Kia 1 Jul 16: Thiepval Mem: * – +: Lived Clifton Ln, Rotherham

MEEK, W: Pte: 28734: OU-1 & 2 Y&L

MEIN, WH: U: Served 12 Y&L 1918

MELLING, H: Pte: 12/993: B: * –: SB: Brother of J Melling

MELLING, J: Pte: 12/1177: D: * +: Brother of H Melling: Lived 62 Brocco Bank

MELLOR, S: Pte: 12/730: C: * +

MELLORS, W: AW02: 40198: A: OU-1nstr 13 Corps Rft Camp, 1 & 2 NFus, 1 15, 6 & 13 Y&L

MELTON, E: Pte: 31333: OU-1 Northants

METHLEY, HA: Pte: 12/185: A: * –

MICKLETHWAITE, W: Cpl: 12/186: OU-2, 6 & 1 O Y&L: Comm Y&L 25 Sep 18

MIDDLEBROUGH, E: Pte: 38582: OU-1 O Y&L

MIDDLETON, JL: Capt: O: DFC: Born Chesterfield 1894: Comm 18 Sep 14: *: Tpt offr OU-RFC

MIDGLEY, WG: Pte: 27530: Born 1887: D 9 Jan 18 with 1/5 Y&L: Aubigny CC Ext: OU-2, 115 & 13 Y&L

MILBURN, W: Pte: 32557: OU-7 & 8 Y&L

MILES, AB: Cpl: 12/731: C: OU-2 Y&L: Comm LFus 28 May 18

MILLER, JS: RSM: D: Ex Regular Coldstream Gds: Served in S African War: Comm 20 NFus Jan 15: Lived 63 Woodstock Rd

MILLER, T: Pte: 12/1478: B: Born St Philips, Sheffield: Kia 1 Jul 16: Queens MC, Serre: * +

MILLERSHIP, HO: Pte: 38034: Born Aston, Birmingham 1887: Kia 14 Nov 16: Sailly au Bois MC: OU-1Fus: Lived Salford

MILLHOUSE, F: Pte: 12/1452: OU-14 Y&L

MILLINGTON, O: Pte: 12/1492: OU-1 Y&L

MILLINGTON, W: Pte: 12/1617: B:

MILLS, CL: Pte: 31328: OU-1 Northants, 2 & 2/5 Y&L

MILLS, JB: Pte: 12/995: D: * +: OU-2 & 13 Y&L

MILLS, JT: Pte: 12/1335: C: Signaller: OU-2 & 13 Y&L

MILLS, PF: Pte: 12/1251: C: Born Upperthorpe, Sheffield: Kia 1 Jul · 16: Euston Rd MC, Colincamps: * +

MILLWARD, GH: Pte: 12/1260: B: Born Rotherham 1890: Kia 17 Jun 17: Arras Mem: Lived Rotherham

MILNE, L: Attended 1918 Reunion Dinner

MILNER, A: Pte: 12/732: C: * –: Sheffield Telegraph Reporter: Bandsman: OU-2/4 Y&L

MILNER, AW: Cpl: 24427: OU-1/4 & 14 Y&L

MILNER, GW: Pte: 12/994: D: W 1 Jul 16: * +: Cook: Lived Rotherham: OU-2 & 13 Y&L

MILTON, C: Pte: 31334: OU-1 Northants

MILTON, H: Cpl: 12/733: C: W 1917: * +

MINCHIN, AL: Sheff Univ Student: Comm 17 N&D 1915

MINNEY, HA: Pte: 36058: OU-2, 1/4 & 6 Y&L

MITCHELL, CA: Pte: 12/1959: A: * –

MITCHELL, G: Capt: MO from Dec 15

MITCHELL, GA: Pte: 12/454: Born Penistone 1891: Kia 17 Jan 17 with 6 Y&L: Thiepval Mem: Lived Penistone: OU-2 & 6 Y&L

MITCHELL, JJ: Pte: 40081: Dow 26 Jul 17 with 9 Y&L: Wimereux CC

MITCHELL, JT: Pte: 12/1632: C: Born Nr Rotherham 1872: Dow 28 Dec 16: Abbeville: CC Ex1: * –

MITCHELL, S: Pte: 17594: OU-6, 7 & 10 Y&L

MOLE, J: Cpl: 27585: OU-1 RWK, 2 & 7 Y&L

MOLYNEUX, GJ: Pte: 12/1830: A: Born Walkley, Sheffield: Kia 1 Jul 16: Thiepval: Mem: * +

MOLYNEUX, R: LCpl: 20534: OU-2 & 7 Y&L

MONK, WR: Sgt: 235644: OU-1 15 Y&L

MONKMAN, J: Pte: 31644: OU-3/5 NStaffs & 7 Y&L

MOODY, F: LCpl: 12/996: D: Born St Barnabus, Sheffield 1888: Kia 31 Ocl18 with 9 Y&L: Tezze MC, Italy: * +: Lived 25 Empire Rd: OU-6 & 9 Y&L

MOONEY, J: Pte: 62294: OU-18 Y&L

MOORE, A: Cpl: 12/997: D: W Jul 16: * –: Lived 65 Wayland Rd

MOORE, AT: Pte: 31335: OU-1 Northants & 13 Y&L

MOORE, R: LCpl: 12/455: OU-1 Y&L

MOORE, REJ: Capt: BCDW 1 Jul 16: * +: Comm 23 Sep 14: 0C 15 Pl: Left 12 Y&L: 2 Sep 17

MOORE, RH: Pte: 31643: OU-3/5 NStaffs & 13 Y&L

MOORE, T: Pte: 205464: OU-1/1 Notts Yeo, 2 London Yeo & 13 Y&L

MOORHOUSE, J: Pte: 12/456: B: * –: OU-2/4 & 13 Y&L

MOORHOUSE, J: Pte: 12/1498: B: W Jul 16

MOORHOUSE, SA: Pte: 12/998: D: W 1 Jul 16: * +: Lived Rotherham: Comm 10 Y&L 29 Aug 17

MOORWOOD, TH: D: Comm 23 N Fus Sep 15: Lived Onslow House

MORETON, WF: LCpl: 12/1 OOO: D: Born Cardiff: Kia 1 Jul 16: Thiepval Mem: * –+: Lived Red House, /ck/es, notherham

MORLEY, HL: Pte: 12/734: C: * –: Comm Y&L 29 Mar 18

MORLEY, CSM: Served 12 Y&L Apr 15

MORLEY Lt: Served 12Y &L Apr 15

MORRELL, JA: Pte: 12/1771: OU-1 & 10 Y&L

MORRIS, FG: 2Lt: Comm 11 Y&L 26 Feb 15: Served 12 Y&L from 15 Dec 16

MORRIS, H: LCpl: 12/735: Sheffield Univ Student: Comm RFus 25 Sep 17

MORRIS, J: Pte: 12/657: OU-2/4 & 6 Y&L

MORRIS, JT: Pte: 12/1682: W Oct 16 with 2 Y&L

MORRIS, SJ: Pte: 12/1 001: D: W 1 Jul 16: * +: Lived 3 Louth Rd: OU-9 Y&L

MORRISON, AL: Cpl: 12/1117

MORRISON, JH: Pte: 37792: A: OU-211 Fd Coy RE

MORRISON, LA: Born 1893: Dow 6 Jan 16 with 4 SLancs: Lijssenthoek MC, Belgium Sheffield Univ StudentComm 3 SLancs Apr 15

MORRISON, R: 2Lt: Served 12 Y&L from Jul 17

MORTE, LV: Pte: 12/1002: D: Born Nr Rotherham: Kia 1 Jul 16: Luke Copse MC Serre: * +: Lived 44 Selwyn St, Rotherham

MORTON, A: Pte: 39116: OU-7 & 10 Y&L

MORTON, F: Pte: 12/1789: A: W 1 Jul 16: * +

MORTON, F: Cpl: 11198: A: Bomber

MORTON, H: Pte: 12/1142: D: * +

MORTON, T: Pte: 12/1872: B: ··

MORTON, W: Pte: 12/1993: OU-2 & 10 Y&L

MORTON, WB: Pte: 12/457: B: * –: Born 1887: Lived 32 Rushdale Rd, Meersbrook OU-221 Div Empl Coy

MOSBY, DP: Sgt: 12/458: A: * +: Comm 13 Y&L 27 Jun 17

MOSES, FS: LCpl: 12/190: A: Born Chester: Kia 1 Jul 16: Thiepval Mem: Sheffield Univ Student* +: Lived 25 Westonville Tce, Weston Park

MOSLEY, E: Pte: 29248: OU-2 Y&L

MOSSMAN, VW: Pte: Sheffield Univ Student

MOTTRAM, D: Pte: 37921: A: 31 Div Clk: OU-7, 9, 13 & 14 Y&L

MOULDS, H: ACpl: 12/736: C: Born Nr Rotherham 1892: Kia 1 Jul 16: Thiepval Mem * +: Lived 28 Ellerton Rd, Firth Park

MOULSON, GH: Pte: 12/1245: D: W 1 Jul 16: * +

MOUNTAIN, AEG: Pte: 12/1836: Born Sharrow, Sheffield 1898: Kia 1 Jul – 16: Queens MC, Serre: Empl G Senior: * +: Brother of H Mountain: Lived 10 Chelsea Rd

MOUNTAIN, H: Pte: 12/1472: C: OU-2 Y&L

MOUNTAIN, H: Pte: 12/1835: A: Born Sharrow, Sheffield 1898: Kia 4 May – 17: Arras Mem: * –: Brother of AEG Mountain

MOUNTFORD Pte: B

MOXEY, EL: Capt: D: Born Sao Paulo, Brazil 1894: Comm 23 Sep 14: MG offr Trans RFC 21 Jul 17: Posthumous GC – WW2

MOXHAM, F: Pte: 12/737: C: Born Sheffield 1897: W I Jul 16 and 2 other occasions: * +: Lived 951 Eccleshall Rd

MOXON, E: Pte: 39131: A: OU-10, 13 Y&L & 94 TMB

MUIRHEAD, W: Pte: 38055

MULFORD, GA: Sgt: 12/1003: D: W I Jul 16: * +: POW I Jul 16: Lived 40 Guset Rd

MULLINS, T: Pte: 235727: A: Bomber: OU-211 Fd Coy RE & 13 Y&L

MUNRO, JB: Pte: 12/738: D: Born Peebles, Scotland 1887: Dow 6 Jul – 16: Beauval CC: * +: Lived 188 Barnsley Rd, Pilsmoor

MURDAY, M: Pte: 12/1684: C: Born Highfields, Sheffield 1895: Dow 8 Jun 16 Abbeville CC: Lived 26 Roach Rd

MURFIN, TH: Pte: 235204: OU-1/4, 2/4 & 7 Y&L

MURPHY, W: Pte: 235216: W Jul 16 and Kia 13 May l7: Arras Mem: OU-1/4 & 2/4 Y&L

MUSGROVE, HH: Pte: 12/461: C: * +: OU-13 Y&L

MUXLOW, EC: LCpl: 12/1 004: D: W 1 Jul 16: Education Dept Clk: * +: Lived Wicker Post Office: OU-2 & 6 Y&L

MYERS, J: ACpl: 8132: D 9 Jun 19: OU-2, 1/4 & 10 Y&L

MYERS, P: Pte: 31331: OU-1 Northants

MYERS, T: Pte: 202605: OU-1/5 & 7 Y&L

MYERSCOUGH, WJ: Pte: 40026: OU-1 & 2 Y&L

MYLCHREEST, J: Pte: 38036: Born Manchesler 1892: Kia 17 Nov l6: Thiepval Mem: OU-1Fus: Lived Manchester

NASH, E: W02: 7583: MM: 1, 2, 114 & 13 Y&L

NASH, JH: Pte: 12/1005: D: * –: Bandsman: OU-2/4 Y&L

NASH, W: Pte: 12/1342: A: W Apr 16 and 1 Jul 16: * +

NAYLOR, J: Pte: 12/462: B: Born Sheffield 1893: D 3 Jan 19 with 9 Y&L: Staglieno MC, Genoa, Italy' * +: OUY-6 & 9 Y&L

NEAL, A: Pte: 12/1812: A: * –: OU-9 & 13 Y&L

NEAL, F: Pte: Sheffield Univ Student

NEEDHAM, A: Pte: 41113: OU-8 Y&L

NEEDHAM, G: Pte: 38038: Born Tottington, Lancs: Dow 12 Dec l6: Couin MC: OU-1Fus: Lived Tottington

NEEDHAM, H: Pte: 12/2102: OU-RAF & 14 Y&L

NEILL, H: Sgt: 12/193: A: Born St Georges, Sheffield 1875: Kia 1 Jul 16 Queens MC, Serre: * +: Lived 21 Whitworth Rd

NEWBOLD, AT: Pte: I211006: D: OU-94 TMB

NEWCOMBE, AF: Lt: Bank Clk: Comm 12 Y&L 27 Jun 15: Ex 12 Y&L OR: OU-15 Y&L

NEWICK, J: Pte: 33559: OU-7 Y&L

NEWSHOLME, TAW: Pte: 12/1007: D: Born St Mar ys, Sheffield 1896: Dow 8 Jul 16 Wimereux CC: * +: Chemist

NEWSOME, H: Pte: 12/1008: D: W Jul 16: OU-2 Y&L

NEWSUM, WB: Sgt22407: OU-2 Y&L

NEWTON, CE: SgtI2/463: B: * –

NEWTON, H: Pte: 12/739: CD: * +: Runner: Comm 2/4 Y&L 30 Jan 18?

NEWTON, L: Pte: 12/740: C: Born Dronfield: Kia I Jul 16: Thiepval Mem: * +: Lived Laurel Holm, Green Ln, Dronfield

NEWTON, P: Pte: 12/1 009: D: Born Nr Manchester: Kia 1 Jul 16: Thiepval Mem: * + Lived Stockport

NICHOL, J: Pte: 12/464: B: * +

NICHOLS, F: Pte: 12/196: A: Born Sheffield 1893: Kia 1 Jul 16: Thiepval Mem: * + Empl Hadfields: Lewis gnr: Lived 23 Tom Ln

NICHOLS, J: Pte: 33547: OU-7 Y&L

NICKERSON, G: Pte: 14/1 018: Kia 15 Sep 18 with 13 Y&L: Pont D'Achelies MC, Nieppe: OU-873 Empl Coy Lab Corps, 13 & 14 Y&L

NIGHTALL, T: Pte: 12/1640: A: * –

NIXON, CEG: ACpl: 46365: OU-1/4 & 2/5 Y&L

NOAKES, TC: CaptComm 19 Dec 14: Served 12 Y&L from 15 Sep 17

NOCK, FJ: Cpl: 12/198: AC: Born Sheffield 1893: SS Jun 16 and Kia 3 Jun 17 with 9 KOYLI: Sunken Rd MC, Boisleux: Comm KOYL127 Mar 17

NORMAN, H: Pte: 22083: B: OU-7 & 14 Y&L

NORMAN, J: Pte: 39487: OU-7, 13 & 14 Y&L

NORRIS, H: Pte: 12/199: A: Born Halifax: Kia 1 Jul 16: Rlwy Hollow MC, Serre * +: Lived 11 Ward Pic, Highfields

NORRIS, CEL: Cpl: I21466: B: * –: OU-HQ 94 Bde

NORTH, A: Pte: 38037: OU-7 Y&L

NORTHERN, MR: Pte: 12/1416: B: * +

NORTON, JW: Pte: 12/200: AW 1 Jul 16: * +: Lived Fulwood Pk: Comm 20 Jun 17

NORTON, H: Attended Reunion 1970

NORTON, J: Pte: Sheffield Univ Student

NOWILL, WE: Pte: 12/202: A: Sheffield Univ Student * –

NUNN, E: Pte: OU-7 Y&L

NUSSEY, B: AW02: 53500: OU-6 KOYLI & 7 Y&L

NUTBROWN, L: Pte: 12/1980: C: W I Jul 16: * +: Also number 63922

OAKDEN, TA: Pte: 39031: B: OU-243 MGC, 10 & 13 Y&L

OAKES, S: Sgt: 12/101o: CD: Born Sheffield 1896: Kia 6 May 17 with Z Spec Coy RE: Beaulencourt MC, Ligny: Sheffield Univ Student * –: Lived Rotherham: Comm EY 1 Oct 16

OAKLEY, RS: Lt: Bank Clk: Comm 12 Y&L 14 Jul 15: OU-15 Y&L

OATES, FH: Pte: 12/467

OATES, GG: LCpl: 12/1240: A: W 1 Jul 16: * +: Lived The Hollins, Rivelin

OBREY, H: Pte: 40071: OU-1 & 9 Y&L

ODDY, W: Pte: 13/1399: OU-2, 2/4, 8 & 13 Y&L

OGLEY, M: Attended 1918 Reunion Dinner

OLDALE, H: Pte: 12/204: A: W I Jul 16: Sheffield Univ Student * +: Comm 7 Y&L 29 Aug 17: Lived 129 Gell St

OLDER, T: Pte: 235700: C: 94 Bde Canteen: OU-13 Y&L

OLDFIELD, J: Pte: 3/4556: OU-2 Y&L: Convicted of desertion 16 Nov 18

OLIVER, A: LCpl: 12/1169: A: Sheffield Univ Student * +

OLIVER, E: Brother of TW Oliver

OLIVER, R: Pte: 12/1 011: D: Born Sheffield: Kia 1 Jul 16: Luke Copse MC, Serre * +

OLIVER, TW: Pte: 12/468: B: Born Sheffield 1889: Dow 27 Jul 16: Rue du Bacquerot Nol MC: * +: Maj Plackett's Batman

OLIVER ,W: Pte: I21205: A: * +: OU-13 & 18 Y&L

OMBLER, R: Pte: 18887: B: 31 Div Water Police

OMLLEN, R: Pte: 9/1857: D

ORME, F: Sheffield Univ Student Comm 1 Garr Bn NFus 1915

ORTTON, JC: Pte: 12/741: Born St Mar ys, Sheffield 1896: D 20 Feb–15: City Rd C, Sheffield: Advertising Agent: Lived 108 Randall St

OSBORN, TE: Pte: 12/206: A: Born Heeley, Sheffield 1891: W 27 Jul 16 & G: 11 Aug 17: Librarian: * +: OU-1 Y&L: Lived 45 Vincent Rd, Sharrow

OSBORNE, A: Pte: 21 045: OU-1/4, 6 & 10 Y&L

OSBORNE, H: LSgt: 12/1565: C: W 1 Jul 16: * –: SB

OTLEY, AC: Pte: 25443

OTTAWAY, WT: RSM: 9489: DCM MID: OU-2 Y&L

OUTRAM, R: LCpl: 12/469: O: * +: POW 1 Jul 16

OVER, T: Pte: 12/1774: OU-2 & 13 Y&L

OWEN, CE: Pte: 12/1523: B: Born Broomhill, Sheff 1895: Kia 1 Jul–16: Rlwy Hollow MC, Serre: * +: Lived 311 Ewing St, Freemont, Ohio, USA

OWEN, GH: Pte: 12/208: D: Born Park, Sheffield 1893: Kia 1 Jul 16: Queens MC Serre: * +: Lived Woodlands Fm, Bank Rd

OWEN, JS: LCpl: 12/1 013: D: Born Sheffield: Kia 9 May 17: Thiepval Mem: * +

OWEN, P: Pte: 14/1173: OU-2& 14 Y&L

OWEN, PW: LCpl: 12/1014: D: Born Darnall, Sheffield 1894: Dow 13 Apr 18 with 13 Y&L: Etaples MC: * –: Bn Tailor

OWEN, RT: Pte: 12/742: C: MM: W 15 May 16

OXLEY, H: Lt: Comm 24 Jul 15: Served 12 Y&L 7 Jun I6-3 Oct I7: Signals offr

OXLEY, H: Pte: 38895: HQ: Special Patrol Pty

PACK, WT: Pte: I211437: C: W 1 Jul 16: * +: Lived 28 Cooksen CI, Parson Cross OU-1/4 & 9 Y&L

PACKARD, J: Pte: 24207: C: * –

PACKWOOD, H: Pte: 31347: OU-1 Northants

PADLEY, W: Pte: 22347: A: * –: Bandsman: OU-2/4 Y&L

PAGETT, WH: Pte: 12/1431: Born Pitsmoor, Sheffield: Kia 1 Jul 16 with 13 Y&L Euston Rd MC, Colincamps

PALETHORPE, J: Pte: 12/1312: C: W May 16: OU-2, 7 & 14 Y&L

PALING, C: Pte: 16879: Born Whittington, Derbys: Kia 4 Nov 16: Sailly au Bois MC: Lived Mexboro: OU-9 Y&L

PARFITT, FA: Pte: 12/1204: C: Born 1897: D 13 Sep 18 with RAF: SI Michaels RC Ch, Sheff: * +: Lived 227 Western Rd: Comm 3 Y&L 28 Aug 17: OU-RAF

PARFITT, HS: LSgt: 20463: OU-2 & 7 Y&L

PARKER, B: Pte: 11318: A: * –

PARKER, H: LCpl: 25799: HQ: Born Boston, Lincs 1896: Kia 25 Mar 18 with 13 Y&L Arras Mem: Signaller: OU-1 0 & 13 Y&L

PARKER, H: Pte: 19495: Born Denaby, Yorks: Dow 15 Mar 17: Varennes MC: Lived Rotherham: OU-2 & 10 Y&L

PARKER, JW: Pte: 12/743: A: Born Attercliffe, Sheffield 1893: Kia 1 Jul 16 Queens MC, Serre: * +: Engineer: Lived Darnall: Brother of R Parker

PARKER, R: Pte: 12/744: C: W 1918: * +: BrotherofJW Parker: OU-2/4 & 13 Y&L Bn Tpt

PARKER, WJ: Pte: 15765: OU-2, 8 & 10 Y&L

PARKIN, HG: LCpl: 12/1161: B: Born Kilburn, Derbys 1888: Kia 1 Jul–16: Thiepval Mem: * +: Lived 4 Carrington Tce, Kiveton Pk

PARKIN, WH: Pte: 12/1384: A: W I Jul 16: * +

PARKINSON, JE: Pte: 12/1290: A: * –: Cook: OU-2, 115, 8 & 10 Y&L

PARR, A: Pte: 12/745: C: Born W Hartlepool: Kia I Jul 16: Thiepval Mem: * +

PARR, W: Pte: 12/1470: C

PARRATT, D: Pte: 235721: A: OU-211 Fd Coy RE & 9 Y&L

PARRINDER H: Pte: 42273: OU-2/4, 6 & 13 Y&L

PARROTT, AE: Pte: 22255: OU-10 Y&L

PARSONS, RE: ACpl: 205405: A: Bomber: OU-2 London Yeo & 13 Y&L

PARSONS, WE: Pte: 12/1209: A: Born Hillsboro, Sheffield 1895: Kia I Jul – 16: Thiepval Mem: Empl Neale & Co: * +: Lived 8 Cemetery Ave

PARTON, J: Pte: 12/210: A: SS Jun 16

PASHLEY, GW: Cpl: 15567: OU-2, 6 & 9 Y&L

PASLEY, E: Pte: Sheffield Univ Student

PASSEY, E: Cpl: 12/471: B: Born Chesterfield 1891: SS Apr 16: Accounts Clk Lived Mill St. Chesterfield

PATRICK, G: Pte: 12/1 016: A: * +: Pioneer

PATTINSON, FA: Sgt: B: Comm to 9 DLI Mar 15: Lived Cragside, Marden Rd

PATTISON, H: Pte: 12/473: B: W 1 Jul 16: * +

PATTLEY, J: Pte: 235648: A

PAWSON, A: Pte: 235701: OU-7 Y&L

PAYLING, G: Pte: 16997: D: * –

PAYLING, GM: Pte: 12/474: B: * +: OU-RFC

PEACE, FH: Pte: 12/475: B: Born Penistone: Kia 1 Jul 16: Thiepval Mem: * +: Lived Penistone

PEACE, NK: 2Lt: Sheffield Univ StudentOC 9 PI: Comm 12 Y&L 11 Nov – 14: OU-Cyclist Corps

PEACOCK, Pte: D: Left 12 Y&L by May 16

PEARSON, Pte: JH: Pte: 1 0391: POW: OU-2 Y&L: Lived 49 Psalter Ln, Rotherham

PEARSON, E: Pte: 12/746: C: Born Maxby, Northants: Kia 1 Jul 16: Luke Copse MC Serre: * +: Lived Maxby

PEARSON, HW: Capt: C: W 1 Jul 16: Sheffield Univ Student: Ex 12 Y&L OR: Comm 12 Y&L 11 Nov 14: * +

PEARSON, J: Pte: 38040

PEASE, J: Pte: 37786: A: Lewis gnr

PEATFIELD, A: Pte: 39132: OU-10 & 13 Y&L

PECK, PH: Pte: 235702: D 6 Jun 18 with 7 Y&L

PEEL, FL: Pte: 12/1447: D

PEET, F: LSgt: 12/476: AB: * –: SB

PEGG, FJ: Pte: 12/1212: W Apr 16: OU-1 Y&L

PEIRSON, L: PteA0072: OU-9 Y&L

PENNEY, G: Pie: 3/3538: OU-7 Y&L

PENNINGTON, FJ: Pte: 12/747: C: * +

PENNOCK, G: Pte: 12/748: W Apr 16

PENNOCK, J: Pte: 38043: Born Manchester 1892: Kia 17 Nov 16: Sailly au Bois MC OU-1Fus: Lived Manchester

PENNY, G: PteA0689: OU-2/4, 2/5 & 8 Y&L

PENNYCOOK, WG: PteA0291: OU-13 & 14 Y&L

PENROSE, RJR: Pte: 12/1520: B: Kia 26 Apr 18 with 1/4 Y&L: Ploegsteert Mem Belgium: * +: Comm 30 Jan 18

PEPPER, FGW: Sgt: 12/1151: OU-2 Y&L: Comm 3 WRiding 31 Jul 17

PERKIN, PK: 2Lt: A: Born 1894: Kia 1 Jul 16: Thiepval Mem: Empl W Hut· ton & Sons: * +: Ex 12 Y&L OR: Comm 14 Sep 15: Served 12 Y&L from 23 Apr 16

PERKINS, C: Pte: 12/477: B: * –: Bandsman

PERRET, W: Pte: 31261: OU-1 Northants

PERRY, C: Pte: 37971: OU-2 Y&L

PHELPS, FA: Pte: 12/214: A: * +

PHILBEY, G: Sgt: 12/1018: C: Born Hallam, Sheffield 1892: Dow 10 Jul–16: Couin MC: * +: Teacher: Lived 67 Duncombe St, Walkley

PHILLIPS, AJ: Pte: 22186: OU-2 Y&L

PHILLIPS, RT: Cpl: 12/749: C: * +: Comm Northants 26 Nov 17

PHILLIPSON, A: Pte: 12/1837: OU-6, 9 & 13 Y&L

PHILPOT, H: Pte: 235196: Kia 22 Sep 18 with 1/5 Y&L: OU-2/4 & 1/5 Y&L

PHIPPS, S: Pte: 12/1978: D: Born W Bromwich, Staffs: Kia 29 Aug 16: St Vaast MC, Richebourg: * +

PICKERING, BW: Cpl: 22152: Comm 3 Y&L 26 Mar 18

PICKERING, H: Pte: 12/478: B: * +: OU-478 & 733 Coy RE.Also number 64191

PICKERING, J: Pte: 12/1 019: A: * +: Lived Pioneer

PICKERING, W: Pte: 29426: OU-2, 1/5 & 14 Y&L

PICKLES, JA: Pte: 12/1463: C: Born Doncaster 1895: Kia 1 Jul 16: Thiepval Mem * +

PILKINGTON, WH: PteA1 075: Kia 21 Apr 18: OU-7 Y&L

PILTON, JG: Pte: 44096: OU-2/4 & 2/5 Y&L

PIMM, CW: 2Lt: Kia 18 May 17: Bailieul Rd MC, Blangy: Comm 1 Mar–17: Served 12 Y&L from 15 Apr 17

PIRKIS, GCML: Capt: Born 1878: W 22 Nov 17: Solicitor: Comm 2 Jun – 15: Served 12 Y&L from 27 Jul 16

PITT, EHP: Capt: MC: Bank Clk: Comm 1 Feb 15: OU-5 & 14 Y&L

PLACKETT, A: Maj: B: W 1 Jul 16: 8anker: 2IC from 30 Nov 14: ACO 1 Jul 16

PLANT, J: Pte: 12/1225: C: 8orn Ranmoor, Sheffield: Kia 1 Jul 16: Luke Copse MC, Serre: * +: Lived 23 Ranmoor Rd

PLATT, F: Pte: 12/480: 8orn Penistone 1888: W May 16 and Kia 9 Oct 16 with 2 Y&L: Thiepval Mem: Lived Wentworth Rd, Penistone

PLATT, H: Pte: 40031: 8orn Milnrow, Lancs 1897: Kia 4 May 17: Arras Mem: OU-WY & 6 Y&L: Lived Leeds

PLATTEN, HG: Pte: 235649: OU-13 Y&L

PLATTS, A: Pte: 12/1515: OU-8 Y&L

PLATTS, E: Attended 1918 Reunion Dinner

PLATTS, G: LCpl: Boxer: PTI

PLATTS, TA: Pte: 12/750: C: W 20 May 16

PLATTS, W: Pte: 12/1852: OU-13 Y&L

PLAXTON, J: Pte: 12/1183: A: 8orn SI Georges, Sheffield: Kia 1 Jul 16-: Thiepval Mem: * +

PLOWRIGHT, B: Sgt: 12/1891: D: * –

PLUMER, S: Pte: 12/1 020: Born Hull 1890: Dow 5 Dec 18 with 1 Y&L: Mikra MC Salonika, Greece: Lived Whitley Bay

POGSON, H: Pte: 12/751: C: W 1 Jul 16: * +: S8: Lived Horncastle

POILE, S: Pte: 12/215: A: Born Ashford, Kent: Kia 1 Jul 16: Thiepva' Mem: * +

POLDEN, C: RSM: 12/480: 8: Comm 12 Y&L 20 Jun 17: 0M: Ex Regular

POLLARD, WD: Pte: 12/1295: A: W 1 Jul 16 with 12 Y&L and D 24 Apr 18 with 15 N&D: Sheffield Gen C: Bank Clk: * +: Comm 15 N&D 30 Oct 17

POOLE, H: Pte: 37981: OU-2 Y&L

POOLE, H: Pte: 12/482: B: * +

POOLE, J: LCpl: 235720: HO: Special Patrol Pty: OU-2 ELancs, 1 Norfolk & 13 Y&L

POPPLEWELL, W: Pte: 38041: OU-7 Y&L

POTTER, AH: Pte: 12/1688: A: Born Derby 1894: Kia 1 Jul 16: Threpval Mem: * +

POTTS, EB: Pte: 12/1506: B

POULTNEY, C: Pte: 12/1319: D: * +: Brother of WJ Poultney: OU-13 Y&L

POULTNEY, WJ: Pte: 12/1 021: D: W 1 Jul 16: * +: 8rother of C Poultney

POWELL, T: Pte: 12/1998: B: * –: Special Patrol Pty

POWNALL, J: Pte: 38042: Born Manchester 1888: Dow 29 Oct 16: Couin MC: OU-1Fus Lived Manchester

PRATT, W: PteA0032: OU-6 & 7 Y&L

PRESTON, A: Pte: 12/752: C: * +: OU-7 Y&L

PRESTON, C: Pte: 23318: OU-2 Y&L

PRESTON, J: Pte: 46446: OU-7 Y&L

PRESTRIDGE, JA: Pte: 12/485: B: * +: OU-13 & 18 Y&L

PRICE, O: Pte: 12/1 022: D: Born Hereford 1896: Kia 1 Jul 16: Thiepval Mem: * + Lived 17 Fisher Rd, Meersbrook

PRIESTLEY, H: Pte: 12/1315: C: Born Pitsmoor, Sheffield 1895: Kia 1 Jul – 16: Queens MC, Serre: * +: 2 Clun Rd, Pitsmoor

PRIOR, CR: LCpl: 235703: A: Born Foulsham, Norfolk: Dow 13 Apr 18 with 13 Y&L: OU-Norfolks, 211 Fd Coy RE & 13 Y&L

PRIOR, HS: Pte: 12/216: A: * –

PRITCHARD, E: Pte: 205403: OU-2/2 London Yeo & 7 Y&L

PROCTOR, W: Pte: 40093: Born 1881: Kia21 Aug 18 with 9 Y&L (attd HQ 70 Inf Bde): Magnaboschi Me, Italy

PRYCE-JONES, R: Pte: 12/217: A: Born 1894: W May 16 with 12 Y&L & Kia 19 Oct 17 with 8 Y&L: 8uttes New MC, Polygon Wood: Comm 28 Aug 17

PRYOR, G: Pte: 22261: 8: * –: OU-7 Y&L

PUMPHREY, CE: 2Lt: Comm unknown unit 16 Jan 15

PURKESS, AJ: 2Lt: Kia 27 Jun 18 with 13 Y&L: Cinq Rues MC, Hazebrouck: Comm 28 Mar 17: Served 12 Y&L from 21 Dec 17

PURSEHOUSE, C: Pte: 31371: OU-1/4, 1/5, 215, 6 & 10 Y&L

PUXLEY, CG: Dmr: 81 01: OU-7 Y&L

QUINN, T: LCpl: 12/1191: A: W 1 Jul 16: * +

RALPH, JA: Pte: 235651: OU-7 & 8 Y&L

RANDALL, TR: Pte: 235652: A: OU-211 Fd Coy RE & 13 Y&L

RAPER, JW: Pte: 52712: OU-2, 2/4 & 13 Y&L

RATCLIFFE, F: Cpl: 12/486: B: * +: Comm EY 13 Aug 18

RATCLIFFE, F: LCpl: 12/1023: D: W 1 Jul 16: * +: Designed 12 Y&L Mem Sheffield Cathedral: OU-10 Y&L

RAWLIN, W: Pte: 12i1152: B: Born Hoyland 1894: Kia 1 Jul 16: Queens MC, Serre * +: lived 17 King St, Hoyland

RAWLINGS, FF: Pte: 12/1753: C: W 1 Jul 16: * +: Lived 70 Cross Bedford St: OU-10 & 14 Y&L

RAYNES, Pte

RAYNES, GE: Sgt: 20013: A: Bomber: OU-211 Fd Coy RE, 2, 6 & 13 Y&L

READ, AE: Pte: 235653: HO: Born Marylebone, M'Sex: Kia 27 Mar 18 with 13 Y&L: Observer: OU-Norfolks

READ, F: Pte: 12/487: B: W 1 Jul 16: Motor engineer: * +: Lived 6 Binfield Rd Meersbrook: OU-2 & 7 Y&L

READ, G: Pte: 38936: HQ: Special Patrol Ply

READ, H: Pte: 25781: OU-10 Y&L

READ, W: Pte: 12/754: C: * +

READ, W: Pte: 13/1435: B: OU-94 Bde War Dogs

REEVE, EA: Pte: 12/218: A: * +: Signaller: Comm EY 28 Nov 17

REEVE, HD: 2Lt: Comm 15 Y&L 27 Apr 15: Lived London

REEVES, W: Pte: 12/2020: B: * –

REGISTER, BJ: Sgt: 12/755: C: Born Crookesmoor, Sheffield 1887: Kia 16 May 16 Sucrerie MC, Colincamps: Teacher: Lived 9 Violet Bank Rd

REID, TR: MC MID: W & G Sep 15: Sheffield Univ Student: Comm KRRC 1915

RELPH, C: Pte: 12/2003: C: Born Sheffield: W 1 Jul 16 with 12 Y&L & Kia 26 Apr 18 with 1/5 Y&L: Suffolk MC, Kemmel, Belgium: * +: OU-1/5 & 9 Y&L

RENWICK, C: Pte: 12/1514: B: W 1 Jul 16: * +

REVILL, A: Pte: 12/1264: A: W 1 Jul 16: * +: Comm 10 Y&L 28 Mar 17

RHODES, GH: Cpl: 12/1 024: D: Born St Georges, Sheffield 1891: Kia 1 Jul 16 Rlwy Hollow MC, Serre: * +: Lived 82 Penrhyn Rd, Ecclesall

RHODES, H: Pte: 12/1724: C: Born Sheffield: Kia 1 Jul 16: Thiepval Mem: * + Lived 10 Court, 9 House, Hodgson St

RHODES, LF: Pte: 12/488: Born Dronfield 1884: Dow 24 May 16 with 2 Y&L: Essex: Fm MC, Boesinghe, Belgium: Bank Clk: Lived Green Lawn, Dronfield

RHODES, N: Pte: 28214: OU-2 Y&L

RHODES, TW: LCpl: 12/489: B: Born Bradfield, Sheffield 1893: Kia 1 Jul 16: Thiepval Mem: * +: Lived Oughtibridge

RIALL, CP: Lt Col: MID: Regular offr EY: Served in S African War: CO Oct 16–May 17

RICHARDS, PB: Pte: 31262: OU-1 Northants

RICHARDS, PC: Pte: 12/757: Born Nr Lincoln 1893: Kia 4 May 16: Sucrerie MC Colincamps: Town Hall Clk: Signaller: Lived 6 Grafton St

RICHARDSON, A: Pte: 12/1594: Born Attercliffe, Sheffield: Kia 9 Oct 17 with 1/5 Y&L: Tyne Cot Mem, Passchendaele, Belgium: OU-1/5, 7, 8 & 10 Y&L

RICHARDSON, J: Pte: 12/490: B: * –: Comm 17 Y&L 26 Aug 16: Pioneer

RICHARDSON, JH: Attended 1932 Reunion Dinner

RICHARDSON, OG: LCpl: 12/491: B: W 1 Jul 16: * +: Lived Alfreton: OU-1 Y&L

RICHARDSON, R: Pte: 12/1314: A: * –: OU-2/4 & 13 Y&L

RICHARDSON, S: Pte: 235705: OU-7 Y&L

RICHARDSON, TC: Cpl: 16659: OU-2 & 8 Y&L

RIDEOUT, FO: Pte: 12/758: C: * +: Comm EY 28 May 18

RIDLEY, OP: Cpl: 12/759: C: Rlwy Accounts Clk: * –: QM Clk: Lived 24 Lennox Rd

RIDLINGTON, AC: 2Lt: Comm 1 Mar 17: Served 12 Y&L from May 17

RIDLINGTON, JF: Pte: 12/760: C: W 1 Jul 16: Bank Clk: * +: Lived Penrhyn Rd

RIDSDALE, S: Pte: 27809: OU-13 & 14 Y&L

RIGG, AK: Pte: 12/1026: D: Born Crowick, Dumfries 1882: Kia 1 Jul–16: Queens MC, Serre: * +: Lived Lea Rigg, Crawick, Sanquhar, Dumfries

RILEY, G: Pte: 12/1027: D: Born Nr Chesterfield 1895: Dow 24 Mar 18 with 2 Y&L: Mons CC, Belgium: * –: Lived Chesterfield

RITCHIE, TH: Pte: 40212: OU-6 & 7 Y&L

RIXHAM, A: LCpl: 12/493: B: Born Sheffield: Kia 1 Jul 16: Thiepval Mem: * +

ROBERTS, AW: Sgt: 12/761: D: W 1 Jul 16: * +

ROBERTS, C: Cpl: 12/762: ABC: W Jul 16: * –: Runner: Comm KOYL128 Mar–17: Lived Oughtibridge: Last President of 12th Club

ROBERTS, EL: 2Lt: Comm 28 Mar 17: Served 12 Y&L from 3 Jun 17

ROBERTS, ES: Empl Cammell Laird: Comm 2/4 Y&L 5 Mar 15

ROBERTS, EW: Sgt: 12/1029: A: * +

ROBERTS, GH: 22254: Born Wilmslow Cheshire 1897: Kia 19 Jul 16 with 1/5 Y&L Authuilie MC: Lived Coverdale Rd, Milihouses: Comm 2 Y&L

ROBERTS, JB: LCpl: 12/763: C: * –: Signaller: Comm Manes 31 Dec 18: OU-N&D

ROBERTS, JC: Pte: 25816: OU-10 Y*L

ROBERTS, JW: Pte: 38044: HQ: Special Patrol Pty

ROBERTS, NW: LCpl: 12/765: A: * –

ROBERTS, RG: Sgt: 12/567: C: Comm RE 17 Mar 17

ROBERTS, W: Pte: 24416: A: * −

ROBERTS, WW: Pte: 44821: Kia 16 Apr 18 with 1 14 Y&L: OU-1 14 & 2/5 Y&L

ROBERTSON, A: Cpl: 12/220: A: Born Edinburgh 1882: Kia 1 Jul 16: Thiepval Mem: * + War Poet

ROBINS, HVL: Lt: Seived 12 Y&L from 8 Dec 17: OU-1 15 ELancs

ROBINSON, AO: Pte: 12/221: A: Kia 21 Mar 18 with 2/8 N&D: Arras Mem: − Bank Clk: * + Comm N&D 1916

ROBINSON, E: ACpl: 46448: OU-7 Y&L

ROBINSON, E: LCpl: 12/1030: D: W 1 Jul 16: * +

ROBINSON, FC: Pte: 12/1031: B: * −

ROBINSON, G: Pte: 12/1219: B: W 6 Apr 18 with 7 Y&L

ROBINSON, G: Pte: 12/123: A: W 1 Jul 16: * +

ROBINSON, H: ACpl: 12/1950: OU-13 Y&L

ROBINSON, JE: Pte: 38056: OU-2 & 14 Y&L

ROBINSON, L: Pte: 12/495: B: Born Dore, Sheffield 1893: Kia 27 Jul 17: Rue du Bacquerot MC: * −: Lived 61 Carterknowle Rd

ROBINSON, P: Pte: 25165: OU-14 Y&L

ROBINSON, PP: Cpl: 12/496: B: Born Sand Hutton 1889: Kia 1 Jul 16: Thiepval Mem * +: Lived Barnsley

ROBINSON, S: Pte: Sheffield Univ Student

ROBINSON, ST: Pte: 12/1815: A: * −

ROBINSON, WS: Left 12 Y&L before May 16

ROCHE, FA: Pte: 12/497: B: * −: SB

RODDIS, H: Pte: 12/1603: A: Born Crookesmoor, Sheffield 1897: W 1 Jul 16 with 12 Y&L & Dow 28 Jun 18 with 13 Y&L: Longvenesse Souvenir MC: * +: OU-2 & 13 Y&L

RODDIS, L: Pte: 39150: OU-7 & 10 Y&L

RODGERS, EG: Pte: 12/767: Born Stafford 1896: Kia 4 May 16: Sucrerie MC, Colincamps

RODGERS, F: Pte: 41 Oil: Kia 17 Sep 17 with 8 Y&L

RODGERS, GH: ASgt: 12/1032: D: * −: OU-14 Y&L: Comm WRiding 28 May 18

RODGERS, J: Pte: 46449: A: Lewis gnr

RODGERS, S: Pte: 12/1310: B: W 1 Jul 16: * +

RODINSON, JR: Pte: 12/1033: D: W 1 Jul 16: * +

ROE, E: Attended 1918 Reunion Dinner

ROE, FN: Pte: 12/768: C

ROGERS, J: Pte: 46449: OU-13 Y&L

ROGERS, W: Pte: 12/1751: Born Meersbrook, Sheffield 1900: Kia 1 Jul 16 with 8 Y&L

ROLLEY, N: ACpl: 12/498: B: SS Apr 16: * −: Comm Y&L 25 Sep 17

ROONEY, GF: Pte: 12/769: C: * −

ROPER, M: Pte: 11567: HO: Special Patrol Pty

ROSE, G: LCpl: 12/499: A: Born Wimbledon 1892: Kia 11 Apr 18 with 13 Y&L Cabaret Rouge Me: * −: Signaller: Lived Worksop

ROSE, HH: Pte: 20541 O: A: Lewis gnr: OU-2 London Yeo & 13 Y&L

ROSE, RN: Pte: 235854: HQ: Barber

ROSS, RM: Pte: 235674: OU-1/4 & 9 Y&L

ROSSOR, A: Pte: 9847: OU-1 & 6 Y&L

ROWLANDS, WH: 2Lt: AB: * −: Comm unknown unit 3 Dec 15: Served 12 Y&L mid 1916–1 Jun 17

ROWLEY, SG: Pte: 12/1036: D: * +: Observer

ROYLE, W: Bank Clk

RUDDLESDEN, G: Pte: 40091: OU-9 & 13 Y&L

RUDDOCK, FA: Pte: Sheffield Univ Student: Signaller

RUDKIN, T: Pte: 12/501: B: MC: W 1 Jul 16: * +: Comm 3 Y&L 26 Jun 18, attd 2 Y&L Lived Chapletown

RUFF, W: Pte: 12/1709: OU-13 Y&L

RUMBELOW, PL: Cpl: 205413: A: Lewis gnr: OU-2/2 London Yeo & 13 Y&L

RUSBY, L: Pte: 12/1558: C

RUSH, B: Pte: 12/770: C: Sheffield Univ Lab Asst: * +: Bandsman: Bde Concert Pty

RUSSELL, CA: Pte: 12/1870: OU-8 Y&L: Comm RLanc 28 Aug 17

RUSSELL, M: ACpl: 12/1173: A
RUSSON, WH: Cpl: 12/502: B
RYLANCE, WL: 2Lt: Comm 27 Sep 17: Served 12 Y&L from 21 Dec 17
RYLETT, A: Pte: 12/1037: 0: * +: Comm Y&L 20 Feb 18

SABBEN, JCF: Pte: 12/772: C: Born Oakengates, Shropshire: Kia 1 Jul–16: Euston Rd MC, Colincamps
SADDLER, GH: Pte: 12/771: C: Born Crookes, Sheffield 1893: Kia 1 Jul–16: Queens MC, Serre: * +: Town Hall Clk: Lived 118 Harcourt Rd
SALISBURY, JAH: Sgt: A
SALISBURY, W: Sgt: 9512: OU-1 & 2 Y&L
SALKELD, CH: LCpl: 12/1038: D: Born Nr Rotherham 1892: Kia 1 Jul 16–: Thiepval Mem: * +: Lived Church St, Kimberworth
SAMPSON, W: Pte: 41097: OU-8 Y&L
SANDERS, N: Pte: 12/1253: D: Born Cardiff: Dow 23 Jun 18 with 1/4 Y&L: Hagle Dump MC, Belgium: * +: OU-1/4 & 10 Y&L
SANDERSON, JW: Pte: 12/504: B: * +: OU-NOJ13 Y&L
SANDERSON, FA: Pte: 12/103f3: 12/10cf3: W 1 Jul 16: * +: Lived 49 Cliffefield Rd: Brother of RW Sanderson
SANDERSON, RW: Pte: 12/1040: D: W 1 Jul 16: * +: Lived 49 Cliffefield Rd: Brother of FA Sanderson
SANDERSON, E: Pte: 12/1549: Born Park, Sheffield 1896: W Jul 16 with 12 Y&L and Kia 22 Jun 17 with 2 Y&L: Philo Sep he MC SATTERTHWAITE E: Pte: 12/1041: D: * +: OU-10 Y&L
SAUL, GW: Pte: 12/2017: C
SAULT, H: Pte: 12/2083: Born Leicester: Dow 27 Dec 17 with 14 Y&L: Aubigny CC Ext: OU-2 & 14 Y&L
SAUNDERS, GP: Pte: 235706: A: Batman: OU-13 Y&L
SAUNDERS, SJ: Pte: 41114: D 2 Jul 18 with 7 Y&L
SAVOURY, W: Pte: 39005: B: OU-41 Mob Vet Sect, 7, 8, 9 & 13 Y&L
SAYLES, B: Pte: 37964: OU-2 Y&L
SAYLES, JP: LCpl: 12/225: A: * –: Mil Postman
SCAIFE, N: Pte: 12/1042: D: W 1 Jul 16: * +: Lived 53 Crookes Rd: OU-13 Y&L
SCALLY, T: Pte: 3/2968: Dow 13 Apr 18 with 1/5 Y&L: Nine Elms MC, Poperinghe Belgium: OU-1/5, 2/5, 7 & 10 Y&L
SCARBOROUGH, H: Pte: 12/773: A: Born 1892: W 1 Jul 16 with 12 Y&L and Kia 17 Sep 18 with 3 WY: Comm WY late 1916: Lived Keighley
SCHOFIELD, H: Pte: 12/1185: A: W 1 Jul 16: * +
SCHOFIELD, J: Pte: 39088: OU-7 & 10 Y&L
SCHOFIELD, JO: Pte: 12/774;C: * –
SCHOLEY, E: Pte: 12/505: B: Barber: * +: Batman: OU-7 Y&L
SCHONHUT, H: Pte: 12/1590: OU-1 14, 6 & 14 Y&L
SCORAH, E: Pte: 12/506: B: * –
SCOTHERN, FJ: Pte: 12/1 044: D: Born Sheffield 1894: Kia 1 Jul 16: Rlwy Hollow MC Serre: * +: Lived 5 Alderson Pic, Highfield
SCOTT, W: Pte: 12/1435: D: Born Swallownest, Sheffield: Kia 1 Jul 16-: Thiepval Mem: * +: Lived Swallownest
SCOTT, WH: Pte: 12/1929: Born Saddler Great, Derbys: Kia 1 Jul 16 with 8 Y&L Blighty Valley MC, Authuille: Lived Rotherham
SCOTT, WR: Pte: 12/1 043: D: W 1 Jul 16: Sheffield Daily Telegraph Reporter: * +
SCROGGS, HH: ASgt: 205424: OU-2/2 London Yeo & 2 Y&L
SEAMAN, R: LCpl: 12/1 045: B: Born Ecclesall1889: Dow 28 Jul 16: Merville CC * –: Lived 781 Ecclesall Rd:
SEARLE, A: Cpl: 39868: A: Signaller: OU-10 & 13 Y&L
SEARLE, WR: Pte: 235711
SEARLES, JW: Pte: 38992: OU-7 & 10 Y&L
SELLARS, D: Sgt: 37975: OU-2 Y&L
SENIOR, B: Pte: 38960: Kia 25 Mar 18 with 7 Y&L: Arras Mem: OU-7 & 9 Y&L

SENIOR, FH: Pte: 12/1216: Born Neepsend, Sheffield 1888: Kia 1 May 16: Sucrerie MC, Colincamps: Sheffield Univ Student

SENIOR, G: Pte

SENIOR, SG: Pte: 37806: A: OU-2, 1/5, 7, 13 & 14 Y&L

SEYMOUR, RWD: Pte: 12/226: A: W 1 Jul 16: * +

SHARMAN, ER: Pte: 12/1868: OU-8 Y&L

SHARP, A: Sgt: 27425: B: Born Darton, Barnsley: Kia 11 Apr 18 with 13 Y&L Ploegsteert Mem, Belgium: Musketry Instr: OU-1 Army School, 2 & 13 Y&L

SHARP, B: Pte: 12/1373: A: W May 16

SHARP, RR: Pte: 12/776: C: Born Pitsmoor, Sheffield: Kia 1 Jul 16: Thiepval Mem: * +

SHARP, W: Pte: 205426: OU-2/2 London Yeo & 7 Y&L

SHARPE, E: Cpl: 12/775: C: * +

SHARPE, JT: Pte: 14/943: OU-10 & 14 Y&L

SHARPE, VE: ACpl: 235708: OU-7 Y&L

SHARPLES, PE: 2Lt: Comm Y&L 31 Jul 15

SHAW, AB: CSM: 12/508: W 1 Jul 16: * +: Lived Red House, Cricket Inn Rd: Comm 8 Y&L 29 Aug 17

SHAW, BGT: Pte: 12/1701: OU-1 Y&L

SHAW, E: Pte: 12/1827: Born Newbold, Chesterfield: Kia 9 Apr 17 with 8 Y&L Lived Chesterfield

SHAW, G: Pte: 37958: OU-2 Y&L

SHAW, H: Pte: 12/777: C: Born Chapletown 1890: W 1 Jul 16 with 12 Y&L and Kia 22 Sep 17 with 9 Y&L: Lijssenthoek MC, Belgium: * +: OU-2, 6, 9 & 14 Y&L

SHAW, H: Pte: 34154: OU-1/5, 8, 10 & 14 Y&L

SHAW, JG: Pte: 12/1182: Born Aston, Sheffield: Kia 1 Jul 16 with 14 Y&L: Thiepval Mem

SHAW, L: Pte: 12/228: A: W 10 May 16

SHAW, T: Pte: 12/1608: D: Born St Philips, Sheffield 1898: Kia 1 Jul 16 Thiepval Mem: * +

SHAW, W: Pte: 12/1555: C: OU-1 Y&L

SHAW, WH: Pte: 235209: OU-1/4, 2/4 & 7 Y&L

SHELDON, B: Pte: 12/510: B: W 1 Jul 16: * +: OU-2 & 14 Y&L: Comm WY 31 Oct 17

SHELDON, S: Pte: 12/1127: A: Born Shalesmoor, Sheffield 1893: Kia 1 Jul 16 Thiepval Mem: * +: Lived Baslow, Derbys

SHELLEY, J: Pte: 12/1912: A: * –: W Sep 16

SHELTON, H: Pte: 12/1395: C

SHELTON, R: Pte: 12/1359: C: OU-2 Y&L

SHEMELD, E: Pte: 25023: MM: Born 1889: Kia 30 Mar 18 with 31 MGC: Arras Mem

SHEPERD, JW: Pte: 12856: D

SHEPHERDSON, AJ: Sgt: 1213: B: W 1 Jul 16: Teacher: * +: Lived 366 City Rd

SHEPHERD, AD: Pte: 205427: A: Kia 12 Apr 18 with 13 Y&L: Lewis gnr: OU-2/2 London Yeo & 13 Y&L

SHEPHERD, GM: CD

SHEPHERD, JW: Pte: 18856: OU-6 Y&L

SHEPHERN, MC: Pte: 12/1134: B: W 1 Jul 16: * +: Lived Old Wheel, Loxley

SHERLOCK, T: Pte: 10569: D

SHERWIN, GA: Cpl: 204340: Kia 29 Sep 18 with 13 Y&L

SHERWOOD, CS: Pte: 12/1867: * –

SHIELDS, FR: Pte: 205425: B: OU-41 Mob Vet Sect, 2 London Yeo & 13 Y&L

SHIELLS, AW: Pte: 23295: Born Sheffield 1885: Kia 1 Jul 16 with 8 Y&L: Thiepval Mem: Teacher: Lived 84 Woodstock Rd, Sharrow

SHIELS, AE: LCpl: 12/1217: B: * –

SHIMELD, H: LCpl: 12/778: C: * –: Bn Ord Rm Clk

SHINN, JW: Cpl: 10051: OU-1, 8 & 9 Y&L

SHIPLEY, A: Pte: 12/779: C: W Jul 16: * –: Empl Cockaynes: OU-14 Y&L

SHIPMAN, G: LCpl: 13/825: OU-2 & 13 Y&L

SHIPSIDE, J: Pte: 12/1451: B: W May 16

SHIRT, JW: Pte: 12/1352: D: Born Crookes, Sheffield 1897: Dow 7 Jul 16 Etretat Chyd: * +: Lived 10 Wadbrough Rd

SHIRT, W: Pte: 41805: HO: Born Sheffield 1894: Runner: OU-6, 7 & 13 Y&L

SHOESMITH, A: Pte: 12/511: Born Skircoat, Haliiax: Kia 27 Jul 18 with 2/4 Y&L: Mar faux MC: OU-2/4 & 6 Y&L

SHOOTER, W: Pte: 12/512: B: * –

SHORT, CE: Cpl: Sheffield Univ Student

SIDDALL, B: Pte: 39081: OU-10 Y&L

SIDDALL, R: Pte: 14/666: Born 1898: D 7 Jul 18 with 1/5 Y&L: Hoyland Nether (Law) St Peter Chyd Ext: OU-2, 1/5, 215 & 14 Y&L: CWGC say he died with 2 Y&L

SIDDONS, A: Pte: 16828: A: Bomber: OU-2, 6 & 13 Y&L

SIDEBOTTOM, H: Pte: 3/3482: OU-7 & 8 Y&L

SIDEBOTTOM, H: Pte: 25481: D: * +: OU-6 Y&L

SIDEBOTTOM, J: Pte: 12/1855: MM: OU-13 Y&L

SIDNEY, No other details: Cpl: 23XP5222: HQ: Special Patrol Pty: OU-2/4, 115 & 13 Y&L

SIMCOX, R: Pte: 12/1 049: SS Apr 16

SIMMONDS, W: Pte: 31267: 01-1 Northants & 13 Y&L

SIMMONITE, C: Pte: 12/1050: D: Born Sheffield: Kia 1 Jul 16: Thiepval Mem: * +: Lived 7 Wharncliffe Rd

SIMONS, SCB: Sgt: 12/513: A: * –: Signalier

SIMONS, LS: Pte: 12/1124: B: W 1 Jul 16: * +: Lived Rotherham: OU-10 & 18 Y&L

SIMPKIN, AL: Pte: 12/1250: A: MC: W 1 Jul 16: * +: Comm 5 Y&L 29 Aug – 17: OU-2/4 Y&L

SIMPSON, A: Pte: 11854: A: Runner

SIMPSON, AA: Sgt: 12/514: B: Born Earsham, Norfolk: Kia 1 Jul 16: Thiepva Mem: * +: Lived Chesterfield

SIMPSON, AJ: LCpl: 235794: A

SIMPSON, AJ: LCpl: 235198: A: OU-1/5 Yorks, 1/4, 214 & 13 Y&L

SIMPSON, C: Pte: 12/1621: OU-14 Y&L

SIMPSON, E: Pte: 12/230: A: W 1 Jul 16: * +: OU-2 & 14 Y&L

SIMPSON, G: Sgt: 12/1726: A: * –

SIMPSON, H: Born 1886: Dow 7 Jul 16 with 6 N&D: St Sever MC, Rouen: Empl Chesterfield Gas & Water Board: Comm N&D late 1915

SIMPSON, VS: CaptMC MID: Kia 13 Apr 18 with 13 Y&L: Outtersteene CC: Ex City Bn OR: OC 20 Pl: Comm 27 Jan 15: Returned 12 Y&L 3 Aug 16

SIMPSON, W: Pte: 12/1394: A: W 1 Jul 16: * +: OU-2 & 10 Y&L: Comm 7 Y&L 27 Jun 17

SIMPSON, W: 2Lt: Comm 27 Jul 17

SIMSON, S: LCpl: 12/1051: D: Born Spalding, Lincs: Kia 1 Jul 16: Thiepval Mem: * +: Bank Clk

SINCLAIR, JM: 2Lt: W 11 May 17: Comm 5 Y&L 25 Oct 16: Served 12 Y&L from 8 Jan 17: OU-Min of Munitions

SISSONS, JM: Pte: 235655: A: Lewis gnr: OU-94 MGC

SKEELS, W: Pte: 12/515: B: W 1 Jul 16: * +: Lived 120 Richmond Rd: OU-2&7 Y&L

SKIDMORE, JW: Pte: 12/233: A: * –: Bn Ord Rm Clk

SKIDMORE, W: Cpl: 12/1052: D: * –: D Coy Barber: OU-1/4, 6 & 9 Y&L

SKINNER, ES: Pte: 12/1053: D: Born Pitsmoor, Sheffield: Kia 1 Jul 16: Luke Copse MC, Serre: * +: Lived 520 Fulwood Rd

SKINNER, J: Cpl: 40196: OU-14 NFus, 6 & 7 Y&L

SLACK, A: Pte: 12/516: B: Born Clay Cross, Derbys 1895: Kia 16 May 16 Sucrerie MC, Colincamps: Lived Chesterfield

SLACK, AE: Bank Clk

SLACK, OE: Pte: 12/2111: A: Born 1896: W 1 Jul 16: * +: Lived 34 Winter St

SLACK, TR: LCpl: 12/234: A: Born Luton 1894: Bank Clk: * +: Lived Hastings Rd, Millhouses: Comm EY 28 Nov 17

SLATER, W: Pte: 12/1778: OU-1 Y&L

SLEIGH, HR: Sgt: 12/1054: D: MSM MID: Sheffield Daily Telegraph Reporter: * –: Bn Ord Rm Clk: OU-ASC attd HQ 94 Bde

SMALLWOOD, TJ: Pte: 12/1934: Born Meersbrook, Sheffield: D 11 Mar 16 with 15 Y&L: Norton C, Sheffield: Lived 64 Woodbank Rd

SMEDLEY, H: Pte: 12/1811: Born Brightside, Sheffield: Kia 15 Oct 17 with 9 Y&L: Godeswaers-Velde MC, Belgium: OU-6, 9 & 13 Y&L

SMITH, A: Pte: 44816: OU-1/4 & 2/5 Y&L

SMITH, AH: Cpl: 12/781: C: Born St Georges, Sheffield 1881: Kia 3 Oct 16: Le Touret MC: * –

SMITH, CS: Cpl: 12/843: D: Sheffield Univ Student * –

SMITH, CW: Pte: 12/1851: OU-13 Y&L

SMITH, DC: Pte: 205468: OU-2 London Yeo & 7 Y&L

SMITH, E: Pte: 12/1956: OU-6, 9 & 13 Y&L

SMITH, F: Pte: 12/235: A: OU-94 TMB

SMITH, FC: Pte: 205418: D 15 Jun 18 with 7 Y&L: OU-2/2 London Yeo & 7 Y&L

SMITH, FJ: Pte: 12/1146: C: W May 16

SMITH, FP: Cpl: 28101: Kia 15 Apr 18 with 1/4 Y&L: Tyne Cot Mem, Passchendaele, Belgium: OU-1/4 & 14 Y&L

SMITH, FP: Pte: 12/1056: D: Born Walkley, Sheffield 1895: Dow 4 Jul 16: Doullens CC Ext No1: * +: Lived 90 Western Rd

SMITH, G: 2Lt: Comm 28 Mar 17

SMITH, GB: Pte: 12/782: C: * –: Comm WY 28 May 18

SMITH, GS: Pte: 12/1208: A: * –: W 13 Apr 18 with 13 Y&L: Comm 15 Y&L 26 Apr 17? or RAF 8 Jun 17?: OU-2/6 NStaffs

SMITH, H: Pte: 12/1787: C

SMITH, J: Pte: 44875: OU-2 & 14 Y&L

SMITH, JL: Pte: 12/517: B: SS 1 Jul 16: * +: Lived 1 Watson Rd, Worksop: OU-8 Y&L

SMITH, R: LCpl: 12/784: C: * +

SMITH, RE: LCpl: 12/1057: D: Born Swinton, Yorks 1890: Kia 16 May–16: Sucrerie MC, Colincamps: Lived Rawmarsh

SMITH, S: Pte: 41 052: OU-8 Y&L

SMITH, S: Pte: 12/2050: OU-NOJ1 Y&L

SMITH, T: Pte: 12/135f3: 12/135

SMITH, T: Pte: 29246: OU-2 Y&L

SMITH, W: Pte: 38962: OU-7 & 10 Y&L

SMITH, W: Pte: 12/2024: A: W 29 Jun 18 with 7 Y&L: Sanitary Man: 12 Y&L until Jun 16

SMITH, W: Pte: 3804o·8orn Rochdale 1888: Kia 12 May 17: Arras Mem: OU-1Fus: Lived Rochdale

SMITH, WJ: Pte: 12/1296: A: Born Westward Ho, Devon 1898: W May 16 with 12 Y&L & Kia 7 May 17 with 13 Y&L: Arras Mem: * –: Lived Nether Green: OU-2 & 13 Y&L

SMITHSON, F: LCpl: 12/1564: W Jul 16: OU-10 & 14 Y&L

SMOUT, WT: Pte: 12/1854: Born Sheffield 1886: Kia 1 Jul 16 with 8 Y&L: Thiepval Mem: Lived Neepsend

SMYTH, GRL: Pte: 45939: OU-11 Suffolk & 7 Y&L

SNEE, J: Pte: 3/4766: MM: OU-1, 2, 6, 7 & 13 Y&L

SNELLING, AL: Pte: 12/519: B: * –

SNELLING, J: 12th Club Member

SNOWDEN, L: Pte: 12/1797: OU-1 Y&L

SOMERSET, RM: Sheffield Univ Med Student: Born 1894: SS 18 Oct – 16: Comm 3 Yorks Jun 15: Lived Fern Cliffe, Carfield Ave: Signals Offr

SOWDEN, HB: Pte: 41771: OU-2 & 14 Y&L

SPARLING, RA: Sgt: 12/1 058: D: MSM: Sheffield Daily Telegraph Reporter: * –: Lived 33 Victoria Rd: OU-13 Y&L

SPEIGHT, W: Pte: 40035: Born Leeds 1890: Kia 4 May 17: Arras Mem: OUWY & 6 Y&L: Lived Leeds

SPENCER, E: Pte: 12/785: C: MM: Born St Georges, Sheffield: Kia 1 Jul 16: Thiepval Mem: * +: Lived 36 Bower Rd, Crookesmoor

SPENCER, HJ: Pte: 12/1477: Born Neepsend, Sheffield 1897: Kia 15 Sep 16 with 2 Y&L: Thiepval Mem

SPENCER, HP: Pte: 12/786: C: * +

SPENCER, J: Pte: 12/1503: Born Neepsend, Sheffield 1894: D 16 Jan 16 with 15 Y&L: Burngreave C, Sheffield

SPERRING, AV: Pte: 23255: OU-2 & 10 Y&L

SQUIRES, EF: Cpl: 12/520: B: MID: * –: Half brother of W Barlow

SQUIRES, JE: Interviewed by J Harris for 'Covenant With Death' in 1961

SQUIRES, WH: Pte: 12/1717: C: * –

STABLES, F: Pte: 21982: Kia 26 Apr 18 with 1/4 Y&L: Suffolk MC Vierstraat, Kemmel, Belgium: OU-1/4, 2/5 & 10 Y&L

STABLES, G: LCpl: 12/237: A: * –: Bandsman

STABLES, V: Pte: 12/1404: C: Born Hutton Pugnall: W Jun 16 and Kia 18 May 17: Arras Mem: Lived Doncaster: OU-10 Y&L

STACEY, AO: Pte: Sheffield Univ Student

STAFFORD, A: Sgt: 12/238: A: * +

STAGG, AC: Pte: 12/1475: B: Born Huddersfield: W 1 Jul 16: * +: Insurance agent: Lived 12 Dover Ad

STALEY, B: Pte: 12/1346: C: SS May 18: * +

STAMP, H: Pte: 12/2122: OU-6, 7 & 10 Y&L

STANBRIDGE, RJ: Pte: 235657

STANCEY, M: Pte: 22001: OU-2& 10 Y&L

STANCILL, A: Sgt: 12/1436: D: * +: OU-6 Y&L

STANCLIFFE, AE: Pte: 12/1738: OU-2 & 13 Y&L

STANIFORTH, CW: Pte: 12/1410: A: W I Jul 16: * +: Lived 93 Beechwood Rd, Hillsboro

STANIFORTH, FC: Pte: 12/1547: W Jul 16: OU-2, 6, 7, 8, 10 & 14 Y&L

STANIFORTH, WR: Pte: 12/787: C: * +

STANLEY, J: Pte: 12/1197: B: Born Firth Pk, Sheffield 1893: Kia 1 Jul–16: Queens MC, Serre: * +: Lived 423 Earl Marshall Rd

STANLEY, JF: Cpl: 38045: A: Bomber

STANSER, JR: Pte: MC: Comm 2/4 Y&L 17 Nov 14

STANTON, A: Pte: 205421: OU-2/2 London Yeo & 7 Y&L

STANTON, A: Pte: 41076: OU-8 Y&L

STAPLEY, E: Pte: 235709: C: 94 Bde Canteen: OU-13 Y&L

STEEL, CL: Pte: 3/3104: A

STEELE, E: LCpl: 24389: Born 1895: Kia 27 Jun 17 with 13 Y&L: Ploegsteert Mem, Belgium: OU-13 & 14 Y&L

STEELE, J: Cpl: 3/3685: OU-1 & 2 Y&L

STENTON, A: LCpl: 12/1313: A: Born Hillsboro, Sheffield 1880: Dow 20 May 18 with 2 Y&L: Etaples MC: * +

STENTON, H: Pte: Sheffield Univ Student

STENTON, TP: Pte: 46366: Kia 14 Apr 18 with 1/5 Y&L: OU-I/5 & 2/5 Y&L

STEPHENSON, T: Pte: 64459: OU-RE, 1 & 2 Y&L

STEPHENSON, W: Pte: 12/788: C: * +

STEVEN, AR: 2Lt: W 13 May l7: Served 12 Y&L from 26 Nov I6: OU-Scot Rfls

STEVENS, F: Pte: 12/789: C: * –: OU-7 Y&L

STEVENSON, JW: Pte: 12/239: A: * +: OU-2/4 Y&L

STEWART, W: Pte: 38963: OU-7 & 10 Y&L

STEWART, W: Pte: 12/1061: D: * +

STIMPSON, A: Sgt: 12/790: C: * +: Gas NCO

STIMSON, CW: Pte: 12/522: B: * +

STINSON, P: Pte: 12/791: C: Born Worksop, Notts: Kia I Jul 16: Thiepval Mem: * +: SB: Lived Worksop

STOCKIL, G: Pte: 12/523: A: Born Heeley, Sheffield 1895: Kia 1 Jul 16: Rlwy Hollow MC, Serre: * +: Lived Rotherham

STOCKWELL, RE: Pte: 37961: Born 1894: Kia 21 Mar 18 with 2 Y&L: Arras Mem

STOKER, F: Pte: 12/792: C: * –

STOKES, F: Pte: 12/1442: B: * +: OU-9 Y&L

STONES, FD: MC: Born 1878: Kia 28 Sep 17 with 2/6 N&D: Mendinghem MC, Belgium: Comm 2/6N&D

STONES, JB: Pte: 12/240: A: * –

STONES, TH: Pte: 12/1696: OU-1 Y&L

STOPPANI, G: LCpl: 12/1 062: D: * –: Refuse Man

STORE, SM: Pte: 25833: OU-10 Y&L

STOREY, CA: Pte: 12/1205: C: W I Jul 16: * +: Lived 111 Stalker Lees Rd: OU-2 & 7 Y&L

STOREY, H: Pte: 12/1378: D: Born Hathersage, Derbys 1897: Dow 28 Jun 16: Bertrancourt MC: Lived 1 Church Hill Rd

STORR, GF: Cpl: 12/793: Born Relford, Notts: W May 16 with 12 Y&L and Kia 23 Apr 17 with 10 Y&L: Arras Mem: Lived Lincoln

STORRY, FWS: Lt: D: MID: W 1 Jul 16: Comm 28 Nov 14: 0C 1 Pl: Lived Wales, Kiveton Pk

STOTHARD, ER: Pte: 12/1491: B: Born Blythe, Notts: Kia 1 Jul 16: Thiepval Mem: * +

STRACHAN, DG: Cpl: 12/1832: OU-2 & 14 Y&L

STREETS, JW: Sgt: 12/525: BD: Born Whitwell, Derbys 1885: Kia 1 Jul–16: Euston Rd MC, COlincamps: Miner: * +: War Poet: Lived 16 Portland St, Whitwell, Derbys

STRICKLAND, J: Pte: 12/1480: B: Born Lancaster 1876: Kia 16 May l6: Sucrerie MC, Colincamps: Lived Barnsley

STRINGER, W: Pte: 12/526: B: * +: OU-7 Y&L

STRONG, RB: Pte: 40202: OU-9 NFus, 2/4 & 6 Y&L

STUBLEY, TW: Pte: 12/1145: B: Born Waltham Abbey, Essex 1889: Kia 16 May 16: Sucrerie MC, Colincamps

SUMMERFIELD, HJ: Pte: 12/243: AB: * –: Bandsman

SUMMERSCALES, W: Pte: 40089: OU-9 Y&L

SURR, H: Pte: 12/1493: B: W 1 Jul 16: * +

SUTHERN, E: Pte: 22149: OU-2 & 14 Y&L

SUTTON, PF: Pte: 31265: OU-1 Northants

SWIFT, CE: LCpl: 12/527: Born Penistone: Kia 18 Sep 16 with 2 Y&L: Thiepval Mem

SWIFT, EE: Pte: 12/2133: Born Ranmoor, Sheffield 1888: Dow 23 Aug 16 with 13 Y&L: Boulogne East MC: Town Hall Education Dept Clk: OU-2 & 13 Y&L

SWIFT, FR: 12/1899

SWIFT, H: Pte: 12/1655: D

SWIFT, J: Pte: 12/794: C: W Jun 16

SWIFT, JS: Pte: 12/1 064: D: Born Barnsley 1885: Kia 1 Jul 16: Luke Copse MC, Serre: Bank Clk: * +: Lived Beech Grove, Barnsley

SWIFT, WW: Pte: 12/1263: A: W Jun 16: * -: Lived Wadsley, Sheffield

SWINDELL, JE: Sgt: 12/244: A: W 1 Jul 16: * +: Lived Bunting Nook, Norton, Sheffield: OU-2 & 6 Y&L

SWINDEN, S: Pte: 12/1065: D: W I Jul 16: * +: Lived 85 Burns Rd, Crookesmoor

SWINSCOE, TC: Pte: 12/795: C: Born Sheffield 1896: Kia 1 Jul 16: Thiepval Mem: * +: Lived 119 Middlewood Rd

SYCAMORE, WJ: Pte: 23571 0: OU-7 Y&L

SYMONDS, H: Pte: 235659: OU-7 Y&L

TAGG, R: Pte: 12/528: C: Born Beighton, Sheffield 1896: Kia 1 Jul–16: AIF Burial Gd, Flers: * +: Lived Scourings Fm, Woodhouse

TALBOT, F: Pte: 31269: OU-1 Northants & 13 Y&L

TALBOT, FS: Pte: 31273: HQ: MM: Shoemaker: OU-Northants & 13 Y&L

TALLANT, S: Pte: 40036: OU-1/5 & 6 Y&L

TATE, A: Pte: 12/1467: B: Born Park, Sheffield: Kia 1 Jul 16: Thiepval Mem: * +

TAYLOR, AL: Lt: Comm 4 Y&L 25 Oct l6: Served 12 Y&L from 8 Jan 17

TAYLOR, AT: Pte: 235722: A: Born South Norwood, Surrey: Kia 27 Mar 18 with 13 Y&L: Lewis gnr: OU-RWKent & 13 Y&L

TAYLOR, C: Pte: 12/1495: B: W 1 Jul 16: * +

TAYLOR, CT: Pte: 12/1402: B: * +

TAYLOR, CW: LCpl: 12/1 066: D: Born E Relford, Notts 1890: Kia 1 Jul 16: Thiepval Mem: Cashier: * +: Lived 58 Cardgate, Retford

TAYLOR, E: Cpl: 12/1997: D: * –

TAYLOR, EN: Capt: A: Comm 19 Dec l6: Served 12 Y&L from 12 Feb 17

TAYLOR, F: Golf Pro at Sickleholme

TAYLOR, FA: Born 1892: Kia 24 Mar 18 with Hood Bn, RND: Arras Mem: Comm RND

TAYLOR, G: Pte: 39104: HQ: Kia 27 Mar 18 with 13 Y&L: Bucquoy Rd Me, Ficheux: Special Patrol Pty: OU-1 0 & 13 Y&L

TAYLOR, GE: PtePte: 12/1300: BEOBALD HC: OU-1 Northants, 1/4, 215 & 6 Y&L

THOMAS, EC: A: Born Bengal, India 1896: Kia 17 Jun 16: Bertrancourt MC: Sheffield: A: OU-13 Y&L

THOMPSON, A: Sgt: 11225: A

THOMPSON, AH: Pte: 12/1363: B: Born Barnsley 1894: Kia 1 Jul 16: Thiepval Mem: * +: Bank Clk: Lived West View, Outwood, Wakefield

THOMPSON, ER: Pte: 31276: OU-1 Northants, 1 15 & 2/5 Y&L

THOMPSON, JS: Pte: MC: Sheffield Univ Student: Comm 1 O Y&L 2 Mar · 15: OU-2 Y&L anMGC

THOMPSON, SE: Pte: 235662: A

THOMPSON, W: Sgt: 12/1 069: C: Born Basford. Notts 1890: Kia I Jul 16: Thiepval Mem: * +: Empl Dixon & Son: Lived 103 Murray Rd: Ex W Yorks TF Arty

THORNE, AJ: Pte: 12/799: C: Born W Bowling 1890: Kia 1 Jul 16: Queens MC, Serre: * +: Lived 28 Marshfield St, Bradford

THORNSBY, HS: Pte: 12/1372: Kia 24 Aug 18\With 10 WY: Vis en Artois Mem: Comm WY 27 Nov 17

THORPE, A: Pte: 12/1 071: BD: Born Park, Sheffield 1891: Dow 10 Jul–16: City Rd C, Sheffield: * +: Lived 21 Manor Ln

THORPE, E: Pte: 23246: D: Born New Sleaford, Lincs: Dow 31 Aug 16– : Merville CC Ext: OU-1incs, 8 & 1 O Y&L: Lived Sleaford

THORPE, F: Pte: 38964: OU-7, 9 & 13 Y&L

THORPE, F: Pte: 38964: HQ: Batman

THORPE, JF: Pte: 28814: OU-2 & 6 Y&L

THORPE, JL: Pte: 12/250: A: Born Norton Lees, Sheffield 1895: Kia 1 Jul 16: Queens MC: * +: Lived 97 Montgomery Ad

THORPE, M: Pte: 38049: OU-6 & 9 Y&L

THRESHER, AW: Pte: 12/1 070: OU-I Y&L

TICKELL, HL: Pte: 205432: A: Lewis gnr: OU-2/2 London Yeo & 13 Y&L

TIFFIN, JJ: CSM: Teacher

TILNEY, JH: Pte: 39039: OU-1 O Y&L: Deserted 26 Jun 18

TIMMONS, TH: Pte: 12/1 073: D: Born St Cuthberts, Sheffield 1891: Dow 3 Nov 17 Depot: Burngreave C, Sheffield: * +

TIMMS, A: Pte: 12/801: A: * +: Observer

TINGLE, A: Pte: 12/1074: B: Born Pitsmoor, Sheffield 1895: Dow 23 Sep 17 with 9 Y&L: Mont Huon MC, Treport: * +: Lived 6 Pitsmoor: OU-6 & 9 Y&L

TINGLE, JH: Pte: 39102: Born 1895: Kia 9 Oct 17 with 1/4: Tyne Cot Mem, Passchendaele, Belgium: OU-2 & 10 Y&L

TIREBUCK, GL: Pte: 12/532: B: * –: Bde Concert Ply

TITTERTON, F: Pte: 91 04: HQ: Regt Police

TOAKLEY, R: Pte: 12/1843: OU-1 & 6 Y&L

TODD, FW: Pte: 203664: A: OU-1/5 & 13 Y&L

TODD, GW: 2Lt: A: Comm 30 May 17: Served 12 Y&L from 2 Aug 17

TODD, H: Pte: 12/802: C: Born Ecclesall, Sheffield 1891: Dow 3 May 16: Sucrerie MC, Colincamps: Bank Clk

TODD, SH: Pte: 12/1218: D: W May 16

TOGHILL, WJ: Pte: 40213: A: Bomber: OU-6 & 13 Y&L

TOMLIN Sheffield Daily Telegraph Reporter

TOMPKINS, C: Pte: 31272: A: Bomber: OU-211 Fd Coy RE

TONGE, F: Lt: MM: W 14 Apr 18 with 13 Y&L: Comm 12 Y&L 16 Feb . 17: Won MM with Manes as LCpl

TOPHAM, GM: LCpl: 12/251: D: Born Newcastle u T 1898: Dow 10 Jul–16: Doullens CC Ext Nol: * –?: Lived Wallsend

TOPHAM, GW: Pte: Sheffield Univ Student

TORRIE, JW: Capt: Comm 17 Apr 15

TOWNSEND, J: LSgt: 12/252: A: Born 1893: Kia 14 Jul 16 with 12WY: Thiepval, Mem: Sheffield Univ StudentITeacher: Comm 12 WY 20 May 16

TOZER, JW: Pte: 205437: OU-2 London, 9 & 13 Y&L

TRANMER, A: Pte: 19139: D: W Jun l6: Lived Leeds: OU-6, 9 & 10 Y&L

TRAPP, G: Pte: 205431: A

TRAYNOR, B: Pte: 12/1237: C: * +: OU-8 & 13 Y&L

TRENAM, A: Pte: 32193: OU-1/4, 10& 14 Y&L

TRICKETT, A: LCpl: 12/804: C: Born Sheffield 1890: Kia 1 Jul 16: Thiepval Mem: * +

TRICKETT, GE: Pte: 12/1075: D: * –: Bank Clk

TRIPP, AH: Pte: 235713: OU-13 Y&L

TRUMAN, JA: Pte: 12/533: OU-1 Y&L

TUCK, GV: Pte: 30049: OU-14 DU, 2 &. 214 Y&L

TUCK, J: Pte: 12/1838: A: Born Nr Cambridge 1897: Kia 1 Jul 16: Thiepval Mem: * +

TUCKER, WHC: Pte: 12/805: Born New Buckingham, Norfolk 1892: Kia 16 May 16: Sucrerie MC, Colincamps: Empl Cockaynes

TUFFNELL, FE: Pte: 12/1 077: D: * +: Sheffield Univ Student

TULK, AL: ACpl: 235664: OU-7 Y&L

TULY, G: Pte: 21889: C: * +

TUNBRIDGE, E: ACpl: 46452: OU-7 & 9 Y&L

TUNBRIDGE, NL: Capt: MID: Born TinwalJ, Stamford 1892: Sheffield UnivStudent: * –: OU-HQ 75 Bde

TURGOOSE, J: Cpl: 14/542: H: OU-13 & 14 Y&L: Signals Instr

TURNBULL, A: Cpl: 34643: 0U.20 DU, 1/4, 2/5, 8, 9 & 10 Y&L

TURNER, A: ASgt: 12/1 078: D: Born Walkley, Sheffield: Kia 9 Mar 17: Thiepval Mem: * +

TURNER, A: 2Lt: Comm 26 Sep l7: Served 12 Y&L from 8 Dec 17: OU-7 Y&L

TURNER, AE: Pte: 235712: HQ: Batman: OU-13 Y&L

TURNER, AR: 2Lt: Comm 3 Y&L 1 Mar l7: Served 12 Y&L from May *17

TURNER, CE: Pte: 12/253: A: W l Jul 16: * +

TURNER, FH: Dmr: 12/1 079: D: * +: Bandsman: OU-2/4 Y&L

TURNER, FW: Sheffield Univ Student

TURNER, H: Pte: 12/1 080: D: W 1 Jul 16: * +

TURNER, H: Pte: 12/1900: B: * –: OU-2/4 Y&L

TURNER, H: Pte: 12/1908: B: * –: OU-94 MGC

TURNER, H: Pte: 12/1428: SS Apr 16

TURNER, HH: Sgt: 12/806: C: * +: Bn Ord Rm Clk

TURNER, J: Pte: 23359: OU-2 & 10 Y&L

TURNER, J: Pte: 12/254: A: Born Sheffield: Kia 1 Jul 16: Thiepval Mem: * +

TURNER, JW: Pte: 12/1611: W Aug I6: OU-8 Y&L

TURNER, R: Cpl: 38319: OU-15 WY, 2/4, 2/5, 8 & 10 Y&L

TURNER, S: Pte: 12/1609: Born Nr Chesterfield 1881: Dow 2 Oct 18 with 2/4 Y&L: St Sever MC Ext, Rouen: Lived Rotherham: OU-2, 2/4 & 13 Y&L

TURNER, SW: Pte: Sheffield Univ Student

TURNER, T: Pte: 12/1767: SS Aug 16: OU-2, 8 & 10 Y&L: Lived Pontefract

TURTON, A: Cpl: 12/1667: A: W 1 Jul 16: * +: Lived Barnsley: OU-13 Y&L

TURTON, A: Pte: 24404: B: * –: OU-2, 6, 9, 1 0 & 13 Y&L

TURTON, JA: Pte: 12/1524: Born St Georges, Sheffield: Kia 1 Jul 16 with 14 Y&L: Thiepval Mem

TURTON, JW: Pte: 12/1081: D: W 1 Jul 16: * +: Lived 176 Cobden View Ad: Runner: OU-HQ 94 Bde, 2 & 13 Y&L

TURTON, O: Pte: 14/922: B: OU-13 Y&L

TWIGG, B: Pte: 12/1 082: D: Born Abbeydale, Sheffield: Kia 1 Jul 16-: Thiepval Mem: * +

TYLER, GH: Pte: 12/1083: D: W I Jul 16: * +: Lived 86 Pickmore Rd, Crookes

TYREMAN, A: Pte: 34332: OU-12 NFus, 2, 8 & 14 Y&L

TYSON, A: Pte: 23373: OU-7 Y&L

TYZACK, EA: Born 1895: Comm 15 Y&L 13 Dec l5: Brotherof WA Tyzack: Lived Ryecroft, Dore New Rd

TYZACK, WA: Lt: Comm 15 Y&L 24 Mar I5: OU-13 Y&L: Brother of EA Tyzack

TYZACK, WH: LCpl: 12/1846: OU-13 Y&L

UNDERHILL, W: Pte: 39094: OU-7 & 10 Y&L

UNWIN, G: Pte: 12/807: C: Born Chapletown 1891: Kia 4 May l6: Sucrerie MC, Colincamps: SB: Lived 25 Oxford St

UNWIN, R: LCpl: 12/535: B: Born Hathersage, Derbys: Kia 12 Apr 18 with 13 Y&L: Ploegsteert Mem, Belgium: * +: OU-ASC: Lived Cotswold, Hathersage

UPTON, A: Pte: 235665: OU-2/4 & 13 Y&L

USHER, AF: LCpl: 21592: W Jul 16: Lived London

USHER, SE: Pte: 21591: Born Holloway, London 1899: Dow 12 Oct 17 with 14 Y&L: Duisans MC: Lived Highbury Pk, London

UTTLEY, HO: Pte: 12/1153: B: OU-10 Y&L

UTTLEY, L: Cpl: 12/1233: Born Ecclesall, Sheffield 1894: Kia 23 Mar 18 with 11 DU: Pozieres Mem

VALENTINE, E: Pte: 37969: OU-2 Y&L

VARDY, A: ACpl: 37979: OU-2 Y&L

VARLEY, JS: Cpl: 12/808: ABC: W Jun 16

VARNEY, W: Pte: 41 017: Dow 30 Jun 17 with 8 Y&L

VAUGHAN, FB: LCpl: 12/256: A: W 1 Jul 16: * +: Comm Indian Army 28 Nov 17

VAUGHTON, EC: Pte: 12/536: Born Penistone 1896: Dow 24 Jan 17 with 2 Y&L: Stottercliffe C, Penistone

VERITY, E: Pte: 235203: OU-1/4, 2/4 & 13 Y&L

VERNER, A: Pte: 12/537: B: Born Staveley, Chesterfield 1886: Kia 1 Jul 16: Thiepval Mem: * +: Civii Engr: Lived Spring House, Calow, Chesterfield: Brother of RH Verner

VERNER, RH: Pte: 12/538: B: Born Woodthorn, Chesterfield 1888: Kia 1 Jul 16: Thiepval Mem: * +: Coliery Manager: Lived Spring House, ealow, Chesterfield: Brother of A Verner

VERNON, JH: Pte: 12/2071: Born Nr Rotherham: Kia 10 Sep 16: Flatiron Copse MC

VICE, AE: Pte: 235666: A: Bomber: OU-2/4, 115 & 13 Y&L

VICKERS, E: Pte: 245254: Born Sheffield 1897: Kia 1 O Jul 17 with 13 DLI: – Menin Gate Mem, Ypres, Belgium: OU-NFus

VICKERS, H: Pte: 12/539: B: W I Jul 16: * +: Lived Rotherham

VICKERS, S: Pte: 12/1118: B: MM: * –: Comm RWFus 25 Apr 17

VILCHES, LH: Pte: 205438: OU-2 London Yeo & 13 Y&L

WADDINGTON, N: Pte: 12/540: OU-2 Y&L

WADDINGTON, WT: Pte: 12/809: C: Born All Sts, Sheffield: Kia 1 Jul 16: Thiepval Mem: * +: Lived 83 Batley St, Pitsmoar and 131 Pickering Rd

WADDINGTON, BSM: 3 W Riding RFA: 12 Y&L recruiter in Sheffield early 1916

WADDLE, E: Pte: 40040: A: OU-6 & 13 Y&L

WADSWORTH, E: Pte: 41039: OU-1/5 & 13 Y&L

WADSWORTH, P: Pte: 12/541: B: * +

WAGSTAFF, D: Pte: 31280: Born 1888: Kia 2 Apr 17 with 1 O Y&L: Arras Mem: OU-2 & 10 Y&L

WAGSTAFFE, GF: Pte: 12/542: BD: W 1 Jul 16 with 12 Y&L and W 31 Mar 18 with 7 Y&L: * +: OU-7 & 13 Y&L

WAIN, AV: Pte: 41802: OU-6 & 7 Y&L

WAIN, J: Pte: 12/2025: SS Aug 16: OU-10 Y&L: Lived Attercliffe, Sheffield

WAIN, J: Pte: 21525: A: * –

WAINWRIGHT, A: Pte: 12/1126: A: * –

WAINWRIGHT, E: Pte: 12/1887: C: 8om Pitsmoor, Sheffield 1896: Kia 1 Jul 16: Thiepval Mem: * +

WAKEMAN, J: Pte: 12/1229: A: * –: Pioneer

WALBY, WD: Pte: 12/1085: D: Bom Nottingham 1893: Dow 9 Oct 17-: Aubigny CC Ext: * +

WALKER, A: Pte: 31338: D 20 Oct 18 with 11 4 Y&L: OU-1 Northants, 1/4 & 2/5 Y&L

WALKER, CS: LCpl: 12/259: A: W 1 Jul 16: Empl Jos Rogers & Co: * +: Lived 55 Endcliffe Rise Rd: OU-2 & 14 Y&L: Comm WY 30 Oct 17

WALKER, F: Pte: I21811: C: W May 16

WALKER, F: LCpl: 12/1084: D: Born St Matthews, Sheffield 1889: Kia 27 May 16: Sucrerie MC, Colincamps: Fish & Poultry dealer: Lived 16 Warwick St, Crookes

WALKER, FW: CSgt: 12/545: B: W 14 May 16

WALKER, H: Pte: 12/812: C: Born Walkley, Sheffield: Kia 1 Jul 16: Thiepval Mem: '+: Lived Crookes 0U_Pte: 30050: OU-2 DU, 2 & 7 Y&L

WALKER, JH: Pte: 19976: OU-2 & 6 Y&L

WALKER, N: Pte: 12/546: 8: W 1 Jul 16: * +

WALKER, NB: Pte: W Jul 16

WALKER, RH: Pte: 12/1268: A: Bom StJohns, Sheffield 1896: Kia 16 May 16: Sucrerie MC, Colincamps: Lived 265 Granville Rd

WALL, E: Pte: 12/1261: D: W Sep 16: * +: Silversmith

WALLACE, F: Pte: 12/1266: C: * –

WALLACE, MB: Capt: Ex 5 Scot Rfls: W 14 Apr 18 with 13 Y&L: Served 12 Y&L from 14 Nov 16

WALSH, H: Pte: 203728: B: OU-243 MGC, 1/5 & 13 Y&L

WALTON, CL: Pte: 235715: OU-7 Y&L

WALTON, E: Pte: 12/814: C: * +: OU-13 Y&L

WALTON, G: Pte: C: Runner: OU-HQ 94 Bde

WARD, A: Pte: 31343: OU-1 Northants

WARD, A: Pte: 12/257: A: * –: OU-9 Y&L

WARD, CG: Pte: 235668: OU-1/4 Y&L

WARD, CW: Pte: 12/815: Bor Scarboro 1888: Kia 28 Aug 17 with 14- Y&L: Douai CC, Cuincy: Bank
Clk: OU-2 & 14 Y&L

WARD, EA: Sheffield Univ Student: Comm 1915

WARD, EE: Pte: 12/1460: B: W I Jul 16: * +

WARD, EN: Cpl: 14/14 70: OU-2, 1/5, 13 & 14 Y&L

WARD, F: Sgt: 12/547: B: W I Jul 16: * +: Lived Market St, Hoyland: Comm 6 Y&L 29 Aug 17

WARD, G: CSgt: 12/1599: W Aug 16: OU-13, 14 & 18 Y&L

WARD, GE: Pte: 12/1882: C: Born Mosboro 1893: Kia 1 Jul 16: Rlwy HolJow MC, Serre: * +: Lived 3
Greenock St, HilJsboro or 327 Woodseats Rd

WARD, HW: Pte: 25797: OU-2, 2/4, 1/5, 2/5, 6 & 13 Y&L

WARD, J: Pte: I211086: D: W I Jul 16: * +

WARD, J: Pte: 12/1622: Born Sheffield: Dow 9 May 18 with 2 Y&L: Arnete MC

WARD, L: Sheffield Univ Student: OU-2 & 14 Y&L

WARD, RA: Pte: 12/1226: C: * –: OU-94 MGC

WARD, TL: Capt: Comm 1 Nov 14: OU-HQ 94 Bde

WARDILL, CH: 2Lt: Born 1877: Kia 1 Jul 16: Thiepval Mem: * +: Comm 15 Y&L 25 Oct 15: Served
12 Y&Lfrom 7 Jun 16: Lived 18 Violet Bank Ad: Brother of SG Wardill

WARDILL, SG: Pte: 12/816: C: Born Ecciesall, Sheffield: Kia 1 Jul 16: Thiepval Mem: * +: Lived 136
Club Garden Rd: Brother of CH Wardill

WARDLE, H: Pte: 11425: OU-8& 14 Y&L

WARNES, W: Pte: 235716: OU-7 Y&L

WARREN, WA: Pte: 31283: OU-1 Northants & 7 Y&L

WATERFALL, J: Pte: 12/817: C: * +: Bank Clk: Comm KOYU29 Jan 18

WATERFALL, N: Pte: 12/1484: C: Born St Philips, Sheffield 1897: Kia 1 Jul 16: Thiepval Mem: * +

WATERHOUSE, J: Pte: 12/1327: Bom Hayford, Stockport: Kia 1 Jul 16 with 14 Y&L: Queens MC,
Serre

WATERHOUSE, JS: ACpl: 235220: A: Lewis gnr: OU-1/4, 214 & 13 Y&L

WATERS, PW: Pte: 11853: D

WATKINS, FE: ALSgtl21548: B: MM: Bom Nr Cheltenham 1884: Kia 1 Jul 16: Thiepval Mem: * +:
Midland Rlwy Clk: Lived Hepthome Ln, Chesterfield

WATSON, A: Pte: 12/1087: D: * +: Cook

WATSON, C: ACpl: 12/549: B: Born St Annes, Sheffield 1890: * –: Lived 77 Bonville St: OU-7 Y&L

WATSON, C: Pte: 12/1937: W Jul 16: OU-13 Y&L

WATSON, HW: Sgt: 12/1210: D: * –: Comm M'Sex 28 May 18

WATSON, J: Pte: 23165: A: Bomber

WATSON, J: Pte: 23165: OU-7 & 13 Y&L

WATSON, JO: Pte: 12/1088: D: Bom Sheffield 1890: Kia 1 Jul 16: Thiepval Mem: • +: Lived 43
Victoria Rd, Broomhall Pk

WATSON, W: Pte: 12/1286: A: SS May 16

WATSON, WG: Attended 1970 Reunion

WATSON, WJ: LCpl: 12/1131: C: * +: Lived Swindon

WATTS, A: Pte: 31345: OU-1 Northants

WATTS, A: Pte: 12/1311: D: W 1 Jul 16: * +

WAYLAND, RB: 2Lt: OU-1l ELancs: Served 12 Y&L from 2 Aug 16

WEBB, WG: Pte: 235729: OU-7 Y&L

WEBBER, EG: Pte: 16691: OU-7, 9 & 10 Y&L

WEBSTER, A: Pte: 12/1165: B: Born Penistone 1888: Kia 1 Jul 16: Queens MC, Serre: Gt Central
Alwy Clk: * +: Lived 5 Rlwy Tee, Penistone

WEBSTER, H: Pte: 12/260: C: W I Jul 16: Lived Hillsboro, Sheffield

WEBSTER, J: Pte: 12/1604: W Jul 16: OU-6, 8 & 9 Y&L

WEBSTER, RC: LCpl: 12/261: A: Comm Jun 16

WEBSTER, TH: Pte: 41761: A: Born Sheffield 1889: Bomber: OU-13 Y&L

WEBSTER, WT: Pte: I21818: C: W 1 Jul 16: * +

WEDDELL, H: Pte: 33544: OU-2 Y&L

WEIGHT, A: Pte: I211 090: D: Born Balham, Surrey: Kia 1 Jul 16: Thiepval Mem: * +

WEIR, E: Pte: 33543

WEIR, JA: Pte: 38050

WELDON, S: Pte: 38732: OU-7 & 10 Y&L

WELDON, S: Attended 1970 Reunion

WELLS, A: Pte: 32496: OU-8 Y&L

WELLS, CH: Sgt: 12/1091: D: W 25 May 16: Accountant

WELLS, J: Pte: 31281: AH: OU-Northants & 13 Y&L

WELLS, JF: Pte: Sheffield Univ Student

WELSH, WA: LCpl: 12/550: B: W 1 Jul 16: * +: Lived Thurlestone

WENMAN, A: Pte: 12/551: B: Hickleton, Derbys 1892-3: * –: Maj Clough's Batman: Lived Hickleton HilJ Green House, Doncaster

WEST, GA: Pte: 31279: OU-1 Northants, 2 & 7 Y&L

WEST, NLW: Pte: 235671: OU-7 Y&L

WEST, PM: Pte: 12/262: A: B()rn Sheffield: W 1 Jul 16 and Kia 12 May–17: Arras Mem: * +: Sheffield Univ Student: Lived 30 Broomgrove Rd: OU-2 Y&L

WESTBURY, WJ: Pte: 31341: OU-1 Northants

WESTBY, FH: 2Lt: Comm 15 Y&L 6 Jan 16: Served 12 Y&L from late 1916

WESTLAKE, SC: Pte: 205448: 0U-2 London Yeo & 13 Y&L

WESTWOOD, H: Pte: 12/1351: A: * +: W Aug 16

WESTWOOD, JW: Pte: 16247: OU-1/5, 9 & 10 Y&L

WEVER, RO: Cpl: MC MID: Born Sharrow, Sheffield 1892: W May 16– : Lived 8 Brincliffe Cres: Comm W Riding Div Signals early 1915

WHARTON, HW: LCpl: 12/264: A: Born St Mary's, Sheffield 1896: Kia 1 Jul 16: Thiepval Mem: * +: Lived 84 Sandford Grive Ad, Netheredge

WHEAT, HA: Pte: 12/1093: D: W Jul 16: * –: Lived Bamford: Comm WY 12 Apr 17

WHIPPLE, HD: ACpl: 12/1411: C: * +: Comm Yorks 23 Aug 18

WHITE, A: Pte: 12/819: B: Born Erith, Kent: Kia 1 Jul 16: Queens MC, Serre: * +

WHITE, A: Pte: 12/1728: C: * +: SignalJer

WHITE, F: Pte: 31351: OU-1 Northants

WHITE, H: Pte: 37837: OU-2 & 6 Y&L

WHITE, HG: Pte: 40074: OU-2 & 2/4 Y&L

WHITE, RH: Pte: 12/1880: B: Born Pitsmoor, Sheffield 1889: Kia 1 Jul 16: Thiepval Mem: * +: OU-13 Y&L

WHITE, WL: Pte: 32332: Born 1897: D 15 Apr 18 with 1/5 Y&L: Wimereux CC: OU-1/5, 2/5 & 10 Y&L

WHITEHALL, JS: Pte: 12/1 094: D: * –: OU-1 O Y&L

WHITEHEAD, HA: Pte: 41706: HQ: Special Patrol PIy: OU-13 Y&L

WHITELEY, AH: Brother of H Whiteley: Comm 3/9DLI Oct 15

WHITELEY, H: Born 1893: Dow 11 Oct 16 with 9DLI: Christ Church Chyd, Sheffield: Sheffield Univ Student: Brother of AH Whiteley: Comm 3/9DLI Oct 15

WHITEWAY, AL: Pte: 12/820: C: W JUL 16: Lived Exeter

WHITLOCK, EF: Pte: 12/553: B: Born W Bridgeford, Notts: Kia 1 Jul 16: Thiepval Mem: * +: Lived Hamsfield

WHITMAN, E: LCpl: 28007: HQ: Gas NCO

WHITNEY, AJ: Pte: 31340: OU-1 Northants

WHITTAKER, AP: 12th Club Member

WHITTAKER, GW: Pte: 12/265: C: Born St Georges, Sheffield: SS & W May 16 with 12 Y&L and Dow 22 Dec 16 with 13 Y&L: OU-7 & 13 Y&L

WHITTAKER, W: Pte: 37984: OU-2 Y&L

WHITTAKER, W: Pte: 12/479: D 28 Jul 15 with 14 Y&L: St Giles Chyd, Whittington, Staffs

WHITTINGTON, GF: Pte: I2/1695: A: * –

WHYMAN, A: Cpl: 12/1281: A

WHYSALL, T: Pte: 12/555: B: Born Waleswood, Sheffield: SS May 16 and Kia 1 Jul 16: Thiepval Mem: * +: Lived Kiveton Pk

WIBBERLEY, G: Cpl: 12/1454: OU-1 Y&L

WIDDOWSON, JH: Pte: 12/1096: D: * +: Runner: Comm Tank Corps 23 Oct 18

WIGLEY, BP: Pte: 39080: OU-7 & 10 Y&L

WILCOCK, N: LCpl: 12/1097: D: Born Sheffield 1893: Kia 1 Jul 16: Queens MC, Serre: * +: Lived 5 Priory Rd, Sharrow

WILCOX, E: Pte: 12/1692: A: W I Jul 16: * +: OU-6, 7, 10 & 14 Y&L

WILCOX, F: Pte: 31339: OU-1 Northants, 2 & 7 Y&L

WILCOX, L: Pte: 31207: Born 1892: Kia 17 Apr 18 with 1/5 Y&L: Tyne Cot Mem, Passchendaele, Belgium: OU-1/5, 215 & 8 Y&L

WILCOX, WG: ALCpl: I2/267: A: Born Holy Trinily 1892: W 1 Jul 16 with 12 Y&L and Kia 25 Sep 17 with 8 Y&L: Tyne Cot Mem, Passchendaele, Belgium: * +: on Hall Clk: Lived 87 BurngreaveRd: OU-8

WILD, AS: Pte: I2/1 098: D: Sheffield Daily Telegraph Reporter: * –

WILD, JE: Pte: 38666: Born 1890: Dow 30 Sep 18 with 2 Y&L: Brie MC: OU-2, 6, 9 & 14 Y&L

WILD, W: Pte: I211939: OU-I, 1/5, 7, 10 & 13 Y&L

WILDSMITH, J: Pte: 27222: OU-10 & 13 Y&L

WILES, P: ACpl: 235717: OU-7 Y&L

WILKINSON, Cpl: Served 12 Y&L 1914

WILKINSON, BC: Pte: I2/822: C: MM: Born Sheffield 1894: Kia 1 Jul 16: Thiepval Mem: * +

WILKINSON, JS: Pte: Sheffield Univ Student

WILKINSON, P: Pte: 12/1790: Born Adwick on Dearne: Kia 25 Jul 16 with 13 Y&L: Pont d'Hem MC, La Gorgue: Lived Bolton on Dearne

WILKINSON, TJ: Pte: 12/1636: Born St Peter's, Sheffield 1878: Kia I Jul 16 with 14 Y&L: Thiepval Mem

WILKS, EH: Pte: 12/268: A: W May 16

WILLFORD, C: LCpl: 12/1100: D: Born Nr Beverley 1881: Dow 14 Jul 16: St Pol CC Ext: * +: Lived 21 Carr Rd, Walkley

WILLIAMS, A: Pte: 12/269: A: * –: Cook

WILLIAMS, CG: Pte: I2111 01: A: * –

WILLIAMS, CH: Pte: 27831: Born 1893: Kia 9 Oct 17 with 1/4 Y&L: Tyne Cot Mem, Passchendaele, Belgium: OU-2, 1/4 & 10 Y&L

WILLIAMS, CH: Pte: 12/823: C: * +: Bandsman: OU-2/4 Y&L

WILLIAMS, E: Pte: 4111 0: OU-2, 2/4 & 8 Y&L

WILLIAMS, EP: Pte: 203037: Born 1886: Kia 24 Apr 18 with 2WY: Crucifix Corner Me, Villers Bretonneux: Lived Milton Rd, Sharrow

WILLIAMS, FW: Pte: 235213: Dow 27 May 18 with 7 Y&L: OU-2/4, 1 15 & 7 Y&L

WILLIAMS, LH: Pte: 21516: HQ: Special Patrol Pty: OU-2, 7 & 13 Y&L

WILLIAMSON, P: Pte: 37966: OU-2 Y&L

WILLIAMSON, P: ASgt: 40073: OU-9 Y&L

WILLIAMSON, TH: Pte: 12/1102: D: W I Jul 16: * +: Lived 9 May Rd, Hillsboro: OU-8 Y&L

WILLIAMSON, WE: Pte: 12/1198: A: Born St Silas, Sheffield 1885: Kia 1 Jul 16: Thiepval Mem: * +

WILLOUGHBY, JA: CSM: 12/1246: D: DCM: W I Jul 16: * +: Lived 41 Albert Rd, Meersbrook: OU-2 & 9 Y&L

WILLS, CA: Pte: 49749

WILSON, A: Pte: I211104: D: * +

WILSON, A: Pte: 12/1953: W Aug 16: OU-13 Y&L

WILSON, A: Pte: 25161: OU-2, 6 & 10 Y&L

WILSON, AN: ACpl: 12/11 05: D: SS May 16 with 12 Y&L & W 5 May 18 with 7 Y&L: * +

WILSON, B: Pte: 39019: HQ: Observer: OU-10 & 13 Y&L

WILSON, E: Pte: 33560: A

WILSON, F: Pte: 37727: Born 1898: D 2 Oct 18 with 1 Y&L: Kirechkoihortakoi MC, Greece: OU-1 & 10 Y&L

WILSON, FB: 2Lt: Born 1892: Dow 7 Aug l7: Aubigny CC Ext: Sheffield Univ Student Comm 7 Jul 15: Served 12 Y&L from 15 Aug 16

WILSON, GHC: Sgt: 12/270: A: W 1 Jul 16: Teacher: * +: Lived 81 or 246 Sandford Grove Rd: OU-94 TMB

WILSON, HA: Pte: I211412: A: Born Leeds 1894: Kia 10 Sep l6: Loos Mem: * –

WILSON, HS: C

WILSON, JF: Pte: 12/2145

WILSON, JW: Pte: 12/824: C: Born Heeley, Sheffield 1882: Kia I Jul–16: Thiepval Mem: * +

WILSON, M: Photo in Y&L Museum

WILSON, M: Pte: 17944: OU-6, 13 & 14 Y&L

WILSON, P: LCpl: 12/1626: A: * –

WILSON, R: Pte: 12/825: C: MM: Born Sheffield 1891: W 16 May 16 with 12 Y&L and Kia 30 Jun 17with 9 Y&L: Rlwy Dugout Burial Gd, Belgium: Lab Asst: Comm 9 Y&L 25 Apr 17

WILSON, TM: Pte: 12/271: A

WILTHREW, WN: Pte: 28773: Born Jesmond, Newcastle u T 1887: Kia 30 Jun 17: Arras Mem: Lived Newcastle u T: OU-2 Y&L

WINDLE, G: Pte: 12/826: OU-6 & 13 Y&L

WINGFIELD, HE: Pte: 12/1602: Born Broomhill, Sheffield: W 1 Jul 16 and Kia 22 Jul 16 with 14 Y&L: Rue du Bacquerot MC: Lived Bexley, Kent

WINN, J: 2Lt: Born 1899: Kia 23 Mar 17 with 7 Y&L: Arras Mem: Comm 26 Sep 17

WINTERBURN, A: Pte: 34277: OU-10 NFus, 1/4, 2/5 & 8 Y&L

WISBEY, E: Pte: 235718: OU-7 Y&L

WISEMAN, C: Pte: 12/272: A: Born Sheffield 1894: Kia 26 May 18 with 2/4 Y&L: Bienvillers MC: Sheffield Univ Student: * –: OU-2/4 & 6 Y&L

WITHERSPOON, JB: Pte: 12/1531: A: Born 1896: W 1 Jul 16: * +: Lewis gnr

WOOD, C: Pte: 13/721: OU-2, 6, 7 & 13 Y&L

WOOD, F: Pte: 12/1803: B: W I Jul 16: * +: OU-2 & 13 Y&L

WOOD, GH: 2Lt: G 12 Nov l7: Comm 19 Dec l6: Served 12 Y&L from 12 Feb 17: OU-13 Y&L

WOOD, H: Pte: 12/1582: Born EcclesalJ, Sheffield: Kia 1 Jul 16 with 8 Y&L: Thiepval Mem

WOOD, H: Pte: 23314: A: Born Nr Barnsley: Kia 29 May l7: Etaples MC: * –

WOOD, J: Pte: 12/1760: Enl underage

WOOD, J: Pte: 12/1808: C: Aunner

WOOD, JF: Pte: 235724: A: Lewis gnr: OU-13 Y&L

WOOD, JH: Pte: 40075: OU-2, 1 15 & 9 Y&L

WOOD, JL: Pte: 37985: OU-2 Y&L

WOOD, JS: Cpl: 12/558: OU-14 Y&L: Comm WRiding 28 May 18

WOOD, JS: Cpl: 12/556: B: * –

WOOD, JS: Cpl: 12/828: C: * –

WOOD, RV: Pte: 12/829: C

WOOD, TH: LSgt: 12/559: B: Born Ecclesfield 1895: Kia 2 Nov 16: Sailly au Bois MC: * –

WOOD, WW: Pte: 12/273: A: W I Jul 16: * +: OU-6 & 9 Y&L: Comm ELancs 28 May 18

WOODBINE, GR: Pte: 31346: OU-1 Northants & 7 Y&L

WOODCOCK, PT: Pte: 12/1136: C: W 1 Jul 16: * +

WOODGER, JA: Pte: 41628: Born Rotherham 1890: Dow 25 Oct l7: Duisans MC: Lived Edinburgh: Labourer

WOODHAMS, CM: Pte: 33546

WOODHEAD, C: Pte: 12/342: OU-13 Y&L

WOODHEAD, EG: Pte: 41 078: OU-8 Y&L

WOODHOUSE, CH: Capt: W 9 Apr 16, 1 Jul 16 with 12 Y&L and Kia 6 Jun 18 with 1/4 Y&L?: Tyne Cot Mem, Belgium: * +: Comm l Nov 14

WOODHOUSE, CW: Pte: 4521: 8

WOODHOUSE, J: Served 12 Y&L early 1915

WOODHOUSE, W: Pte: 12/1324: A: * +

WOODING, WC: Pte: 205441: OU-2 London Yeo & 7 Y&L

WOODLAND, H: Pte: 37973: Dow 17 Apr 17 with 2 Y&L

WOODS, W: Pte: 236670: Kia 31 Oct 18 with 1 15Y &L

WOODWARD, FH: LCpl: 12/1143: D: Sanitary Man

WOOLHOUSE, EGG: Capt: Comm 18 Sep 14: * –

WOOLHOUSE, G: Pte: 12/1992: C: W 30 Sep 18 with 13 Y&L: Comm Y&L 30 Jan 18

WOOLLARD, EJ: Pte: 31277: OU-1 Northants
WOOLLIN, F: Sgt: 14/1132: OU-2, 13 & 14 Y&L
WOOLMER, HW: Sgt: 31337: A: Lewis gnr: OU-Northants & 13 Y&L
WORMLEIGHTON, CE: Cpl: 235719: OU-2 Y&L
WRAGG, J: Pte: 201928: OU-1/5 Y&L
WRAGG, JA: Pte: 12/1574: W Jul 16: OU-2 & 14 Y&L
WRAGG, JW: Pte: 12/1911: OU-2/5 & 8 Y&L
WRAY, CR: 2Lt: Comm 26 Sep 17: Served 12 Y&L from 21 Dec 17: OU-7 & 1/4 Y&L
WRAY, WG: Pte: 27835: A: Lewis gnr
WRIGHT, A: Pte: 12/1090: D: 8orn Balham, Surrey: Kia 1 Jul 16: Thiepval Mem: * +
WRIGHT, AW: Pte: 12/274: A: W I Jul 16: * +: Lived Broad Oaks
WRIGHT, BA: Pte: 31543: OU-2 & 14 Y&L
WRIGHT, F: Pte: 12/1187: C: W 1 Jul 16: * +: OU-1 Y&L
WRIGHT, FW: Pte: 12/11 09: D: * +: Sheffield Univ Student
WRIGHT, GC: Pte: 12/275: A: DCM: W 1 Jul 16: * +: Bank Clk: Runner: Lived 15 Grange Rd:
    Comm DU 29 May 17
WRIGHT, H: Pte: 41709: HQ: Born Rotherham 1882: Dow 30 Jun 18 with 13 Y&L: Observer
WRIGHT, JA: Pte: Sheffield Univ Student
WRIGHT, JH: Pte: 37968: OU-2 & 13 Y&L
WRIGHT, JH: Pte: 12/1110: D: +: Bandsman
WRIGHT, JR: Cpl: 12/833: C: Born Walkley, Sheffield 1892: Kia I Jul 16: Thiepval Mem: * +: T
    eacher: Lived 192 School Rd
WRIGHT, WH: Pte: 12/21 08: B: * –: W Sep I6: OU-2 & 13 Y&L
WRIGHT, WW: Cpl: 235223: A: Kia 24 Mar 18 with 13 Y&L: OU-2/4, 1 15 & 13 Y&L
WYNNE, RJ: 2Lt: Comm 17 Apr 15
WYRILL, EF: 2Lt: Comm 29 Aug 17: Served 12 Y&L from 8 Dec I7: OU-7 Y&L
YATES, E: Pte: 38051
YELF, RH: Pte: 31342: Born Bloomsbury, London: Kia 28 Oct 16– : Hebuterne MC: OU-Northants:
    Lived Tooting
YORK, CT: Pte: 13315: B
YOUNG, AA: 2Lt: Comm 17 Apr 15
YOUNG, GW: Pte: 235672: A: OU-211 Fd Coy RE, 8 Norfolk & 13 Y&L
YOUNG, JF: Pte: 12/1612: OU-2 Y&L
YOUNG, W: Pte: 12/1613: Deserted 4 Feb I8: OU-14 Y&L
YOUNGS, RW: Pte: 235673: A: OU-13 Y&L

Battalion Strength

DATE	OFFRs	Ors	Remarks
5 Dec 14	30	1034	
13 May 15	34	1070	ORs break down; 6 WOs, 41 Sgts, 40 Cpls and 983 LCpls and Ptes Plus 2 + 19 attached
20 Dec 15	29	1025	Plus 2 + 19 attached
26 Jan 16	29	982	Possibly does not include attached personnel
16 Mar 16	30	986	Plus 8 ORs left in Egypt
30 Jun 16	36	1036	
7 Jul 16	18	541	Incls 75 with minor wounds and draft of 56 ORs arrived that day
31 Mar 17	23	806	Actually serving with the Battalion, detached not mentioned
16 Aug 17	31	559	Trench strength was 21 + 427, with 10+ 132 detached etc.
17 Sep 17	?	595	ORs trench strength was 475
31 Nov 17	19	460	Probably does not include detached personnel
31 Jan 18	39	667	Trench strength was 25 + 431, with 14 + 236 on leave, courses and detached etc.

This is a copy of the last letter written to his
Sweetheart Miss Dora Clegg by Captain W.S.Clark.
Sadly Capt.Clark was killed leading "A" company
on that fateful day, the 1st of July 1916. He is
burried in Serre Road cemetery No.2.

There is a sequel to this story which started when Private Thomas Leefe,
a member of "A" company was seriously wounded, losing his sight. He was
crawling about in No Mans Land from shell-hole to shell-hole searching
for water bottles on bodies. The only way he could distinguish between
night and day was, the birds song by day and at night he could hear the
swish of the very-lights. After three days he was finaly taken prisoner
by the germans. He was treated in various hospitals. When his recovery
allowed him to be moved he was repatriated to England in Otober1916,
and eventually to be discharged from the army. In later years his
housekeeper knew Dora Clegg, Capt.Clark's fiance. The couple were
introduced and in time were married.

Sources and Acknowledgements

1. OFFICIAL SOURCES

a. Details of medal citations etc, from MS1b, Stanmore, Middlesex, and the Army Medal Office in Droitwich.

b. The Commonwealth War Graves Commission for records of burials and memorials.

c. The Public Record Office in Kew for the various War Diaries consulted, and the Medal Rolls.

d. 'The Official History of the Great War', compiled by Brig-Gen Sir J. E. Edmunds. Various volumes were consulted.

e. 'Order of Battle of Divisions', compiled by Maj A. F. Becke as an accompaniment to the Official Histories.

f. 'Soldiers Died in the Great War 1914-19, Part 61-The York and Lancaster Regiment'. Other parts were also consulted, including 'Officers Died in the Great War'.

g. 'The Army List', August 1914 to January 1919.

2. PUBLISHED SOURCES.

Barrie A. 'War Underground'. (Frederick Muller Ltd. 1962).

Blunden E. 'Under-Tones of War'. (William Collins & Sons Ltd. Glasgow 1965).

Broaston C. B. OBE, Lt Col J. H. (Editor) 'Sir Douglas Haig's Despatches'.

Caffery K. 'Farewell Leicester Square'. (Andre Deutsch 1980).

Carrington C. 'Soldiers From The Wars Returning'. (Hutchinson & Co. Ltd. 1965).

Chapman G. 'Passionate Prodigality'. (Ivor Nicholson & Watson Ltd. 1933).

Churchill, The Right Hon. Winston S. 'The World Crisis 1911-1918 Vol. 1 and 2'. (Thornton & Butterworth Ltd. 1927).

Congreve B. Edited by Terry Norman 'Armageddon Road'. (William Kimber & Co. Ltd. 1982).

Craster, J. M. 'Fifteen Rounds a Minute'. (Macmillan London Ltd 1976).

Crutwell, C. R. M. F. 'A History of the Great War'. (Oxford Clarendon Press 1936).

Dewar G. A. B. 'Sir Douglas Haig's Command Vol. 1 and 2'. (Constable & Co. Ltd. 1922).

Farrar-Hockley A. H. 'The Somme'. (Pan Books Ltd. 1983).

Gibbs P. 'Realities of War'. (William Heinemann 1920).

Giles J. 'The Ypres Salient Then and Now'. (Picardy Publishing Ltd. 1979).

Giles J. 'The Somme Then and Now'. (Bailey Brothers and Swifen Ltd. 1977).

Gladden N. 'Somme 1916'. (William Kimber & Co. Ltd). 1974).

Gladden N. 'Ypres 1917'. (William Kimber & Co. Ltd. 1976).

Glubb J. 'Into Battle'. (Book Club Associates by arrangements with Cassell Ltd. 1978).

Graves R. 'Goodbye To All That'. (Penguin Books Ltd. 1984).

Greenwell G. H. 'An Infant In Arms'. (Penguin Press, Alan Lane 1972).

Haig R. H. and Turner P. W. 'Not For Glory'. (Pergamon Press Ltd. 1962).

Hamilton Lord E. 'The First Seven Divisions'. (Hurst and Blackett Ltd. 1916).

Hammerton Sir J. Editor 'World War 1914-1918 Vol 2'. (Amalgamated Press Ltd).

Hitchcock M. C. Capt. F. C. 'Stand Too' A Diary of The Trenches. (Hurst & Blackett Ltd. 1937).

Horne A. 'The Price Of Glory, Verdun 1916'. (Penguin Books 1964).

Longworth P. 'The Unending Vigil'. (Constable & Co. Ltd. 1967).

Manning F. 'Middle Parts of Fortune'. (Peter Davis Ltd 1937).

Nash D. B. 'Imperial German Army Handbook 1914-1918'. (Ian Allan Ltd. 1980).

Nettleton J. 'The Anger Of The Guns'. (William Kimber & Co. Ltd. 1979).

Norman T. 'The Hell They Called High Wood'. (William Kimber & Co. Ltd. 1984).

Pitt B. '1918 The Last Act'. (Cassell & Co. 1962).

Reppington Lt Col CaCourt 'The First World War 1914-1918 Vol. 1 and 2'. (Constable & Co. Ltd. 1920).

Richards F. 'Old Soldiers Never Die'. (Faber & Faber Ltd. 1933).

Rogerson S. 'Twelve Days'. (Arthur Barker Ltd. London).

Sassoon S. 'Memoirs Of An Infantry Officer'. (Faber & Faber Ltd. 1933).

Tucker J. F. 'Johnny Get Your Gun'. (William Kimber & Co. Ltd. 1978).

Williams J. 'The Home Fronts 1914-1918'. (Constable London 1972).

Wolf L. 'In Flanders Fields'. (Longmans, Green & Co. 1959).

3. OTHER PUBLISHED SOURCES

a. Extracts from 'The Tiger and Rose', the York and Lancaster Regiment's magazine, 1919-1986.

b. 'History of the 7th Service Battalion York and Lancaster Regiment (Pioneers)', by M. Gilvary.

c. 'History of the 9th (Service) Battalion The York and Lancaster Regiment 1914-1919', by J. B. Montagu.

d. 'History of the 12th Service Battalion York and Lancaster Regiment', by R. A. Sparling.

e. 'Pals — 13th and 14th Battalions York and Lancaster Regiment'. A History of the Two Battalions raised by Barnsley in World War One, by Jon Cooksey.

f. 'A Town for Four Winters', by C. J. & G. P. Whitehouse. The story of the Cannock Chase World War One Army camps.

g. 'The First Day on the Somme', by M. Middlebrook.

h. 'Somme', by Lyn McDonald.

i. Numerous articles from the 'Sheffield Daily Telegraph', August 1914 to date.

j. Various articles from the 'Sheffield Independent', printed during the war.

k. 'University of Sheffield, Roll of Service January 1916'.

l. 'The Accrington Pals - 11th (Service) Battalion, (Accrington) East Lancashire Regiment' by William Turner.

4. PRIVATE SOURCES

a. The diary of 12/1137 Cpl J. Dixon, kindly loaned by Mr D. Martin of South Anston.

b. The diary of 12/847 Pte W. G. Alflat, kindly loaned by his son, Mr D. J. Alflat of Worksop.

c. The diary of 12/156 Pte T. C. Hunter, kindly made available by Mr D. Martin of South Anston from Hunter's son, Mr T. J. Hunter of Inverness.

d. The diary of Capt J. L. Middleton, kindly made available by his daughter Mrs G. W. J. Tunbridge of Baslow.

e. The diary of 12/807 Pte G. Unwin, kindly loaned by his nephew, Mr R. F. Unwin of Sheffield.

f. Extract from the lifestory of 12/1299 Pte A. H. Hastings kindly loaned by his daughter Mrs J. Clarke of Tadcaster.

g. Copies of the letters and poems of 12/525 Sgt J. W. Streets kindly loaned by Mr I. Seaton of Whitwell.

h. The letters and sketches of 12/877 Cpl O. Bradshaw, kindly loaned by his daughter, Mrs B. Tew of Oakham.

i. The account of the war service of 12/141 Pte L. A. Hill, kindly loaned by his son Mr W. A. Hill of Sheffield.

j. The recorded interviews of 12/70 Sgt D. E. Cattell, kindly loaned by his son Mr F. Cattell of Baslow.

k. The recorded interviews of 12/300 RQMS T. Bingham, kindly loaned by his daughter, Mrs B. Burnett.

l. The letters and documents of 12/338 Pte Corthorn, DCM, kindly loaned by his grandson Mr. R. Redmile of Sheffield.

m. The photo album of 12/697 L/Cpl F. Jameson kindly loaned by his son Mr. P. Jameson.

n. The photo album of 12/946 Sgt J. Hastings kindly loaned by his son Mr. J. Hastings.

5. OTHER ACKNOWLEDGEMENTS

a. The following people, in no order of merit, made a significant contribution to the research for this book; Mr Laurie Milner, Imperial War Museum; Mr S. Eastwood and Mr D. Scott of the York and Lancaster Regimental Museum; Mr P. Markie and Mr S. McClarence of Sheffield Newspapers; the staff of the Local Studies Section and the Archives of the Sheffield Central Library; the Western Front Association; Mr P. Linacre and Mr P. Healy of Sheffield University; Mr P. Smithhurst, the curator of the Kelham Island Industrial Museum, Sheffield; the staff of the Prince Consort's Military Library in Aldershot; Mr J. Harris, author of the novel, 'Covenant with Death'; Mr G. Dorling of James Dixons, Sheffield; Mr G. Buxton of Sheffield; Mr G. Rhodes of Rotherham, Mr Peter Taylor of Barnsley, Mrs M. Cahill, Mr D. E. Owen, Mrs E. Rose, Mr D. W. Linsley, Mrs B. Thorpe, Mr J. T. Armes, Mrs D. P. Brisbane, Mrs J. M. Barton, Miss E. Pack, Mrs B. Burnett, Mr H. R. Allcard, Mr D. Bertaut, Mrs W. M. Burwell, Mrs P. Radley, Mrs J. Davy, Mr I.C. Pearson, Miss K. Osborn, Mr L. Shipley, Mrs B. L. Lombardy, Mrs A. Crum, Mr H. L. Gent, Mrs A. Mortimer, Mr J. S. Horrax, Mrs W. Hyde, Misses J. and M. Sparling, Mr G. C. Hinckley, Miss W. E. G. Gapes, Mr H. O. Chaddock, Mr G. T. Bescoby, Mrs C. Allcard, Mrs W. A. Hagon, Mr M. V. Kerrigan, all of Sheffield and its surrounding districts; Mr C. G. Parker of Guildford; Mrs M. Taylor of Leamington Spa; Mr A. D. Baynes of Worksop; Mr G. S. Passey of Croydon; Mrs P. Taylor of Scarborough; Miss C. Wenman of Thurnscoe; Mrs K. M. Woodhead of Chesterfield; Mr J. Cuthill of Wickersley; Mrs M. Tupling of Rotherham; Mr M. Middlebrook of Lincolnshire; Mr C. F. Cavill of Worthing, Sussex. If anyone has been missed it was not done intentionally and may we offer our apologies.

b. The following veterans gave freely of

their time and added much of the background information, the amusing, and the not so amusing anecdotes of their time in the City Battalion; Mr J. R. Glenn of Oughtibridge; the late Mr O. P. Ridley of Rotherham; Mr J. B. Roberts of Folkestone; Mr H. Hall of Sheffield; Mr D. Cameron of Sheffield; Mr H. N. Hobson of Harrogate; Mr E. Passey of Southsea.

c. Finally we would like to acknowledge Mrs K. Purdy of Coal Aston, who sent a parcel of her father's documents and photographs to help our research.

Sadly the parcel never arrived, it was lost in the post. Nothing can ever replace these family treasures and we offer our sincere regrets and thanks for her trouble.

Further Information

Further information is available to accompany this book. This includes: A Biographical list of all known members of the Sheffield City Battalion.

A chart of the Army Organisation and Ranks and further official documents produced relating to the Sheffield City Battalion.

If you would like to receive this information please contact the publishers. This information is priced at £10 including postage and packaging.

Pen & Sword Books Ltd
47 Church Street
Barnsley
South Yorkshire S70 2AS
Tel: 01226 734222
email: enquiries@pen-and-sword.co.uk